T0300260

ROUTLEDGE LIBRARY EDITIONS:
ACCOUNTING

Volume 46

STUDIES IN CASH FLOW ACCOUNTING AND ANALYSIS

STUDIES IN CASH FLOW ACCOUNTING AND ANALYSIS

Aspects of the Interface between Managerial Planning, Reporting and Control and External Performance Measurement

Edited by
G.H. LAWSON

LONDON AND NEW YORK

First published in 1992

This edition first published in 2014
by Routledge
2 Park Square, Milton Park, Abingdon, Oxon, OX14 4RN

and by Routledge
711 Third Avenue, New York, NY 10017

Routledge is an imprint of the Taylor & Francis Group, an informa business

British Library Cataloguing in Publication Data
A catalogue record for this book is available from the British Library

ISBN: 978-0-415-53081-1 (Set)
eISBN: 978-1-315-88628-2 (Set)
ISBN: 978-0-415-71712-0 (Volume 46)
eISBN: 978-1-315-87152-3 (Volume 46)

Publisher's Note
The publisher has gone to great lengths to ensure the quality of this book but points out that some imperfections in the original copies may be apparent.

Disclaimer
The publisher has made every effort to trace copyright holders and would welcome correspondence from those they have been unable to trace.

STUDIES IN CASH FLOW ACCOUNTING AND ANALYSIS

Aspects of the Interface between Managerial Planning, Reporting and Control and External Performance Measurement

Edited by
G.H. Lawson

Garland Publishing, Inc.
New York and London 1992

Library of Congress Cataloging-in-Publication Data

Studies in cash flow accounting and analysis: aspects of the interface between managerial planning, reporting, and control and external performance measurement / edited by G.H. Lawson.
p. cm.—(New works in accounting history)
Includes bibliographical references.
ISBN 0-8153-0687-3
1. Cash flow—Accounting. 2. Managerial accounting. I. Lawson, G.H. (Gerald Hartley)
II. Series.
HF5681.C28S78 1992 92-5927
658.15'11—dc20

All volumes printed on acid-free, 250-year-life paper.
Manufactured in the United States of America.

Design by Marisel Tavarez

CONTENTS

Acknowledgments

The editor and publisher wish to thank the following joint authors, journals and publishers for their kind permission to reprint copyright materials in this volume:

J. van den Berge and the *Journal of Oil and Gas Accountancy* for "Contract costing and the negotiation of contract prices," © 1986;

R. C. Stapleton and *Managerial Finance* for "The Pricing of Non-competitive Government Contracts," © 1984;

Managerial Finance for the revised version of "The Mechanics, Determinants and Management of Working Capital Investment," © 1984;

P. Barnes (ed.) and Simon & Schuster for "Zones, Ltd.," from *Case Studies in Financial Analysis*, © 1990.

E. Gaugler, H. G. Meissner and N. Thorn (eds.) and C. E. Poeschel Verlag for "The valuation of a business as a going concern," from *Zukunftsaspekte der anwendungsorientierten Betriebswirtschaftslehre*, © 1986;

Lafferty Publications Ltd. for "Was Woolworth ailing?" © 1982, "Why the current UDS takeover bids became inevitable," © 1983, "Call for SSAP 10 reform," © 1983;

Accounting and Business Research for "The Measurement of Corporate Performance on a Cash Flow Basis: A Reply to Mr. Egginton," © 1985;

A. W. Stark and *Lloyds Bank Review* for "Equity Values and Inflation, Dividends and Debt Financing," © 1981;

A. Aziz and D. C. Emanuel and *The Journal of Management Studies* for "Bankruptcy Prediction - An Investigation of Cash Flow Based Models," © 1988.

The editor of this volume is also extremely grateful for generous financial support he has received from the Esmée Fairbairn Charitable Trust in London for various studies he has initiated in the last twenty years or more. Many of the ideas contained in the following pages stem from this work.

Last but not least, the encouragement and help in the completion of this book from faculty and secretarial colleagues at SMU, and from the series editor, Richard Brief, should also be recorded. None of them should be held responsible for the deficiencies which remain.

Gerald H. Lawson
Edwin L. Cox School of Business
Southern Methodist University
Dallas, Texas, December, 1991

INTRODUCTION

1. Subject-matter

This collection of papers reflects its editor's long-standing interest in the creation of ownership value and the system of performance measurement which is logically-implicit in that objective, namely, cash flow-market value accounting.

The first paper is divided into two main parts which are supplemented with two appendices (A and B). Part 1 of Paper 1 contains a detailed description and appraisal of cash flow-market value accounting by reference to the desiderata of traditional accounting models. Part 2 discusses ways of assessing corporate dividend and debt-financing policies in a cash flow-market value accounting framework. Appendix B is an interpretation of the 1984-89 cash flow-market value performance and financial policies of Texas Instruments, Inc. and is intended to illustrate some of the main issues raised in both parts of Paper 1.

The second paper (on best practice in financial management and wealth maximization) also divides into two distinct halves. The first of these contains an outline of a normative wealth-maximizing (ownership value creation) framework which, in turn, is supplemented with questionnaire survey responses that are summarized in the second half of the paper.

Papers 1 and 2 therefore constitute a pair of related frameworks to which all twelve of the remaining papers can be related. These divide roughly equally between aspects of value creation on the one hand and the measurement and interpretation of financial performance (including the evaluation of financial policies) on the other.

In that a great deal of economic activity is organized in the form of individual contracts and projects, the third and fourth papers are deliberately intended to illustrate the implementation of the value creation objective in that context.

Paper 3 is basically concerned with the obviating of the possible adverse economic consequences of contract costing and pricing systems that ignore the cost of capital. It outlines a general contract pricing formula from which, starting with the risk-adjusted cost of capital, contract prices for any given (target) net present value can be derived.

Paper 4 deals with a rather more specific case of contract costing and pricing, namely, the pricing of non-competitive government contracts. The main issue to be resolved here turns on the rate of return which should be allowed to a contractor who undertakes a government contract in the absence of a competitive price-setting process. The relevant macroeconomic principle which should be invoked is that the contractor should be allowed a risk-commensurate return.

The risk which characterizes <u>any</u> contract is the likelihood that cost estimates will be exceeded. If the contractee agrees to absorb all cost overruns himself under some type of cost-plus pricing formula, the contractor enjoys a riskfree return and should be allowed to earn slightly more than the rate of return which can be obtained from a riskfree security of comparable cash flow time-profile and similar duration. However, if the contractor is required to bear the entire contract risk, he should be allowed a (higher) return which is <u>at least</u> commensurate with the risks characterizing the individual contract in question. Thus, as discussed in Paper 4, non-competitive contracts should be costed in a risk-return (cash flow) framework and priced at a level which offers a "more than risk-commensurate rate of return," i.e., positive net present value. This is, of course, subject to the proviso that regardless of the nature of the contract, a contractor should always (legitimately) attempt to charge any such higher price as the market will bear.

The fifth paper describes a multiperiod financial model which has many important practical and educational applications including the various analyses described in Papers 2, 6, 7 and 8. The model's specification accommodates multiperiod accruals-cash flow relationships together with changes in cost, price, output and investment, liquidity adjustments, inventory policy and corporate taxation. It can therefore evaluate any number of alternative scenarios from which, in turn, it projects multiperiod sequences of future income, cash flow and balance sheet statements - in about the same degree of detail as that contained in published annual reports. The model's outputs are therefore an eminently suitable means of summarizing alternative plans for presentation to boards of directors and a virtual _sine qua non_ for a 'top-down' planning approach which culminates in detailed operational plans.

In addition to the evaluation of alternative plans, other managerial uses of this kind of multiperiod model include: standard and target setting for reporting and control purposes, the analysis and management of working capital, internal corporate valuation, the valuation of take-over targets and other related external financial analysis, dividend policy analysis, the timing of external financial-raising; and, the resolution of 'what if' questions.

Apart from its obvious educational uses in elucidating the latter problem areas, the multiperiod model described in Paper 5 has powerful academic research applications. Thus, an obvious way of testing the multiperiod effects of accounting policy changes on financial statements is simply to include them in a multiperiod sequence of financial (output) statements which, in turn, can be compared under alternative economic scenario assumptions with the outputs of 'base case' accounting policy assumptions, i.e., each alternative economic scenario can be combined with "base case" and alternative accounting policies respectively. To the extent that accounting policy changes cause changes in corporate cash flows and therefore shareholder and/or lender cash flows, market value changes, i.e., real economic consequences of accounting policy changes, can also be anticipated.

A particularly powerful research application of the model described in paper 5 concerns the determinants of the degree of association between alternative measures of periodic cash flow and periodic profit measured on an accruals basis. Papers 6 and 7 include formal analyses and numerical examples of these determinants and therefore represent an approach which differs from that adopted in recent empirical work.

Using simple four-period examples, Paper 6 outlines a multiperiod analysis of working capital investment and attempts to clarify the objects of working capital management by reference to ownership value maximization. (The model specified in Paper 5 can be used to undertake precisely the analysis which is described in Paper 6.)

Periodic working capital investment can be defined as: periodic change in [receivables minus payables plus inventory]. Such periodic investment also constitutes the difference between (a) periodic profit (before interest, depreciation and tax expense and extraordinary items) alias funds from operations (before tax and interest expense) and (b) periodic operating cash flow (before interest and tax payments). Hence, an analysis of the determinants of periodic working capital investment is synonymous with an analysis of the relationship between periodic funds from operations (before interest and tax expense) and periodic operating cash flow (before interest and tax payments).

Introducing time-lags into this relationship, and making appropriate mathematical substitutions, results in framework with which an important FASB contention can be examined, namely, that conventionally-computed periodic profits are superior to coterminous periodic cash flows as a basis for predicting future cash flows. We return to this problem at the end of this introduction in commenting on the direction that ought perhaps to be taken by future empirical research on the association between accruals-based periodic earnings and periodic earnings measured on a cash flow basis.

The main conclusions that are drawn in Paper 6 stem from the following accruals-cash flow relationships.

i. Conventionally-measured periodic profit (before depreciation, interest and tax), HCP_j^*, characteristically overstates periodic operating cash flow, OCF_j, i.e., in general $HCP_j^* > OCF_j$ $(j = 1, 2...)$.

ii. As a consequence of i, a situation in which, on a continuing basis, $HCP_j^* > 0$ and $OCF_j < 0$ cannot be precluded. That is to say, whilst continuously reporting conventionally-measured profit, a firm may not be financially-viable. Such a firm can survive as a going concern if, and only if, it can access external sources of finance on a continuing basis.

iii. A further possible consequence of i is that when used as ranking criteria, HCP_j^* and OCF_j may give different rankings for alternative plans (A and B), i.e., $HCP_j^{*(A)} > HCP_j^{*(B)}$ but $OCF_j^{(A)} < OCF_j^{(B)}$ $(j = 1, 2, ...)$. As also suggested in Paper 2, this raises the presumption that the rankings of the respective sequences of projected ROIs (profit divided by capital employed) of alternative plans will at times conflict with their present value rankings.

iv. The characteristic excess of HCP_j^* over OCF_j is a function of about eight variables, including the periods of credit given to, and taken from, customers and suppliers respectively, periodic rates of change in costs, selling prices, and output ,etc.[1]

It also follows from the analysis contained in Paper 6 that break-even price-output conditions measured on an accruals basis will generally deviate from those that are derived from a cash flow break-even analysis. For any given selling price (output), the break-even cash flow output (price) will generally be higher than its accruals counterpart. This problem area, further analysis of the relationship between accruals and cash flow variables, and relevant empirical evidence have recently been examined in more detail elsewhere.[2]

As already indicated, Paper 7 is also concerned with the accruals-cash flow relationship. It reports the manner in which a (subsidiary) company involved in North Sea oil exploration, drilling and platform maintenance introduced cash flow break-even analysis. The company's preference for the latter was dictated by two considerations:

i. by a recognition that an accruals-based break-even analysis will usually not satisfy self-financing policy constraints because of the characteristic excess of periodic profit over periodic cash flow earnings; and,

ii. by a group financial constraint requiring each constituent subsidiary within the group to achieve a self-financing status within a five-year period, commencing January 1985, i.e., be able to operate as a going concern without resorting to inter-company and external financing other than short-term debt-financing for short-term contracts, the pricing of which fully allow for the cost of capital (see Paper 3).

It turns out that the somewhat capricious properties of the company's cash flow identity raise doubts about the reliability of single-period cash flow break-even analysis. The company's break-even conditions therefore need to be elucidated with the type of multiperiod financial model that is described in Paper 5.

Paper 8, "The valuation of a business as a going concern," is primarily intended to alert practitioners to much-neglected economic fundamentals. Going concern valuation and ownership value creation are closely related problem-areas that can be handled in identically the same valuation framework. The main valuation approach described in Paper 8 (the discounting of a stream of projected entity cash flows and horizon value) is, as already mentioned, a direct application of the multiperiod model outlined in Paper 5. A going concern valuation can thus be based upon numerous alternative scenario assumptions, e.g., those of potential buyers and sellers who may have different synergistic objectives. Alternatively, given the asking price of a going concern that is up for sale, the leading question may be: under what range of alternative scenarios will a buyer get his money back and, allowing for a risk-commensurate cost of capital, how long will it take?

Papers 9, 10 and 11 are case studies on the interpretation of the cash flow market value performances and financial policies of three major companies (two U.K. and one U.K./Dutch).

Paper 9 exemplifies the classic case of a company (Woolworth) which, going by its published income statements, seems to have turned in a good average performance during a five-year period (1977-82). Thus, its interest expense was covered no less than six times by its profit (before interest and taxes) during this half-decade and it apparently suffered tax at the seemingly modest average rate of 32 per cent. Additionally, with an average pay-out ratio of 52 percent it was (on paper) able to reinvest 48 percent of its net profits in the expectation of future earnings growth for its shareholders.

Woolworth's 1977-82 cash flow performance tells a somewhat different story. The true incidence of taxation amounted to 49 percent of pre-tax entity cash flow and 30 percent of shareholder cash flow was financed by lenders who also financed their own contractual and real interest payments. Furthermore, even though average periodic capital expenditure exceeded average periodic depreciation by 61 percent during 1977-82, it cannot in any real economic sense be said that profits were reinvested on the shareholders' behalf. Far from increasing the value of the business, actual capital expenditure could not prevent a real decline of about 26 percent in its total market value. The 53 percent decline in the real market value of equity (roughly £141.3 mill.) was not offset by the distribution of real aggregate shareholder cash flows of £112.6 mill. Shareholders therefore suffered substantial real capital erosion.

The decline in the Woolworth's total market value (market value of debt _plus_ market value of equity) was probably only a mild symptom of the much more serious illness which led to its take-over. At that time, the disposal value of its net assets exceeded the former value by at least a factor of two.

Paper 10 illustrates a further case in which the picture painted by a company's five-year sequence of income statements is largely inconsistent with its coterminous cash flow-market value performance. In each of the five years (1977-82) the company (UDS) reported positive, albeit declining, profits. Its aggregate (inflation-adjusted) post-tax entity cash flows amounted to £74.7 mill. whilst its (inflation-adjusted) total market value declined by £88.9 mill. UDS therefore sustained a five-year economic loss, i.e., change in market value _plus_ entity cash flow[3] of £14.2 mill. and suffered a _negative_ five-year entity rate of return of 1.15% p.a. (expressed in real terms).

Unlike the subject of Paper 9, UDS did not (partially) finance shareholder cash flows with debt and its interest payments were also internally financed. However, whilst, in these respects, UDS managed its dividend and debt-financing policies with some skill, its shareholders were nevertheless the victims of reverse leverage, i.e., a situation in which the rate of return on debt exceeds the entity rate of return, and, in the event, sustained a negative five-year rate of return of 2.46% p.a. (expressed in real terms).

The purpose of Paper 11 was to answer six alleged shortcomings of cash flow accounting.[4] Like Papers 9 and 10, it also illustrates the measurement and interpretation of the multiperiod (in this case seven-year) cash flow-market value performance of a large listed company, namely, Royal Dutch/Shell. The inferences which are drawn are typical examples of crucially important relationships which tend not to be brought out into the open by analyses of conventional income and balance sheet statements. They include:

i. a near confiscatory seven-year tax burden;

ii. the financing of 56 percent of shareholder and minority interest cash flows by lenders who also financed their own interest-payments; and,

iii. a significant degree of reverse leverage in the five-year sequence 1976-81.

Paper 12 was written in early 1983. It is an abridged version of a lengthier (1980) submission to the U.K. Accounting Standards Committee.[5] Both the original version and Paper 12 itself emphasize the shortcomings of the U.K. Statement of Standard Accounting Practice No. 10. (Sources and Application of Funds Statements) that was finally abandoned in 1991. They also enter a strong plea for the replacement of that statement with a full-blooded cash flow statement. Such a statement should, if is contended, distinguish between the cash flow implications of commercial activity on the one hand, and financial policies on the other, and thereby facilitate separate inferences about the efficiency of each.

Paper 13 (by Lawson and Stark) contains an interpretation of the 1961-77 aggregate cash flow performance of about 1,000 U.K. listed companies. It was originally written as a reply to another author.[6] The substance of Paper 13 can be summarized as follows, "...the [1961-77] financial behavior of U.K. companies is a classic example of what is nowadays known as the economic consequences of accounting data. In the post-war period, U.K. companies and the tax authorities behaved as though historic cost profit (before interest) constituted the amount that could be distributed on a continuing basis in the form of interest, taxes and dividends. However, a persistent, significant excess of pre-interest profit over entity cash flows resulted in a sequence of payments which could not be financed internally. The resultant deficit was virtually institutionalized as a feature of the system and, being debt-financed, therefore caused debt-equity substitution which, in turn, was reflected in a commensurate decline in real equity values."[7]

Paper 14 reports the results of research on the use of cash flow models for corporate bankruptcy prediction. This research was motivated by the belief that corporate insolvency is predominately, if not exclusively, a cash flow-market value phenomenon. Thus, the higher a company's expected (entity) cash flow generating capacity the higher will be its total market value and vice versa. Consequently, downward revisions to expectations hitherto held will not only cause a fall in total market value but, if great enough, will also result in an erosion of lenders' capital. Thus, if the market value of a corporation's expected cash flow stream falls below the realizable market value of lenders' collateral, no amount of debt rescheduling can generate a market value for lenders which exceeds the realizable value of their collateral and bankruptcy proceedings may become unavoidable.

Implicit in the use of <u>ex post</u> cash flow data in corporate bankruptcy prediction is the assumption that such data actually enter the expectations-formation process; and, that a deterioration in cash flow performance will be embodied in such expectations accordingly.

Recalling, as illustrated in Paper 6, that the characteristic excess of conventionally-measured periodic profit over periodic cash flows can take the form of positive profit and negative cash flows; there is thus at least one *a priori* reason why cash flow performance may be a better predictor of the onset of insolvency.

The results indicate that, as predictors of corporate bankruptcy, cash flow models compare at least favorably with other bankruptcy prediction models and that they are more accurate at longer ranges.

2. *Implications for further study*

The study of any problem area invariably lends to the conclusion that particular facets of the subject require further attention.

Mainly as a result of the pioneering efforts of Alfred Rappaport,[8] the ownership value creation approach to business management is now beginning to receive the attention it deserves from practitioners, academicians and students alike. Implicit in the adoption of this objective is the use of an *ex post* cash flow-market value accounting model for measuring the performance of the system, i.e., company specified as a multiperiod *ex ante* cash flow system. Put another way; a cash flow-market value model is the *ex post* analog of the system that is to be optimized.

In that, as emphasized in Paper 1, a cash flow-market value accounting model explicitly incorporates the observable financial relationship between a company and its owners, it complies with the criteria of representational faithfulness more stringently than do other accounting models. (This is also true of the ownership value creation objective vis à vis other objectives.) The conspicuous absence of a firm's owners from all other accounting models can indeed be counted as one of their most distinctive and perplexing features. It is a non-sequitur which deserves the serious attention of academicians and practitioners alike.

It is difficult to avoid the conclusion that the increasing popularity of the ownership value creation approach to corporate financial management will eventually lead to the recognition, as in operational research, that the performance of a system which is to be optimized should be measured in the very dimensions in which that system is specified. It might therefore be reasonably speculated that cash flow-market value performance indices will, in the fulness of time, supercede, or supplement, the bottom line of the income statement as the principal means of measuring ownership returns. Moreover, in that modern risk measures are also market-based, cash flow-market value accounting may well become the first two-parameter (risk-return) accounting model. This suggests some fairly obvious research possibilities.

A further avenue for research is sketched out in the second part of Paper 1. An accounting model which faithfully represents the financial relationship between a company and its owners ought to facilitate an appraisal of the efficiency of corporate dividend and debt-financing policies. Whilst such an acounting objective may, at first sight, appear to be outside the domain of that which is practically feasible in the forseeable future, it seems to have close affinities with the Miller-Modigliani divided prescription,[9] the specification of distributable income and Jensen's free cash flow theory.[10] Moreover, this latter theory may itself be a suitable subject for analysis in a multiperiod cash flow-market value framework; or constitute a basis for interpreting the economic expediency of ex post financial policies.

Thus, whilst it is perhaps unrealistic to expect the world's accounting bodies to promulgate an accounting standard on cash flow-market value accounting in the very near term, the growing influence of the ownership value creation approach to financial management, Jensen's free cash flow theory and agency theory should not be underrated. Efforts by accounting researchers on this front could yield new accounting prescriptions that would put some practitioners well ahead of statutory and other official requirements.

2.1 Current earnings and future cash flows

An issue which probably deserves further attention is the FASB's contention that historical earnings are superior to historical cash flows as a predictor of future cash flows. The FASB argument runs as follows:[11]

i. The primary objective of accounting data is to "...provide information to help present and potential investors, creditors and others assess the amounts, timing and uncertainty of prospective net cash inflows to the related enterprize (paragraph 37)."

ii. "Information about enterprize earnings based on accrual accounting generally provides a better indication of an enterprize's present and continuing ability to generate favorable cash flows than information limited to the financial aspects of cash receipts and payments" (p. ix).

iii. The [earnings-cash flow] relationship may be identified in a two-stage process for the assessment of future cash flows: a) reports of past earnings are used for the assessment of future earnings b) an adjustment is then made to the assessment of future earnings to derive an assessment of future cash flows (paragraph 8).[12]

The FASB's view is tantamount to asserting that the track record of a firm measured on an accruals accounting basis constitutes the best guidance on the formation of expectations about its future cash flows; or, alternatively, that a firm's cash flow track record is inferior to its accruals track record as a basis for the formation of cash flow expectations.

In the absence of corporate income taxes, and in corporate tax regimes in which taxable earnings are, in compliance with the principles of tax neutrality, measured on a cash flow basis, the FASB's view is counter-intuitive and readily controvertible. Under tax neutrality conditions, accruals accounting measurement is not a necessary part of the cash flow expectations-forming process. In the real world, corporate taxable earnings are universally measured on an accruals accounting basis - a measure which, as is well-known, violates corporate tax neutrality criteria. Equally significant in the present context is the previously-emphasized, non-stationary relationship between periodic entity cash flows and periodic accruals income.

In that the characteristic (relative) excess of pre-tax periodic accruals income over pre-tax entity cash flows is a function of about ten different variables, it varies enormously across companies and over time. Corporate income tax assessments based on taxable earnings measured on an accruals basis, therefore, not only cause considerable "fiscal drag," i.e., result in upward leverage on the effective rate of tax on pre-tax entity cash flows; such assessments also cause significant serial and cross-sectional variations in the relative burden of corporate income taxation on pre-tax entity cash flows (and thereby adversely influence the resource allocation process). Consequently, expected corporate tax payments cannot, as a rule, be directly estimated from pre-tax entity cash flow and must, therefore, be derived from expected taxable earnings - an accruals income variant. Indeed, only if taxable earnings measured on an accruals basis are incorporated into the cash flow expectations-forming process will financial markets correctly capture the true unsystematic incidence of corporate taxation on pre-tax entity cash flows.

The upshot of the previous two paragraphs is that accruals measures of periodic income enter the cash flow expectations-forming process only because the world's corporate tax systems do not comply with the principles of tax neutrality. Periodic income measured on an accruals basis is a convenient starting point for an elaboration of this contention.

As indicated by Appendix A of Paper 1, periodic historic cost profit, HCP_j, can, ignoring minority interests, be defined as:

$$HCP_j = d_j - (a_{j-1} + b_j - a_j) - L_j - F_j - t_j + (Y_j - X_j) \qquad (1)$$

A firm's periodic cash flow identity can be expressed as:

$$(k_j - h_j) - (A_j + R_j - Y_j) - t_j - H_j \equiv (F_j - N_j - M_j) + (D_j - B_j) \qquad (2)$$ [13]

In comparing and contrasting (1) and (2) in the light of the FASB propositions enumerated above, pre-depreciation profit (alias funds from operations before interest and tax expense) can be juxtaposed with operating cash flow (before tax and interest), i.e.,

$d_j - (a_{j-1} + b_j - a_j)$ can be compared with $k_j - h_j$.

Similarly, periodic depreciation plus the written down value of assets displaced, $L_j + X_j$, can be compared with capital expenditure $A_j + R_j$. (The proceeds of assets displaced, Y_j, can be ignored since they appear in both (1) and (2).) We return to taxes[14] on page 23.

2.1.1. Pre-depreciation profit and operating cash flow

The multiperiod relationships between the constituents of pre-depreciation profit on the one hand and the constituents of operating cash flow on the other, might be expected to elucidate their respective predictive powers, i.e., the predictive power of current pre-depreciation profit and current operating cash flow as predictors of future operating cash flows.

2.1.2 Accrued sales and sales receipts

The inter-period relationship between periodic accrued sales d_j ($j=1,2...$), is of the form:

$$d_j = d_{j-1}\,(1+v_j)(1+sp_j)$$

where, in period j,

v_j = change in sales volume; and, sp_j = change in selling price.

The corresponding sequence of sales receipts, k_j, (j=1,2...) is of the form:

$$k_j = \phi d_{j-1} + (1-\phi)d_j$$
$$= \phi d_{j-1} + (1-\phi)d_{j-1}(1+v_j)(1+sp_j)$$

where ϕ denotes the period of credit given to customers.

Thus,

$$k_{j+1} = \phi d_j + (1-\phi)d_j(1+v_{j+1})(1+sp_{j+1})$$
$$= \phi d_{j-1}(1+v_j)(1+sp_j) + (1-\phi)d_{j-1}(1+v_j)(1+sp_j)(1+v_{j+1})(1+sp_{j+1})$$

Therefore, k_{j+1}/k_j is given by:

$$\frac{k_{j+1}}{k_j} = \frac{(1+v_j)(1+sp_j)[\phi+(1-\phi)(1+v_{j+1})(1+sp_{j+1})]}{\phi + (1-\phi)(1+v_j)(1+sp_j)}$$

If v_j and sp_j and ϕ (j=1,2...) are serially constant, the relationship between k_j and k_{j+1} reduces to:

$$k_{j+1} = k_j(1+v_j)(1+sp_j).$$

Summarizing the foregoing analysis; estimated sales receipts k_{j+1} can, given estimates of v, sp_j and ϕ, be directly derived from k_j. Moreover, the relationship between k_j and k_{j+1} is entirely independent of current and future values of accrued sales (d_j and d_{j+1} respectively). This conclusion is diametrically opposed to the FASB's view.

2.1.3 Cost of sales and operating payments

The multiperiod relationship between the cost of sales, c_j, given by:

$$c_j = a_{j-1} + b_j - a_j$$

and operating payments, h_j, is rather more complex than the multiperiod relationship between accrued sales, d_j, and sales receipts, k_j.

Making the distinction between (periodic) fixed and variable costs, the periodic cost of sales, c_j, may be expressed as:

$$c_j = a_{j-1} + b_j^{(f)} + b_j^{(v)} - a_j.$$

Purchases, $b_j^{(f)} + b_j^{(v)}$ is therefore given by:

$$b_j^{(f)} + b_j^{(v)} = c_j + a_j - a_{j-1}$$

The corresponding sequence of operating payments, $h_j,(j=1,2,..)$ is of the form:

$$h_j = \gamma[\ b_{j-1}^{(f)} + b_{j-1}^{(v)}\ ] + (1-\gamma)[\ b_j^{(f)} + b_j^{(v)}\ ]$$

where γ denotes the period allowed by suppliers which, without loss of generality, can be assumed to be the same for both the fixed and variable components of purchases.

In showing that h_{j+1} can be directly derived from h_j it is convenient to partition operating payments into three components, namely:

payments $h_j^{(f)}$ in period j in respect of fixed costs

payments $h_j^{(v)}$ in period j in respect of the variable costs of sales

payments $h_j^{(i)}$ in period j in respect of periodic inventory adjustments.

Payments in respect of fixed costs

Payments, $h_j^{(f)}$, in period j in respect of fixed costs are given by:

$$h_j^{(f)} = \gamma b_{j-1}^{(f)} + (1-\gamma)b_j^{(f)}$$

$$= \gamma b_{j-1}^{(f)} + (1-\gamma)b_{j-1}^{(f)}\ (1+fc)$$

where fc denotes the rate of change in fixed costs in period j.

Similarly, $h_{j+1}^{(f)}$ is given by:

$$h_{j+1}^{(f)} = \gamma b_j^{(f)} + (1-\gamma)b_{j+1}^{(f)}$$

$$= \gamma b_{j-1}^{(f)}(1+fc_j) + (1-\gamma)b_{j-1}^{(f)}(1+fc_j)(1+fc_{j+1})$$

Therefore, $h_{j+1}^{(f)}/h_j^{(f)}$ is given by:

$$\frac{h_{j+1}^{(f)}}{h_j^{(f)}} = \frac{(1+fc_j)[\gamma+(1-\gamma)(1+fc_{j+1})]}{\gamma + (1-\gamma)(1+fc_j)}$$

and, as a function of the period of credit taken γ and the rates of change in fixed costs (fc_j, fc_{j+1}) in periods j and j+1, is independent of accrued fixed expense.

Payments in respect of the variable costs of sales

Re-arranging the above expression for periodic purchases, $b_j^{(f)} + b_j^{(v)}$, into its variable cost of sales, $c_j^{(v)}$, and inventory change, (a_j-a_{j-1}), components facilitates the specification of payments $h_j^{(v)}$ in respect of the variable cost of sales. Thus,

$$b_j^{(v)} = [\ c_j - b_j^{(f)}\ ] + (a_j - a_{j-1})$$

$$= c_j^{(v)} + (a_j - a_{j-1}).$$

Operating payments $h_j^{(v)}$ in period j in respect of the variable costs of sales are therefore given by:

$$h_j^{(v)} = \gamma c_{j-1}^{(v)} + (1-\gamma)c_j^{(v)}$$

$$= \gamma c_{j-1}^{(v)} + (1-\gamma)c_{j-1}^{(v)}(1+v_j)(1+vc_j)$$

where vc_j denotes the rate of change in unit variable costs in period j.[15]

Similarly, $h_{j+1}^{(v)}$ is given by:

$$h_{j+1}^{(v)} = \gamma c_j^{(v)} + (1-\gamma)c_{j+1}^{(v)}$$

$$= \gamma c_{j-1}^{(v)}(1+v_j)(1+vc_j) + (1-\gamma)c_{j-1}^{(v)}(1+v_j)(1+vc_j)(1+v_{j+1})(1+vc_{j+1})$$

Therefore, $h_{j+1}^{(v)}/h_j^{(v)}$ is given by:

$$\frac{h_{j+1}^{(v)}}{h_j^{(v)}} = \frac{(1+v_j)(1+vc_j)[\gamma+(1-\gamma)(1+v_{j+1})(1+vc_{j+1})]}{\gamma + (1-\gamma)(1+v_j)(1+vc_j)}$$

The interperiod relationship $(h_j^{(v)}, h_{j+1}^{(v)})$ is therefore independent of the variable cost of sales and any other accruals accounting measure.

Payments in respect of periodic inventory adjustments

Operating payments $h_j^{(i)}$ in period j in respect of inventory adjustments are given by:

$$\begin{aligned} h_j^{(i)} &= \gamma(a_{j-1}-a_{j-2}) + (1-\gamma)(a_j-a_{j-1}) \\ &= a_{j-1}(2\gamma-1) + a_j(1-\gamma) - \gamma a_{j-2} \\ &= a_{j-2}(1+v_{j-1})^{½}(1+vc_{j-1})(2\gamma-1) \\ &\qquad + a_{j-2}(1+v_{j-1})^{½}(1+vc_{j-1})(1+v_j)^{½}(1+vc_j)(1-\gamma) - \gamma a_{j-2} \end{aligned}$$

[The ½ exponential adjustment to the sales volume factors $(1+v_{j-1})$ and $(1+v_j)$ is the assumption that the firm's inventory policy conforms to the EOQ model]. Operating payments $h_{j+1}^{(i)}$ in respect of inventory adjustments are defined in the same manner as $h_j^{(i)}$. After first substituting for a_{j-1}, a_j and a_{j+1} in the expression for $h_{j+1}^{(i)}$, the ratio $h_{j+1}^{(i)}/h_j^{(i)}$ reduces to:

$$\frac{h_{j+1}^{(i)}}{h_j^{(i)}} = \frac{(1+v_j)^{½}(1+vc_j)[2\gamma-1+(1+v_{j+1})^{½}(1+vc_{j+1})(1-\gamma)]-\gamma}{[2\gamma-1+(1+v_j)^{½}(1+vc_j)(1-\gamma)]-\gamma/(1+v_{j-1})^{½}(1+vc_{j-1})}$$

That is to say, the relationship between $h_j^{(i)}$ and $h_{j+1}^{(i)}$ is a function of the period of credit, γ, taken from suppliers, periodic rates of change in inventory volume e.g., $(1+v_j)^{½}-1$, and the periodic rates of change in unit variable costs. Thus, as is also true of future payments in respect of fixed operating costs and the variable cost of sales, future payments in respect of periodic inventory adjustments can be estimated directly from the corresponding current payments and wholly independently of the corresponding current and future accruals measures. This conclusion is also diametrically opposed to the FASB's view.

Summing up the implications of the foregoing analysis; expectations about a firm's future operating cash flows (sales receipts, k_j, minus operating payments, h_j,) can be based directly upon its operating cash flow track record and can thus be formed entirely independently both of its *ex post* profits (before depreciation, interest and taxes) and future profit expectations. This contention is entirely at odds with the FASB's assumptions.

2.1.4. Periodic depreciation and other amounts written off versus periodic capital expenditure

Although the FASB does not actually state that current periodic depreciation should be used to forecast future periodic depreciation (as a basis for estimating future periodic capital expenditure), such a contention seems to be implicit in the last of the three FASB propositions enumerated above. In any event, this view does not appear to stand up to serious analysis.

Periodic depreciation is typically an aggregation of fractions of the historic costs of an asset stock which, in the case of manufacturing industry has an average life of about 20 years with a standard deviation of approximately 7 years. Conservative accounting practice typically results in depreciation policy that is based on asset life-estimates averaging about two thirds of actual service lives. Thus, current periodic depreciation (plus other amounts written off) is probably an accurate estimate of future periodic depreciation because periodic depreciation is a (fairly slow) moving-average. However, in deciding whether future periodic depreciation is an acceptable proxy for the same period's capital expenditure, the leading question is: does an aggregation of fractions of the successive values of a historic time-series of capital expenditures constitute a reasonable basis for the formation of expectations about future capital expenditure? It is therefore helpful to distinguish between expectations of zero growth (steady-state), growth and decline.

A zero-growth situation can here be regarded as one in which, roughly speaking, a firm maintains a constant scale of productive and trading capacity over time, by undertaking replacement investment, in the expectation of an approximately constant future sales volume. Such expenditure is, subject to embodied technological progress, principally a function of the age-structure and remaining service lives of the individual constituents of its existing productive (and trading) asset stock which have their own individual replacement cycles.

A growth situation can thus be regarded as one in which a firm increases its scale of trading and productive capacity in preparation for expected sales volume growth. In these conditions, periodic capital expenditure comprises both replacement and growth investment. Growth investment will, in turn, set up its own replacement cycles.

A business that is on the decline can be type-cast as one which anticipates a continuous fall in future sales volume. In this situation some, albeit serially-declining, replacement investment might be expected as trading and productive capacities are tailored to the declining sales volume.

It can readily be shown that in steady state and growth situations, periodic capital expenditure will typically exceed periodic depreciation by significant orders of magnitude.[16] This characteristic excess is a positive function of: periodic nominal rate of increase in asset acquisition costs, the age-structure of existing assets and their replacement cycles (useful service lives), growth capital expenditure (which is also a function of current idle capacity) and assumed asset-lives for depreciation policy purposes. Thus, if future periodic depreciation is to be used as a basis for forecasting future capital expenditure, the issue to be resolved is as just implied: the amount by which (in the case of steady-state and growth situations) the future depreciation charge must be scaled up in order to compensate for the characteristic excess of periodic capital expenditure over periodic depreciation. But to answer this question it is first necessary to estimate the future level of periodic capital expenditure which is a function of about six different variables. To estimate the capital expenditure-depreciation relationship under conditions of decline, it is also necessary to make an independent estimate of future periodic capital expenditure.

In that the variables which determine the characteristic excess of periodic capital expenditure over periodic depreciation take on different values across companies, and over time, the possibility of obtaining direct estimates of the excess of the former over the latter can be ruled out. There is no stationary parameter value which can be used for this purpose[17] and there are therefore no serious grounds for assuming that future periodic depreciation is an accurate predictor of the same period's capital expenditure. In other words, accruals accounting depreciation policy is not a necessary part of the cash flow expectations-formation process.

Additionally, it should be noted that the characteristic excess of periodic capital expenditure over periodic depreciation is usually greater than, but nevertheless compounds, the characteristic excess of periodic pre-depreciation profit over periodic operating cash flow. There are, therefore, serious grounds for the utmost scepticism about the second of the two FASB propositions enumerated above solely because it reveals no awareness of a significant 'feature of the system,' namely, a characteristic excess of conventionally-measured periodic earnings over periodic entity cash flows. Contrary to popular belief, this periodic excess is, therefore, typically cumulative and is not a self-reversing timing-difference. Indeed, it is precisely because of this "feature of the system" that the multiperiod effective rate of tax on pre-tax entity cash flows usually exceeds the multiperiod ratio of tax expense (excluding provisions for deferred taxation) to pre-tax income (before interest) measured on an accruals basis. (See Paper 1, Appendix B and Papers 9, 11 and 13).

We can now return to the contention that accruals accounting measures enter the cash flow expectations-formation process solely because of the universally non-neutral character of corporate income tax systems. As shown above, accruals accounting measures are not a necessary part of the formation of expectations about the operating cash flow, $k_j - h_j$, and capital expenditure, $A_j + R_j - Y_j$, constituents of future entity cash flows. [The expected periodic liquidity change, H_j, can be assumed to be a function of operating and capital expenditure transactions, $(k_j - h_j)$, $(A_j + R_j - Y_j)$].

In a neutral corporate tax regime, pre-tax entity cash flows, $(k_j - h_j) - (A_j + R_j - Y_j) - H_j$, need only be multiplied by a serially-constant tax factor $(1-T^*)$ in deriving post-tax entity cash flows, i.e., in such a regime post-tax entity cash flows, $ENCF_j^*$, are given by:

$$ENCF_j^* = [(k_j - h_j) - (A_j + R_j - Y_j) - H_j](1-T^*).$$

In a non-neutral corporate tax regime, in which taxable earnings are measured on an accruals basis, periodic post-tax entity cash flows, $ENCF_j$, are given by:

$$\begin{aligned} ENCF_j &= (k_j - h_j) - (A_j + R_j - Y_j) - H_j - T_j[d_j - (a_{j-1} + b_j - a_j) - TDA_j - F_j + Y_j] \\ &= (k_j - h_j) - (A_j + R_j - Y_j) - H_j - T_j TE_j \end{aligned}$$

Where T_j, TDA_j and TE_j respectively denote the corporate tax rate, tax depreciation allowances and taxable earnings in year j.

As typically, $d_j - (a_{j-1} + b_j - a_j) > k_j - h_j$ and $A_j + R_j > TDA_j$ then, as a rule,

$$d_j - (a_{j-1} + b_j - a_j) - TDA_j - F_j + Y_j > (k_j - h_j) - A_j + R_j - Y_j) - H_j.$$

More to the point, however, is that, in a non-neutral corporate tax regime, the market capitalization process should be specified as:

$$TMV_0 = \sum_{j=1}^{\infty} \frac{(\bar{k}_j - \bar{h}_j - (\bar{A}_j + \bar{R}_j - \bar{Y}_j) - \bar{H}_j - \bar{T}_j \overline{TE}_j}{(1+\bar{r})^j}$$

That is to say, the normative valuation model should incorporate the universal feature of corporate income tax systems, namely, taxable earnings measured on an accruals basis. Reiterating the substance of this section; the non-compliance of corporate income tax systems with the principles of tax neutrality is the sole justification for the FASB's contention to the effect that accruals income measurement is a necessary part of the cash flow expectations-formation process - the FASB is right but for the wrong reason!

We conclude this section by suggesting that considerable mileage should be gained from further empirical research in the areas outlined above commencing, perhaps, with projections from a multiperiod financial model.

A related possibility which could also be explored with the aid of the model outlined in Paper 5 lies in the multiperiod relationships between cash flow and accruals variables in alternative economic scenarios. Thus, to the extent that earnings changes (which may be associated with market value changes) are proxying for cash flow changes, the non-stationary relationship between accruals and cash flow variables may explain the variability of earnings response coefficients. The outputs of a multiperiod financial model might give some guidance on the kind of empiricism that would convincingly demonstrate that earnings response coefficients have genuine economic content and are not merely accounting artifacts.

2.2 Evidence of the relationship between earnings and cash flows

This section contains comments on the direction taken by some of the reported research on the relationship between earnings and cash flows.

One of the most frequently cited papers on this subject is the 1986 contribution by Bowen, Burgstahler and Daley (BBD) who address themselves to three specific questions namely:

1. Are the traditional CF measures used in previous research highly correlated with alternative measures of cash flow that have recently been advocated by academics and practitioners?
2. Are accrual accounting earnings and cash flow measures highly correlated?
3. Does earnings or a CF variable best predict future cash flows?

BBD define five measures of cash flow. Each of these can in fact be expressed in terms of the constituent variables of historic cost profit (equation (1) above) and/or variables in equation (2) (periodic cash flow identity). BBD's cash flow measures, CF(1), CF(2), CF(3), CF(4) and CF(5) are therefore given by:

$$CF(1) = d_j - (a_{j-1}+b_j-a_j) - F_j - t_j^* + (Y_j-X_j)$$

$$CF(2) = d_j - (a_{j-1}+b_j-a_j) - F_j - t_j^*$$

$$CF(3) = [\phi d_{j-1} + (1-\phi)d_j] - [\gamma b_{j-1}] + (1-\gamma)b_j] - F_j - t_j$$

$$= k_j - h_j - F_j - t_j$$

$$CF(4) = [\phi_{j-1} + (1-\phi)d_j] - [\gamma b_{j-1} + (1-\gamma)b_j] - F_j - t_j - (A_j+R_j-Y_j)$$

$$= k_j - h_j - F_j - t_j - (A_j+R_j-Y_j)$$

$$CF(5) = H_j$$

[t_j^* denotes periodic tax expense as opposed to periodic tax payment t_j.]

None of these five definitions specifies periodic entity cash flow. This is significant in that a company's observable total market value, i.e., market value of debt plus market value of entity, is usually assumed to be a function of its future entity cash flows. Of the above five measures, CF(4) is the closest approximation of periodic entity cash flow. It includes interest payments, F_j, but excludes periodic liquidity change H_j. Thus, CF(4) = $ENCF_j - F_j + H_j$.

Though commonly described as such, the first two definitions are not cash flow specifications at all; they are pure accruals income variants.

The third measure CF_3 is indeed a pure cash flow specification. It is nevertheless objectionable in that it contains interest payments which are a function of financial policy. As a discretionary variable, financial policy should arguably be separated from the prediction of future cash flow generating capacity - a process which is preeminently a matter of commercial logic that is independent of financial policy.

To describe liquidity change CF(5) as a cash flow measure is to assume that it is a dependent variable. A central proposition of financial economics is that a company's liquidity level should be a function of transactions, precautionary and speculative motives. Periodic liquidity changes should therefore reflect adjustments stemming from changes in the intensities of these motives. In other words, periodic liquidity changes are, like capital investment, an independent variable and ought to be interpreted as such. To treat liquidity changes as a dependent variable is to assume that firms ignore transactionary, precautionary and speculative considerations. Casual observations of the serial and cross-section behavior of liquidity levels negates any such assumption. It should nevertheless be noted that, as an independent variable, periodic liquidity changes can be expected to be positively correlated with CF(1), CF(2), CF(3) and CF(4). Why? Because the constituents of each of these measures is a rough and ready surrogate for the scale of a firm's transactions.

The correlation among the other CF measures can virtually be predicted from the similarities between their respective specifications. Precisely the same point can be made about BBD's (Question 2) analysis of the correlation between periodic (accruals) earnings and periodic cash flows. It might, therefore, reasonably be questioned whether, in researching the issues raised by BBD's three questions, immediate resort should be made to statistical analysis. In that the interrelationships between periodic earnings and periodic cash flow measures, with or without time-lags, can be precisely specified in simple algebraic terms, that kind of analysis ought to precede the statistical tests. Moreover, in that this relationship is a function of about ten different variables, e.g., periodic changes in sales volume, selling prices, costs, capital expenditure, etc.[18] which may change significantly over time, these variables ought to be separately controlled for if convincing conclusions are to be derived from empirical analysis. In other words, empirical analysis ought to follow a formal analysis of the relevant explanatory variables and this approach might also be expected to constitute a sound basis for the interpretation of empirical results.

2.3 Evidence on stock market reactions to the cash flow and accruals components of periodic earnings

One of the best known papers on this subject is the contribution by Bernard and Stober.[19] In commenting on previously-reported evidence they state, "Prior studies of the information in cash flows and accruals [Wilson, 1986 and 1987; Rayburn, 1986; and Bowen et al., 1987] can be interpreted within a common framework. Each decomposed accounting earnings as follows:

  Cash Flow from Operations
+ Current Accruals
= Working Capital from Operations
+ Noncurrent Accruals
= Accounting Earnings.

Here, current accruals include such items as increases in inventories and receivables and decreases in payables, while depreciation and deferred income taxes are (negative) noncurrent accruals."[20]

As indicated in the first paper in this anthology,[21] the cash flow-accruals dichotomy adopted by Bernard and Stober (and the others cited above) is an under-specification which cannot be directly embodied in a cash flow valuation framework. This dichotomy is, therefore, an inadequate basis for the analysis and interpretation of stock price reactions to unexpected changes in the cash flow and accruals components of periodic earnings.

A study by McConnell and Muscarella[22] provides evidence that (except in the oil industry) stock prices respond positively to announcements of increased investment expenditures and negatively to reduced expenditures. Thus, the absence of capital expenditure from the earnings dichotomy used by Bernard and Stober (and others) must be regarded as a serious deficiency.

The formulation of a dichotomized cash flow-accruals earnings measure which is directly related to the normative valuation model, and which therefore embodies capital expenditure, can begin with a firm's periodic cash flow identity, namely,

$$(k_j-h_j) - (A_j+R_j-Y_j) - t_j - H_j \equiv (D_j-B_j) + (F_j-N_j-M_j)$$

or,

$$ENCF_j \equiv SHCF_j + LCF_j$$

The normative cash flow valuation model can thus be represented as:

$$\sum_{j=1}^{\infty} \frac{\overline{ENCF_j}}{(1+\bar{r})^j} \equiv \sum_{j=1}^{\infty} \frac{\overline{SHCF_j}}{(1+\bar{r}_e)^j} + \sum_{j=1}^{\infty} \frac{\overline{LCF_j}}{(1+\bar{r}_d)^j}$$

or,

$$TMV_o \equiv MV^{(e)} + MV_o{}^{(d)}$$

Ex post periodic income measured on a cash flow-market value basis (economic profit), $ENPROF_j$ is, therefore, given by:

$$ENPROF_j = ENCF_j + TMV_j - TMV_{j-1}$$

$$= [(k_j-h_j) - (A_j+R_j-Y_j) - t_j - H_j] + TMV_j - TMV_{j-1}$$

Historic cost profit (before interest), $HCP_j{}^{\dagger}$, is given by:[23]

$$HCP_j{}^{\dagger} = d_j - (a_{j-1} + b_j-a_j) - L_j - t_j + (Y_j-X_j)$$

$$= RE_j + D_j + F_j$$

$$= (NW_j-NW_{j-1}) - (B_j+N_j-M_j) + D_j + F_j$$

$$= NW_j - NW_{j-1} + ENCF_j.$$

Thus, whilst dichotomized economic profit and dichotomized historic cost profit (before interest) contain the same (entity) cash flow component, they have different periodic "change in value" components. The former contains the observable periodic change in market values whereas the latter contains the periodic change in (entity) net book values, ΔNW_j. The periodic change, ΔNW_j can, in turn, be represented as the increase in the net book value of fixed assets plus periodic working capital investment (including liquidity change) and is given by:

$$\begin{aligned}\Delta NW_j &= HCP_j{}^{\dagger} - ENCF_j \\ &= (A_j+R_j-L_j-X_j) + [(d_j-k_j) + (a_j-a_{j-1}) - (b_j-h_j) + H_j] \\ &= \text{periodic change in } \{(\text{net book value of fixed assets}) \\ &\quad + (\text{receivables} + \text{inventory} - \text{payables} + \text{liquidity})\}\end{aligned}$$

It is important to emphasize that the normative valuation model represents the capitalization of an expected entity cash flow stream and not the capitalization of expected economic profits. The capitalization of the latter would, in fact, constitute double-counting - a possibility that can be ruled out in a market that is semi-strong efficient. Likewise, the capitalization of an expected $HCP_j{}^{\dagger}$ stream would also constitute a greater or lesser degree of double-counting and can also be ruled out. Thus, it follows that a periodic entity cash flow specification constitutes the best guidance as to the nature of the expectations-forming and capitalization processes which generate observable market values. These processes include the estimation of the future incremental entity cash flow stream that can be expected from currently-recorded increases or decreases in capital expenditure or, perhaps more directly, the net present values attributable thereto.

This line of argument raises the presumption that the accruals component of periodic income has little or no information content and that unexpected changes therein should have no significant effect on a company's market value.

A consideration of the constituents of the periodic change in net book value, ΔNW_j, provides some support for this hypothesis. Thus, whereas the inventory and liquidity components of periodic working capital investment may be symptomatic of planned adjustments to the level of transactions in the forthcoming period, the receivables and (non-inventory change) payables components are a direct function of the previous period's transactions. As demonstrated in Paper 6, given the periods of credit given and taken, receivables less payables (excluding the inventory change component) constitute a sunk cost of supporting an existing activity level. Merely to maintain that activity level (in a world of continuously increasing (nominal) costs and selling prices) necessitates further (nominal) periodic working capital investments on a continuing basis.

As regards the periodic change in the net book value of fixed assets, it seems unlikely that this constitutes information which is incremental to that embodied in periodic entity cash flow $ENCF_j$. That is to say, the periodic depreciation charge probably has no information content because, as a (relatively slow) moving-average of fractions of historic time-series outlays, it can hardly spring surprises. Moreover, as periodic historic cost depreciation significantly understates the same period's replacement investment, the periodic change in the net book value of fixed assets is not an acceptable approximation of periodic growth capital expenditure.

A recognition that the periodic change in net book value, ΔNW_j, i.e., the accruals component of periodic income, can be regarded as a proxy for the corresponding periodic change in market value also raises doubts about the information content of ΔNW_j. If NW_{j-1} and NW_j are, at best, proxies for observable market values (TMV_{j-1}, TMV_j), changes in the former are unlikely to provide information which is incremental to that contained in TMV_{j-1} and TMV_j.

We conclude this introduction by reiterating the view that empirical research in accounting might contribute rather more to the body of knowledge were it to be preceded by careful attention to a conceptual framework that is solidly based on fundamentals of financial economics. It is probably no exaggeration to state that the explosion in empirical research in accounting which has been a feature of the last two decades has not been without considerable opportunity cost to the conceptual foundations of the subject. Stock market reactions to periodic earnings surprises and the notion of earnings response coefficients are typical examples of research directions that have probably added little to a genuine understanding of the economic consequences of accounting numbers.

Notes

[1]It is only a short step to the conclusion that the introduction of periodic depreciation, L_j, and other periodic amounts written off, X_j, into HCP_j* on the one hand, and periodic capital expenditure, $A_j + R_j$, and periodic liquididty change, H_j, into OCF_j on the other, increases the excess of periodic accruals earnings over periodic cash flows. The latter periodic excess can then be expressed as a function of at least two more variables, namely, periodic nominal rate of change in asset prices and real rate of change in periodic capital expenditure.

[2]See Schweitzer, Trossmann and Lawson (1991), pp. 256-277.

[3]See Paper 1, page 12.

[4]See page 99 (original pagination).

[5]Lawson (1980).

[6]B. J. Moore (1980). Professor Moore also published two replies (1981a and 1981b). Lawson and Stark added a rejoinder (1981b) to the present paper.

[7]Lawson and Stark (1981b), p. 43.

[8]See for example, Rappaport (1986).

[9]Miller and Modigliani (1961).

[10]Jensen (1986).

[11]FASB (1978).

[12]FASB (1979). The FASB's position on this issue in 1987 was as follows, "Some investors and creditors may assess future cash flows in part by first estimating future income based in part on reports of past income and then converting those future income estimates to estimates of future cash flows by allowing for leads and lags between cash flows and income. Information about similar leads and lags in the past are likely to be helpful in that process." (paragraph 36).

[13]See Paper 1, page 3.

[14]Periodic tax expense reported in the income statement may deviate from periodic tax payments shown in the cash flow identity (because of deferred taxation provisions, preceding year basis of taxation, etc.).

[15]The product $(1+v_j)(1+vc_j)$ is an (accurate) approximation of $c_j^{(v)}/c_{j-1}^{(v)}$ which is in fact given by:

$$c_j^{(v)}/c_{j-1}^{(v)} = (z_j y_j - a_{j-1} vc_j)/(z_{j-1} y_{j-1} - a_{j-2} vc_{j-1})$$

$$\simeq z_{j-1} y_{j-1}(1+v_j)(1+vc_j)/z_{j-1} y_{j-1}$$

where y and z denote unit variable cost and sales volume respectively.

For example, putting $z_{j-1}y_{j-1} = 10{,}000$, $a_{j-2} = 1{,}000$, $vc_{j-1} = 0.04$, $vc_j = 0.05$, , $v_{j-1} = 0.045$ and $v_j = 0.035$;

$$c_j^{(v)}/c_{j-1}^{(v)} = \frac{z_{j-1}y_{j-1}(1+v_j)(1+vc_j) - a_{j-2}(1+v_{j-1})^{1/2}(1+vc_{j-1})vc_j}{z_{j-1}y_{j-1} - a_{j-2}vc_{j-1}}$$

$$= \frac{10{,}000(1.035)(1.05) - 1{,}000(1.045)^{1/2}(1.04)(0.05)}{10{,}000 - 1{,}000(0.04)}$$

$$= 1.08578$$

whereas,

$$(1+v_j)(1+vc_j) = (1.035)(1.05) = 1.08675.$$

[16]Evidence and a formal analytical basis for this contention are given in Schweitzer, Trossmann and Lawson op.cit., p. 259-60.

[17]This is also true of the characteristic inter-period and cross-section excess of periodic pre-depreciation over periodic operating cash flow.

[18]See Schweitzer, Trossman and Lawson, op.cit.

[19]Bernard and Stober (1989).

[20]Bernard and Stober, op. cit., pp. 625-6.

[21]See pages 3-8.

[22]McConnell and Muscarella (1985).

[23]See Paper 1, Appendix A for an elaboration of the analysis which follows.

References

Bernard, V. L. and Stober, T. L., "The Nature and Amount of Information in Cash Flows and Accruals," The Accounting Review, Vol. LXIV, No. 4, October 1989, pp. 624-652.

Bowen, R. M., Burgstahler, D. and Daley, L. A., "Evidence on the Relationships Between Earnings and Various Measures of Cash Flow," The Accounting Review, Vol. LX1, No. 4, October 1986, pp. 713-725.

Financial Accounting Standards Board, Objectives of Financial Reporting by Business Enterprizes, 1978.

______, Discussion Memorandum: An Analysis of Issues Related to Reporting Earnings, 1979.

______, Statement of Financial Accounting Standards No. 95: Statement of Cash Flows, 1987.

Jensen, M. C., "Agency Costs of Free Cash Flow, Corporate Finance, and Takeovers," American Economic Review, Vol. 76, No. 2, May 1986, pp. 323-329.

Lawson, G. H., "Memorandum on statement of standard accounting practice SSAP10 (funds statement) to the Accounting Standards Committee (U.K.) in Hicks, B. E. and Hunt, P. (eds) Cash Flow Accounting, The Research and Publication Division, School of Commerce and Administration, Laurentian University, 1981, pp. 172-214.

Lawson, G. H., and Stark, A. W., "Equity Values and Inflation: A Rejoinder," Lloyds Bank Review, October 1981, No. 142, pp. 39-43.

McConnell, J. J. and Muscarella, C. J., "Corporate Capital Expenditure Decisions and the Market Value of the Firm," Journal of Financial Economics, 14, No. 3, 1985.

Miller, M. H. and Modigliani, F., "Dividend Policy, Growth and the Valuation of Shares," Journal of Business, 34, 1961, pp. 411-433.

Moore, B. J., "Equity Values and Inflation: The Importance of Dividends," Lloyds Bank Review, July 1980, No. 137, pp. 1-15.

______, "Equity Values and Inflation: Reply," Lloyds Bank Review, January 1981, No. 139, pp. 55-57.

______"Equity Values and Inflation: Reply," Lloyds Bank Review, October 1981, No. 142, pp. 44-45.

Rappaport, A., Creating Shareholder Value: The New Standard for Business Performance, The Free Press, New York, 1986.

Schweitzer, M., Trossmann, E. and Lawson, G. H., Break-even Analyses: Basic Model, Variants, Extensions, John Wiley & Sons, 1991, pp. 256-277.

Assessing economic performance and corporate financial policies on a cash flow-market value basis

by

G. H. Lawson

Contents

Assessing economic performance and corporate financial policies on a cash flow-market value basis†

Introduction

The first part of this paper justifies the use of an operationalized *ex post* analog of the normative discounted cash flow valuation model in meeting two preeminent objectives of accounting:

i. the disclosure of information to facilitate the formation of investor expectations about corporate cash flows; and,

ii. income measurement.

This *ex post* cash flow-market value (CF-MV) model is evaluated by reference to such familiar notions as distributable income and capital maintenance, representational faithfulness, recognition criteria, etc.

The second part of the paper discusses ways of assessing corporate dividend and debt-financing policies in a CF-MV accounting framework. It first considers the possible economic consequences of a "Lintner-type" dividend policy. Previous studies have suggested that the characteristic excess of historic cost profit over entity (i.e., corporate) cash flows may, result in dividends (net of new equity raised) which are financed with debt. Debt-financed dividends substitute debt for equity and may cause shareholder wealth losses and/or wealth transfers from shareholders to lenders. Unlike other corporate

---

†Originally presented by the author, as one of two principal speakers, at an international conference sponsored by the Universite de Nice and Banque Populaire de la Côte d'Azur on cash flow accounting at Nice, December, 1990.

I am grateful to my accounting colleagues at SMU for their lively and constructive criticisms of the first draft of this paper and to Michael Vetsuypens (Finance Department, SMU) for his constructive criticism and editorial work on the previous draft. The remaining objectionable parts are entirely my responsibility.

accounting models, the CF-MV model presented here can be used to analyze the efficiency of dividend and debt-financing policies.

Part 1: Cash flow expectations and performance measurement

The value and continuity of a business enterprise and the returns it can provide for its owners depend upon its cash flow-generating capacity. This implies that the past performance of a going concern and *ex post* ownership returns ought to be measureable on a cash flow basis. A distinction, which is crucial from an operational standpoint, between a *pure* cash flow accounting model and a cash flow-market value accounting model can, however, be made.

The foregoing propositions can be elaborated by reference to two paramount objectives of external financial reporting, one modern the other ancient, i.e.,

- the disclosure of such information as facilitates the formation of investor expectations about the main determinant of a firm's market value, namely, its future cash flow generating capacity; and,

- the measurement of *ex post* periodic income.

1.1 Formation of expectations about future cash flows

The stream of cash flows generated by a business enterprise (hereafter 'entity') is divided between lenders and stockholders in a ratio which reflects its dividend and debt-financing policies. This partitioning of (entity) cash flows also divides total (entity) market value into the market values of its debt and equity.

The distinction between entity and claimholder cash flows on the one hand, and between entity and claimholder market values on the other can be expressed as two simple identities. As argued hereafter, these distinctions should be explicitly allowed for in reporting performance as a guide to the formation of expectations and in measuring *ex post* income.

For any year j, an entity's cash flow identity, allowing for minority interests (if any), is defined as:

entity cash flow(j)	≡	lender cash flow(j)	+	shareholder cash flow(j)	+	minority interests cash flow(j)

or, in more compact shorthand form,

$ENCF_j \equiv LCF_j + SHCF_j + MICF_j$;

or, in more detailed accounting form,

$$(k_j-h_j) - (A_j+R_j-Y_j) - t_j - H_j \equiv (F_j-N_j-M_j) + (D_j-B_j) + [D_j^{(MI)}-B_j^{(MI)}] \quad (1)$$

where, in year j,

k_j-h_j = operating cash flow represented by cash collected from customers, k_j, and operating payments, h_j;

$A_j+R_j-Y_j$ = replacement investment, A_j, growth investment, R_j, and the proceeds from assets displaced, Y_j;

t_j = corporate income tax payments;

H_j = liquidity change, i.e., change in cash and cash equivalents;

F_j = interest payments;

N_j = medium and/or long-term debt raised (-ve) or repaid (+ve);

M_j = short-term debt raised (-ve) or repaid (+ve);

D_j = dividends paid to shareholders;

B_j = equity capital raised (-ve) or repaid (+ve);

$D_j^{(MI)}$ = dividends paid to minority interests; and,

$B_j^{(MI)}$ = equity capital raised (-ve) from, or repaid (+ve) to, minorities.

The latter cash flow identity can be contrasted with the cash flow classification prescribed by the FASB (1987) and followed by the British ASC in Exposure Draft 54 (1990), namely (ignoring minority interests),

$$(k_j-h_j-F_j-t_j) - (A_j+R_j-Y_j) - (D_j-B_j-N_j-M_j) \equiv H_j$$

i.e.,

operating cash flow net of interest and taxes paid	-	net capital expenditure	-	dividends paid net of equity and debt financing	≡	liquidity change

The FASB-ASC cash flow classification can be criticized on at least four grounds:

(i) It erroneously treats contractual interest payments as an operating cost and thereby fails to allow for the "Fisher effect", i.e., the fact that contractual interest payments embody a significant element of lenders' principal which is repaid accordingly.† The FASB-ASC classification therefore generally understates "true" operating cash flow and does not facilitate direct inter-company operating cash flow comparisons.

(ii) In treating tax payments as a constituent of operating cash flow, rather than as a separate variable, it fails to recognize that tax payments are a function of a company's financial policy. Moreover, the separate disclosure of taxes facilitates a direct assessment of the effective incidence of corporate taxation in accordance with well-established principles of tax neutrality.

(iii) It wrongly treats the periodic change in cash balances as a dependent variable. A long-established principle of financial economics is that a firm's liquidity level should be a function of transactions precautionary and speculative motives. Hence, revisions to

---

†See Modigliani and Cohn (1979).

expectations concerning these motives will cause liquidity adjustments which are therefore an independent variable in the same sense as capital expenditures. (In fact the ASC advocates the inclusion of some, or all, of M_j with H_j and thereby confuses liquidity, which is an asset, with the way in which that asset is financed).

(iv) As a consequence of (i) and (iii), the FASB-ASC classification fails to separate the entity cash flows which are generated by a firm's commercial activities from the partitioning of those flows between lenders and shareholders which is a separate financial policy decision.

The entity and ownership valuation identity (at end-year 0) which corresponds to cash flow identity (1) is:

entity market value	≡	market value of debt	+	market value of equity	+	market value of minority interests.

i.e., $TMV_o \equiv MV_o^{(d)} + MV_o^{(e)} + MV_o^{(MI)}$ (2).

Thus, the FASB-ASC cash flow classification can therefore be further faulted because its individual categories do not directly correspond to the entity-ownership components of the corporate valuation model.

If the equity of a parent company and that of its subsidiaries are, together with parent and subsidiary company fixed interest debt,† listed on stock exchanges, the three values shown on the RHS of the valuation identity

†The MV of variable interest rate debt is usually close to its book value. If fixed interest debt is not listed, its value can be estimated by reference to corporate debt interest rates, by taking the present value of the interest payments and principal repayments that are specified in debt contracts.

(and therefore the TMV_o on the LHS) thus represent the observable values of capitalized expectations. That is to say, the observable market values of a company's debt and equity reflect a complex market capitalization process in which the collective cash flow expectations, that are formed by individual market participants about an individual company, are transformed into a present value equivalent which is simultaneously partitioned into the market values of its debt and equity.

Using the foregoing identities this capitalization process can be illustrated† as follows:

$$\sum_{j=o}^{\infty} \frac{\overline{ENCF}_j}{(1+\bar{r})^j} \equiv \sum_{j=o}^{\infty} \frac{\overline{LCF}_j}{(1+\bar{r}_d)^j} + \sum_{j=o}^{\infty} \frac{\overline{SHCF}_j}{(1+\bar{r}_e)^j} + \sum_{j=o}^{\infty} \frac{\overline{MICF}_j}{(1+\bar{r}_{MI})^j} \qquad (3)$$

or, in more detailed operational form,

$$\sum_{j=o}^{\infty} \frac{(\bar{k}_j-\bar{h}_j)-(\bar{A}_j+\bar{R}_j-\bar{Y}_j) - \bar{t}_j - \bar{H}_j}{(1+\bar{r})^j}$$

$$\equiv \sum_{j=o}^{\infty} \frac{\bar{F}_j-\bar{N}_j-\bar{M}_j}{(1+\bar{r}_d)^j} + \sum_{j=o}^{\infty} \frac{\bar{D}_j-\bar{B}_j}{(1+\bar{r}_e)^j} + \sum_{j=o}^{\infty} \frac{\bar{D}_j^{(MI)}-\bar{B}_j^{(MI)}}{(1+\bar{r}_{MI})^j} \qquad (4)$$

$$\text{or, } TMV_o \equiv MV_o^{(d)} + MV_o^{(e)} + MV_o^{(MI)} \qquad (2)$$

where, $\bar{r}, \bar{r}_d, \bar{r}_e$ and $\bar{r}_{MI}$ respectively denote entity, (group) lender, shareholder and minority interest costs of capital; and, the bars denote expected values.

---

†This particular formulation of a normative valuation model implies that periodic cash flows are serially independent. However, they are more likely to be serially correlated. If so, the capitalization process needs to be formulated in conditional probabilistic terms.

Note also that even if expected entity cash flows are serially independent their quality may not be stationary. Furthermore, a company's debt ratio may also be serially variable. The single-period values corresponding to $\bar{r}$, $\bar{r}_d$ $\bar{r}_e$ and $\bar{r}_{MI}$ are therefore unlikely to be serially constant.

These points are, however, technicalities which do not negate the substance of the argument adduced hereafter.

Cast in detailed operational form, a normative valuation model implies that in forming expectations about a future entity cash flow stream $\overline{ENCF}_j$ (j=1,2...), individual market participants form expectations about each of its constituents by reference to their determinants. For example, sales receipts, k_j, are a function of a firm's price-output policies in end-product markets that are characterized by their own supply and demand conditions. On the other hand, operating payments, h_j, are a function of the supply and demand conditions in its respective factor input markets. It can reasonably be presumed that in using information to form expectations about each entity cash flow constituent, market participants will derive entity cash flow expectations which are at least as accurate as a direct estimate of the latter. Hence, if, as is generally assumed, market participants use a company's track record in forming expectations about its future performance, it is arguable that companies should disclose past cash flow performance data in detailed constituent form.[†] A detailed cash flow disclosure classification which, at least in principle, is the analog of equation (4), is probably the most suitable guidance to investors on the complex capitalization process which generates market prices. Whilst minimal, unsystematic disclosure may not cause biased market values, fuller disclosure can be expected to result in market values that are more precise and therefore perhaps less risky. Moreover, as elaborated in part 2, a necessary prerequisite for an assessment of the efficiency of past dividend and financing policies is the separate disclosure of the constituents of lender and shareholder cash flows and such information as facilitates an estimate of the market value of unquoted fixed interest rate debt.

[†]To the extent that detailed corporate financial disclosure puts a country at an international competitive disadvantage, such contensions should be qualified.

1.2 Periodic income measurement

The previously-mentioned distinction between a pure cash flow accounting model and a cash flow-market value accounting model can be clarified by reference to a definition of periodic income which has gained almost universal acceptance, namely,

periodic income	≡	end-period value of business	*minus*	beginning of period value of business
	plus	distributions to owners during the period	*minus*	contributions from owners during the period

or, in symbolic form,

$$I_j = (V_j - V_{j-1}) + [F_j + D_j + D_j^{(MI)}] - [N_j + M_j + B_j + B_j^{(MI)}]$$

$$= (V_j - V_{j-1}) + ENCF_j \qquad (5)$$

=	periodic change in value of business	*plus*	periodic entity cash flow

It is worth emphasizing that this result cannot be derived by using the FASB-ASC cash flow classification.

In the case of a wealth-maximizing firm, periodic entity cash flow, i.e., the periodic income component that is actually distributed to, or financed by, its owners is a dependent variable. Such a firm must first provide for its periodic income tax payment before determining its investment level and liquidity adjustment by reference to its wealth-maximizing objective function. Thereafter, taking cognizance of its debt-servicing obligations, it arranges its lender and shareholder cash flows accordingly. This is precisely the prescription that specifies distributable profit - a concept that has eluded accountants for decades. Note, however, that even if entity cash flow (distributed periodic income) is not optimally determined in the foregoing sense, periodic income is still defined by equation (5). In that case, the end-period valuation will reflect the non-optimal distribution and its effect will be captured in periodic income accordingly.

Perhaps the most important feature of the latter formulation is that it indicates that <u>all</u> measures of periodic income constitute a dichotomized measure, one component of which, entity cash flow, <u>is common to all</u>. In that entity cash flow constitutes the component of periodic income that is actually delivered directly by a company to, or received from, its owners, it directly affects the company's end-period valuation, however defined. More to the point, however, is the fact that different accounting models generate different measures of periodic income only because they vary with respect to the choice of beginning and end-period valuations.

In the last half century, at least five different business valuations have been proposed in the literature as a basis for income measurement. These include:

exit values (Sterling and, more recently, Scottish ICA)

current cost values (Edwards and Bell and, more recently, Solomons)

cash equivalent values (Chambers)

discounted present value (Solomons)

market values (Lawson).

To the foregoing "asset-liability" approaches to income measurement can be added the (historic) "accruals" or "matching principle" approach attributed to Paton-Littleton.[†] For comparative purposes this measure can be represented as a dichotomized historic cost measure of periodic income comprising periodic entity cash flows and a periodic change in total net worth (or total capital employed) measured on a historic cost (entity) basis. Expressed symbolically historic cost (entity) profit, $HCP_j + F_j + MI_j$, that is, post-tax profit before interest, F_j, and group profit ascribable to minorities, MI_j, is therefore given by:

$$HCP_j + F_j + MI_j = NW_j^{(en)} - NW_{j-1}^{(en)} + [F_j + D_j + D_j^{(MI)}] - [N_j + M_j + B_j + B_j^{(MI)}]$$

$$= \Delta NW_j^{(en)} + ENCF_j \qquad (6)$$

This formulation of periodic historic cost profit (before interest) not only shows that a firm's income, cash flow and balance sheet statements, are interrelated, and that profit is computed accordingly, it also casts doubt on the ASC's[††] contention that, "...a cash flow statement also gives information which is in addition to that provided by the profit and loss account and balance sheet." As indicated by (6), a firm's profit and loss account embodies either the left or right hand side of its cash flow identity. That identity can itself be fully derived by differencing end- and beginning-of-period balance sheets as, indeed, can the periodic change in net worth.[†††] Thus, efficient market theorists would doubtless question whether cash flow statements provide any information that is not already impounded in prices which

---

[†]The matching principle was developed in Germany by Schmalenbach about 40 years earlier. See, for example, Schmalenbach (1926).

[††]Op cit. (1990) page 5.

[†††]See Appendix A.

are generated in a semi-strong efficient market because such a market understands the accounting relationships between financial statements. A cogent counter-argument is that not all companies are listed in semi-strong efficient markets and that an overwhelming majority is not listed at all. But even if this were not so, the disclosure of an appropriately-classified cash flow statement giving direct guidance to the typical user of *ex post* financial statements on the nature of the cash flow-generating capacity, and capitalization processes, which provide ownership returns would, at the very least, serve an important educational purpose.

The view that cash flow statements should be presented as one of two components of a dichotomized periodic income computation will doubtless be contested. Be this as it may, implicit in the discussion which follows is the contention that, except for a cash flow-market value income measure, the entity cash flow component of *any* periodic income measure is the best index of income quality.

The essential difference between a pure cash flow accounting model and a cash flow-market value accounting model, namely, the use of discounted (expected) cash flows as beginning and end-period values in the former and the use of actual observable values in the latter can now be emphasized.

Beginning and end-period DCF valuations are estimates of the value of a business as a going concern, i.e., estimates of the values that would be realized were that business to be sold at arms length. DCF valuations should only be used in measuring *ex post* periodic income when it is not possible to obtain the necessary market values. The only justification for using a DCF valuation is that it represents the most theoretically-defensible basis for simulating the market capitalization process which generates market values. If such values can be more accurately and conveniently estimated from some alternative information source, that source should generally be preferred to DCF estimates.

The periodic income measure implicit in the *ex post* (single-period) normative valuation model can be derived as follows:

$$TMV_o = \frac{ENCF_1}{1+r} + \frac{TMV_1}{1+r} \tag{7}$$

whence,

$$r = \frac{ENCF_1 + (TMV_1 - TMV_o)}{TMV_o} \tag{8}$$

and,

$$rTMV_o = ENCF_1 + (TMV_1 - TMV_o) \tag{9}$$

The latter measure can, in turn, be partitioned into measures of periodic equity, lender and minority interest income. Thus,

$$\begin{array}{lcl} r_d\, MV_o^{(d)} & = & LCF_1 + [MV_1^{(d)} - MV_o^{(d)}] \\ r_e\, MV_o^{(e)} & = & SHCF_1 + [MV_1^{(e)} - MV_o^{(e)}] \\ r_{MI} MV_o^{(MI)} & = & MICF_1 + [MV_1^{(MI)} - MV_o^{(MI)}] \\ \hline rTMV_o & = & ENCF_1 + (TMV_1 - TMV_o) \end{array}$$

As indicated by equations (7) and (8), the single-period rate of return is directly related to periodic income. The former is equal to the latter divided by the beginning of period value of the business. Half-matrices of multiperiod (market-based) rates of return which measure multiperiod rates of profitability from both entity and ownership standpoints can obviously be derived from the multiperiod version of equation (7).[†]

[†]See Appendix B, Table B.5.

Illustration 1

Discounted cash flow accounting model

Assumptions

i. A company's entity cash flows grow at the rate of 8% p.a. and amount to 1000, 1080,1166...ad inf. in years 1,2,3,.....

ii. The latter series is net of capital expenditures in years 1,2,3... of 400,420,441...

iii. For simplicity, though without loss of generality, periodic tax payments and liquidity changes are ignored.

iv. The company is wholly equity-financed.

v. The company's cost of capital is 10% p.a.

Collating these five assumptions, and adopting an end-period discounting convention, the position which emerges is:

	end-year	0	1	2	3	...
(a)	operating cash flow	-	1,400	1,500	1,607.4	...
(b)	net capital investment	-	400	420	441.0	...
(c)	entity cash flow		1,000	1,080	1,166.4	...
(d)	market value†	50,000	54,000	58,320	62,986	...
(e)	periodic income††	-	5,000	5,400	5,832	...

Notes

†The market values are derived from the formula for the present value of an infinite series that is growing at a constant annual rate g which is less than the (constant) annual discount rate r. For example, the end-year 0 market value of 50,000 is given by:

$1{,}000/(r-g) = 1{,}000/(0.1-0.08) = 50{,}000.$

††Periodic income is equal to the periodic change in market value plus periodic entity cash flow.

1.3 Specific attributes of a cash flow-market value accounting model

Whilst a pure cash flow accounting model which utilizes beginning and end-period DCF values may be subject to significant estimation error, the arithmetic of that model under conditions of certainty nevertheless offers important insights into why the cash flow-market value model transcends all other accounting models. Consider the situation depicted in Illustration 1.

The measure of periodic income which is computed in Illustration 1 is, as already stated, a dichotomized income measure. It comprises:

(i) an entity cash flow that is delivered directly by a company to its owners†; and,

(ii) a change in market value which can only be realized by a company's owners via capital market transactions.

Although the two components of periodic income take on positive values in Illustration 1, both can, for a variety of reasons, take on positive, zero or negative values depending upon the case in question. Whilst this point is pursued further at the end of the discussion which follows, it should first be noted that the latter distinction not only specifies distributable income (as already mentioned) but also yields an operational concept of capital maintenance.

1.4 Distributable income and capital maintenance

The notions of distributable income and capital maintenance have traditionally been regarded as integrally-related aspects of periodic income measurement. Whilst it may seem axiomatic to the layman that a full

---

†As previously shown, periodic entity cash flow is equal to periodic distributions to owners less periodic ownership contributions.

distribution of periodic income should not result in some form of capital erosion or significant refinancing, accountants have long contemplated the possible adverse economic consequences of a full distribution of income. This apprehension has not, of course, led to an abandonment of the search for a measure of fully-distributable periodic income containing in-built safe-guards which ensure that capital is maintained intact.

It is not, in fact, possible to specify an undichotomized periodic income which, as a general rule, is wholly distributable by a firm itself. The essential characteristic of the income dichotomization shown in Illustration 1 is, as already emphasized, that it partitions periodic entity income into that component which is distributable by a firm itself; and, a second component which, can only be accessed by a company's owners via market transactions. The specification of the latter income component, the periodic change in market value, automatically provides for the maintenance of ownership capital when that periodic change is positive (or zero). A periodic decrease in total market value measures the additional investment in marketable assets (of any kind) which owners themselves need to undertake in order to maintain their capital intact. In short, a firm's owners can take action which maintains their capital intact whereas a firm is unable to do so. The apparent dilemma in which a firm generally finds itself when it attempts simultaneously to distribute the full (undichotomized) periodic income and maintain ownership capital intact is, in fact, indicative of a problem that is intractable because it is mis-specified.†

In the circumstances depicted by Illustration 1, the firm in question could neither finance the distribution of the succession of periodic changes

†Though apparent rather than real, this dilemma is, as evidenced by a 1989 publication of the Institute of Chartered Accountants in England and Wales by David Solomons (see pages 57-58), undoubtedly very resilient.

in market value internally, nor by raising new money from lenders or shareholders, nor by selling assets (or forgoing investment).

The raising of new debt and/or equity capital to finance the distribution (by means of interest and/or dividend payments) of the periodic change in market value would not affect the LHS of the cash flow identity (equation (1)). Such transactions would amount to lenders and shareholders financing their respective interest and dividend payments and/or a change in the ratio of lender to shareholder cash flows, i.e., a change in the firm's debt ratio. That is to say, the net result would be an overall no-change situation, i.e., the situation depicted in Illustration 1 would continue to emerge; and, shareholders and lenders would collectively receive zero distributions in excess of periodic entity cash flows. For example, assume that at end-period 2 the firm raises a perpetual loan of 4,320 at an interest rate of 5% p.a. and immediately distributes that amount to shareholders in addition to the period 2 entity cash flow of 1,080. If no further capital is raised externally after period 2, the position emerging would be as in Illustration 1A.

Illustration 1A

Distributions exceeding entity cash flow

end-year	0	1	2	3	4
(c) entity cash flow	-	1,000	1,080	1,166.4	1,259.7
lender cash flow	-	-	-4,320	216.0	216.0
shareholder cash flow	-	1,000	5,400	950.4	1,043.7
(d) total market value	50,000	54,000	58,320	62,986	68,025
market value of debt†	-	-	4,320	4,320	4,320
market value of equity	50,000	54,000	54,000	58,666	63,705
(e) periodic income = (c) + Δ(d)	-	5,000	5,400	5,832	6,298.7

Note

†Assuming its market interest rate remains constant.

Turning to the disposal of assets (including existing liquidity levels) as a possible means of financing the distribution of periodic increases in market value; two separate points can be made. First, should a firm possess surplus assets†, the realization of their disposal values, which would, of course, be impounded in the firm's total market value, could possibly finance the distribution of periodic market value increases in the short-term. Such a policy could not be continued indefinitely and clearly cannot be regarded as a general solution.

The disposal of non-surplus assets (including liquidity) and/or a reduction in periodic investment levels as a means of financing the distribution of periodic increases in market value would conflict with wealth-maximizing investment and liquidity decision rules. Thus, the use of assets to finance the distribution of a periodic increase in market value can generally be expected to lower end-period market value by more than the (pre-distribution) periodic increase in market value. In other words, the disposal of an existing asset, or reduction in investment which appears profitable *ex ante*, will normally result in the forgoing of a positive NPV, i.e., income reduction.†† This is precisely the substance of the dividend decision-making

---

†Surplus assets are here defined as those which contribute in no way to the generation of a firm's entity cash flow stream.

††This can be demonstrated by reference to Illustration 1. Assume that a reduction of 100 in period 1 investment causes as reduction in all future periodic entity cash flows of 11. The distribution of 1100 in period 1 (instead of the initially contemplated 1000) would have the following consequences:

	end-year	0	1	2	3	...
(c)	entity cash flow	(-	+1,000	+1,080	+1,166.4	...
		(	+100	-11	- 11.0	...
(d)	market value	49,991	53,890	58,210	62,876	...
(e)	periodic income	-	4,999	5,389	5,821	...

rule promulgated by Miller and Modigliani (1961) when they stated, ".....given a firm's investment policy, the dividend payout policy it chooses to follow will affect neither the current price of its shares nor the total return to its shareholders," i.e., the distributable component of periodic income is a dependent variable which is a function of internal investment and liquidity decisions.†

To complete this section, reference is made to a dichotomized periodic income having constituent components with opposite signs. Thus, a company which is formed to exploit a wasting asset can, in the very nature of things, be expected to have (positive) periodic entity cash flows and market values, both of which decline in real terms over the bigger part of the company's finite life. Hence, its positive (distributed) entity cash flow will typically exceed the periodic decline in its market value and ipso facto its periodic income too. In these circumstances, investors can maintain their capital intact by reinvesting the requisite amount elsewhere and, if periodic income is positive, will be in a position to do so. The relationship between positive and negative periodic income constituents and periodic income itself can be depicted more generally as in Illustration 2.

In the latter illustration, positive periodic incomes are represented by positive combinations of periodic entity cash flow and periodic change in market value, namely, the combinations to the right of the 45° line.

All periodic incomes in the two upper quadrants of Illustration 2 contain

---

†The gist of the foregoing paragraphs was originally outlined in Lawson (1975) in response to an erroneous sugestion of the U.K. Inflation Accounting Committee (1975) (see page 30) to the effect that a company can distribute $(V_j - V_{j-1}) + ENCF_j$ on a continuing basis. It would not be necessary to controvert this contention again were it not for the fact that the committee's error is repeated in Arthur Young (1989) (see page 32).

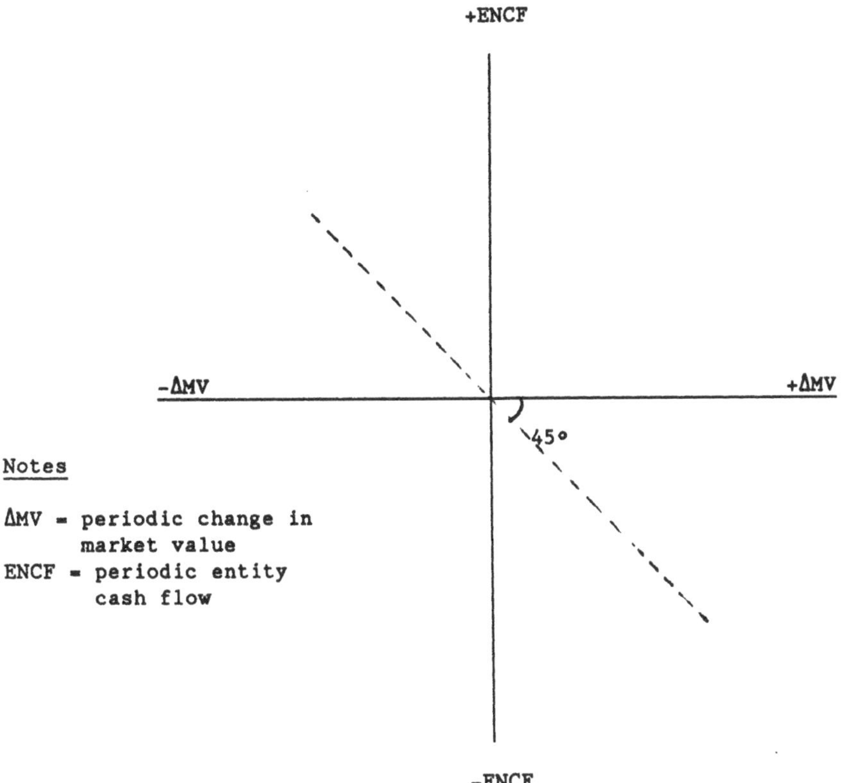

Ilustration 2: positive and negative components of periodic income

a positive (distributed) entity cash flow component which is indicated by the ENCF axis.

All points in the lower quadrants denote negative entity cash flows which necessitate additional net financing by lenders and/or shareholders, i.e., represent situations in which lender and shareholder cash flows are collectively negative.

The very special cases in which periodic income is fully distributable are indicated by all points on the positive ENCF axis. These are situations in which the periodic changes in market value are equal to zero.

It should perhaps finally be questioned whether the substitution of any of the other four business valuations that are enumerated on page 9 (above) results in a measure of periodic income which, if fully distributed, will cause neither capital erosion nor a change in a firm's financial structure. As shown above, all other measures of *ex post* periodic income can be dichotomized into a (distributed) periodic entity cash flow and an "undistributable" periodic change in business value (however defined). Hence, regardless of the way in which the periodic change in the value of a business is computed, a full distribution of periodic income will generally violate wealth-maximizing decision rules in the manner illustrated in the penultimate footnote. Moreover, as described hereafter, replacement, disposal and historic book values generally fail to comply with the criterion of representational faithfulness in a strict economic sense.

1.5 Representational faithfulness

The "faithful representation of any phenomenon implies that the representation is complete. But completeness is a relative term..................All that faithful representation requires is that there shall be no *material* omissions of relevant information."†

Wherever capitalism is to be found so too is the joint stock enterprise. The joint stock enterprise organizes the greater part of economic activity in a capitalistic economy and has become one of the most obvious manifestations of private property rights in such a system precisely because of the

†Solomons (1989), page 33.

special advantages which, as a vehicle of economic organization, it confers on its owners. It is therefore difficult to avoid the inference that, in fulfilling its income measurement function, financial reporting ought to take explicit cognizance of the latter environmental postulate and precisely recognize the financial relationship that subsists between a joint stock enterprise and its owners. This is simply a plea for the faithful representation within an accounting model of the principal *dramatis personae* to whom the enterprise is accountable. An individual generally acquires a debt or equity participation in a joint stock enterprise by transacting in the market place. That same individual can divest himself of his proprietory rights by transacting in the same way. The return to such an owner thus derives from entry and exit (secondary capital market) values and the stream cash flows (distributions *minus* further capital contributions) that spans the two. If, and only if, an accounting model dove-tails with the observable financial relationship which subsists between an enterprise and its owners, as does a cash flow-market value model, does the model comply with the criterion of representational faithfulness in a strict, material economic sense.† The possibility of temporary under- or over-valuations stemming from the withholding of (inside) information in no way negates the use of market values in income measurement. Whether "correctly" valued or not, market values

†The long established financial reporting practice of neglecting the true financial relationship between an enterprise and its owners can be contrasted with the wealth-maximizing *ownership* prescription of financial economics.

Such a divergence of *ex ante* and *ex post* measures is not encountered in operational research. A cardinal OR principle is that *ex post* performance should be measured in the same dimensions as the antecedent objective function. It is tempting to suggest that in accounting the measurement of *ex post* performance preceded the formulation of an objective function; and, that the misspecification of ownership interests which is a feature of the former was, as evidenced by such corporate objectives as ROI, carried over into the latter.

constitute the only means whereby investors can become the owners of a company or divest themselves of their proprietorship rights in a company.

It follows by definition that accounting models based on current cost, disposal or historic book values are not faithful representations in the foregoing sense since none of these values appears in the financial relationship between an enterprise and its owners. There may, of course, be occasions when a firm's going concern value is closely approximated by its current cost value, in particular on its formation. On other occasions, for example, immediately before it has become a take-over target, a firm's going concern value may be equal to, or perhaps even less than its net asset disposal (exit) value. In the latter event the firm's liquidation may be in its owners' best interests in which case exit asset values would constitute the appropriate terminal value for the terminal periodic income computation.

1.6 Compliance with recognition criteria

A recent authoritative enunciation of the conventional accounting wisdom on recognition criteria runs:

> "The essential building blocks from which financial statements are constructed are an entity's assets and liabilities. It is from these that all of the subelements shown in the statements are derived. Once the criteria for recognizing assets and liabilities have been agreed, therefore, it should be easy to answer questions about the recognition of the subelements. Problems concerning the recognition of revenues and expenses, gains and losses, are really problems about recognizing changes in assets and liabilities.
>
> An item should be recognized in financial statements if:
>
> (a) it conforms to the definition of an asset or liability or of one of the subelements derived therefrom; and
>
> (b) its magnitude as specified by the accounting model being used can be measured and verified with reasonable certainty; and

(c) the magnitude so arrived at is material in amount.

Nothing needs to be said in the criteria for recognition about the probability that, if the item is an asset, it will yield economic benefits or, if the item is a liability, that there will be a future transfer of assets or service to others, for if the probability of a yield or a transfer of future benefits is zero or very small, the items will not conform to the definitions, and the first criterion will not be satisfied; whilst great uncertainty as to the yield or transfer of the benefits will either make verifiable measurement of the item impossible, leaving the second criterion unsatisfied, or it will be taken into account in the measurement of the item.

It is clear from the second criterion for recognition that questions about recognition and measurement are typically not separable, for if an item cannot be measured with reasonable certainty, it will not be recognized."†

This quotation is a symptom of the dilemma in which accountants apparently find themselves when faced with the need to value expectations. It is precisely the dilemma that is posed by the subjective formation and capitalization of expectations in the derivation of DCF valuations. Compliance with conditions (a), (b) and (c) is at best the adoption of a rather crude subjective probabilistic approach which may introduce biases in favor of conservative valuations: either because of the deliberate exclusion of uncertain elements of valuation, or, because some elements simply defy the comprehension of the preparers of financial statements. However, in that objective verifiability is not always completely attainable, (a), (b) and (c) may also not preclude upward valuation biases.

A cash flow-market value model is more likely to satisfy recognition criteria in an economic sense of that expression than are other accounting models. Thus, going concern market values, especially those generated in an

---

†Solomons (1989), page 43.

informationally-efficient market, might usually be expected to impound positive and negative elements of value that are signalled by information sources going well beyond the attention, or indeed span of comprehension, of the preparers of published financial reports. Moreover, whilst the existence and ownership of particular assets, which are an integral part of the productive capacity of a going concern may not be in doubt, they may lack a piece-meal current cost or exit value because they are not physically displaceable. Other assets in place may not have readily quantifiable exit and current cost values because they are rarely traded, if at all. Thus, to the extent that an asset's technical features do not preclude exit value and current cost assessments, the latter may nevertheless entail enormous expense and necessitate considerable subjective judgement compared with the costless objective going concern valuations that are available to listed companies.

Judged against recognition criteria, the principal defect (from an income-measurement standpoint) of current cost, (asset) exit, and indeed historic cost values, thus lies in the fact that they are the outcome of subjective assessments which may, therefore, vary quite significantly from one company to the next. Such assessments are prone to errors both of omission and under or over-valuation. In other words, current cost, (asset) exit and historic cost values are derived, or estimated, by a small number of accountants within a company whilst a company's market value reflects an overall market consensus. Thus, when the shortcomings, as measured by recognition criteria, of current cost, (asset) exit and historic cost values are added to their failure to comply with the criterion of representational faithfulness, the case against their use in periodic income measurement begins to look quite formidable. But this is by no means the end of the story.

1.7 Other attributes of the cash flow-market value accounting model

In addition to the above-mentioned merits of cash flow-market value accounting as a means of measuring economic performance, its other advantages as a measure of both single-period and multiperiod performance can be briefly enumerated as follows:†

- a CF-MV model uses data that are wholly objectively measureable
- a CF-MV model completely circumvents the allocation problem
- a CF-MV model is the only accounting model that can accommodate both relative price changes and inflation in correct economic terms
- a CF-MV model reveals the incidence and burden of corporate taxes measured in accordance with the classic principles of tax neutrality. The CF-MV model can therefore indicate: the discriminatory character of any corporate tax system, i.e., the true burden of taxation on, and its dispersion across, companies; and, whether state fiscal incentives embodied in a corporate tax system are actually having their intended effect.

1.8 Summary and conclusions

The first part of this paper has attempted to demonstrate the superiority of a cash flow-market value accounting model vis à vis other accounting models, by reference to conventional accounting desiderata, and from basically two standpoints, namely, (i) income measurement; and, (ii) the presentation of a company's track record consistent with the best guidance on the expectations - forming and capitalization processes which generate the market-value of a company as a going concern.

†See Lawson (1985) and Lawson and Stark (1981a and 1981b).

Following well-established principles of financial economics, a clear distinction was made between the total market value of a company as an economic entity, and, the market values of the respective ownership participations of lenders and shareholders that reflect the financial policies over which a corporate directorate may exercise considerable discretion. Exactly analogous to the latter distinction is the classification of a company's cash flow identity into entity, lender, shareholder and, if any, minority interests cash flows. Entity cash flows are a reflection of economic activity and can be sub-divided accordingly. Lender, shareholder and minority interest cash flows are, like the corresponding market values, a consequence of financial policies; and, unless they are clearly separated from entity cash flows, will blur an entity's economic performance by mixing up economic and financial policy variables. The importance of this principle has apparently escaped the attention of both the FASB and the British ASC. It therefore constitutes an important starting point for determining the respects in which the cash flow statements promulgated by those bodies are deficient.

The popular supposition that cash flow statements and income statements are, or should be, addressed to somewhat different, though related, problems can be questioned. Thus, the long-standing maxim, "liquidity and profitability are opposing considerations" ought to be stringently qualified. As has been shown, periodic entity cash flow is one of two dichotomized components of all concepts of periodic income. There is therefore every reason why a suitably-classified entity cash flow statement should be fully incorporated into the income measurement process. Moreover, entity cash flow constitutes the component of periodic income that is directly generated by a firm and which incisively summarizes the cash flow consequences of the totality of is commercial decisions as an economic entity. This said it should perhaps be repeated that, with the exception of a cash flow-market value measure of income, periodic entity cash flow is probably the best index, albeit subject to adjustments, of income quality. In short, there are strong grounds for arguing that entity cash flow ought in fact to be the main focus of corporate financial reporting.

As a means of measuring ex post performance, accounting models have traditionally taken the form of a single-parameter (income measurement) model. As yet, accountants have not attempted to report performance in a risk-return framework. In that modern concepts of risk are also market-based, it is reasonable to speculate that, in the forseeable future, a cash flow market-value accounting model will accommodate the risk dimension and report risk-adjusted returns. In the meanwhile, the devising and empirical testing of a two-parameter cash flow-market value accounting model ought to be a fruitful avenue for research.

Part 2: Assessing the efficiency of dividend and debt-financing policies

2.1 Introduction

The evaluation of the efficiency of dividend and debt-financing policies has not evolved as an integral part of enterprise accountability. This may be ascribable to the previously-emphasized fact that accounting models other than a CF-MV model do not faithfully represent the ownership-entity relationship in financial terms.

As illustrated by cash flow identity (1), the cash flow consequences of dividend and financing policies can be expressed in terms of the ratio in which a firm's (entity) cash flow stream is simultaneously partitioned into lender, shareholder and minority interest (if any) cash flows. In practice the partitioning of entity cash flows is mainly, though perhaps not entirely, a consequence of dividend policy.

2.2 Dividend policy

Empirical studies have consistently suggested that the dividend policies of British and American companies have hitherto been based on post-tax historic cost profit and generally conform to the original Lintner† model, namely,

$$D_j = \alpha\ \gamma\ HCP_j + (1-\alpha)\ D_{j-1} \tag{10}$$

where,

D_j denotes the dividend in year j;

α is the rate of adjustment of dividends to current earnings ($1>\alpha<0$);

γ stands for the firm's target pay-out ratio; and,

HCP_j is post-tax historic cost profit (net of interest).

Lintner's descriptive model gives effect to two well-known dividend policy aims, namely, the adjustment of dividends to current earnings and continuity of established dividend policy. The higher the value of the adjustment factor, α, the greater is the weight attaching to the current earnings determinant and vice versa. However, as the previous year's dividend, D_{j-1} may be written:

$$D_{j-1} = \alpha\ \gamma\ HCP_{j-1} + (1-\gamma)\ D_{j-2} \tag{11}$$

then, after substituting (11) into (10) and making similar substitutions for D_{j-2}, D_{j-3} etc., D_j can be expresed wholly in terms of earnings, namely,

$$D_j = \alpha\gamma HCP_j + (1-\alpha)HCP_{j-1} + (1-\alpha)^2 HCP_{j-2} + \ldots\ldots + (1-\alpha)^n HCP_{j-n} \tag{12}$$

The financial and economic consequences of this type of dividend policy

---

†Lintner (1956), Theobald (1978). See also, Theobald and Cadle (1990).

will normally be revealed by the CF-MV model. Recall that historic cost profit (before interest), i.e., entity profit, HCP_j+F_j, can, ignoring minority interests, be represented as:

$$HCP_j + F_j = NW_j^{(en)} - NW_{j-1}^{(en)} + (D_j+F_j) - (B_j+N_j+M_j)$$

$$= \Delta NW_j^{(en)} + ENCF_j. \qquad (6)$$

Hence, typically, $HCP_j > ENCF_j - F_j$

But if, as in cases reported elsewhere,† historic cost profit, HCP_j, consistently exceeds entity cash flows by a large margin, dividends (net of capital raised or repaid), D_j-B_j, may well exceed entity cash flows over long periods of time. That is to say,

$$\text{if } HCP_j > ENCF_j - F_j \qquad (13)$$

and, assuming for convenience, $\alpha = 1$, then,

$$\alpha\,\gamma\,HCP_j - B_j > ENCF_j - F_j \qquad (14)$$

provided,

$$\gamma > \frac{ENCF_j - F_j + B_j}{HCP_j} \qquad (15)$$

For example, put $ENCF_j = 600$, $B_j = 0$ (since B_j will usually, though not always, take on a value of zero) $HCP_j = 1000$ and $F_j = 200$. Thus, if $\gamma > 0.4$ some part of dividends D_j, will necessitate external debt-financing, $N_j + M_j$, given by:

$$N_j + M_j = (D_j - B_j) - (ENCF_j - F_j) \qquad (16)$$

---

†Lawson (1980, 1982, 1983), Lawson and Stark (1981), Lawson, Möller and Sherer (1982).

Put another way; if the ratio of periodic dividends (less periodic equity raised) to historic cost profit is greater than the ratio of periodic entity cash flow (less interest) to historic cost profit, i.e., if

$$\frac{D_j - B_j}{HCP_j} > \frac{ENCF_j - F_j}{HCP_j}, \tag{17}$$

shareholder cash flow, D_j-B_j, will be uncovered by an amount equal to $(D_j$-$B_j)$ - $(ENCF_j$-$F_j)$, etc.

2.3 Shareholder wealth losses and wealth transfers to lenders

A continuous debt-financed shareholder cash flow shortfall will result in a (total) accumulation of corporate debt, the market value of which may increase or decrease relative to a firm's total market value (i.e., market value of debt and equity). Hence, a dividend policy based on a firm's historic cost profits may cause a debt-financed dividend shortfall which, in turn, causes an increase in its debt ratio. Such an increase represents the substitution of debt capital for equity or, what amounts to the same thing, the repayment of shareholders' capital in the guise of dividends. However, the repayment of shareholders' capital via dividend payments which are taxed as income in a classical system of corporation tax, like that of the U.S., causes an obvious wealth loss. Moreover, if shareholder cash flow shortfalls are financed with new tranches of debt that are underpriced i.e., issued at interest rates above the securities market line, there will be a wealth transfer from shareholders to lenders.

The extent to which debt is underpriced in practice is an empirical question which, because of the lacunae in corporate financial disclosure regulations, cannot be accurately resolved in quantitative terms. The disclosure issue is taken up below. The point emphasized here is that much of the debt, especially short-term debt, which is raised by companies is priced in bilateral negotiations between companies and lending institutions. This process is inefficient in the sense of the semi-strong version of the efficient market model and biased in favour of full-time professional money lenders. In short, there is a general presumption that companies pay over the odds for a great deal of corporate debt.

Wealth transfers from shareholders to lenders stemming from debt-financed shareholder cash flows are depicted by Illustrations 3 and 4 which differ in one fundamental respect. In Illustration 3 it is assumed that, over a sequence of five years, the company in question raises additional tranches of "correctly-priced" debt to finance dividend payments in excess of entity cash flows. ("Correctly-priced" debt is here defined as debt that is issued at a _zero_ discount to the price at which it can be traded in an efficient market immediately following its issue). By contrast, the situation contemplated in Illustration 4 is one in which the new tranches of debt are underpriced because lenders are able to obtain a market discount which they can realize by transacting, i.e., borrowing or selling, in an efficient market.

The substance of Illustration 3 is mainly to be seen in the half-matrices of rates of return that are contained in part (d). Thus, whilst the entity's rate of return is constant over all holding periods within the five-year sequence considered, the (correctly-priced) successive tranches of debt (which are used to finance part of the dividend payments) increase its debt ratio and successively leverage up the (risk-commensurate) shareholder IRRs accordingly. In a neutral tax regime such dividend-induced debt-equity substitution would cause neither shareholder wealth losses, nor wealth transfers from shareholders to lenders, because it is tantamount to be repayment of shareholder capital at its (correctly-priced) market value.

Illustration 3

Dividends financed with correctly-priced debt

Assumptions (everything expressed in real terms)

i. A company generates a constant annual (entity) cash flow of £1000. Its cost of capital is 10% p.a. and at end-year 0, when it has zero debt in issue, its entity and equity market values are, therefore, both equal to £1000/0.1 = £10000.

ii. At end-year 1 the company raises perpetual debt of £1000 at 1% p.a. to finance dividend payments. At end-years 2, 3, 4 and 5 further tranches of perpetual debt of £2250 at annual interest rates of 4.25%, 8.75%, 13.25% and 17.75% respectively are raised for the same purpose. All five tranches of debt are assumed to be correctly priced† and, at end-year 5, the company is, therefore, wholly owned by lenders.

iii. The company's (entity) cost of capital is assumed to be independent of its debt ratio whereas, as indicted by ii, the average cost of debt is assumed to increase linearly from 1% p.a. at the 10% debt ratio to 10% p.a. at the 100% debt ratio.

iv. Bankruptcy costs are ignored.

Analysis

Collating the forgoing assumptions the picture which emerges is:

(a) interest paid to lenders

end-year 2	(0.01) (1000)	= 10
" " 3	10 + (0.0425) (2250)	= 105.625
" " 4	105.625 + (0.0875) (2250)	= 302.5
" " 5	302.5 + (0.1325) (2250)	= 600.625
" " 6 (and thereafter)	600.625 +(0.1775) (2250)	= 1000

(b) average cost of debt

end-year 1	10/1000	= 1% p.a.
" " 2	105.625/3250	= 3.25% p.a.
" " 3	302.5/5500	= 5.5% p.a.
" " 4	600.625/7750	= 7.75% p.a.
" " 5	1000/10000	= 10% p.a.

---

†That is to say, the debt is raised at the price that would emerge were it to be traded in an efficient market.

Illustration 3 (continued)

(c) cash flow statement

end-year	1	2	3	4	5
i. entity cash flow	+1,000	+1,000	+1,000	+1,000	+1,000
ii. shareholder cash flow:					
internally-financed	-1,000	- 990	- 894	- 698	- 399
debt-financed	-1,000	-2,250	-2,250	-2,250	-2,250
iii.= i.+ii lender cash flow	-1,000	-2,240	-2,144	-1,948	-1,649
lender cash flow comprises:					
interest received		-10	-106	-302	-601
new debt contributed	+1,000	+2,250	+2,250	+2,250	+2,250
	+1,000	+2,240	+2,144	+1,948	+1,649

(d) market values

end-year	0	1	2	3	4	5
	1,000/0.1	1,000/0.1	1,000/0.1	1,000/0.1	1,000/0.1	1,000/0.1
entity market value	=10,000	=10,000	=10,000	=10,000	=10,000	=10,000
	1,000/0.1	990/0.11	894.375/0.1325	697.5/0.155	399.375/0.1775	
equity market value	=10,000	=9,000	=6,750	=4,500	=2,250	0
		10/0.01	105.625/0.0325	302.5/0.055	600.625/0.0775	1,000/0.1
debt market value	0	=1,000	=3,250	=5,500	=7,750	=10,000

Note

As the debt is assumed to be correctly priced, the average cost of debt is simply end-year annual interest divided by beginning of year market value, e.g., at end-year two the average cost of debt is: 105.625/3,250 = 0.0325; or, (0.01) (1,000/3,250) + (0.0425) (2,250/3,250).

Illustration 3 (continued)

(e) half-matrices of rates of return

Using the above sequences of cash flows and market values, the following half-matrices of entity, shareholder and lender internal rates of return (IRRs) can be derived. These IRRs cover all possible holding periods within, and including, the five-year sequence in question.

entity IRRs

bought end-year	sold 1	2	3	4	5
0	10.00	10.00	10.00	10.00	10.00
1		10.00	10.00	10.00	10.00
2			10.00	10.00	10.00
3				10.00	10.00
4					10.00

shareholder IRRs (assuming new debt is efficiently priced)

bought end-year	sold 1	2	3	4	5
0	10.00	10.45	11.10	11.63	11.93
1		11.00	11.90	12.59	12.99
2			13.25	14.08	14.59
3				15.50	16.18
4					17.75

lender IRRs (assuming new debt is efficiently priced)

bought end-year	sold 1	2	3	4	5
0	--	--	--	--	--
1		1.00	2.71	4.25	5.71
2			3.25	4.64	6.03
3				5.50	6.78
4					7.75

Note

The five-year shareholder IRR of 11.93% p.a. is the value of 100r which satisfies the equation:

$$10,000 = \frac{2,000}{1+r} + \frac{3,240}{(1+r)^2} + \frac{3,144}{(1+r)^3} + \frac{2,948}{(1+r)^4} + \frac{2,649}{(1+r)^5}$$

Illustration 4

Debt-financed dividends and reverse leverage

Assumptions (everything expressed in real terms)

i. As in Illustration 3.

ii. The company divides its (internally-generated) entity cash flow as in Illustration 3. However, it issues new tranches of perpetual debt which are distributed as dividends at end-years 1, 2, 3, 4 and 5 at prices of 1,000, 2,002.5, 1,929.375, 1,867.5 and 2,030.625 respectively. The marginal costs of these five tranches of debt, the last four of which lie above the securities market line, are therefore:

10/1,000	= 1% p.a.
(105.625-10)/2,005.5	= 4.775% p.a.
(302.5-105.625)/1,929.375	= 10.2% p.a.
(600.625-302.5)/1,867.5	= 15.965% p.a.
(1,000-600.625)/2,030.625	= 19.668% p.a.

iii. As in Illustration 3.

iv. As in Illustration 3.

Analysis

The picture which emerges in this case is:

(a) interest paid to lenders

As in Illustration 3.

(b) cash flow statement

end-year	1	2	3	4	5
i. entity cash flow	+1,000	+1,000	+1,000	+1,000	+1,000
ii. shareholder cash flow:					
internally-financed	-1,000	-990	-894	-698	-399
debt-financed	-1,000	-2,003	-1,929	-1,868	-2,031
iii.= i.+ii lender cash flow	-1,000	-1,993	-1,823	-1,566	-1,430
lender cash flow comprises:					
interest received	-	-10	-106	-302	-601
new debt contributed	+1,000	+2,003	+1,929	+1,868	+2,031
	+1,000	+1,993	+1,823	+1,566	+1,430

Illustration 4 (continued)

(c) market values

As in Illustration 3

(d) half-matrices of rates of return

entity IRRs (as in Illustration 3)

bought end-year	sold 1	2	3	4	5
0	10.00	10.00	10.00	10.00	10.00
1		10.00	10.00	10.00	10.00
2			10.00	10.00	10.00
3				10.00	10.00
4					10.00

shareholder IRRs†

bought end-year	sold 1	2	3	4	5
0	10.00	9.21	9.04	8.78	8.74
1		8.25	8.35	8.08	8.07
2			8.50	7.93	7.32
3				7.00	7.32
4					8.00

lender IRRs†

bought end-year	sold 1	2	3	4	5
0	--	--	--	--	--
1		25.75	16.45	14.35	12.83
2			13.12	12.72	11.80
3				12.45	11.41
4					10.58

†Assuming that the rates of interest on debt raised at end-years 2,3,4 and 5 lie above the securities market line (see assumption ii).

2.4 Estimating wealth transfers ascribable to mis-priced debt issues

Illustration 4 exemplifies a wealth transfer from shareholders to lenders that is caused by debt-financed dividend payments. The extent of such a transfer can be measured by reference: either to the IRR half-matrices shown in part (d) or to the differences between the tranches of debt shown in part (b) compared with the corresponding amounts of new debt shown in Illustration 3, part (c). Thus,

	debt-financing				
end-year	1	2	3	4	5
Illustration 3	1,000	2,250	2,250	2,250	2,250
Illustration 4	1,000	2,003	1,929	1,868	2,031
shareholder wealth losses	-	247	321	382	219

Were companies required to disclose the issue and concurrent market prices of new tranches of debt, or given such information from an alternative source, it would be possible to estimate the absolute amounts of wealth transferred from shareholders to lenders via the dividend-debt financing mechanism.

A more readily observable symptom of wealth transfers stemming from debt-financed dividend payments that are reported in cash flow statements is the concomitant reverse leverage that is indicated by an excess of lender IRRs over some, or all, of the corresponding IRRs for shareholders (and for the entity as whole).†

A comparison of Illustrations 3 and 4 clearly indicates that, although the wealth transfers in the latter situation are initially triggered by the dividend decision, they are entirely ascribable to the mispricing of debt. However, in

†See Illustration 4, part (d).

that many corporate loans are bilaterally negotiated by borrowers and lenders for other purposes, wealth transfers from lenders to shareholders which are caused by the mispricing of debt are unlikely to be triggered by dividend policy alone.

The alternative circumstances in which a company may resort to debt-financing can be summarized by reference to the periodic cash flow identity, i.e., (ignoring minority interests)

$$ENCF_j \equiv SHCF_j + LCF_j$$

or,

$$ENCF_j \equiv (D_j - B_j) + (F_j - N_j - M_j) \; .$$

The six possible sign-structures of this identity are:

$$ENCF_j \equiv (D_j - B_j) + (F_j - N_j - M_j)$$

	$ENCF_j$	$(D_j - B_j)$	$(F_j - N_j - M_j)$
case 1	+	+	+
case 2	+	+	-
case 3	+	-	+
case 4	-	-	-
case 5	-	-	+
case 6	-	+	-

Case 1 is a situation in which a company's dividend and debt-financing policies enable it to deliver positive cash flows to both shareholders and lenders. Note, however, that even in this case the lender cash flow could comprise interest and a somewhat smaller new tranche of debt. Moreover, maturing debt which supplements interest payments to lenders may be refinanced in the same period. In fact, in all six of the above cases, lender cash flow may include new debt raised which if mispriced, will cause wealth transfers.

In cases 3, 4 and 5 shareholders are net contributors to the company and apparently finance their own dividends (if any). However, Lintner's descriptive dividend model implies that the dividend decision is independent of equity financing decisions. If so, and if debt-financing is the ultimate dependent variable, the dividend component of a negative shareholder cash flow (new equity in excess of dividends) could, in fact, cause an equal (or lesser) amount of incremental debt-financing. For example, in 1987, the abridged cash flow identity of Texas Instruments was:†

$$\begin{aligned} \text{ENCF (1987)} &\equiv \text{SHCF (1987)} + \text{LCF (1987)} \\ &\equiv (D - B) + (F + N - N) \\ -411.4 &\equiv (72.8 - 279.3) + (33.4 + 23.3 - 261.6) \\ -411.4 &\equiv -206.5 - 204.9 \end{aligned}$$

Thus, on the foregoing assumptions and in the absence of the divided payment of 72.8, the following position would have emerged:

$$\begin{aligned} \text{ENCF (1987)} &\equiv \text{SHCF (1987)} + \text{LCF (1987)} \\ -411.4 &\equiv -279.3 + (33.4 + 23.3 - 188.8) \\ -411.4 &\equiv -279.3 - 132.1 \end{aligned}$$

That is to say, a lesser amount of debt would have been raised and the mispricing potential would have been reduced accordingly.

Summarizing the foregoing paragraphs; if dividend policy is an active decision variable and debt-financing is the ultimate dependent residual, new tranches of debt may typically be raised for three separate purposes or for some combination of the three. These are: financing a dividend shortfall, financing an entity cash flow deficit to which may be added the financing

---

†See page 52.

requirements for an established dividend policy; and, the refinancing of maturing debt. Debt-financing for any of these reasons exposes shareholders to the danger that some of their wealth will be transferred to lenders. Whereas it would be entirely unrealistic to suggest that, in the interests of shareholders, companies should generally seek to avoid debt financing, the wisdom of debt-financed dividend payments is at least questionable. It is tempting to argue that dividend policy should be based upon and constrained by, projected entity cash flows, i.e., be a dependent variable in the MM sense.

As the previous discussion has also emphasized, other aspects of financial policy may expose shareholders to the danger of wealth losses. Whilst a multiperiod cash flow-market value analysis does not of itself provide calibrated measures of the efficiency of dividend and financing policies it nevertheless constitutes the kind of framework in which those issues can be raised and subjected to a preliminary analysis.

2.5 Wealth losses and wealth transfers caused by declining entity returns

In discussing criteria for assessing the efficiency of dividend and financing policies, reference should also be made to shareholder and/or lender wealth losses, and reverse leverage, that may be caused by a decline in entity returns. Such a deterioration may be due to a fall in the cash flow generating capacity of ongoing operations that may have been exacerbated by the acceptance of new capital projects which do not generate risk-commensurate returns. The nature and possible effects of a decline in an entity's cash flow stream are depicted in Illustration 5.

A decline in entity returns, which, as indicated by Illustration 5, can of itself cause reverse leverage, may be coterminous with the financing of dividend payments with new tranches of debt issued at a market discount. In such a case reverse leverage is caused by two contributory factors. That is to

Illustration 5

Declining entity returns: wealth losses and wealth transfers

Assumptions (everything expressed in real terms)

i. At end-year 0 a company expects a constant annual (entity) cash flow of £1000.

ii. At end-year 0 the company's cost of capital is 10% p.a. when, in accordance with existing debt contracts, its entity cash flow is divisible between lenders and shareholders in the ratio: 302.5: 697.5.

iii. At its end-year 0 debt ratio the company's costs of debt and equity are 5.5% p.a. and 15.5% p.a. respectively. Its entity, debt and equity market values at end-year 0 are therefore given by:

MV entity ≡ MV debt + MV equity

$$\frac{1{,}000}{0.1} \equiv \frac{302.5}{0.055} + \frac{697.5}{0.155}$$

$$10{,}000 \equiv 5{,}500 + 4{,}500$$

iv. During year 1, the entity cash flow generating capacity declines to £800 p.a. whilst suffering no deterioration in quality. However, the consequent rise in the company's debt ratio causes the costs of debt and equity to increase to 6.09% p.a. and 16.4% p.a. respectively. At end-year 1 the resultant market values are therefore:

MV entity ≡ MV debt + MV equity

$$\frac{800}{0.1} \equiv \frac{302.5}{0.0609} + \frac{497.5}{0.164}$$

$$8{,}000 \equiv 4{,}967 + 3{,}033$$

Analysis

On the foregoing assumptions, the entity, lender and shareholder internal rates of return which are generated in year 1 are thus:

$$\text{entity IRR} = \frac{800 + 8{,}000 - 10{,}000}{10{,}000} = -12\%$$

$$\text{lender IRR} = \frac{302.5 + 4{,}967 - 5{,}500}{5{,}500} = -4.2\%$$

$$\text{shareholder IRR} = \frac{497.5 + 3{,}033 - 4{,}500}{4{,}500} = -21.5\%$$

Illustration 6

Declining entity returns and underpriced debt

Assumptions (everything expressed in real terms)

i. The company in Illustration 5 pays a dividend at end-year 1 of 797.5 whilst simultaneously raising further perpetual debt of 300 at 15% p.a. to finance the resultant shortfall.

ii. The costs of capital and market values emerging at end-year 1 are:

MV entity ≡ MV debt + MV equity

$$\frac{800}{0.1} \equiv \frac{347.5}{0.0654} + \frac{452.5}{0.1684}$$

$$8{,}000 \equiv 5{,}313 + 2{,}687 \quad .$$

Analysis

(a) As a consequence of the end-year 1 dividend and debt-financing decisions, the market value of debt rises on that date by:

5,313 - 4,967 (see Illustration 5, assumption iv) = 346

and the new tranche of debt was therefore underpriced by:

346 - 300 = 46 .

(b) The lender and shareholder internal rates of return for year 1 (which respectively allow for the end-year 1 debt issue of 300 and the dividend payment of 795.5) are:

$$\text{lender IRR} = \frac{302.5 - 300 + 5{,}313 - 5{,}500}{5{,}500}$$
$$= -3.4\%$$

$$\text{shareholder IRR} = \frac{497.5 + 300 + 2.687 - 4{,}500}{4{,}500}$$
$$= -22.6\% \ .$$

The effect of the debt underpricing (compared with the situation in Illustration 5) is therefore to increase the lender IRR by - 4.2 + 3.4 = 0.8% and decrease the shareholder IRR by - 21.5 + 22.6 = 1.1%.

(c) Had the debt been issued at its correct price of 346, the respective lender and shareholder IRRS would, as in Illustration 5, have been:

$$\text{lender IRR} = \frac{302.5 - 300 - 46 + 5{,}313 - 5{,}500}{5{,}500}$$
$$= -4.2\%$$

$$\text{shareholder IRR} = \frac{497.5 + 300 + 46 + 2{,}687 - 4{,}500}{4{,}500}$$
$$= -21.5\% \ .$$

say, reverse leverage may be symptomatic of a wealth transfer from shareholders to lenders resulting from a decline in entity cash flow generating capacity which is compounded by a wealth transfer stemming from debt issued at a market discount. Thus, if the market discount on new tranches of debt is ascertainable, wealth transfers from shareholders to lenders that are caused by debt-financed dividend payments and/or other debt financing can be separated out. Hence, after adjusting shareholder cash flows in respect of the market discount on new debt, the shareholder IRR half matrix can be recomputed accordingly. It will then reveal shareholder wealth losses (if any) stemming from a deterioration in entity cash flow performance and from any market perceived decline in *ex ante* (entity) cash flow generating capacity that is impounded in entity market values. These possibilities are illustrated in Illustration 6.

2.6 Summary and conclusions

Corporate financial and dividend policies constitute the vehicles with which a corporate directorate delivers the cash flow component of a (dichotomized) entity income to its owners, i.e., to its lenders and shareholders. It is therefore natural to ponder whether reliable operational criteria for measuring the economic efficiency of these policies can actually be specified.

The fundamental dividend policy aspect of this question can be illustrated more concretely by contemplating a situation in which judging by its (risk-adjusted) entity IRR half matrix vis à vis the market portfolio IRR half matrix, a company is generating risk-commensurate returns.† However, as a consequence of a dividend policy (based on reported post-tax profits) which is

†See page 59-60.

financed with debt that is issued at a market discount, the company's shareholders suffer reverse leverage (as in Illustration 4). The debt-financing aspect of this question can also be pursued by reference to a company which, in the absence of internal financial resources, raises a new tranche of debt to finance a capital expenditure program.

As regards dividend policy, it can be contended that in accordance with the Miller-Modigliani irrelevance proposition,†† a company should first determine its level of investment [and liquidity adjustment] by reference to a wealth maximization objective. Should finance remain thereafter, dividend payments and/or a reduction in debt levels are indicated. Thus, as a general principle, dividend payments should not be externally financed with either debt or equity. Non-compliance with the MM dividend irrelevance proposition, and the financing of dividend payments with debt, exposes shareholders to the risk that some part of their wealth will be transferred to lenders. Moreover, as already noted, debt-financing in general exposes shareholders to exactly the same kind of risk.

The decision to finance a new program of capital expenditure with specifically earmarked incremental debt can in fact be separated from the capital investment decision itself. Thus, a capital expenditure program is acceptable if it promises a positive net present value at its risk-adjusted cost of capital. The market price of the incremental debt depends upon whether that debt is to rank _pari passu_ with pre-existing debt. Whether or not this is the case, the earmarked incremental debt should be incrementally priced as indicated by Illustrations 3 and 4 -- after first superimposing the new program's incremental entity cash flows on the pre-existing (expected) entity cash flow stream.

---

††Op cit.

The appearance of debt-financed shareholder cash flows in cash flow statements and coterminous reverse leverage (indicated by lender and entity half-matries) are consistent with wealth transfers from shareholders that are ascribable to debt issued at a market discount. The conclusive evidence of such transfers is, of course, the market discount itself which, in the case of unlisted debt, can only be estimated. Wealth transfers that are imputable to new debt raised for other purposes can, at least in principle, be measured in the same way. However, information on, or facilitating estimates of, such market discounts is not usually ascertainable from corporate financial reports. Moreover, the dearth of information in those same reports on the terms of existing debt contracts frequently precludes accurate estimates of the market value of unlisted fixed interest rate debt. The upshot of these lacunae in corporate disclosure regulations is three-fold, namely,

(i) the resultant inaccuracies in estimates of the market value of unlisted corporate debt have a consequential effect on the accuracy of both lender and entity IRR matrices;

(ii) as a result of (i), any (apparent) reverse leverage indicated by companisons of entity and lender IRR matrices may need to be treated with caution; and,

(iii) estimates of the wealth transfers from shareholders to lenders that are imputable to debt-financed dividends, and/or debt-financing otherwise induced, are of dubious reliability.

At its present stage of evolution, corporate financial reporting does not yet constitute a reliable basis for measuring the efficiency of corporate debt policy. Additional disclosure provisions on new debt issues would appear to be in the best interests of the investing public. These could include regulations requiring companies to disclose detailed information on, or facilitating, accurate estimates of:

- the market values of all short, medium and long-term interest-bearing debt; and
- market discounts (or premia) on all new debt issues.

It should, of course, be recognized that the present far-reaching absence of accurate measures of the market value of (interest-bearing) corporate debt (at the level of the individual listed company) restricts the cash-flow market value basis of income measurement discussed in part 1 of this paper which is illustrated in Appendix B hereafter.

Appendix A: Cash flow-accruals accounting relationships

The intra-period relationships between a firm's income, balance sheet and cash flow statements can be expressed in simple symbolic terms.

1. Income statement for year j

Post-tax historic cost profit, HCP_j, for any year j can be defined as:

$$HCP_j = d_j - (a_{j-1}+b_j-a_j) - L_j - F_j - t_j + (Y_j-X_j) - MI_j \qquad \text{(i)}$$

where in year j,

d_j = accrued sales;

$a_{j-1} + b_j - a_j$ = cost of sales (a_{j-1}, a_j denote opening and closing inventories and b_j is accrued purchases);

L_j = historic cost-based depreciation;

F_j = interest expense;

t_j = corporate income tax charged (here assumed to be equal to tax paid);

$Y_j - X_j$ = profit or loss on assets displaced (Y_j and X_j denote the proceeds and written down book value of assets displaced respectively); and,

MI_j = share of group profit ascribable to minority interests.

Thus,

$$HCP_j + F_j + MI_j = D_j + F_j + RE_j + MI_j \qquad \text{(i(a))}$$

i.e., entity profit = dividends + interest + retained earnings + profit ascribable to minorities

$$= \Delta NW_j^{(en)} + ENCF_j \qquad \text{(i(b))}$$

= change in (entity) net worth *plus* entity cash flow.

The proof of equation (i(b)) is contained in section 2 (see page 49).

2. Balance sheet at end-year j and funds flow statement for year j

The end-year j balance sheet of a company formed at end-year -x can be expressed as:

$$\sum_{t=-x}^{j} [(A_t + R_t - L_t - X_t) + (d_t - k_t) + H_t] + a_j$$

$$\equiv \sum_{t=-x}^{j} [B_t + RE_t + N_t + (b_t - h_t) + M_t + (MI_t - MICF_t)] \qquad \text{(ii)}$$

Differencing the end-year j and end-year j-1 balance sheets yields the funds flow statement:

$(A_j+R_j-L_j-X_j)$	$+ (d_j-k_j)$	$+ H_j$	$+ (a_j - a_{j-1})$
Δ in NBV of fixed assets	+ Δ in receivables	+ Δ in liquidity	+ Δ in inventories

$\equiv B_j$	$+ N_j$	$+ (b_j-h_j)$	$+ M_j$	$+ (MI_j-MICF_j)$	$+ RE_j$	(iii)
Δ in equity capital	+ Δ in med/long debt	+ Δ in payables	+ Δ in short-term debt	+ Δ in minority interests	+ retained earnings	

where, in year j,

$A_j + R_j$ = capital expenditure comprising replacements A_j and growth investments R_j;

k_j = sales receipts;

h_j = operating payments; and,

$MICF_j$ = minority interests cash flow comprising dividends $D_j^{(MI)}$ paid to, and new capital $B_j^{(MI)}$ raised from, minorities.

Retained earnings, RE_j, are defined by equation (iii) (funds flow statement) as:

$$RE_j = (A_j + R_j - L_j - X_j) + (d_j - k_j) + H_j + (a_j - a_{j-1}) - B_j - N_j - (b_j - h_j) - M_j - (MI_j - MICF_j)$$

$$= \Delta NW_j^{(en)} - B_j - N_j - M_j - (MI_j - MICF_j) \qquad \text{(iii(a))}$$

= change in (entity) net worth <u>minus</u> new equity and debt capital <u>minus</u> change in minority interests.

Thus, equation (i(a)) (periodic entity income), namely,

$$HCP_j + F_j + MI_j = D_j + F_j + RE_j + MI_j \qquad (i(a))$$

can, after substituting for RE_j, be written:

$$HCP_j + F_j + MI_j = D_j + F_j + MI_j + \Delta NW_j{}^{(en)} - B_j - N_j - M_j - (MI_j - MICF_j)$$
$$= \Delta NW_j{}^{(en)} + ENCF_j \qquad (i(b)).^{\dagger}$$

It should be noted that equation (iii(a)) defines the change in entity net worth, $\Delta NW_j{}^{(en)}$, as:

$$\Delta NW_j{}^{(en)} = (A_j+R_j-L_j-X_j) + (d_j-k_j) + H_j \quad + (a_j-a_{j-1}) - (b_j-h_j) \qquad (iii(b))$$

Δ in NBV fixed assets	+ Δ in receivables	+ Δ in liquidity	+ Δ in inventories	− Δ in payables

3. Cash flow statement for year j

Substituting RE_j as defined by equation (i) namely,

$$RE_j = d_j - (a_{j-1}+b_j-a_j) - L_j - F_j - t_j + (Y_j-X_j) - MI_j - D_j \qquad (i(c))$$

into equation (iii) (funds flow statement) and rearranging, yields the cash flow identity:

$$(k_j-h_j) - (A_j+R_j-Y_j) - t_j - H_j \equiv (F_j-N_j-M_j) + (D_j-B_j) + MICF_j \qquad (iv)^{\dagger}$$

$$\text{i.e., } ENCF_j \equiv LCF_j + SHCF_j + MICF_j$$

4. Relationship between the three financial statements

Substituting equation (iii(b)) (change in entity net worth) and the left hand side of equation (iv) (entity cash flow) into the entity income statement defined by (i(b)), i.e., into:

---

† See page 3.

$$HCP_j + F_j + MI_j = \Delta NW_j^{(en)} + ENCF_j \qquad (i(b))$$

$$HCP_j = [(A_j+R_j-L_j-X_j) + (d_j-k_j) + H_j + (a_j-a_{j-1}) - (b_j-h_j)]$$
$$+ [(k_j-h_j) - (A_j+R_j-Y_j) - t_j - H_j] - F_j - MI_j$$
$$= d_j - (a_{j-1}+b_j-a_j) - L_j - t_j + (Y_j-X_j) - F_j - MI_j \qquad (i)$$

The characteristic excess, $\Delta NW_j^{(en)}$, of post-tax entity profit, $HCP_j + F_j + MI_j$, over entity cash flow, $ENCF_j$, i.e., $(HCP_j+F_j+MI_j) - NW_j^{(en)} = ENCF_j$ can also be derived by deducting the left hand side of (iv) from the right hand side of (i) after adding $F_j + MI_j$ to both sides of the latter. Thus,

$$HCP_j + F_j + MI_j = d_j - (a_{j-1}+b_j-a_j) - L_j - t_j + (Y_j-X_j) \qquad (i(d))$$

and,

$$ENCF_j = (k_j - h_j) - (A_j+R_j-Y_j) - t_j - H_j \qquad (iv(a))$$

Deducting (iv(a)) from (i(d)) gives:

$$HCP_j+F_j+MI_j - ENCF_j = (d_j-k_j) + (a_j-a_{j-1}) - (b_j-h_j) + (A_j+R_j-L_j-X_j) + H_j$$

= Δ in receivables + Δ in inventory − Δ in payables + depreciation shortfall + Δ in liquidity

= periodic working capital investment + depreciation shortfall† + Δ in liquidity

†The depreciation shortfall can, as indicated by equation (iii), also be defined as the periodic increase in the net book value of fixed assets.

Appendix B: Interpretation of the 1984-89 financial performance and financial behavior of Texas Instruments, Inc.

To facilitate multiperiod comparisons, cash flow and market value statements must be restated at a base-year price level as in Tables B.2 and B.4.† Thereafter, the corresponding (real) half-matrices of entity, lender and shareholder IRRs and economic profits can be derived accordingly (see Tables B.5 and B.6).

TI's cash flow statement (Table B.2) gives the distinct impression that the company stood still throughout the six-year period 1984-89. TI's sales receipts which, like those of any other company, measure the level of its economic activity in its end-product markets, fell somewhat in the middle of that period before returning to approximately their initial (1984) level. Whereas there was some variation in the level of operating payments (expressed as a percentage of sales receipts), the dispersion about the average percentage was not significant. Operating cash flow therefore also declined towards the middle of the period before returning to its 1984 level.

The trend of TI's 1984-89 capital expenditure was similar to that of its operating cash flows - an initial decline followed by a return to its 1984 level. TI's relatively constant operating cash flow and capital expenditures during 1984-1989, which are prima facie evidence of a "stand still" economic performance, seem to have been interpreted by the stock market as signals that the company is likely to give a repeat performance in the future. Thus, TI's (real) total market value increased by a modest 4.5 percent over the entire six-year period. This said it ought to be emphasized that TI suffered an enormous tax burden in the six years to December, 1989. Its total tax payments amounted to $603 million and thus converted a pre-tax entity cash

†See footnote on page 64.

TABLE B.1

CASHFLOW STATEMENT

	1984	1985	1986	1987	1988	1989
SALES RECEIPTS	5622.1	5115.1	4933.8	5621.0	6382.7	6521.1
OPERATING CASH OUTFLOW	4851.9	4614.2	4678.3	5075.4	5550.3	5607.9
OPERATING CASH FLOW	770.2	500.9	255.5	545.6	832.4	913.2
PUR OF FIXED ASSETS	704.7	484.8	445.8	462.8	628.1	862.5
DISP OF FIXED ASSETS	0.0	0.0	-119.7	0.0	0.0	0.0
CAPITALIZED INTEREST	-10.0	-14.6	-14.1	-12.7	-14.9	-14.8
NET CAPITAL OUTLAY	694.7	470.2	312.0	450.1	613.2	847.7
OP CASH FLOW-NET CAP OUTLAY	75.5	30.7	-56.5	95.5	219.2	65.5
TAX PAID	-112.7	-82.0	-63.0	-62.0	-133.0	-85.0
LIQUIDITY CHANGE	-89.5	115.6	-55.7	-448.0	-118.0	146.8
POST TAX ENTITY CASHFLOW	-126.7	64.3	-175.2	-414.5	-31.8	127.3
DIVIDEND-NEW EQUITY RAISED	-21.0	-6.2	-265.2	-206.5	7.1	50.5
LENDER CASHFLOW	-105.7	70.5	90.0	-208.0	-38.9	76.8
INTEREST PAID	-58.9	-55.0	-48.4	-30.3	-44.8	-44.5
NEW-REPAID MED,LT LOANS	156.3	2.6	-86.6	261.6	116.4	-32.3
CHANGE IN ODRAFTS, ST LOANS	8.3	-18.1	45.0	-23.3	-32.7	0.0
LENDER CASHFLOW	105.7	-70.5	-90.0	208.0	38.9	-76.8

INDEXATION FACTORS

	1983	1984	1985	1986	1987	1988	1989
MID ACCTING YEAR RPI		103.700	107.600	109.500	113.500	118.000	124.100
END ACCTING YEAR RPI	1.000	105.300	109.300	110.500	115.400	120.400	126.100
LATEST ACCTING YEAR END RPI	0.000	126.100	126.100	126.100	126.100	126.100	126.100
INDEX FACTOR CASHFLOWS		1.216	1.172	1.152	1.111	1.069	1.016
INDEX FACTOR MARKET VALUES	1.245	1.198	1.154	1.141	1.033	1.047	1.000

Texas Instruments, Inc.

TABLE B.2

CASHFLOW STATEMENT 1989 PRICES	1984	1985	1986	1987	1988	1989	Average
SALES RECEIPTS	6837	5995	5682	6245	6821	6626	6367
OPERATING CASH OUTFLOW	5900	5408	5388	5639	5931	5698	5661
OPERATING CASH FLOW	937	587	294	606	890	928	707
PUR OF FIXED ASSETS	857	568	513	514	671	876	
PUR OF INVESTMENTS	0	0	0	0	0	0	
DISP OF FIXED ASSETS	0	0	-138	0	0	0	
CAPITALIZED INTEREST	-12	-17	-16	-14	-16	-15	
NET CAPITAL OUTLAY	845	551	359	500	655	861	629
OP CASH FLOW-NET CAP OUTLAY	92	36	-65	106	234	67	78
TAX PAID	-137	-96	-73	-69	-142	-86	-101
LIQUIDITY CHANGE	-109	135	-64	-498	-126	149	-85
POST TAX ENTITY CASHFLOW	-154	75	-202	-461	-34	129	-108
PURCHASE OF MINORITY INTEREST	0	0	0	0	0	0	
DIVIDEND-NEW EQUITY RAISED	-26	-7	-305	-229	6	51	-85
LENDER CASHFLOW	-129	83	104	-231	-42	78	-23
INTEREST PAID	-72	-64	-56	-34	-48	-45	-53
NEW-REPAID MED,LT LOANS	190	3	-100	291	124	-33	79
CHANGE IN ODRAFTS, ST LOANS	10	-21	52	-26	-35	0	-3
LENDER CASHFLOW	129	-83	-104	231	42	-78	23

Texas Instruments, Inc.

TABLE B.3

ESTIMATED MARKET VALUES

	1983	1984	1985	1986	1987	1988	1989
DEBT < 1 YEAR	36.6	44.9	26.8	72.9	54.1	22.9	42.7
DEBT > 1 YEAR	225.1	380.7	381.9	191.4	486.5	623.8	617.5
TOTAL DEBT CAPITAL	261.7	425.6	408.7	264.3	540.6	646.7	660.2
MARKET VALUE OF EQUITY	2895.3	3018.6	2656.8	3032.1	4373.1	3306.5	3444.7
MINORITY INTEREST	0.0	0.0	0.0	0.0	0.0	0.0	0.0
TOTAL MARKET VALUE	3157.0	3444.2	3065.5	3296.4	4913.7	3953.2	4104.9
DEBT RATIO	8.30%	12.40%	13.30%	8.00%	11.00%	16.40%	16.10%

TABLE B.4

EST MKT VALUES DEC 1989 PRICES

	1963	1984	1985	1986	1987	1988	1989
DEBT < 1 YEAR	46	54	31	83	59	24	43
DEBT > 1 YEAR	280	456	441	218	532	653	618
TOTAL DEBT CAPITAL	326	510	472	302	591	677	660
MARKET VALUE OF EQUITY	3604	3615	3065	3460	4779	3463	3445
MINORITY INTEREST	0	0	0	0	0	0	0
TOTAL MARKET VALUE	3930	4124	3537	3762	5369	4140	4105

TABLE B.5 INTERNAL RATES OF RETURN 1984-89 EXPRESSED IN REAL TERMS

ENTITY RATES OF RETURN

	SOLD	1984	1985	1986	1987	1988	1989
BOUGHT	1983	1.04%	-6.07%	-3.88%	4.06%	-2.85%	-1.92%
	1984		-12.43%	-6.18%	5.04%	-3.73%	-2.45%
	1985			0.66%	15.00%	-0.81%	0.01%
	1986				30.49%	-1.46%	-0.18%
	1987					-23.52%	-11.51%
	1988						2.27%

LENDER RATES OF RETURN

	SOLD	1984	1985	1986	1987	1988	1989
BOUGHT	1983	17.07%	12.21%	2.86%	5.90%	6.32%	6.87%
	1984		8.75%	-2.36%	2.79%	4.21%	5.33%
	1985			-14.05%	-0.99%	2.50%	4.43%
	1986				19.24%	11.84%	10.69%
	1987					7.62%	8.33%
	1988						8.99%

SHAREHOLDER RATES OF RETURN

	SOLD	1984	1985	1986	1987	1988	1989
BOUGHT	1983	-0.41%	-8.24%	-4.65%	3.87%	-3.99%	-3.11%
	1984		-15.41%	-6.68%	5.29%	-4.80%	-3.59%
	1985			2.93%	16.95%	-1.30%	-0.71%
	1986				31.47%	-3.11%	-1.75%
	1987					-27.37%	-14.39%
	1988						0.95%

Table B.6 Texas Instruments, Inc. Economic profits 1984-1989

	1984	1985	1986	1987	1988	1989
change in total market value	194	-587	225	1607	-1229	-35
entity cash flow	-154	75	-202	-461	-34	129
economic profit	40	-512	23	1146	-1263	94
change in market value of debt	184	-38	-170	289	86	-17
lender cash flow	-129	83	104	-231	-42	78
lender profit	55	45	-66	58	44	61
change in market value of equity	11	-550	395	1319	-1316	-18
shareholder cash flow	-26	-7	-305	-229	8	51
shareholder profit	-15	-557	90	1090	-1308	33
reported net income	276	-141	63	321	366	292
re-stated net income	335	-165	73	357	392	296

flow deficit of $44 million into a corresponding post-tax deficit of $647 million.

"Fiscal Drag" on the scale suffered by TI during 1984-89 is a classic example of the economic consequences of corporate taxable earnings measured on a conventional historic cost basis.† Thus, as shown in Appendix A, periodic historic profit before interest, $HCP_j + F_j + MI_j$, usually <u>exceeds</u> periodic entity cash flow, $ENCF_j$, by an amount representing the periodic change in net worth $\Delta NW_j^{(en)}$,

$$\text{i.e., } HCP_j + F_j + MI_j = \Delta NW_j^{(en)} + ENCF_j.$$

†Empirical evidence of this phenomenon is reported elsewhere. See, for example, Lawson (1980), Lawson and Stark (1981), Lawson, Möller and Sherer (1982)

Hence, as $NW_j^{(en)}$ is usually much greater than $F_j + MI_j$, a tax imposed on HCP_j† will generally exert very considerable leverage on the effective incidence of taxation on $ENCF_j$. It is difficult not to infer from TI's 1984-89 cash flow statement that the company was caught in a fiscal trap. If so, there must be serious doubts as to whether TI could have provided adequate entity returns during 1984-89 and, indeed, whether the company can avoid a fiscal trap in the future. The possible ways of ameliorating this problem ought to be the subject of a thorough-going analysis by TI's financial managers.††

TI increased its level of liquidity during the six-year period 1984-89 by $513 million. Expressed as a percentage of operating cash flow, a liquidity increase of this magnitude is relatively high compared with those of other companies. In that TI's level of transactions remained relatively constant during the period, its continuous (real) increase in liquidity is apparently ascribable to precautionary and/or speculative motives, i.e., the expectation that the company was steadily moving into a more risk-laden environment which might nevertheless present unforseen new opportunities. An alternative explanation could be that, during 1984-89, TI pursued a conservative liquidity policy and that it accumulated cash in excess of its needs for transactions, precautionary and speculative motives. But this does not

---

†To be precise HCP_j should read: HCP_j with tax depreciation allowances substituted for depreciation <u>plus</u> the written down book value of assets displaced.

††On 31st December, 1989, TI had accumulated unabsorbed tax-deductible items amounting to $757 million which probably have a present value of about $170 million that is already impounded in the company's market value.

imply that, in measuring performance, periodic entity cash flows should be reduced in respect of "excess" liquidity changes. Any such "excesses" are impounded as surplus assets, and are thereby offset by commensurate increases, in a company's total market value. Put another way; a company's market value embodies, and thus countervails, any "excess" liquidity investments included in the periodic liquidity increases (outlays) that are reported in its cash flow statement.

In judging TI's six-year performance as an economic entity, its (real) entity cash flows must be linked to its (real) market value performance. TI's six-year negative cash flow of $647 million more than offset the coterminous increase in its total market value of $175 million and it therefore reported a six-year economic (entity) loss of $472 million. This cumulative six-year loss is, of course, reflected in the proliferation of negative rates of return in TI's half-matrix of entity IRRs.

The six-year negative entity IRR of 1.92% p.a. shown at the head of the 1989 entity IRR matrix column indicates that TI was generally unprofitable throughout the six-year period.† This rate of return can also be interpreted as a six-year compound rate of ownership wealth erosion. In that profitability is essentially a risk-relative concept, a more accurate assessment of TI's 1984-89 performance is probably provided by a juxtaposition of its risk-adjusted (real) entity half-matrix with the market portfolio IRR half matrix.

---

†As emphasized in the next section, TI's six-year entity IRR is a function of the closing market value of its debt which is an estimate. However, because of TI's relatively low debt ratio during 1984-89, variations in the debt valuation of plus or minus 30% result in a (negative) entity IRR of 1.92% p.a. plus or minus 0.75 percent.

TI's equity beta coefficient averaged 1.15 during 1984-89[†] and, as indicated by Table B.3, it operated with a relatively low debt ratio throughout that six-year period. A direct comparison of its (real) <u>entity</u> IRR matrix with the coterminous market portfolio (real) half matrix is therefore reasonable. This contention can be clarified as follows:

TI's 1984-89 average <u>entity</u> beta coefficient, β_{en}, can be approximated as:

$$\beta_{en} = \frac{MV(debt)}{TMV} \beta(debt) + \frac{MV(equity)}{TMV} \beta(equity).$$

Putting $\beta_{(debt)} = 0.2$[††], $\beta_{(equity)} = 1.15$ and $MV_{(debt)}/TMV = 0.12$,

$$\beta_{en} = (0.12)\ (0.2) + (0.88)\ (1.15)$$
$$= 1.06.$$

The comparison of TI's (real) unadjusted entity half matrix for 1984-89 with that of the market portfolio tells its own story. Not to put too fine a point on it, TI does not appear to have generated risk-commensurate returns during 1984-89. Whereas the real rate of return on the market portfolio averaged 13.7% p.a., TI's entity rate of return was approximately <u>minus</u> 2% p.a. plus or minus roughly 0.75% p.a.

The efficiency of TI's debt-financing and dividend policies

Debt-financing

A comparison of TI's three IRR half matrices suggests that, throughout the six-year period 1984-89, the company consistently generated negative (real) entity returns that were below its real cost of debt which was

---

[†]TI's seven "<u>Value Line</u>" equity beta values at end-years 1983 to 1989 were respectively: 1.05, 1.05, 0.95, 0.95, 1.25, 1.4 and 1.4.

[††]This may be on the high side because TI's (real) lender IRR half matrix for 1984-89 was probably somewhat below the corresponding IRR half matrix for long-term government bonds.

Table B.7 Real rates of return on U.S. common stocks 1984-89

bought end-year	sold end-year 1984	1985	1986	1987	1988	1989
1983	2.21%	14.1%	15.2%	11.3%	11.5%	13.7%
1984		27.4%	22.2%	14.5%	13.9%	16.1%
1985			17.2%	8.7%	9.7%	13.5%
1986				0.8%	6.2%	12.3%
1987					11.9%	18.6%
1988						25.7%

Source: Corresponding nominal values in Ibbotson Associates SBBI 1990 Yearbook

Table B.8 Real rates of return on U.S. long-term corporate bonds 1984-89

bought end-year	sold end-year 1984	1985	1986	1987	1988	1989
1983	11.9%	18.8%	18.8%	12.5%	11.2%	11.1%
1984		26.1%	22.4%	12.6%	10.9%	10.9%
1985			18.5%	6.3%	6.3%	7.5%
1986				-4.5%	0.7%	4.0%
1987					6.0%	8.5%
1988						11.1%

Source: Corresponding nominal values in Ibbotson Associates SBBI 1990 Yearbook

positive. Thus, shareholders apparently suffered a rather extreme form of reverse leverage.

It is important to reiterate that the computed values in the lender IRR matrix are a direct function of the seven estimated end-year market values of its interest-bearing debt. However, although TI's (estimated) debt ratio (measured on a market value basis) seems to have doubled over the six-year period, it was no higher than about 16% plus or minus 4 percentage points in December 1989. Hence, errors in the debt valuation estimates can only have a negligible effect on the accuracy of the entity IRR matrix which is arithmetically equal to the weighted average of the debt and equity half matrices. For example, allowing TI's December 1989 debt valuation estimate to vary by plus or minus 30% puts its (real) six-year lender IRR in the range 14.6% p.a. to 2.36% p..a. The corresponding entity IRR range is minus 1.26% p.a. to minus 2.84 p.a.

Equally important in the present context is the fact that significant errors in the debt valuation estimates do not alter the conclusion that lenders enjoyed real positive returns whereas shareholders suffered real negative returns throughout 1984-89. There appears to be a two-fold reason for this extreme degree of reverse leverage. TI evidently raised debt at real positive interest rates and invested both debt and equity internally at negative real rates of return. Put another way; shareholders not only financed internal investments generating negative real rates of return, they also subsidized lenders. On the other hand, even allowing for a 30 percent increase in TI's December 1990 debt valuation, a comparison of its lender half-matrix with the coterminious IRR half matrix for U.S. corporate loans provides no obvious evidence that TI's 1984-89 debt issues have been underpriced, i.e., issued at a market discount.

It should finally be noted that TI's 1984-89 entity cash flow deficit of $647 million was jointly financed by lenders and shareholders in the respective amounts of $137 million and $510 million. The $137 million negative lender cash flow comprises interest payments of $319 million and new debt amounting to $456 million. Lenders therefore financed their own interest payments.

Dividend policy

The constituent components of TI shareholder cash flows (1984-89) elucidate aspects of its dividend policy during those years.

Table B.9 TI shareholder cash flows expressed at December 1989 prices

$ million	1984	1985	1986	1987	1988	1989	average
common and pref. dividends	+58.73	+58.36	+69.90	+80.88	+93.18	+98.87	+76.65
pref. stock issue			-339.84	-245.86			-97.62
common stock issue	-84.27	-63.63	-35.47	-64.44	-85.59	-47.55	-63.49
shareholder cash flows	-25.54	- 7.27	-305.41	-229.42	+ 7.59	+51.32	-84.46

Whilst TI's common and preference dividends increased at a compound annual rate of about 11 percent in real terms, the company simultaneously raised new equity. Common stockholders provided new equity each year whilst, in the two middle years (1986 and 1987) preferred stockholders contributed sums which in total amounted to twice as much as the equity raised from common stockholders over the entire six-year sequence. As already noted, stockholders thus financed no less than $510 million (78 percent) of TI's $647 million entity cash flow deficit. Additionally, stockholders financed the entire six-year dividend sequence that was paid out by TI.

If, as a matter of financial policy, TI intended to raise from shareholders the net amounts of cash represented by the above shareholder cash flows, shareholders should have been invited to provide such net amounts directly in order to obviate substantial tax leakages resulting from dividend payments. Alternatively, the intention may have been to raise gross amounts of capital from shareholders in the belief that new equity issues and concurrent dividend payments are somehow unrelated, e.g., because dividend policy

Table B.10: Texas Instruments, Inc. - Income Statements 1984-89

$ millions	1984	1985	1986	1987	1988	1989
net sales billed	5,741.6	4,924.5	4,974.0	5,594.5	6,294.8	6,521.9
other income	9.6	17.0	9.4	205.0	181.8	59.0
	5,751.2	4,941.5	4,983.4	5,799.5	6,476.6	6,580.9
cost of sales	4,793.2	4,500.2	4,445.9	4,997.0	5,537.0	5,748.8
depreciation	422.6	515.9	426.2	380.1	389.8	453.7
interest expense	48.9	40.4	24.1	20.7	33.4	23.6
pre-tax profit	486.5	(115.0)	87.2	401.7	516.4	354.8
tax paid	112.7	82.0	63.0	62.0	133.0	85.0
post-tax profit	373.8	(197.0)	24.2	339.7	383.4	269.8
extraordinary item	--	--	(10.8)	--	--	--
dividends paid	48.3	49.8	60.7	72.8	87.2	97.3
retained earnings	325.5	(246.8)	(47.3)	266.9	296.2	172.5

Table B.11: TI's income statements expressed at December 1989 prices

$ millions	1984	1985	1986	1987	1988	1989	average
net sales billed	6,981.8	5,771.0	5,728.1	6,215.5	6,726.6	6,626.9	6,341.7
other income	11.7	19.9	10.8	227.8	194.3	59.9	87.4
	6,993.5	5,790.9	5,738.9	6,443.3	6,920.9	6,686.8	6,429.1
cost of sales	5,828.5	5,273.8	5,119.9	5,551.7	5,916.8	5,841.4	5,588.7
depreciation	513.9	604.6	490.8	422.3	416.5	461.0	484.9
interest expense	59.5	47.3	27.8	23.0	35.7	24.0	36.2
pre-tax profit	591.6	(134.8)	100.4	446.3	551.8	360.4	319.3
tax paid	137.0	96.1	72.6	68.9	142.1	86.4	100.5
post-tax profit	454.6	(230.9)	27.8	377.4	409.7	274.0	218.8
extraordinary item			(12.4)	--			(2.1)
dividends paid	58.7	58.4	69.9	80.9	93.2	98.9	76.7
retained earnings	395.9	(289.3)	(54.5)	296.5	316.5	175.1	140.0

per se is in some sense desirable. If so, TI's dividend policy affected the level of debt raised (or repaid) and increased its debt ratio accordingly. However, as already suggested, there is no evidence of underpriced debt issues during 1984-89 and therefore no reason to suppose that debt-financed dividends, and/or other forms of debt-financing, caused wealth transfers from shareholders to lenders which exacerbated shareholder wealth losses attributable to dividend tax leakages.

Comparison of TI's reported profits with its cash flow performance 1984-89

The conventionally-measured profit performance of TI for 1984-89 is shown in Table B.10. The same six-year sequence of income statements, restated at December 1989 prices, is given in Table B.11. The specific reason for this latter transformation should first be emphasized. Restated at a base-year price level, periodic historic cost income is not amenable to economic interpretation. This is also true of periodic historic cost-based income itself. Unlike the constituents of a periodic cash flow statement, the constituents of historic cost-based periodic income are not expressed in a common periodic purchasing power. Restating historic cost profit at a base-year price level is therefore not a transformation which corrects for the purchasing power heterogeneity of its periodic constituents whilst simultaneously allowing for changes in the purchasing power of money.†

Periodic historic cost profit which is restated at a base-year price level is, however, a legitimate basis for the averaging of historic cost accounting

---

†Restating multiperiod cash flow performance at a base-year price level is an economically-meaningful transformation because the cash flows of any individual period are, as just stated, measured in a common purchasing power. A succession of periodic cash flow statements therefore automatically captures relative price changes. Hence, to restate an actual multiperiod cash flow statement at a base-year price level, i.e., in real terms, it is merely necessary to resort to index numbers which measure changes in the purchasing power of money.

performance over a succession of periods for comparisons with the corresponding average periodic cash flow performance. The average "conventionally-reported" and average "cash flow" performances of TI for 1984-89 can therefore be juxtaposed as in Table B.12.

A conventional interpretation of the historic cost accruals-based summary shown in Table B.12 might run as follows. During the six-year period 1984-89, TI apparently generated pre-tax profit (after interest) averaging $320 million (expressed at December 1989 prices) on which it paid taxes at the (optically) modest rate of 33%. TI distributed 35 percent of its post-tax profit to its shareholders as dividends and apparently reinvested the remaining 65 percent in the business in order to increase earnings on its shareholders' behalf.

Plausible though the latter interpretation may seem, it does not accurately reflect the real economic events underlying TI's performance during 1984-89. Nevertheless, accruals accounting numbers generally have significant economic consequences because they are used for an array of decision-making purposes at the managerial, corporate and macroeconomic levels. Table B.12 provides some indication of the possible economic consequence of historic cost accruals income measures at the corporate-macroeconomic levels.

Corporate interest cover is widely, albeit erroneously, defined as pre-tax profit (before interest) divided by interest expense. Thus measured, TI's interest cover averaged (320 + 36) ÷ 36 = 9.9 during 1984-89. In that interest cover is essentially a cash flow concept, TI's 1984-89 <u>ex post</u> interest cover should be inferred from the cash flow column of Table B.12. Furthermore, tax payments are based on taxable earnings which are net of (tax-deductible) interest payments; and, in accordance with statutory law, tax payments take precedence over interest payments. Hence, cash flow interest cover is measured by entity cash flows divided by <u>contractual</u>, as opposed to

Table B.12

Average income and cash flow statements of Texas Instruments, Inc. 1984-89

	accruals basis	cash flow basis	
net sales billed	6,342	6,367	sales receipts
cost of sales (less other income)	5,501	5,661	operating payments (less other income)
pre-depreciation profit	841	707	operating cash flow
depreciation	485	629	net capital expenditure
		85	liquidity change
interest expense	36	37	real interest (see note i)
pre-tax profit	320	(44)	
tax paid (32%)	101	101	tax paid
post-tax profit	219	(145)	
dividends paid (35%)	77	(85)	shareholder cash flow
retained earnings	142	(60)	debt-financing (see note ii)

Notes

i. real interest = (interest expense + capitalized interest) x [1 - (average inflation rate ÷ average interest rate)]

= (38+15)[1-(0.037 ÷ 0.1194)]

ii. net of lenders' principal of 16 repaid (via the "Fisher effect") as a component of contractual payments of (38 + 15).

real, interest payments. As TI sustained a negative entity cash flow of $647 million during 1984-89 (expressed at December 1989 prices), its interest expense was totally uncovered and, in the event, was financed by lenders themselves. In sum, both TI and its lenders may, given the company's investment intentions, have been under entirely the wrong impression about its debt-servicing capacity during 1984-89.

The incidence of taxation on TI's pre-tax entity cash flows has already been mentioned. Here it is only necessary to repeat that taxes assessed on taxable earnings -- a near relation of pre-tax (dichotomizable) reported income -- must, taking one year with another, be financed from internally-generated cash, i.e., from pre-tax entity cash flow. But entity cash flow is one of the two (dichotomizable) components of taxable earnings. It is therefore virtually inevitable that the proportion of pre-tax entity cash flow which is syphoned off by way of taxes on a continuing basis constitutes a much higher effective tax burden than is signalled by the tax charges reported in a company's income statement.

The possible consequences of dividend policies based upon historic cost accruals accounting income measures have also already been discussed at length and need not be reiterated in detail here. It ought nevertheless to be emphasized that the six-year income statement gives an entirely misleading impression about dividend policy. Far from being the recipients of a 35 percent payout, who could look forward to dividend growth from a 65 percent plough-back, shareholders were net cash contributors to an entity cash flow deficit. A small part of this deficit was countervailed by the 4.5 percent real increase, in the company's total market value. Shareholders obviously did not receive commensurate market value increases for their deficit financing because their real market value declined by 4.4 percent.

Summing up; at the corporate-macroeconomic level three major policies which have direct cash flow consequences, namely, debt-financing, taxation and dividend distribution are generally based on accruals-based measures of corporate income. Such (virtually universal) custom and practice seems to reflect an implicit assumption that accruals income measures are an appropriate basis for decisions which have direct cash flow consequences and/or that income measured on an accruals basis is a reasonable proxy for cash flow income. Both of these assumptions are patently invalid. It is therefore perhaps not surprising that conventional accounting numbers can have extremely serious adverse, or unintended, economic consequences; and, that, as a means of measuring economic performance, and of reporting the efficiency of dividend and debt-financing policies, they are chronically deficient.

Table B.13 Texas Instruments, Inc. and Subsidiaries

Balance Sheet	December 31 1989	December 31 1988
Assets		
Current assets:		
Cash and cash equivalents	$ 418.2	$ 541.3
Short-term investments	219.2	239.1
Accounts receivable, less allowance for losses of $41.7 in 1989 and $49.0 in 1988	942.9	942.1
Inventories (net of progress billings)	806.4	769.7
Prepaid expenses	59.7	56.4
Total current assets	2,446.4	2,578.6
Property, plant and equipment at cost	3,641.1	3,073.7
Less accumulated depreciation	(1,511.4)	(1,347.6)
Property, plant and equipment (net)	2,129.7	1,726.1
Other assets	228.3	152.8
Total assets	$4,804.4	$4,427.5
Liabilities and Stockholders' Equity		
Current liabilities:		
Loans payable and current portion long-term debt	$ 42.7	$ 22.9
Accounts payable and accrued expenses	1,210.7	1,091.0
Income taxes payable	24.4	39.0
Accrued pension and profit sharing contributions	7.5	28.9
Dividends payable	17.5	17.6
Total current liabilities	1,302.8	1,199.4
Long-term debt	617.5	623.8
Accrued pension costs	128.9	115.2
Deferred credits and other liabilities	270.3	245.5
Stockholders' equity:		
Preferred stock, $25 par value.Authorized-10,000,000 shares.		
Market auction preferred (stated at liquidation value). Shares issued and outstanding: 1989 and 1988 - 3,000	300.0	300.0
Convertible money market preferred (stated at liquidation value). Shares issued and outstanding: 1989 and 1988 - 2,208	220.8	220.8
Participating cumulative preferred. None issued	--	--
Common stock, $1 par value.Authorized-300,000,000 shares. Shares issued:1989-81,606,649; 1988-80,746,272	81.6	80.8
Paid-in capital	483.1	437.1
Retained earnings	1,403.9	1,209.4
Less treasury common stock at cost. Shares: 1989 - 102,754; 1988 - 100,182	(4.5)	(4.5)
Total stockholders' equity	2,484.9	2,243.6
Total liabilities and stockholders' equity	$4,804.4	$4,427.5

References

Arthur Young, UK GAAP: Generally Accepted Accounting Practice in the United Kingdom, Longman, London, 1989.

Accounting Standards Committee, Proposed Statement of Accounting Practice, ED54: Cash flow statements, London, 1990.

Baumol, W. J., "The Transactions Demand for Cash: An Inventory Theoretic Approach," Quarterly Journal of Economics, 66: 545-556, 1952.

Chambers, R. J., "Evidence for a Market-Selling Price-Accounting," in Sterling, R. R., (ed.) Asset Valuation and Income Determination - a Consideration of Alternatives, Scholars Book Co., 1972.

Chambers, R. J., Accounting, Evaluation and Economic Behaviour, Prentice-Hall, 1966.

Edwards, E. O. and Bell, P. W. The Theory and Measurement of Business Income, University of California Press, 1961.

Financial Accounting Standards Board, Statement of Financial Accounting Standards No. 95, Statement of Cash Flows, 1987.

Ibbotson Associates, Stocks, Bonds, Bills and Inflation Yearbook, 1990.

Inflation Accounting Committee, Inflation Accounting, HMSO London, 1975.

Lawson, G. H., "Initial Reflections on Sandilands - I," Certified Accountant, November, 1975, pp. 583-588 and 634.

Lawson, G. H., "The Measurement of Corporate Profitability on a Cash Flow Basis," The International Journal of Accounting, Fall, 1980, pp. 11-46.

Lawson, G. H., and Stark, A. W., "Equity Values and Inflation, Dividends and Debt Financing," Lloyds Bank Review, No. 139, January 1981(a), pp. 40-54.

__________ "Equity Values and Inflation: A Rejoinder," Lloyds Bank Review, No. 142, October, 1981(b), pp. 39-43.

Lawson, G. H., Möller, H. P. and Sherer, M., "Zur Verwendung anschaffungswertorientierter Aufwand-Ertrag-Rechnungen als Grundlage für die Bemessung von Zinsen, Steuern und Dividenden" in Lück und Tromsdorff (eds.), Internationalisierung der Unternehmung Erich Schmidt Verlag, Berlin, 1982, 643-662.

Lawson, G. H., "The measurement of corporate performance on a cash flow basis: a reply to Mr. Egginton," Accounting and Business Research, Vol. 15, No. 58, Spring 1985, pp. 99-108.

Lee, T. A., Income and Value Measurement: Theory and Practice, Nelson, London, 1974.

Lee, T. A., Cash Flow Accounting, Van Nostrand Reinhold (U. K.) Co. Ltd., Wokingham, England, 1984.

Lintner, J., "Distribution of Income of Corporations Among Dividends, Retained Earnings and Taxes," American Economic Review 46: 97-113, 1956.

Miller, M. H., and Modigliani, F., "Dividend Policy, Growth and the Valuation of Shares," Journal of Business 34: 411-433, 961.

Miller, M. H., and Orr, D., "A Model of the Demand for Money by Firms," Quarterly Journal of Economics 80: 413-435, 1966.

Modigliani, F., and Cohn, R. A., "Inflation, Rational Valuation and the Market," Financial Analysts Journal, 1979.

Paton, W. A. and Littleton, A. C., An Introduction to Corporate Accounting Standards, American Accounting Association, 1940.

Rappaport, A., Creating Shareholder Value: The New Standard for Business Performance, The Free Press, New York, 1986.

Stern, J., "Stop Paying Dividends," Corporate Finance, January 1989.

Schmalenbach, E., Dynamische Bilanz, 4th edition, Gloeckner, Leipzig, 1926. [Republished in English as Dynamic Accounting by Murphy, G. W., and Most, K. S., (translators), Gee and Company, London, 1959].

Solomons, D., "Economic and Accounting Concepts of Income," The Accounting Review, 374-383, 1961.

Solomons, D., Guidelines for Financial Reporting Standards, Institute of Chartered Accountants in England and Wales, London, 1989.

Sterling, R. R., "Costs (Historical versus Current) versus Exit Values," Abacus 17: 93-129, 1981.

Theobald, M., "Intertemporal dividend models: An empirical analysis using recent U. K. data," Journal of Business Finance and Accounting, 123-135, 1978.

Theobald, M., and Cadle, J., "Corporate Dividend Policies in the U. K." (forthcoming).

Ownership value creation and the evaluation of alternative plans

by

G. H. Lawson and Henry Chong

Manchester Business School

Contents

Ownership value creation and the evaluation

of alternative plans

1. Introduction

This paper contains five main parts. Section 2 contrasts the cash flow valuation basis of the normative wealth maximisation model with the accruals basis of measurement; and, questions the use of an accruals accounting model as a framework for the financial evaluation of alternative plans.

Section 3 contains the conceptual foundations of an aide memoire covering the systematic sequence of steps that should be taken in the financial evaluation of alternative corporate plans by reference to any corporate financial objective. Whether such steps are in fact taken is the empirical issue which the questionnaire survey described in section 5 was intended to elucidate.

Section 4 is concerned with corporate dividend and debt-financing policies. It contains brief discussions of the possible economic consequences of dividend policies based on conventionally-measured earnings and of debt ratios measured on a balance sheet basis.

The results that are reported in section 5 were obtained from a postal questionnaire survey which was undertaken in the summer of 1984 as part of a student MBA project. Accepting the deficiencies of questionnaire methodology, the intention was to obtain a very broad indication of the extent to which U.K. practice in the evaluation of corporate plans conforms to a normative wealth maximisation approach - alias shareholder wealth creation. It was assumed from the outset that because U.K. corporate financial management tends to be dominated by accountants, evidence elicited on the financial evaluation corporate plans would probably reveal strong accounting influences which themselves constitute a departure from normative wealth-maximising behaviour. To some extent this assumption determined in the way in which questions were formulated and, in turn, produced a number of affirmative replies about what is actually done in practice. Had the questions focused solely on the operational implications of adopting a wealth maximisation objective, it is likely that the responses would have been largely in the negative.

In section 6 some tentative conclusions are drawn from the responses obtained in the postal survey. The questionnaire that was circulated to samples of small, medium and large companies is reproduced as an appendix.

2. Valuation and wealth maximisation

Assuming a firm's paramount objective is the maximisation of ownership wealth, (alias market value maximisation) the net present value rule constitutes its exclusive decision-making prescription. As outlined in section 3, this framework readily accommodates the economist's traditional short run analysis of cost, price and output as well as the (long run) analysis of capital projects.

The market value of a firm is usually defined as the present value of its expected cash flow stream.[1] For example, the Modigliani-Miller[2] valuation model may, under a neutral corporate tax regime, be expressed as:

$$\sum_{j=1}^{\infty} \frac{(\bar{k}_j-\bar{h}_j)-(\bar{A}_j+\bar{R}_j-\bar{Y}_j)-\bar{t}_j-\bar{H}_j}{\prod_{t=1}^{j}(1+\bar{r}_t)} \equiv \sum_{j=1}^{\infty} \frac{\bar{D}_j-\bar{B}_j}{\prod_{t=1}^{j}\{1+\bar{r}_t(e)\}} + \sum_{j=1}^{\infty} \frac{\bar{F}_j-\bar{N}_j-\bar{M}_j}{\prod_{t=1}^{j}\{1+\bar{r}_t(d)\}} \qquad (1)$$

or $\qquad V_o \equiv V_o(e) + V_o(d)$

that is, market value of entity ≡ market value of equity + market value of debt

---

[1]An individual project's net present value is the amount its implementation is expected to add to its implementer's market value.

[2]Modigliani and Miller (1958).

or, present value of entity cash flows $\equiv$ present value of shareholder cash flows + present value of lender cash flows

where (using bars to denote expected values),

$\bar{r}_t$, $\bar{r}_t^{(e)}$ and $\bar{r}_t^{(d)}$ the single period costs of entity, shareholder and lender capital respectively; and, V_o is independent of the ratio $V_o^{(d)}/V_o$.

In year j,

$k_j - h_j$ = operating cash flow represented by cash collected from customers, k_j, and operating payments, h_j;

$A_j + R_j - Y_j$ = replacement investment, A_j, growth investment, R_j, and the proceeds from assets displaced, Y_j;

t_j = corporate income tax payments;

H_j = liquidity change;

F_j = interest payments;

N_j = medium and/or long term debt raised or retired;

M_j = short term debt raised or repaid;

D_j = dividends paid to shareholders; and,

B_j = equity capital raised or repaid in year j.

A wealth maximising firm may therefore be defined as one which, faced with alternative financial plans (each of which may be regarded as a different path through time), chooses the plan offering the highest present value. Put another way, the objective function of a wealth maximising firm can be expressed as:

$$\text{Max!} \sum_{j=1}^{\infty} \frac{(\bar{k}_j - \bar{h}_j) - (\bar{A}_j + \bar{R}_j - \bar{Y}_j) - \bar{t}_j - \bar{H}_j}{\prod_{t=1}^{j} (1+\bar{r}_t)} \tag{2}$$

The latter statement is based on three specific assumptions. First, the assumption of a neutral tax regime in which case the tax payment, t_j, on the

LHS of (1) is independent of the debt-financing and dividend policies reflected in the division of cash flows between lenders and shareholders shown on the RHS of (1). Second (and third), that an entity's (single period) cost of capital, $\bar{r}_t$, is independent both of its debt ratio and its dividend policy.

On the foregoing assumptions, a company's dividend policy and its lender cash flow stream (debt ratio) are both independent variables and should be simultaneously determined. If either one is treated as a separate independent variable, the other clearly becomes a dependent variable. If the foregoing assumptions do not hold, three decisions, namely, those concerning the choice of plan, dividend policy and debt ratio must be simultaneously determined. Whether the foregoing assumptions hold or not, the valuation identity (1) makes it quite clear that dividend policies and debt-servicing capacity, i.e., debt ratios, ought to be settled simultaneously by reference to <u>expected</u> entity cash flows. We return to financial policy in section 4.

The cash flow basis of measurement which is the essence of the valuation identity can be contrasted with the accruals-based historic cost accounting model. Historic cost profit for any period j is given by:

$$HCP_j = d_j - (a_{j-1}+b_j-a_j) - L_j - F_j + (Y_j-X_j) - t_{j+1} \qquad (3)$$

where, in year j,

d_j = accrued sales;

a_{j-1}, a_j = beginning and end-year inventory book values;

b_j = total accrued revenue expenditure;

L_j = depreciation based on historic cost;

t_{j+1} = provision for corporate income tax paid one year later; and

Y_j-X_j = accounting profit on assets displaced (X_j represents their written down book value).

For any year j entity cash flows, $ENCF_j$, are as indicated by the LHS of (1), given by:

$$ENCF_j = (k_j - h_j) - (A_j + R_j - Y_j) - T_j - H_j \qquad (4)$$

Ignoring taxes and assuming the case of a wholly equity-financed company; the difference between periodic entity cash flow and historic cost profit, $HCP_j - ENCF_j$, is given by:

$$HCP_j - ENCF_j = (d_j - k_j) + (a_j - a_{j-1}) - (b_j - h_j) + (A_j + R_j - L_j - X_j) + H_j \qquad (5)$$

that is,

$HCP_j - ENCF_j$ = periodic change in (receivables, inventories, and payables) + periodic depreciation shortfall + periodic liquidity change

The constituents of this difference are such that there are strong a priori reasons for assuming that HCP_j will characteristically overstate $ENCF_j$. This contention can be demonstrated empirically[3] and by generating hypothetical data using multiperiod computer-based simulation models. Thus, contrary to common supposition, a characteristic excess of historic cost profit over cash flow earnings tends to be a permanent difference rather than a self-reversing timing difference.

Given the relationships between the cash flow and profit & loss statements that are represented by equations (3), (4) and (5), it is perhaps not surprising that in a comparison between alternatives (say) A and B, it may turn out that the sequence of historic cost profits for A ($HCP_j^{(A)}$; $j=1,2,\ldots$) may dominate the historic cost profit sequence of B but that the ranking by entity cash flows, $ENCF_j$, is reversed, i.e.,

$HCP_j^{(A)} > HCP_j^{(B)}$

but, for $j=1,2,\ldots$.

$ENCF_j^{(A)} < ENCF_j^{(B)}$

---

[3]See Lawson, Möller and Sherer (1982) and Lawson and Stark (1981).

It is only a further short step to the conclusion that similar rankings may well emerge if the sequences of HCP_j are divided through by the corresponding sequences of capital employed ($CE_j^{(A)}$, $CE_j^{(B)}$) and entity cash flow sequences are discounted at the firm's cost of capital. In short, ROI maximisation and wealth maximisation objectives may give conflicting signals to managers who are attempting to choose between alternative corporate financial plans.

A further possibility should also be mentioned, namely, $HCP_j > 0$ whilst, simultaneously, for the same plan, $ENCF_j < 0$. That is to say, a plan that looks profitable may not be financially viable. This is another way of referring to a 'profitable' plan that requires a continuing financial subsidy.

3. Operational implications of wealth maximising behaviour

Whatever financial objective is used as a basis for evaluating and choosing between alternative plans, a firm needs to have a conceptual framework that is capable of depicting the alternatives from which a choice is to be made. As illustrated by Figures (1), (2) and (3), alternative financial plans are variations, each of which can be regarded as the exploration of an alternative path through time, on the theme of price, cost, output and investment.

Figure 1 illustrates the notion of a multiperiod demand curve expressed in money terms. The gaps between the individual curves could be explained by a world of rising prices and/or expected growth in sales volume which, in turn, may be attributable to total market growth and/or increases in market share. The path labelled I reflects a policy emphasising high price and low volume increases compared to path II. As paths I and II both imply significant increases in output over the four-year period, the firm needs to assess its capacity requirements and, as the case may be, create additional capacity accordingly.

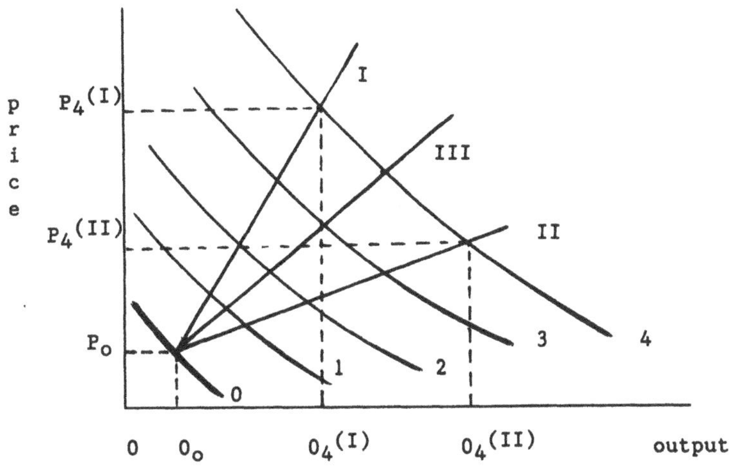

Figure 1 multiperiod demand curve

i. Curves 0, 1, 2, 3 and 4 denote demand curves expressed in money terms in periods 0, 1, 2, 3 and 4 respectively.

ii. The lines, I, II and III represent alternative paths through time, i.e., alternative multiperiod price/output plans. In period 0 the firm sold output 00_o at price $0P_o$. In period 4 the price/output combinations are $[00_4^{(I)}, 0P_4^{(I)}]$ and $[00_4^{(II)}, 0P_4^{(II)}]$ for plans I and II respectively.

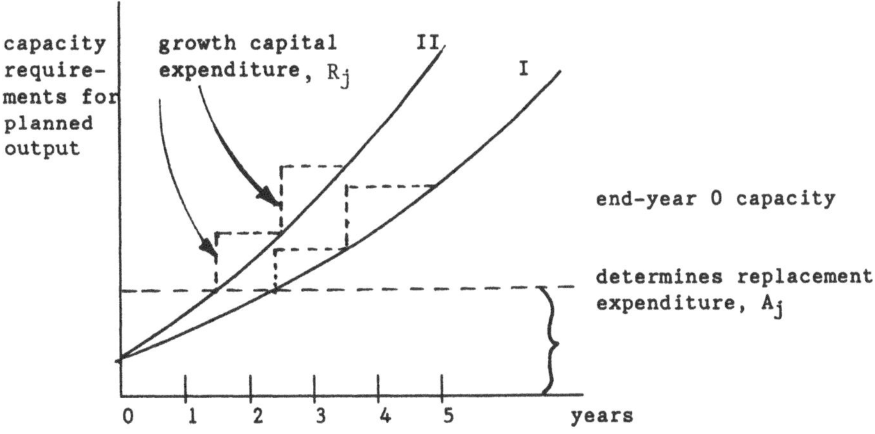

Figure 2 Capacity and capital expenditure for alternative plans

Note

Curves I and II denote the capacity requirements for plans I and II assuming that in period 0 the firm was operating below capacity.

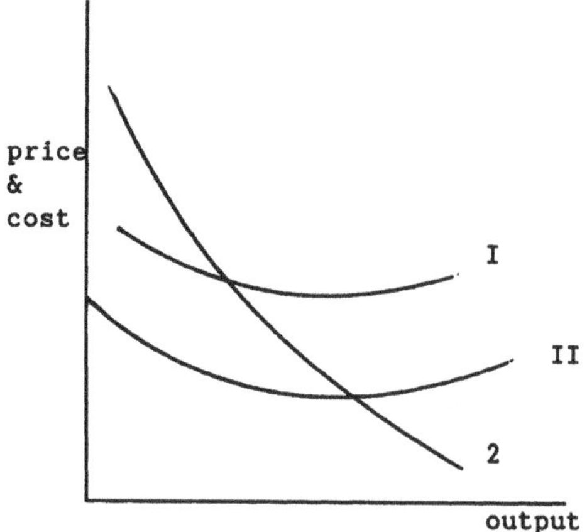

Figure 3 Operating costs associated with alternative plans

Notes

i. I and II denote (average) operating cost functions of plans I and II respectively in period 2.

ii. Curve 2 is the period 2 demand curve.

The relationship between output, existing (end-year 0) capacity and required additional capacity is shown in Figure 2. Future capital expenditure programmes therefore comprise the replacement investment, A_j, which is primarily a function of the age-structure and expected lives of the end-year 0 asset stock; and, growth investment, R_j, which creates additional capacity. Growth investment will itself result in replacement expenditure in the fullness of time.

Figure 3 illustrates the possibility that the different scales of productive capacity that are required for different paths through time have different operating cost functions. Thus, in Figure 3, the operating cost function for period 2 of path I is higher than that of path II. (Curve 2 represents the period 2 demand curve.)

Each individual path through time represents a scenario of prices, costs, outputs and investment which can be expressed as sequences of profit & loss, balance sheet and cash flow statements.[4] Such sequences can nowadays be generated rapidly with computer-based financial models. Thus, as already stated by reference to (2), a wealth-maximising firm should apparently choose the alternative plan which promises the sequence of entity cash flows offering the highest present value. This prescription is subject to two important qualifications. First, if a choice between alternative plans is to be based upon (say) a five-year planning horizon, a terminal (i.e., end-year 5) valuation problem has to be faced.[5] This said, there is always the possibility that the entity cash flow sequence of one alternative may not only dominate those of all other alternatives, but also have a higher implicit terminal value because it requires higher investment levels.

The second qualification is that different plans may reflect different levels of risk, which may perhaps be attributable to different levels of operating leverage, and therefore have different costs of capital.

A third qualification that should be entered concerns the relationship between planning and budgeting. Given its financial objective a company should first choose a plan. Thereafter, the first year of the plan should be divided into weekly/monthly budgets etc. In many companies the preparation of the forthcoming year's budgets seems to precede planning; and, the plans for subsequent years are an extrapolation of the budget. Such a 'cart before the horse' approach is inconsistent with wealth-maximising behaviour.

4. Corporate financial policy decisions: dividend and debt ratio policies

As has been emphasised elsewhere,[6] the effects of corporate dividend policies are a classic example of the economic consequences of accounting.

---

[4]See Paper 5, pages 17-21.

[5]See Paper 8.

[6]Lawson (1980).

Empirical studies have consistently suggested that the dividend policies of British and American companies have hitherto been based on post-tax historic cost profit and generally conform to the original Lintner[7] model, namely,

$$D_j = \alpha \gamma HCP_j + (1-\alpha) D_{j-1} \quad (6)$$

where,

D_j denotes the dividend in year j;

α is the rate of adjustment of dividends to current earnings ($1>\alpha<0$);

γ stands for the firm's target pay-out ratio; and,

HCP_j is post-tax profit.

Lintner's descriptive model gives effect to two well-known dividend policy aims, namely, the adjustment of dividends to current earnings and continuity of established dividend policy. The higher the value of the adjustment factor, α, the greater is the weight attaching to the current earnings determinant and vice versa. However, as the previous year's dividend, D_{j-1} may be written:

$$D_{j-1} = \alpha \gamma HCP_{j-1} + (1-\alpha) D_{j-2} \quad (7)$$

then, after substituting (7) into (6) and making similar substitutions for D_{j-2}, D_{j-3} etc., D_j can be expressed wholly in terms of earnings, namely,

$$D_j = \alpha\gamma[HCP_j+(1-\alpha)HCP_{j-1}+(1-\alpha)^2HCP_{j-2}+ \ldots\ldots+(1-\alpha)^nHCP_{j-n}] \quad (8)$$

To determine the financial and economic consequences of an (accruals) earnings-based dividend policy (including equity capital raised or repaid), it is of course necessary to refer to a multiperiod cash flow statement. Thus, if as in cases reported elsewhere,[8] post-tax historic cost profit, HCP_j, consistently exceeds post-tax entity cash flows by a large margin, dividends (net

---

[7]Lintner (1956), Theobald (1978).

[8]Lawson (1980, 1982, 1983), Lawson and Stark (1981), Lawson, Möller and Sherer (1982).

of capital raised or repaid), $D_j - B_j$, may well exceed entity cash flows over long periods of time. That is to say,

$$\text{if } HCP_j > ENCF_j$$

and assuming for convenience, $\alpha = 1$,

$$\text{then } \alpha\ \gamma\ HCP_j - B_j > ENCF_j$$

provided,

$$\gamma > \frac{ENCF_j + B_j}{HCP_j}$$

For example, put $ENCF_j = 600$, $B_j = 0$ (since B_j will usually, though not always, take on a value of zero) and $HCP_j = 1000$. Thus, if $\gamma > 0.6$, some part of dividends, D_j, and the whole of interest, F_j, will need to be externally financed with debt, i.e.,

$$(D_j - B_j) - [(k_j - h_j) - (A_j + R_j - Y_j) - t_j - H_j] - F_j = N_j + M_j \qquad (9)$$

A continuous debt-financed dividend shortfall will, in turn, cause an accumulation of corporate debt, the market value of which may increase or decrease relative to a firm's total market value (i.e., market value of debt and equity). An increase in the market value of debt relative to a firm's total market value represents a rise in its debt ratio. In other words, a dividend policy based on a firm's historic cost profits may cause a debt-financed dividend shortfall which in turn causes an increase in its debt ratio. But such an increase represents the substitution of debt capital for equity or, what amounts to the same thing, the repayment of equity to shareholders.

So far as one can tell, dividend policy is supposed to provide a return on shareholders' capital and is not intended to return their capital to them.[9]

---

[9]This seems to be a firmly established principle of company law in several of the countries in which the joint stock enterprise is to be found.

However, dividend policies based on accounting earnings may result in exactly the latter consequence.

We conclude this section by referring to a different aspect of debt financing but which also has to do with the economic consequences of accounting.

In the sequence of events just postulated, dividend policy is clearly the active decision variable and debt financing is the dependent residual. In other cases dividends may be the dependent variable because a firm actively seeks to maintain a stable debt ratio. An important aspect of such a financial policy objective is clearly the way in which a firm actually measures its debt ratio.

If the financial summaries that are contained in published company accounts are anything to go by, not to mention SSAP 16,[10] it is widely assumed that a debt ratio is, or should be, measured by reference to a company's balance sheet. Balance sheet measures of debt ratios are, at best, only rough approximations of the correct market value basis on which a debt ratio should be measured. A debt ratio is pre-eminently intended to reveal the proportions in which the total market value of a firm is divided between lenders and shareholders. Among other things, it reveals how much wealth shareholders can sell to (buy from) lenders before the latter (former) become the sole owners of the firm in question. This is clearly a matter that can only be resolved by reference to market values.

Alternatively, it can be said that a market value-based debt ratio reflects the capitalised value of the preferential claims of lenders on expected entity cash flows. If a firm's multiperiod (entity) cash flow stream is highly variable (widely dispersed about the multiperiod expected value

---

[10]Statement of Standard Accounting Practice No. 16, Accounting Standards Committee (U.K.), 1980.

sequence), the avoidance of corporate bankruptcy may dictate a relatively low debt ratio. In an efficient stock market, revisions of expectations about both the expected value and variability of future cash flows are quickly impounded into market-based debt ratios which ought therefore to be taken seriously by financial managers.

The potential economic consequences of debt ratios measured on a balance sheet basis lie in the possibility that a balance sheet measure may seriously understate its market value counterpart. Thus, a firm entering a period of financial difficulty resulting in a decline in market value (LHS of (1)) may find that, because of the reverse leverage effect on the market value of equity, both the absolute and relative decline in its equity market value (second term on the RHS of (1)) are very significant and may actually fall below the balance sheet value of its equity. It is hardly necessary to emphasise that balance sheet debt ratios do not respond in this way.

The danger to a firm in these circumstances is the likelihood that lenders will base their decisions on the balance sheet and actually exacerbate the situation already accurately reflected in its market value-based debt ratio by advancing a further tranche of debt.

5. The questionnaire survey

The postal questionnaire was circulated to samples of small, medium and large companies as defined by the 1981 U.K. Companies Act. The companies were selected at random from Key British Enterprise '84 British Top 20,000 Companies published by Dun & Bradstreet Ltd. This book lists all U.K. companies in alphabetical order and includes information on turnover, number of employees, etc.

The overall response rate was 27 percent. The individual response rates were:

company size	no. of questionnaires circulated	response rate percent
large	350	29
medium	350	31
small	350	20

Questionnaire responses should always be qualified with an important caveat if, as in this case, they have not been cross-checked with interviews. In the absence of follow-up interviews, the researcher can never be sure that the respondents have fully understood the questions or that he (she) correctly understands the responses.

The questionnaire was designed to elicit information on five main aspects of corporate financial planning, namely,

I. The preparation of financial plans

II. Corporate financial objectives

III. The preparation of alternative financial plans

IV. Internal financial reporting

V. Corporate financing (including dividend policy).

The main inferences suggested by the survey responses about best practice in the above five areas[11] are set out below.

I. & III. The preparation of financial plans (including alternatives)

(a) High percentages of the respondents to Question 1 in all three samples (91 percent overall) stated that their companies prepare financial plans. The affirmative and negative responses within class sizes are as in Table 1.

---

[11]In fact, (I) and (III) are both concerned with the preparation of plans. The three questions about the preparation of alternative plans were deliberately separated from the five questions in section (I) in an attempt to maintain the interest of the respondent by not dwelling on one subject to an excessive degree.

Table 1: <u>Percentage of respondents preparing a financial plan</u>

	small percent	medium percent	large percent	total percent
affirmative	78	92	97	91
negative	18	8	3	8
no answer	4	-	-	1
	100	100	100	100

(b) In all three sizes categories a projected profit & loss account seems to be the main basis for expressing financial plans whilst projected cash flow statements and projected balance sheets appear to play an important, albeit lesser, role. As a planning framework, projected funds flow statements appear to rank well behind the other projected statements. The details are as in Table 2 from which it can be inferred that about 56 percent of all respondents use a combined profit & loss, balance sheet and cash flow planning framework.

Table 2: <u>Manner in which financial plans are expressed</u>

	small percent	medium percent	large percent	total percent
projected profit & loss accounts	72	90	97	89
projected balance sheets	44	66	81	68
projected funds flow statements	28	48	59	49
projected cash flow statements	56	71	80	72

(c) Whereas high proportions of the companies in all three samples appear to divide their first year plan into monthly, quarterly or half-yearly budgets, significant, though somewhat lower, proportions appear to prepare their budgets in advance of their financial plan. As noted previously, this rather puts the cart before the horse. The relevant responses are summarised in Tables 3 and 4.

Table 3: Percentages of respondents which divide the first year of the plan into monthly/quarterly/half-yearly budgets

	small percent	medium percent	large percent	total percent
affirmative	58	78	77	74
negative	20	15	20	18
no answer	22	7	3	8
	100	100	100	100

Table 4: Percentages of respondents preparing budgets in advance of first year of plan

	small percent	medium percent	large percent	total percent
affirmative	48	49	36	44
negative	30	44	61	48
no answer	22	7	3	8
	100	100	100	100

(d) The more distant the planning year, the less detailed that year's plan appears to be.

(e) A relatively small percentage of the respondents to Question 9 (12 percent overall) stated that they prepare alternative financial plans. (See Table 5).

Table 5: Percentage of respondents preparing alternative plans

	small percent	medium percent	large percent	total percent
affirmative	2	13	16	12
negative	94	87	83	87
sometimes	-	-	1	-
no answer	4	-	-	1
	100	100	100	100

(f) The responses to Question 12 suggest that large majorities of companies in all three class sizes revise their financial plans at intervals from three to twelve months. The responses to Question 12 are given in Table 6.

Table 6: Frequency at which respondents revise plans

	small percent	medium percent	large percent	total percent
monthly	2	8	9	7
quarterly	32	31	30	31
half-yearly	22	25	23	24
annually	20	26	34	28
whenever necessary	2	4	2	3
no answer	22	6	2	7
	100	100	100	100

II. Corporate financial objectives

(a) It is hardly necessary to state that Question 6 was intended to provide direct evidence of wealth maximising behaviour. Companies were asked to rank their financial objectives in descending order of importance. The principal financial objectives of U.K. companies appear to be ROI maximisation and the maximisation of the "bottom line" of the profit & loss account. A comprehensive picture of the responses to Question 6 is provided by Tables 7, 8, 9, 10 and 11.

Table 7: Paramount financial objective of respondent companies

	small percent	medium percent	large percent	total percent
ROI maximisation	44	40	53	46
conventional profit maximisation	38	45	38	41
sales maximisation	16	11	4	9
market value maximisation	-	1	4	2
no answer	2	3	1	2
	100	100	100	100

Table 8: Second financial objective of respondent companies

	small Percent	medium Percent	large Percent	total Percent
ROI maximisation	18	24	19	21
conventional profit maximisation	26	19	28	24
sales maximisation	10	22	15	17
market value maximisation	2	3	3	3
no answer	44	32	35	35
	100	100	100	100

Table 9: Third financial objective of respondent companies

	small percent	medium percent	large percent	total percent
ROI maximisation	8	13	10	11
conventional profit maximisation	12	7	10	9
sales maximisation	12	21	21	19
market value maximisation	2	2	5	3
no answer	66	57	54	58
	100	100	100	100

Table 10: Fourth financial objective of respondent companies

	small percent	medium percent	large percent	total percent
ROI maximisation	-	-	1	-
conventional profit maximisation	-	-	3	1
sales maximisation	4	2	3	3
market value maximisation	8	8	6	7
no answer	88	90	87	89

Table 11: Percentages of respondents stating that none of the four enumerated objectives is applicable

	small percent	medium percent	large percent	total percent
ROI maximisation	28	25	15	22
conventional profit maximisation	22	30	22	25
sales maximisation	52	45	57	51
market value maximisation	82	89	81	85

(b) Judging from Tables 7, 8 and 9, sales maximisation appears to have a significant influence on corporate financial targetry.

(c) The responses summarised in Tables 7 to 11 (inclusive) provide rather uncomfortable evidence that U.K. companies are not wealth maximisers. Since operationally speaking, ROI and post-tax profit objectives cannot be relied upon to signal the same set of decisions as a wealth maximisation objective, it is tempting to conclude that U.K. best practice in corporate financial planning may be responsible for a significant loss of ownership wealth. However, in the absence of systematically-generated alternatives, the idea of alternative decision sets is something of a non-sequitur.

(d) Eighty-four percent of the respondents to Question 7 in each size category stated that they had not changed their corporate financial objectives in recent years.

IV. Internal financial reporting

(a) The responses to the questions on financial reporting were rather predictable. Eighty-five percent of respondents intimated that they report on a monthly basis. The other responses are summarised in Table 12.

Table 12: Frequency of financial reporting by respondent companies

	small percent	medium percent	large percent	total percent
monthly	72	86	90	85
quarterly	10	10	7	9
half-yearly	6	-	1	2
annually	6	2	2	3
bi-monthly	2	2	-	1
	100	100	100	100

(b) Reporting actual results against the budgeted profit & loss account appears to be almost universal practice (89 percent of the respondents as shown in Table 13).

Fifty-three percent of the respondents stated that they report actual balance sheets against budgeted balance sheets. This practice varies in intensity within the size categories.

Whereas cash budgets seem to be slightly more popular than balance sheets as a basis for comparing actual outcomes, projected funds flow statements appear to be less popular. The respondent's use of the latter and other statements as a basis for comparison within the size categories is summarised in Table 13.

Table 13: Respondent company bases for comparing actual results

	small percent	medium percent	large percent	total percent
profit & loss account	76	88	96	89
balance sheet	36	47	68	53
funds flow statement	20	42	47	39
cash flow statement	46	51	68	57

(c) The analysis of deviations between budgets/projections and actuals is arguably an integral part of the implementation of a plan in the pursuit of any kind of financial objective. Such analysis allegedly indicates the appropriate managerial response when things do not go according to plan. Question 15 was intended to reveal information on how companies react to deviations. In the event it seems to have elicited information on the deviation magnitudes that would stimulate an analysis of deviations. The responses are summarised in Table 14.

Table 14: Action on deviations between budget and actual

	percentage of respondents			
	small percent	medium percent	large percent	total percent
all deviations are investigated	2	21	20	17
5-10% deviations are investigated	36	29	27	30
no procedure	2	10	14	10
different standard for different parts of the company	8	5	3	5
"significant" deviations only	12	3	14	9
depends on absolute level of deviation	0	3	4	3
controllable items only	0	3	0	2
no answer	40	26	18	24
	100	100	100	100

(d) Question 16 was intended to elicit information on the use of financial data generated in the budgetary/planning process. If such data are really taken seriously they should constitute financial targets and authorisation levels for particular time-intervals. The overall 76 percent affirmative response does, in fact, suggest a widespread use of budgets and/or plans in this way. The responses within categories are indicated in Table 15.

Table 15: Respondents' use of budgets and plans for expenditure authorisation

	small percent	medium percent	large percent	total percent
affirmative	50	78	84	75
negative	20	16	13	15
other	8	-	-	2
no answer	22	6	3	8
	100	100	100	100

V. Corporate financing

(a) Question 17 is based on the assumption that bank overdraft financing is a short term problem that should be controlled, negotiated and kept under continuous surveillance by reference to a company's cash budgets. The replies from the respondent companies to Question 17 suggest that the use of cash budgets as a basis for negotiating and altering bank overdraft limits is by no means universal practice. The affirmative and negative responses to the question are summarised in Table 16.

Table 16: Use of cash budgets for negotiating bank overdrafts

	small percent	medium percent	large percent	total percent
affirmative	44	53	54	52
negative	30	35	37	35
not applicable	4	6	6	5
no answer	22	6	3	8
	100	100	100	100

(b) The use of financial plans to estimate the amounts and/or timing of new equity and medium/long term loans appears to be even less common than the use of cash budgets for negotiating bank overdrafts. As Table 17 shows, most of the responses to this question were in the negative.

Table 17: Use of financial plans to estimate the amounts and/or timing of new equity issues and medium/long term loans

	small percent	medium percent	large percent	total percent
affirmative	4	18	31	20
negative	64	55	50	54
not applicable	10	21	17	17
no answer	22	6	3	8
	100	100	100	100

(c) Question 19 was intended to reveal whether the companies giving the affirmative answers in Table 17 determine their debt ratios by reference to projected balance sheets. Small, though nevertheless significant, percentages in all three size categories appear to do so. (See Table 18.)

Table 18: Percentage of respondents determining debt ratios by reference to projected balance sheets

	small percent	medium percent	large percent	total percent
users of projected balance sheets	6	9	19	11
non-users of projected balance sheets	38	31	33	34
not applicable	34	53	46	45
no answer	22	7	2	10
	100	100	100	100

(d) Although the idea of a target debt ratio is popular among textbook writers, the virtual absence of responses to Questions 20 and 21 suggest that it is a much less familiar notion in practice.

(e) The final two questions sought information on the basis of company dividend policies. The responses seem to suggest that dividends are determined independently of target debt ratio levels (if any) mainly by reference to established dividend policy or by reference to established dividend policy and current profits. The responses to Question 22 are given in Table 19.

Table 19: Basis of respondent company dividend policies

	small percent	medium percent	large percent	total percent
by reference to				
established dividend policy	20	21	23	21
established dividend policy and current profits	28	30	41	34
last year's dividend and the rate of inflation	4	2	4	3
expected future cash flows	2	6	5	5
none of the above	30	41	27	33
no answer	16	-	-	4
	100	100	100	100

No company offered a definition of expected future cash flows in response to Question 23.

Summing up the evidence on dividend policies; the dividend policies of about 55 percent of the respondent companies appear to conform to something akin to a Lintner type of model. If so, it can in turn be inferred that they are prone to the possible consequences outlined in section 4.

6. Conclusions

The information summarised in the previous section contains few surprises. If, as in the U.K., corporate financial management is dominated by accountants it is almost inevitable that financial plans will be expressed mainly in terms of the profit & loss account. It is also inevitable that corporate financial objectives will be expressed in terms of such accounting yardsticks as ROI and "conventional" profit maximisation. Even though 72 percent of the respondents (56, 71 and 80 percent for small, medium and large companies respectively) state that they also express their plans as a sequence of cash flow statements, their choice of financial objectives strongly suggests that cash flow is either a dependent variable or constraint. As already emphasised, accounting criteria will generally not signal the same set of decisions as will a wealth maximisation approach. Furthermore, whereas the essence of wealth maximisation is a choice between alternatives, the responses summarised in Table 5 indicate that companies generally do not prepare alternative plans from which a choice could be made.

Further evidence of a departure from wealth maximising behaviour is the habit of preparing budgets ahead of plans (48 percent of the respondents).

Turning to the right hand side of the normative wealth maximisation model; about 50 percent of the respondents intimated that they use cash budgets as an aid to short term financing and control. By contrast, only 20 percent of the respondents (4, 18 and 31 percent for large, medium and small respectively) use financial plans to estimate the amounts of new equity issues and/or medium and long term loans.

Whilst about 12 percent of the respondents appear to determine debt ratios by reference to balance sheets, there is no evidence that companies utilise target debt ratios. Moreover, about 58 percent of the respondents seem to determine dividend payments by reference to past profits and/or established dividend policy. Thus, whereas the financing and dividend decisions should be simultaneously determined by reference to expected entity cash flows, the former seems to be based on post-tax historic cost (actual) profits and the latter appears to be a dependent variable.

Returning finally to evidence of departures from wealth maximising behaviour; it is scarcely necessary to state that any resultant wealth loss is not directly observable. If a company's market value reflects the discounted value of its expected (entity) cash flows, that market value will clearly depend upon the cash flows expected from the preferred plan regardless of whether its selection criterion (corporate financial objective) is economically defensible. In other words, whatever plan a company chooses, that company will be valued on a cash flows basis; and, the net wealth loss resulting from any preferred plan can only be estimated by attempting to measure the discounted incremental cash flows that could have been accessed by the choice of a superior alternative expected entity cash flow stream.

April, 1985.

References

Lawson, G. H. "The Measurement of Corporate Profitability on a Cash-Flow Basis," The International Journal of Accounting Education and Research, 1980.

Lawson, G. H. "Was Woolworth Ailing?," The Accountant, 1982.

Lawson, G. H. "Why the Current UDS Takeover Bids Became Inevitable," The Accountant 1983.

Lawson, G. H., Möller, P. and Sherer, M. "Zur Verwendung anschaffungswertorientierter Aufwand-Ertrag-Rechnungen als Grundlage für die Bemessung von Zinsen, Steuern und Dividenden," Internationalisierung der Unternehmung, Erich Schmidt Verlag, GmbH, 1982.

Lawson, G. H. and Stark, A. W. "Equity Values and Inflation: Dividends and Debt Financing," Lloyds Bank Review, 1981.

Lintner, J. "Distribution of Incomes of Corporations Among Dividends, Retained Earnings and Taxes," American Economic Review, 1956.

Modigliani, F. and Miller, M. H. "The Cost of Capital, Corporation Finance and the Theory of Investment," American Economic Review, 1958.

Theobald, M. "Intertermporal Dividend Models - An Empirical Analysis Using Recent UK Data," Journal of Business Finance and Accounting, 1978.

Appendix

Questionnaire on the financial evaluation of corporate plans

I. Preparing financial plans

1. Does your company prepare a one/two/three/four/five† -year financial plan? Yes ☐ No ☐

2. If the answer to Question 1 is 'yes', is your company's financial plan expressed as sequences of:

   (a) projected profit & loss accounts? Yes ☐ No ☐

   (b) projected balance sheets? Yes ☐ No ☐

   (c) projected funds flow statements? Yes ☐ No ☐

   (d) projected cash flow statements? Yes ☐ No ☐

3. [Please read both parts of this question before answering it.]

   (a) If the answer to Question 1 is 'yes', is the first year of your company's financial plan divided into monthly/quarterly/half-yearly† budgets? or, Yes ☐ No ☐

   (b) Does the first year of your company's financial plan represent the sum of the monthly/quarterly/half-yearly† budgets that are prepared in advance of your financial plan? Yes ☐ No ☐

---

† Please delete the alternative(s) that do(es) not apply.

4. If your company prepares a financial plan, is the second year of the plan as detailed as the first year? Yes ☐ No ☐

5. [Please answer this question if it applies.]

How detailed are the third and subsequent years of your company's financial plan?

3rd year: equally as/less† detailed as/than† year 2

4th year: equally as/less† detailed as/than† year 3

5th year: equally as/less† detailed as/than† year 4.

II. Corporate financial objectives

6. What is your company's principal financial objective?

[If your company pursues more than one of the following objectives please rank them in order of importance using 1 to denote most important, 2 to denote next most important, etc. If it pursues objectives not listed here, please enumerate and rank them under (e) below.]

(a) Improving its rate of return on capital employed? ☐

(b) Maximising the sequence of post-tax profits in the projected profit & loss accounts? ☐

(c) Maximising the level of sales? ☐

---

† Please delete the alternative(s) that do(es) not apply.

(d) Maximising the company's market value? ☐

(e) Other(s) (please describe) ____________________

____

7. Has your company changed its financial objective(s) in recent years? Yes ☐ No ☐

8. If the answer to Question 7 is 'yes' please describe the change ____________________

____

III. <u>Preparing alternative financial plans</u>

9. Does your company prepare two or more alternative financial plans? Yes ☐ No ☐

10. If the answer to Question 9 is 'yes', how does your company choose between the alternatives? ____________________

____

11. If the answer to Question 9 is 'yes' please briefly describe the procedure with which the alternatives are generated ____________________

____

12. How often are your financial plans revised?

monthly ☐ quarterly ☐ half-yearly ☐

annually ☐

IV. Internal financial reporting

13. How often are financial reports presented in your company?

monthly ☐ quarterly ☐ half-yearly ☐ annually ☐

14. In your company are actual results reported against:

(a) budgeted profit & loss accounts? Yes ☐ No ☐

(b) budgeted balance sheets? Yes ☐ No ☐

(c) budgeted funds flow statements? Yes ☐ No ☐

(d) cash budgets? Yes ☐ No ☐

15. If the answer to Question 14 is 'yes', please describe briefly how deviations between 'budget' and 'actual' are acted upon, e.g., "A 5 or 10 percent deviation will be investigated and subsequent action will depend upon whether or not it occurred for reasons within the company's control."

16. Are your company's budgets and/or plans used as a basis for expenditure authorisation and/or approval? Yes ☐ No ☐

Additional comment ______________________________

____

V. Corporate financing

17. Are your company's first year's cash budgets used as a basis for negotiating and/or altering bank overdraft and short term loan limits? Yes ☐ No ☐

18. Does your company use its financial plan to estimate the amounts and/or timing of new equity issues and medium/long term loans? Yes ☐ No ☐

(Please amplify as necessary) ____________________

____

____

19. If the answer to Question 18 is 'yes', does your company decide between equity and loan capital by reference to debt ratios revealed in projected balance sheets? Yes ☐ No ☐

20. If the answer to Question 19 is 'yes', what is your company's target debt ratio and how do you define it?

debt ratio = ; debt ratio definition =

21. If the answer to Question 19 is 'no', how do you determine your debt ratio?

____

____

22. Is your company's dividend determined by reference to

    (a) established dividend policy? Yes ☐ No ☐

    (b) established dividend policy and current profits? Yes ☐ No ☐

    (c) last year's dividend and the rate of inflation? Yes ☐ No ☐

    (d) expected future cash flows? Yes ☐ No ☐

23. If your answer to Question 22(d) is 'yes', please give your definition of expected future cash flows ______________________

    ____

    ____

Thank you for your collaboration. All information received will be anonymised.

Contract costing and the negotiation of contract prices

Joop van den Berge, Chief Financial Executive, the Dietsmann Group, and G. H. Lawson, Professor of Business Finance, Manchester Business School, and Non-Executive Director, Dietsmann (UK) Ltd. on how to approach price negotiations.

Van den Berge

Lawson

The costing and pricing of contracts provide interesting examples of the potential conflict between traditional accounting and the discounted cash flow (DCF) approach which has gained increasing use as a capital budgeting framework in the last 25 years. Such a conflict, and its implications for contract costing, pricing, price negotiations and financial control are elaborated below by reference to a numerical example based on figures provided by a large UK public company.

Not to put too fine a point on the substance of this paper at this juncture, it is nowadays usually assumed that, in terms of financial logic, the DCF approach is the more defensible computational method. Thus, sole reliance upon the conventional accounting approach to contract costing and pricing could result in financial penalties that might otherwise have been avoided. Conversely, joint reliance on both the conventional and DCF frameworks may suggest ways of improving the financial returns from contracts.

Related financial aspects

Contract costing and pricing have at least three related financial aspects:

1 Contracts are usually costed on a conventional accounting basis with profit mark-ups expressed accordingly.

2 The intrinsic profitability of a contract is measured by its net present value, ie the discounted value of the inflows and outflows associated therewith. Thus, whatever conventional

accounting mark-up has been negotiated, a contract's intrinsic profitability depends upon the timing of the payments and receipts associated therewith. Hence, any slippage in the collection of price instalments will, regardless of the predetermined conventional profit mark-up, which is unaffected thereby, reduce intrinsic profitability. Conversely, any acceleration in the collection of price instalments and/or down-payments will raise intrinsic profitability and, again, will not affect the conventional profit mark-up.

3 Contract negotiators may find themselves in a situation in which, given the competition, etc, they are under pressure to reduce the conventional profit mark-up but, in so doing, may be able to persuade a contractee to agree to a 'sweetener' in the form of a down-payment or, for example, monthly instead of two-monthly instalments. Alternatively, a contract negotiator may occasionally wish to take the initiative and propose a reduction in conventional profit mark-up if the contractee will agree to a different payments schedule. Possible trade-offs between conventional profit mark-up and changes in the time-profile of contract price instalments should be computed explicitly as an aid to contract price negotiations.

Some of the more important implications of these aspects are illustrated and analysed below.

Conventional profitability and net present value

If, as already stated, a contract's intrinsic profitability is represented by its net present value, contracts should be costed and priced on a cash flow (present value) basis. However, if the language of contract negotiations is conventional contract costing and pricing, the cash flow numbers need to be translated accordingly; and the resultant conventional profit mark-up should be expressed in the usual way. Thus, a contractor's negotiators* should be able to analyse contract costs, prices, profit margins and profitability in both conventional and cash flow terms. That is to say, they need to understand the possible trade-offs between conventional mark-up on the one hand, and possible alternative price instalment schedules and net present value on the other. These propositions can be illustrated arithmetically as in illustrations **1** and **2**.

Illustration 1

Assumptions

1 Expressed in money terms, the estimates for a contract with an expected duration of two years are:

* Purely for convenience everything which follows is written from a contractor's standpoint. Clearly that same viewpoint is at least as pertinent to a contractee.

labour: £4,660 a month for 24 months
material: £4,980 a month for 24 months
plant acquisition cost £24,000 (estimated residual market value after two years: £13,000).

2 The DCF rate of return required on the contract (expressed in money terms) is 23 per cent per annum and is determined by reference to the (risk-free) rate of interest on Government bonds (9 per cent) *plus* a risk premium (say 10 per cent) that is commensurate with the contract's degree of market risk (here assumed to be average) *plus* a pure profit margin of four percentage points.* (The contract's risk-adjusted cost of capital is thus assumed to be 19 per cent p.a.).

3 The contract price is payable in four half-yearly instalments in arrears.

Given the foregoing assumptions, the contract's price, P, should be derived from the following (summarised) cash flow computation.

Month	**0**	**6**	**12**	**18**	**24**
1 Price instalment	—	+P/4	+P/4	+P/4	+P/4
2 Capital expenditure	−24,000	—	—	—	+13,000
3 Labour £4,660 monthly					
Material £4,980 monthly					
£9,640 monthly					

The present value computation from which the contract price, P, is derived, is therefore:

present value at 23 per cent of four half-yearly price instalments of P/4 (in arrears)

plus

present value at 23 per cent of plant worth £13,000 at end year 2

minus

present value at 23 per cent of *monthly* labour and material costs, and capital expenditure of £24,000 at end year 0.

Using present value formulae this computation can be written as:

$$24{,}000 = \frac{P}{4}\left[\frac{1-(1.23)^{-2}}{(1.23)^{1/2}-1}\right] + \frac{13{,}000}{(1.23)^{2}} - 9{,}640\left[\frac{1-(1.23)^{-2}}{(1.23)^{1/12}-1}\right]$$

*The technicalities of market risk, etc., are elaborated elsewhere and need not be repeated here. See Lawson and Stapleton. (1984) It should be emphasized that a contract's estimated cost of capital must, by definition, be commensurate with its characteristic degree of risk. However, the required rate of return must *exceed* the cost of capital because a contract which promises a rate of return that is equal to the cost of capital has a zero net present value. Such contracts do not add to the value of a firm.

whence,

$$P = 4\left[\frac{(1.23)^{½}-1}{1-(1.23)^{-2}}\right]\left\{24{,}000 - \frac{13{,}000}{(1.23)^2} + 9{,}640\left[\frac{1-(1.23)^{-2}}{(1.23)^{1/12}-1}\right]\right\}$$

= £261,699

If the cost of capital for the contract is 19 per cent per annum as assumed above, its net present value, NPV, is given by:

$$NPV = \frac{261{,}699}{4}\left[\frac{1-(1.19)^{-2}}{(1.19)^{½}-1}\right] + \frac{13{,}000}{(1.19)^2} - 9{,}640\left[\frac{1-(1.19)^{-2}}{(1.19)^{1/12}-1}\right] - 24{,}000$$

= £2,584

The contract's profitability is stated in conventional accounting form as in *Illustration 2*.

Illustration 2: Contract profitability expressed in conventional accounting form

		£
Contract price		261,699
Labour cost	111,840	
Material cost	119,520	
		231,360
		30,339
Depreciation (24,000-13,000)		11,000
Conventional mark-up		**£19,339**
Profit on sales 7.39 per cent		
Profit on cost 8.0 per cent		

Before turning to the possible variations that can be analysed by reference to Illustrations 1 and 2, the contract's conventional and DCF profitability values should be briefly commented upon:

1 The contract's present value of £2,584 can be interpreted as the capital gain that is immediately enjoyed by the firm (if all the assumptions of the illustration hold) by undertaking that contract; and, in theory, the firm's market value will increase accordingly.

2 The contract's conventional profit (mark-up) of £19,339 measures its net present value at a *zero* cost of capital. In that such a NPV effectively ignores the cost of capital, it

characteristically overstates intrinsic profitability. However, as illustrated by both the graph and *Table 1*, the conventional mark-up may occasionally *understate* profitability. Thus, as detailed analysis would confirm, no consistent relationship between NPV and conventional profit can be presumed and the latter should not be used as a surrogate for the former.
3 The contract's required rate of return of 23 per cent per annum is directly comparable with interest rates quoted in money and capital markets. Its accounting rates of return of 7.39 per cent on sales and 8.0 per cent on cost cannot be interpreted by reference to quoted interest rates and have no economic significance. It cannot be assumed that a contract's DCF rate of return will characteristically exceed its accounting rate(s) of return by a constant factor and, indeed, an excess of the latter over the former cannot be precluded. Thus, a contract's accounting rates of return should never be used as a surrogate for its DCF rate of return.
4 If as a matter of universal practice, contract profit rates are measured as in *Illustration* 2, their use in contract negotiations cannot be avoided. As already suggested, this aspect of the conventional approach may afford opportunities to contract negotiators who also know how to evaluate contracts on a DCF basis and can translate from the one basis of evaluation to the other.

Trading-off conventional profit mark-up against present value

This is perhaps the leading question that can be elucidated by reference to numerical examples of the previous type. Assume that, in the previous case, contract negotiators believe that, given the competition, a six per cent profit on cost would clinch the deal. They also believe that the contractee would agree to pay the half-yearly (equal) instalments of the contract price, in advance, ie, making a down payment followed by payments after six, 12 and 18 months respectively.

The contract price would reduce by £4,797 to £256,902 as in *Illustration 3*.

The present value of the contract would, again assuming a risk-adjusted cost of capital of 19 per cent p.a. *increase* by:

$$- \frac{261{,}699}{4}\left[\frac{1-(1.19)^{-2}}{(1.19)^{1/2}-1}\right]$$
$$+ \frac{256{,}902}{4}\left[1 + \frac{1}{(1.19)^{1/2}} + \frac{1}{1.19} + \frac{1}{(1.19)^{1\frac{1}{2}}}\right]$$

= **£14,994**

Illustration 3. Alternative terms of contract

		£
Contract price		256,902
Labour cost	111,840	
Material cost	119,520	
		231,360
		25,542
Depreciation (24,000-13,000)		11,000
Conventional mark-up		£14,542
Profit on sales 5.67 per cent		
Profit on cost 6 per cent		

In other words, if the contractee could be persuaded to pay one of the four instalments of the contract price in advance, in return for a 1.8 percentage points reduction in the contract price, the contractor would increase the contract's net present value by a factor of (14,994 + 2,584)/2,584 = 6.8, ie the contract would become more than six times as profitable!

Put yet another way, instead of adding only £2,584 to the total market value of the contractor firm, the contract would, if the price instalments were paid in advance, add £14,994 + £2,584 to contractor's market value. All of this is, of course, contingent upon the other assumptions being maintained. But even if they are not, the *lower* contract price of £256,902 associated with the payment in advance, and three remaining instalments after six, 12 and 18 months respectively, is still the superior strategy.

Alternative down-payments

A comparison of Illustrations 1 and 2 with Illustration 3 makes it quite clear that, in the case in question, the conventional profit margin could be reduced very considerably as a trade-off against a down-payment (four half-yearly payments in advance) as opposed to four equal half-yearly payments *in arrears* – while increasing the contract's net present value.*

Furthermore, contracts can have many different possible durations and progress payments may be other than half-yearly. This implies that the number of possible combinations of contract price instalments in relation to any given accounting profit mark-up may be quite enormous. The size of the combinatorial problem

* If paid in four equal half-yearly instalments in advance, the contract's price could be reduced to any value exceeding £239,899 to give a net present value greater than the £2,584 obtained in Illustration 1. At the latter contract price (payable in four equal instalments in advance) the net present value is equal to £2,584 and the conventional mark-up is a *loss* of £(239,899-242,360) =£2,461.

should not, however, be over-emphasized and it can easily be kept within manageable proportions by resorting to pre-computed tables that can handle any contract duration. Also, as just illustrated, the analysis is mainly concerned with the revenue side since the control of payments can be handled as a separate issue whatever price and progress payment schedule is negotiated.

A further factor that will tend to reduce the scale of the computational problem is custom and practice. For example, if, in the industry in question, progress payments are customarily made monthly in arrears, it may at best only be possible to negotiate about the level of a down-payment with the balance payable in equal monthly instalments in arrears.

In comparing Illustrations 1 and 2 with Illustration 3, the rather dramatic difference between four half-yearly payments in arrears and four (somewhat lower) half-yearly payments in advance provides a fairly obvious clue that the weakness in the conventional approach illustrated above lies in its failure to allow for the time-value of money via an interest charge.*

Thus, in proposing radical changes in the time-profile of price instalments in return for a reduction in conventional mark-up, a contractor may give the game away. Less radical adjustments, eg, a small down-payment of contract price in return for a (less than commensurate) reduction in conventional profit mark-up, may not arouse a contractee's suspicions while nevertheless redistributing a contract's returns in favour of the contractor. This clearly implies the need for a general formula which facilitates rapid calculations of the trade-off between changes in conventional mark-up on the one hand and price instalments and net present value on the other.

Derivation of a general formula

It is assumed that the general case is one in which:

1 Some capital expenditure is incurred at the start of the contract and may have a positive or negative residual value on the contract's termination.

2 Other costs are incurred and paid monthly.

3 The contract price is payable in instalments, subject to the deduction of retentions, comprising a down-payment and the balance in equal monthly instalments in arrears over the duration of the contract.

4 Half of the retentions are released on the completion of the contract and the remaining half some months later.

---

* The authors' experience is that interest charges are rarely included in conventional contract costing computations. Indeed, their exclusion is officially sanctioned in the UK. See, for example, *Review Board for the Government Contracts (1984)*. It can in fact be contended that the entire analytical basis adopted by the latter is deficient.

Table 1 **Contract price minima as a function of varying down-payments (with a constant net present value of 993)**

Rate of down-payment, 100 x %	0%	2.2%	5%	7½%	10%	12½%	15%	20%	22½%
Minimum contract price, £P*	252,294	251,157	250,003	248,859	247,725	246,602	245,489	243,293	242,210
Total conventional cost £	242,360	242,360	242,360	242,360	242,360	242,360	242,360	242,360	242,360
Conventional profit £	9,934	8,797	7,643	6,499	5,365	4,242	3,129	933	(150)
Profit on sales %	3.94%	3.50%	3.06%	2.61%	2.17%	1.72%	1.27%	0.38%	—
Profit on cost %	4.1%	3.63%	3.15%	2.68%	2.21%	1.75%	1.29%	0.38%	—

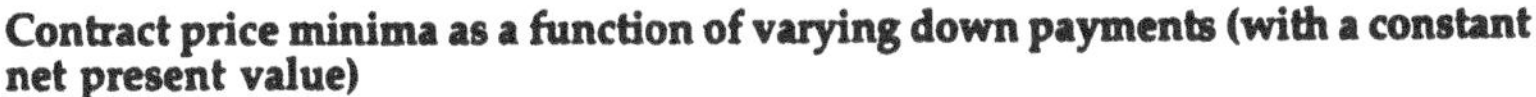
Contract price minima as a function of varying down payments (with a constant net present value)

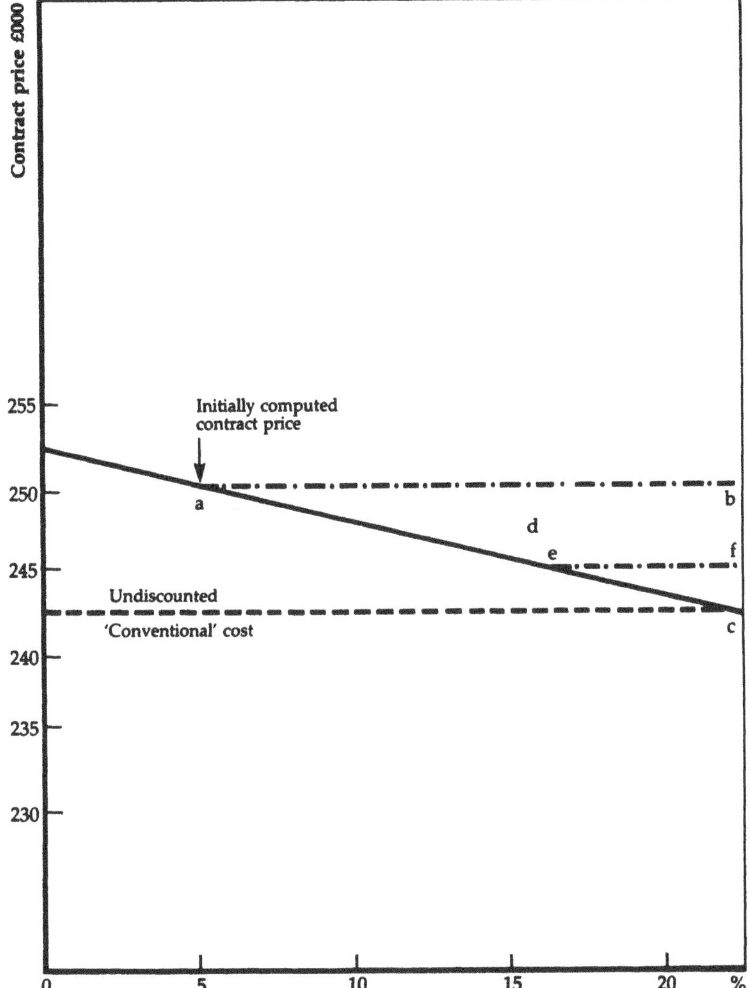

Down-payment expressed as a percentage of contract price.

Note:
The initially computed contract price (at a 5 per cent down-payment) offers a DCF rate of return of 23 per cent

Viewing the position from the standpoint of a contractor, the total contract price, P, for any required or target rate of return, r, is therefore given by:

$$CE_o = xP(1-y) + \frac{(1-x)P(1-y)}{t} \left[\frac{1-(1+r)^{-t/12}}{(1+r)^{1/12}-1}\right] + \frac{yP}{2(1+r)^{t/12}}\left[1 + \frac{1}{(1+r)^{w/12}}\right] + \frac{RV_t}{(1+r)^{t/12}} - \sum_{i=1}^{t} \frac{h_i}{(1+r)^{t/12}} \qquad \text{.......... (1)}$$

whence,

$$P = \frac{CE_o + \sum_{i=1}^{t} \frac{h_i}{(1+r)^{i/12}} - \frac{RV_t}{(1+r)^{t/12}}}{x(1-y) + \frac{(1-x)(1-y)}{t}\left[\frac{1-(1+r)^{-t/12}}{(1+r)^{t/12-1}}\right] + \frac{y}{2(1+r)^{t/12}}\left[1 + \frac{1}{(1+r)^{w/12}}\right]} \qquad \text{..........(2)}$$

where, expressing all payments and receipts in money terms,

CE_o is capital expenditure at end-month O;
RV_t is the residual value of capital expenditure at end-month t;
t denotes the contract's duration in months;
h_i stands for monthly expenditures;
x is the down-payment expressed as a proportion of the contract price;
y denotes the proportion of the contract price instalments retained by the contractee;
w stands for the number of months following the completion of the contact at which the *second* instalment of the retentions is released by the contractee.

Having initially determined a target contract price, P, from equation (2), the contract's NPV can be computed from equation (1) by substituting the (lower) cost of capital, k, for r. (The contract's NPV is the resultant excess of the RHS of (1) (re-computed at k) over CE_o).

Trading-off conventional profit mark-up against an improved down-payment

A target contract price, P, and its corresponding NPV having been computed from equations (2) and (1) respectively (from the contractor's standpoint), equation (2) can then be adjusted to determine the maximum reduction in conventional mark-up, ie reduced contract price, P^*, that would be justified by any given improvement in the down-payment, ie increase to x^*. This reduced price, P^*, is given by:

$$P^* = \frac{NPV + CE_o + \sum_{i=1}^{t} \frac{h_i}{(1+k)^{i/12}} - \frac{RV_t}{(1+k)^{t/12}}}{x^*(1-y) + \frac{(1-x^*)(1-y)}{t}\left[\frac{1-(1+k)^{-t/12}}{(1+k)^{1/12}-1}\right] + \frac{y}{2(1+k)^{t/12}}\left[1 + \frac{1}{(1+k)^{w/12}}\right]} \quad \text{.....(3)}$$

where,

NPV denotes the net present value derived from equation (1); and, k stands for the cost of capital.

Although the originally-computed price, P, is greater than the price P^*, which allows for a higher rate of down payment x^*, the alternative contracts have equal NPVs at the cost of capital k. It therefore follows that a contract price having been initially agreed at P, a contractor can, for any improved rate of down payment, x^*, accept any price, P^1, that is equal to, or greater than, P^*. It can be assumed that, in general, a contractee will only be convinced he is being offered an acceptable trade-off in return for a higher rate of down payment if the revised price, P^1, is less than P. Thus, when a contractee shows a willingness to negotiate any given rate of down-payment x^*, the alternative prices, P and P^* therefore demarcate the practical limits to price negotiations.

The use of equations (1), (2) and (3) is illustrated under the next heading.

Numerical illustration of the use of equations (1), (2) and (3)

1 Using equation (2), determine a contract's total price, P, if contractor's *required rate of return*, r, is 23 per cent p.a. and, CE_o = £24,000; RV_t = £13,000; t = 24 months; h_i = £9,640; x = 0.05 (ie 5 per cent); y = 0.04; and w = 9 months.

$$P = \frac{24{,}000 + 9{,}640\left[\dfrac{1-(1.23)^{-2}}{(1.23^{1/12}-1}\right] - \dfrac{13{,}000}{(1.23)^{2}}}{0.05(1-0.04) + \dfrac{(1-0.05)(1-0.04)}{24}\left[\dfrac{1-(1.23)^{-2}}{(1.23)^{1/12}-1}\right] + \dfrac{0.04}{2(1.23)^{2}}\left[1 + \dfrac{1}{(1.23)^{9/12}}\right]}$$

= £250,003

2 Having determined the total contract price of £250,003 as in part **1**, the contract's NPV is computed from equation (1) at a cost of capital of 19 per cent as follows:

$$\begin{aligned} NPV = & -24{,}000 + (0.05)\ 250{,}003\ (1\text{-}0.04) \\ & + \frac{(1-0.05)\,250{,}003\,(1-0.04)}{24}\left[\frac{1-(1.19)^{-2}}{(1.19)^{1/12}-1}\right] \\ & + \frac{(0.04)(250{,}003)}{2(1.19)^{2}}\left[1 + \frac{1}{(1.19)^{9/12}}\right] + \frac{13{,}000}{(1.19)^{2}} \\ & - 9{,}640\left[\frac{1-(1.19)^{-2}}{(1.19)^{1/12}-1}\right] \end{aligned}$$

= £993

3 Putting the NPV of equation (3) equal to £993 (the value just computed), P^* can be expressed as a function of the rate of down payment x. That is to say, from a negotiating standpoint, CE_o, h_i, RV_t, y, k, t, and w can now be treated as constants, ie given the lower limit to the required NPV, the object of the exercise is to determine from equation (3) the trade-off between the contract price/conventional mark-up and rate of down-payment. For example, putting NPV=993, CE_o=24,000, h_i=9,640, RV_t=13,000, y=0.04, k=0.19, t=24 and w=9 in equation (2) gives:

$$P^* = \frac{993 + 24{,}000 + 9{,}640\left[\dfrac{1-(1.19)^{-2}}{(1.19)^{1/12}-1}\right] - \dfrac{13{,}000}{(1.19)^{2}}}{x(1-0.04) + \dfrac{(1-x)(1-0.04)}{24}\left[\dfrac{1-(1.19)^{-2}}{(1.19)^{1/12}-1}\right] + \dfrac{0.04}{2(1.19)^{2}}\left[1 + \dfrac{1}{(1.19)^{9/12}}\right]}$$

$$= \frac{209{,}962}{0.1544x + 0.83212}$$

..........................(4)

and,

$$x = \frac{1}{0.1544}\left(\frac{209{,}962}{P^*} - 0.83212\right) \qquad \text{.........................(5)}$$

The contract price line shown in the graph is derived from the latter expression for P* for rates of down-payment, x, ranging from 0 to 22½ per cent. The graph is amplified by *Table 1* which is self-explanatory.

As a basis for indicating the manner in which the graph might be used by a contract negotiator, assume that a contractee states that the maximum price he is willing to pay is £245,000 (conventional profit £2,640). The contractor should therefore attempt to move as far as possible in the direction of **f** along the line **ef**. Alternatively, assume that a contractor *provisionally* negotiates a price of £250,000 when a 5 per cent down-payment is initially contemplated (point **a** in the graph as computed in part (i) above).

If the contractee is willing to improve the rate of down-payment in return for a price reduction, the contractor should attempt to attain some point in the region bac. For example, if the contractor can attain point d (price of £247,500 and 15 per cent down-payment) he would raise his (initially negotiated) net present value of £993 by 173 per cent to £2,713.*

But what of the contractee? At a price of £247,500, the conventional mark-up is reduced by 33 per cent from £7,643 to £5,140 and the profit percentages to 2.08 and 2.12 on cost and sales respectively. If the conventional accounting numbers really are taken seriously by the contractee they might well have an adverse effect on his negotiating stance.

Other implications

In the approach to contract pricing outlined above, a contractor was assumed initially to derive a contract price from a required or target DCF rate of return based on a contract's cost of capital. This contract price was, in turn, used to determine the contract's NPV and its conventional profitability.

In practice the conventional accounting approach to contract costing and pricing tends to predominate and a probable price, or price range, having been determined on a conventional basis, a contract's DCF rate of return and its NPV constitute dependent variables. This by no means implies that, as dependent

* The NPV of £2,713 is derived from equation (4) by putting $P^* = £247{,}500$ and $x = 0.15$.

$$\text{Thus } 247{,}500 = \frac{(209{,}962 - 993) + NPV}{(0.1544)(0.15) + 0.83212}$$

whence, NPV = 2,713.

variables, the latter criteria are rendered redundant. On the contrary, they should be computed in any event to determine whether the contract really is worth having and to facilitate further price negotiations.

The point is that a contract's intrinsic profitability is measured by its NPV and, as already suggested, no consistent relationship between conventional accounting profitability and DCF criteria can be presumed. The DCF criteria alone can accurately reveal contracts that are marginally profitable and, by the same token, accurately determine the lower limit to an acceptable contract price – a matter of crucial importance when competition is acute.

Finally, it should perhaps also be emphasised that there may be occasions when a modest-looking conventional mark-up, that is acceptable to a contractee, is associated with a DCF rate of return that handsomely exceeds a contractor's target DCF rate of return. Such occasions must surely be a considerable source of satisfaction to a contractor who understands the use of DCF analysis.

Summary and suggestions

The foregoing discussion suggests the following approach to contract pricing and price negotiations:

1 Starting with the minimum rate of return required from a contract (23 per cent in the previous examples), determine a provisional contract selling price, P, using the discounted present value approach.

2 Restate the contract's costs and selling price on a conventional accounting basis showing the conventional profit mark-up.

3 If the conventional profit mark-up looks rather modest in the circumstances, or if the market will bear a higher price, adjust the conventional profit mark-up accordingly.

4 If the contractee is willing to make a down-payment after the conventional profit mark-up has first been agreed, the aim should be to secure the highest percentage down-payment consistent with the non-alienation of the contractee.

5 If the contractee is a haggler, the object of the negotiations should be to secure such a down-payment as is necessary at least to compensate for the reduction in the conventional mark-up that is necessary to secure the deal, using the present value method of measuring trade-offs between the two.

References

Lawson, G. H., and Stapleton, R. C., 'The Pricing of Non-competitive Government Contracts', *Managerial Finance*, vol. 10, No. 3/4, 1984, pp. 40-48.

Review Board for Government Contracts, *Report on the Fourth General Review of the Profit Formula for Non-competitive Government Contracts*, HMSO, London, 1984.

The Pricing of Non-competitive Government Contracts

by G. H. Lawson and R. C. Stapleton

Introduction

This paper is based on a response to the 1982 general invitation from the Review Board for Government Contracts. It is concerned with the general economic principles that are germane to the five items enumerated in the terms of reference outlined by Mr. Leon Brittan on 6th April 1982, in a written Parliamentary answer, namely,

(a) the principle of practical application of comparability including the extent to which the target rate of return of these contracts should reflect changes in economic factors and the rate of profitability of other sectors of British industry;

(b) the appropriate definition of the rate of profit, including the accounting conventions relating thereto and the balance between remunerating capital and cost;

(c) the extent to which risk contracts should not only attract a higher rate of profit than non-risk contracts, but should differentiate if at all for varying degrees of risk;

(d) the obstacles to earlier pricing of various kinds of contracts;

(e) whether having regard to the purposes for which they were intended, the post-costing arrangements should be modified.

Our major contention is that the pricing of Government contracts has hitherto been deficient in at least two fundamental respects.

One deficiency stems from the use of the historic cost (accruals) accounting model as a computational framework for the costing and pricing of non-competitive Government contracts. In our view all forms of accruals accounting, including current cost accounting, are methodologically objectionable for contract costing, especially for the costing and pricing of medium and long term contracts.

The second deficiency, namely the use of *ex post* accounting rates of return for estimating target rates of return, has two facets which can, and should, be examined separately. More precisely, *ex post* and *ex ante* accounting rates of return are theoretically deficient and poor approximations from a measurement standpoint; and, *ex post* accounting rates of return constitute a very crude basis for estimating *ex ante* accounting rates of return. Moreover, whether correctly computed or not, *ex post* rates of return can be improved upon as a basis for estimating target rates of return for risk and non-risk contracts.

A cash flow basis of contract costing

As already suggested, none of the generally-recognised alternative forms of accruals accounting constitutes a valid computational framework for contract costing and pricing.

A multiperiod contract is *par excellence* an example of the investment decision. Such a contract therefore needs to be accounted for (either *ex post* or *ex ante*) in a framework which is rooted in capital theory, namely, a multiperiod cash flow accounting system. The latter is of course familiar as the capital budgeting framework that is extensively used in conjunction with discounted cash flow investment criteria in companies in Britain, America, Germany and in scores of other places around the globe.

It clearly cannot be correct to contend that (multiperiod) accruals accounting is a (or the) valid basis for contract costing and pricing, whereas (multiperiod) cash flow accounting is the theoretically defensible basis for investment analysis. That a contract is an example of an investment is evidenced by the fact that individual contracts can be and frequently are, floated off as separate companies.†

†The internal rate of return, alias Keynes' marginal efficiency of capital, was invented about 350 years ago by merchants who attempted to determine the annual rate of profit on Far Eastern ventures with durations exceeding three or four years.

Stated in more detail, the theoretical and operational justification for a cash flow computational basis for contract costing runs as follows. Assuming that a firm is primarily interested in economically-efficient resource allocation, it should, ignoring the question of externalities, seek to maximise its total market value (market value of debt plus market value of equity). Operationally speaking, this objective is synonymous with the maximisation of the present value of lender and shareholder cash flows which, as dependent variables, need to be specified by reference to a firm's total cash flow statement.

A firm's total cash flow statement *for any year j* can be represented with the identify:

$$(k_j - h_j) - (A_j + R_j - Y_j) - H_j - t_j = (F_j - N_j - M_j) + (D_j - B_j) \quad (1)$$

that is,

$$\text{entity cash flows} = \text{lender cash flows} + \text{shareholder cash flows}$$

where,

$k_j - h_j$	denotes operating cash flow in year j represented by cash collected from customers, k_j, and operating cash outflows, h_j;
$A_j + R_j - Y_j$	stands for replacement investment, A_j, growth investment, R_j, and the proceeds from assets displaced, Y_j, in year j;
t_j	stands for all taxes assessed on the corporation that are actually paid in year j;
H_j	denotes liquidity change in year j;
F_j	represents period j interest payments;

N_j	is medium and/or long term debt raised or retired in year j;
M_j	is short term debt raised or repaid in year j;
D_j	represents dividends paid to shareholders in year j; and,
B_j	is equity capital raised or repaid in year j.

Stated symbolically the theory of corporate valuation can therefore be represented as:

$$\sum_{j=1}^{\infty} \frac{(\bar{k}_j - \bar{h}_j) - (\bar{A}_j + \bar{R}_j - \bar{Y}_j) - \bar{H}_j - \bar{t}_j}{(1+\bar{r})^j} = \tag{2}$$

$$\sum_{j=1}^{\infty} \frac{\bar{F}_j - \bar{N}_j - \bar{M}_j}{(1+\bar{r}_d)^j} + \sum_{j=1}^{\infty} \frac{\bar{D}_j - \bar{B}_j}{(1+\bar{r}_e)^j}$$

that is,

present value of expected entity cash flows	=	present value of expected lender cash flows	+	present value of expected shareholder cash flows
or, total market value, TMV_o	=	market value of debt $MV^{(d)}$	+	market value of equity $MV^{(e)}$

where,

the bars denote expected values; and, $\bar{r}$, $\bar{r}_d$ and $\bar{r}_e$ represent the firm's weighted average cost of capital, its cost of debt and the cost of its equity respectively. (For simplicity $\bar{r}$ is assumed to be constant over time)

Following Modigliani and Miller (MM) and the capital-asset pricing model (CAPM), the weighted average cost of capital $\bar{r}$ is, in a neutral corporate tax regime, assumed to be independent of its debt ratio $MV^{(d)}/(MV^{(d)} + MV^{(e)})$. This is another way of saying that, in a neutral corporate tax regime, a firm's total market value is independent of its debt ratio.††

Both the MM hypothesis and the CAPM imply that a firm's weighted average cost of capital is a function of its risk class. There are however conceptual differences between the MM and CAPM notions of risk. The latter is more readily reconcilable with observable market behaviour and also offers a realistic practical approach to risk measurement.

We raise some risk considerations that are germane to the costing and pricing of non-competitive Government contracts in the following two sections. Here we return to the practical implications of the wealth maximisation objective.

†The use of discrete end-year discounting implies, for example, that all capital expenditure undertaken between end-years 0 and 1 is included in $A_1 + R_1 - Y_1$ etc.

††One implication of this in the present context is that the assessment of the allowed rate of return on a non-competitive Government contract should be separated from the manner in which that contract might be financed.

To gain an incisive understanding of wealth maximisation from an operational standpoint it is necessary to focus attention on the left hand sides of (1) and (2) i.e. on the constituents of the entity cash flows that are the focus of managerial planning and control and which, in turn, are the determinants of proprietor cash flows. Thus, efficient commercial management can be defined as the choice of one of perhaps many alternative paths through time that results in the generation of a time-profile of entity cash flows which maximises the total market value, TMV_o, given by:

$$TMV_o = \sum_{j=1}^{\infty} \frac{(\bar{k}_j - \bar{h}_j) - (\bar{A}_j + \bar{R}_j - \bar{Y}_j) - \bar{H}_j - \bar{t}_j}{(1+\bar{r})^j} \tag{3}$$

Now if, as in the case of non-competitive Government contracts, the contractor is a cost-plus price maker, sales receipts, k_j, are, given the volume of activity, the associated capital expenditure programme, $A_j + R_j - Y_j$, the value of existing assets and the target (or allowed) rate of return, $\bar{r}$, the dependent variable. Moreover, contracts have a finite life, n.

Two aspects of this proposition requiring clarification are, first, the quantification of the rate of return to be allowed within this cost-plus formula; and, second, the valuation of those of a firm's existing assets (TMV_o in (3) above) as are to be deployed on the contract.

The capital budgeting theory that is relevant to contract costing may be stated as follows.

The utilisation by a firm of part, or all, of its existing productive capacity on a non-competitive Government contract is the use of capacity which can be sold now as a going concern i.e. literally hived off and sold or hired out, as opposed to being sold on the completion of the contract. The clearest example of this idea is a hypothetical contract which would fully occupy the capacity of (say) an entire division within a divisionalised organisation. Note that, to satisfy the notion of division in an economic sense, it (the division) must be salable as a separate productive and/or trading entity i.e. as a going concern. Such a division has a realisable market value which can therefore be substituted for TMV_o in (3) above. Similarly, since the contract has a finite life of n years, the estimated end-year n market value of the division, TMV_n, can be estimated accordingly. The contract should therefore be priced by reference to equation (4) from which the k_js (contract price instalments) can be derived as a sequence of dependent variables.

$$TMV_o = \sum_{j=1}^{n} \frac{(\bar{k}_j - \bar{h}_j) - (\bar{A}_j + \bar{R}_j - \bar{Y}_j) - \bar{H}_j - \bar{t}_j}{(1+\bar{r})^j} + \frac{T\bar{M}V_n}{(1+\bar{r})^n} \tag{4}$$

To the extent that the contract requires replacement or additional equipment (less the proceeds of assets displaced) $A_j + R_j - Y_j$, which will enhance the value of the division, it should be allowed for accordingly in the estimation of $T\bar{M}V_n$.

In reality Government contracts are unlikely to be consistently undertaken in organisational segments which neatly satisfy the economic idea of divisionalisation. Moreover, divisions are frequently defined by reference to accounting rather than to economic criteria, are frequently not geographical by separate, and usually enjoy common organisational facilities. The economic notion of divisionalisation nevertheless points to the principle which should be invoked in estimating the market value of that part of a firm's existing fixed capital stock that is to be deployed on a Government contract.

If the alternative to a Government contract is a capacity reduction, estimates of the capital that would be disinvested (including redundancy payments (if any)) can be made on precisely the same basis as an assessment of the cash flow consequences of the sale of a division as a going concern.

The implications of a third possibility, namely, the use of available capacity on a private contract as an *alternative* to its use for a Government contract should also be considered, rare though such an alternative may be. If after treating as an initial capital outlay the capital that would be realised on a capacity reduction (or sale of division) the alternative private contract has a positive net present value, the latter should be counted as additional (opportunity cost) outlay in respect of the Government contract.

For clarity, the salient financial aspects of what in fact constitutes four† possible alternatives may be summarised as in Table 1.

†A fifth possibility, namely, a situation in which a contractor has no available capacity should also be contemplated. In such a case, expenditure incurred in creating the requisite additional capacity, and the market value of that capacity on the termination of the contract, need to be taken into account.

TABLE 1

USE OF DIVISIONAL AND OTHER CAPACITY ON GOVERNMENT AND PRIVATE CONTRACTS

Alternative 1: No prospect of Government or alternative contracts

action: (a) reduce capacity, sell assets including working capital (if any) realising an amount, Y_j, and make redundancy payments RP_j;
or,
(b) sell a division at the higher of its going concern or asset value realising Y_j, and incurring redundancy payments RP_j (if any)

Alternative 2: Government contract and no prospect of alternative contract

action: (a) estimate the value of fixed capital to be deployed on Government contract by reference to (a) or (b) in alternative 1, namely, $Y_j - RP_j$.
(b) treat as part of the contract cost, wage and salary costs and all other operating costs, hj, that become payable because of the continued use of capacity or a division
(c) treat capital expenditure (less disposals), $A_j + R_j - Y_j$, incurred during, and by virtue of, the contract as part of contract cost.
(d) allow for tax payments Δt_j that result from the contract by reference to the incremental taxable earnings that are ascribable thereto
(e) allow for the incremental periodic change in liquidity ΔH_j that is ascribable to the contract
(f) estimate TMV_n

Alternative 3: Private contract as an alternative to a Government contract

action (a) as in steps (a) to (f) in alternative 2
(b) given the contract price and/or agreed profit margin, estimate the contract's net present value

Alternative 4: Government contract as an alternative to a private contract

action (a) as in alternative (2)
(b) add the net present value of alternative (3) to $Y_j - RP_j$.

The estimation of the target rate of return for non-risk contracts

If the entire risk of a non-competitive Government contract is borne by the Government itself, the contractor should be allowed to earn a riskfree rate of return. Such a rate is approximately equal to the redemption yield on a Government bond that matures on a date that is coterminous with the date on which the final instalment of the contract price is received by the contractor.

The qualification "approximately" is necessary because a redemption yield is a geometric mean rate of interest which is a function of the time-profile of the bond's interest payments. For example, if two British Government bonds with a common maturity date have different coupon rates, their market prices will be such that they offer different gross redemption yields. Thus, Treasury 12½% '93 and Funding 6% 1993, were priced at 114¾ and 80½ on 29th October 1982, when their gross redemption yields were 10.73% and 9.0% respectively.

Part of the divergence between these two yields is ascribable to their different tax burdens. Thus, the Treasury 12½% '93 would suffer tax on annual interest of £12.5 per £114¾ invested whereas the Funding 6% would bear tax on annual interest of £6 per £80½ invested. Hence, £9,237.375 invested in Treasury 12½% '93 would yield annual interest of £1,006.25 whereas the same amount invested in Funding 6% would produce annual interest of £688.5. Allowing for tax at (say) 30%, the post-tax annual interest would be £704.375 and £481.95 respectively.

The redemption yields stated on this net of tax basis are the values of r_T and r_F given by

$$£9{,}237.375 = £704.375\left[\frac{1 - (1+r_T)^{-11}}{r_T}\right] + \frac{8{,}050}{(1+r_T)^{11}}$$

and, (5)

$$£9{,}237.375 = £481.95\left[\frac{1 - (1+r_F)^{-11}}{r_F}\right] + \frac{11{,}475}{(1+r_F)^{11}}$$

whence,

$$r_T = 6.82\% \text{ and } r_F = 6.88\%.$$

In that the (multiperiod) riskfree interest rate is a function of the time-profile of a (riskfree) bond's interest payments and redemption value, all of which are fixed in money terms, an important practical question arises. Which bond yield should be used as a yardstick in quantifying the target rate of return on a non-competitive Government contract?

The time-profile of the net cash flows of a Government contract which, as argued below, should be specified in money terms, may rarely correspond to the cash flows on a Government bond of similar duration. There is in fact a theoretical solution to this problem, namely, the use of a sequence of single period riskfree interest rates r, $r_2,....r_n$ for the years corresponding to the duration of the contract. Substituting such a sequence into equation (4) gives:

$$TMV_o = \frac{CCF_1}{1+r_1} + \frac{CCF_2}{(1+r_1)(1+r_2)} + ... + \frac{CCF_n + TMV_n}{(1+r_1)(1+r_2)...(1+r_n)} \quad (6)$$

where,
CCF_j is the contract cash flow of year j given by:

$$CCF_j = (k_j - h_j) - (A_j + R_j - Y_j) - H_j - t_j.$$

The sequence of single-period interest rates can be estimated recursively, from the yield curve (average gross redemption yields as a function of maturity) for British Government Funds, commencing with the derivation of r_2.

To end this sub-section; the affinities between riskfree Government bonds held to maturity and a non-competitive Government contract should be qualified in at least one important respect. The market rate of interest on a Government bond *held to maturity* is absolutely riskfree in that the owner is entitled to a stream of contractually-determined interest payments and redemption price. Such an investor is by definition immune to interest rate risk i.e. the risk that interest rates will rise after the bond's purchase.

By contrast, a non-risk contractor is guaranteed a (multiperiod) riskfree rate of return if, and only if, he is protected by price escalation clauses which allow actual costs to be substituted for the estimates that were initially tendered and for the instalments of the contract price to be recomputed in relation to the allowed rate of return. But price escalation clauses are inherently dangerous from a contractee's standpoint. Whereas it is easy to make the rather abstract distinction between cost increases that are outside a contractor's control and those which are not, the reality is frequently a large grey area in which special cases abound. As far as we are aware, there is little in modern managerial theory which throws light on the efficient regulation and administration of price escalation clauses in a risk-return framework.†

†A detailed analysis of alternative forms of escalation clause is provided by Gee (1981).

The target return on risk contracts: the CAPM approach

Leaving aside administrative considerations, the essential difference between risk and non-risk Government contracts turns mainly, if not entirely, on the rate of return that should be allowed to the contractor.

The most modern theory that is germane to risk contracts is the capital-asset pricing model (CAPM). The essence of the CAPM is that the expected performance of any real, or financial, investment should be measured on two dimensions, namely, non-diversifiable risk and return. The higher an investment's perceived degree of non-diversifiable risk, the higher will be the return expected therefrom and its market value will reflect the situation accordingly.

The required (or expected) return on a risky investment can clearly be directly related to the rate of return obtainable on a riskfree investment which, by definition, must set the lower limit to the former. In other words the question is: What manner and amount of risk premium should be added to the riskfree interest rate to compensate for the risks inherent in a risky investment? The CAPM answers this question by reference to the (weighted) average rate of return that can be obtained on investment in general (the so-called expected rate of return on the market portfolio). Since 1919, the excess of the return on the market portfolio over the riskfree interest rate has in the U.K. averaged roughly 9 percentage points and has taken on a similar value in the USA.†

Thus, leaving aside personal taxes, this implies that if the n-year redemption yield on a Government bond stands at 10 per cent, the allowed rate of return (expressed in money terms) on an n-year Government contract of average risk should be about 19 per cent.

The degree to which an individual investment's setwins covary with average market setwins is, adopting the CAPM approach, measured by its beta coefficient.†† Simply described, an investments' beta coefficient is the factor by which the (historical) 9 per cent excess return on the market portfolio is multiplied to give the risk premium applicable to the individual risky investment. Stated symbolically the required rate of return, $\bar{r}_e$, on a risky investment is given by:

$$\bar{r}_e = i + (\bar{r}_m - i)\beta_e \qquad (7)$$

where,

i is the single period riskfree interest rate

$\bar{r}_m$ stands for the (single period) expected rate of return on the market portfolio; and

β_e is the beta coefficient of a risky investment e which, in turn, is given by

$$\beta_e = \frac{\text{covariance } (\bar{r}_m, \bar{r}_e)}{\text{variance } (\bar{r}_m)}$$

The beta coefficient, β_e, can alternatively be regarded as a measure of the sensitivity of the market value of a risky security to general market movements. For example, if a risky investment has a beta coefficient of 1.5 then a 10 per cent rise in the level of the market as a whole would be associated with a 15 per cent rise in that investment's market value and *vice versa*.

†See, for example, Brealey & Myers (1981), ch. 7, and Dimson and Brealey (1978).

††Strictly speaking covariation is measured with the statistical measure known as covariance. As stated hereafter, an investment's (or project's) beta coefficient is given by the covariance of its returns with the returns on the market portfolio *divided* by the variance of the returns on the latter. Dividing by the variance of the returns on the market portfolio is simply a device for ensuring that the market portfolio has a beta coefficient of unity. Hence, investments (or projects) that are more risky than the market portfolio have a beta coefficient greater than one and vice versa.

The latter idea can perhaps be clarified more concretely by contemplating a situation in which a company is specifically formed to undertake risky Government contracts on a continuing basis. Assume further that the company achieves a stock exchange listing on, or before, the start of its contracting work and that, by and large, the entire succession of contracts it undertakes is characterised by the same degree of risk. The degree to which the market value of the company might be expected to covary with the level of the stock market as a whole provides a basis for estimating its beta coefficient.

Whilst clearly presenting greater difficulty, the case of the individual contract that is not to be undertaken by a specially constituted quoted company is the same in principle. At least two alternative approaches can be followed in attempting an estimate of the beta coefficient in such a case.

One prescription starts from the assumption that an individual contract can be regarded as a scaled-down version of a well-established listed contracting company whose beta coefficient is therefore a relevant yardstick for estimating the required contract beta coefficient. In the absence of such companies, the quantification problem remains unresolved.

An alternative approach is to focus on the factors that might be expected to determine an asset's, or risk contract's beta coefficient. This in turn leads to an examination of the covariability of the level of a contract's (cash flow) earnings with the level of (cash flow) earnings in the economy as a whole. The jump from the covariability of risky and market portfolio *rates of return* as measured by the covariance $(\bar{r}_e, \bar{r}_m)$ is in fact no more than a short step. This is simply because the definition of $\bar{r}_e$ embodies a firm's expected cash flows. Thus, $\bar{r}_e$ is also given by:

$$\bar{r}_e = \frac{\bar{D}_1 + (\bar{P}_1 - P_0)}{P_0}. \tag{8}$$

where,

- P_0 is the acquisition cost (market value) of a risky investment at end-year 0;
- $\bar{D}_1$ is the dividend expected from that investment at end-year 1; and,
- $\bar{P}_1$ is the expected market value (exit price) of the investment at end-year 1.

However, assuming that the firm is internally financed and has no outstanding debt,† $\bar{D}_1$ is given by:

$$\bar{D}_1 = (\bar{K}_1 - \bar{h}_1) - (\bar{A}_1 + \bar{R}_1 - \bar{Y}_1) - \bar{t}_1 - \bar{H}_1$$

and, (9)

$$\bar{P}_1 = \sum_{j=2}^{\infty} \frac{(\bar{K}_j - \bar{h}_j) - (\bar{A}_j + \bar{R}_j - \bar{Y}_j) - \bar{t}_j - \bar{H}_j}{(1 + \bar{r}_e)^j}$$

Hence, the covariance $(\tilde{r}_e, \tilde{r}_m)$ reflects the covariability of a firm's cash flows with the market portfolio's cash flows.

†New debt and new equity can readily be accommodated in the analysis (see identity (1)).

The relevance of the foregoing analysis to the factors which influence a risk contract's beta coefficient can readily be illustrated by reference to, rare though such a contract may nowadays be, the "classic type of fixed price contract (i.e. one on which the contractor bears the full risk of incurring higher costs than he bargained for and receives the full benefit of any savings which he may be able to achieve)".†

Given that the contractor has a captive-market in the case of a non-competitive fixed price Government contract, the risk he bears is clearly the risk that stems from unanticipated cost increases which may, in turn, be primarily a function of unanticipated inflation. On the other hand, to the extent that raw materials, and other contract inputs, are purchased in world markets (as opposed to domestic markets), such elements of cost have their own particular influences on contract risk and should be dealt with accordingly.

Assume first that all inputs to a contract are purchased in U.K. factor markets and mainly represent finished and semi-finished components, domestic energy, labour and a variety of overheads. The costs of such factor inputs emerge from a pricing process which typically reflects the weighted average rate of increase in costs borne by suppliers. The rate of increase of domestic supply price increases will, in these circumstances, therefore tend to the rate of inflation.

†*Review Board for Government Contracts,* (1980), page 29.

On the other hand, if the cost structure of a risk contract includes the costs of raw and other materials that are bought in world markets at prices which are highly volatile, such a contract may initially appear to be characterised by a higher risk class than that described in the previous paragraph. However, if the market price behaviour of the raw material in question is not highly correlated (or is perhaps even negatively correlated) with changes in the domestic price level or, more specifically, is not highly correlated with changes in the prices of other contract factor inputs, the degree of risk exposure characterising a fixed-price Government contract, may to a greater or lesser extent, be diversified away.

The substance of the foregoing paragraphs is that the risk which characterises the 'classic type of fixed-price contract' is a function both of its cost structure and the degree to which the prices of its cost constituents are (positively or negatively) correlated. The latter in turn determines the degree to which a contract's cash flow earnings are correlated with the cash flow earnings on the market portfolio. If the contract's cash flow earnings are perfectly correlated with the market portfolio's cash flow earnings, the contract has a beta coefficient of unity. Higher or lower degrees of correlation which, as just described, are directly traceable to the covariability of the contract's cost structure with the cash flow earnings on the market portfolio, should lead to beta estimates which reflect the situation accordingly.

The practical implication of the above analysis is that the cost specification (which parallels the specification of a contract's inputs in physical terms) should have at least two features. On the one hand, it should reflect the contractor's best estimates, expressed in money terms, of the costs of physical inputs of labour, materials, energy, (incremental) overhead expenditure, machines, etc. – given the contractor's expectations about the course of inflation over the duration of the contract.

On the other hand, drawing upon available historic time-series data, the cost specification should reveal the degree to which the contract costs are assumed to covary with the cash flow earnings on the market portfolio. Contracts can be ranked by this criterion and their beta coefficients may be assessed accordingly. Given an agreed estimate of a contract's beta coefficient, its target rate of return is automatically determined – as is the contract price.

An important qualification to this and the previous section must now be entered. A contract which is expected to earn an actual return that is exactly equal to a risk-commensurate target return has a zero net present value (NPV). Such a contract will not enhance the value of a contracting firm, to which it is therefore of no commercial interest. Unfortunately the CAPM cannot specify the magnitude of the NPV which should be allowed on a non-competitive Government contract to stimulate commercial interest. Hence, what has previously been described as a target rate of return should be designated "minimum required rate of return".

Illustration of the incidence of fixed price contract risk

The incidence of fixed price contract risk in the sense in which the expression is used in the forgoing paragraphs can be illustrated in terms of the range of possible rates of return that such a contract may achieve *ex post.*

Assumptions

i. A contractor assumes that a particular fixed price (five-year) contract, e, is of average risk i.e. $\beta_e = 1$.
ii. The contractor observes that redemption yields on five-year Government bonds currently average 12 per cent per annum.
iii. The contractor also knows that historically the excess return on the market portfolio has averaged 9 percentage points.
iv. The contractor's other estimates are:
initial capital deployed on the contract: 5,000;
residual value of the former at end-year 5: 2,000;
annual operating costs at end-years 1, 2..., 5: 800, 880,

968, 1,064.8, 1,171.28.

Analysis

i. The minimum required rate of return, $\bar{r}_e$, is given by:

$$\bar{r}_e = i + (\bar{r}_m - i)\beta_e$$
$$= 12 + (9)(1) = 21\%$$

ii. If the contract price is to be paid in 5 end-year instalments $k_1, k_2, \ldots, k_5$, minimum values of the latter should satisfy the equation:

$$5{,}000 = \frac{k_1 - 800}{1.21} + \frac{k_2 - 880}{(1.21)^2} + \frac{k_3 - 968}{(1.21)^3}$$
$$+ \frac{k_4 - 1{,}064.8}{(1.21)^4} + \frac{k_5 - 1{,}171.28 + 2{,}000}{(1.21)^5}$$

However, assuming that the contractor desires annual contract price instalments which increase at the same rate as the estimated rate of increase in operating costs, namely 10% per annum, the five instalments (minima) should be derived from:

$$5{,}000 = \frac{k_1 - 800}{0.21 - 0.1}\left[1 - \frac{(1.1)^5}{(1.21)^5}\right] + \frac{2{,}000}{(1.21)^5}$$

whence, $k_1 = 2{,}027.14$
and, $k_2 = 2{,}229.85$, $k_3 = 2{,}452.84$, $k_4 = 2{,}698.12$, $k_5 = 2{,}967.94$.

iii. But if the actual operating costs increase at 14% annually after year 1 and the residual value of the contract at end-year 5 is only 1,500, its actual rate of return, r_e, is given by:

$$5{,}000 = \frac{2{,}027.14}{r_e - 0.1}\left[1 - \frac{(1.1)^5}{(1 + r_e)^5}\right] + \frac{1{,}500}{(1 + r_e)^5}$$
$$- \frac{800}{r_e - 0.12}\left[1 - \frac{(1.14)^5}{(1 + r_e)^5}\right]$$

whence,

$$r_e = 17.92\%.$$

By contrast, an initial over-estimation on the cost side of the calculation would, other things being the same, result in a higher achieved rate of return than 21 per cent.

A Digression on "forecasting risk"

The previous example also appears to suggest that the degree of risk that characterises a fixed price contract is a function of the accuracy of contractors' forecasts. But it must be emphasised that the CAPM concept of market risk is solely concerned with the covariability of a contract's cash flow earnings with the cash flow earnings on the market portfolio, and takes no account of the differences in contractors' skills in financial forecasting.

If the authors' own experience is anything to go by, forecasting expertise varies to a considerable degree in practice. In some firms, forecasting ranges from pure guesswork to crude statistical extrapolations, which have no underlying economic model, to highly sophisticated econometric/stochastic approaches which reflect a defensible economic rationale.

Strange as it may perhaps seem, some corporate planning departments apparently do not recognise the importance of the distinction between inflation and relative price changes and how that distinction can be clarified by reference to historic time series data. It is also not widely appreciated that future inflation can be forecast quite accurately for periods of up to 3 or 4 years; and, that there may be fairly stable relationships between inflation and particular factor input prices e.g. unit labour cost, which can perhaps be turned to good advantage in forecasting contract costs. Thus, regardless of the way in which target rates of return for risk contracts should be estimated, it is arguable that the whole basis of financial forecasting for contract costing should be held up to close scrutiny.

Recommendations

The substance of the foregoing discussion is two-fold, namely,

(a) the costing of non-competitive Government contracts should be based on a normative capital budgeting framework, i.e. a multiperiod cash flow accounting framework; and,
(b) minimum required rates of return should be estimated by reference to a capital-asset pricing framework.

Postscript: the adequacy of ex post returns

The adequacy of the profit margins which have been earned hitherto on non-competitive Government contracts should be assessed by reference to the market-based real rates of return that have been obtained by lenders and shareholders in the companies in question.

Achieved entity, lender and shareholder rates of return are defined by the *ex post* version of equation (2) (see page 41). That is to say, all values in the numerators are actual values, the superscript . is replaced with n; and, exit and entry market values also need to be taken into account. For example, an *ex post* equity rate of return, r_e, is given by:

$$MV_0^{(e)} = \sum_{j=1}^{n} \frac{D_j - B_j}{(i + r_e)^j} + \frac{MV_n^{(e)}}{(1 + r_e)^n}$$

For any n-period sequence there are: $n + (n-1) + \ldots\ldots + (n - n + 1)$ possible holding periods. Thus, when $n = 5$ there are, as illustrated by Tables 2A, 2B and 2C, fifteen different rates of return, namely,

5 one-year, 4 two-year, 3 three-year, 2 four-year and 1 five-year.

The steps involved in the computation of such rates of return are illustrated in detail elsewhere† and need only be briefly summarised here. They are:

(i) The derivation of multiperiod *ex post* cash flow statements in accordance with identity (1) in money and, in turn, in real terms.
(ii) The estimation of the end-period market values, corresponding to the multiperiod cash flow statements referred to in (i), of debt and equity (and therefore total corporate capital).
(iii) The computation of half matrices of rates of return from (i) and (ii).

†See, for example, Lawson (1983).

Whilst emphasising that the company in question, namely, U.D.S., does not undertake Government contracts, inferences that might be drawn from Tables 3A, 3B and 3C for the five-year period considered include:

i. U.D.S. did not earn adequate real returns on total proprietorship capital (Table 3A);
ii. U.D.S. lenders received real returns which just about maintained their capital intact (Table 3B); and,
iii. U.D.S. shareholders suffered a reverse leverage effect and a significant erosion of real capital (Table 3C).

Had the above results referred to a company engaged solely on non-competitive Government contracts, they would have constituted *prima facie* evidence that the profit margins allowed to the contractor had not maintained his real capital intact.

Whilst a preponderance of negative real rates of return (as in Tables 3A and 3C) can be directly interpreted, the more general question is whether a firm has earned risk-commensurate returns. Sequences of abnormal returns, i.e. differences between actual returns and required returns (derived from beginning of the period *ex post* beta coefficients), can be used in an attempt to answer this question.

TABLE 2A

UDS ENTITY RATES OF RETURN (PER CENT PER ANNUM)

		sold on 31st January				
		1978	1979	1980	1981	1982
	1977	42.15	21.58	12.62*	10.09	10.85
bought	1978		3.73	−0.69	0.47	3.43
on	1979			−5.43	−1.24	3.32
31st	1980				2.75	7.98
January	1981					14.60

**See footnote to Table 2c.*

TABLE 2B

UDS LENDER RATES OF RETURN (PER CENT PER ANNUM)

		sold on 31st January				
		1978	1979	1980	1981	1982
	1977	17.90	10.75	11.87	12.82	12.84
bought	1978		4.40	8.33	10.97	11.29
on	1979			14.66	15.55	14.93
31st	1980				16.56	15.12
January	1981					13.00

TABLE 2C

UDS SHAREHOLDER RATES OF RETURN (PER CENT PER ANNUM)

		sold on 31st January				
		1978	1979	1980	1981	1982
	1977	57.8	28.48	13.12	8.31	9.68
bought	1978		3.37	−5.76	−4.88	−0.14
on	1979			−14.54	−8.59	−1.24
31st	1980				−3.36	5.13
January	1981					15.23

The rate of return for any holding period is derived from the entry and exit market values and cash-flows corresponding thereto. For example, the three-year entity rate of return of 12.62% pa for 31.1.77. to 31.1.80. is the value of r which satisfies the equation:

$$155.5 = \frac{3.239}{1+r} + \frac{24.121}{(1+r)^2} + \frac{(208.4-17.547)}{(1+r)^3}$$

TABLE 3A

UDS ENTITY RATES OF RETURN (PER CENT PER ANNUM) EXPRESSED AT JANUARY 1982 PRICES

		sold on 31st January				
		1978	1979	1980	1981	1982
	1977	29.36	11.19	0.39	−1.90	−1.15
bought	1978		−4.67	−12.54	−11.20	−8.33
on	1979			−20.66	−14.54	−9.67
31st	1980				−8.55	−3.65
January	1981					2.61

TABLE 3B

UDS LENDER RATES OF RETURN (PER CENT PER ANNUM) EXPRESSED AT JANUARY 1982 PRICES

		sold on 31st January				
		1978	1979	1980	1981	1982
	1977	7.10	1.41	0.31	1.11	1.09
bought	1978		−3.68	−3.10	−1.07	−0.76
on	1979			−2.36	0.72	0.77
31st	1980				4.34	2.97
January	1981					0.93

TABLE 3C

UDS SHAREHOLDER RATES OF RETURN (PER CENT PER ANNUM) EXPRESSED AT JANUARY 1982 PRICES

		sold on 31st January				
		1978	1979	1980	1981	1982
	1977	43.73	17.43	0.45	−3.88	−2.46
bought	1978		−5.21	−17.57	−16.35	−11.75
on	1979			−28.96	−21.21	−13.75
31st	1980				−14.26	−6.28
January	1981					3.27

Appendix I
Deriving a contract's single-period beta coefficient

(a) *Covariability of contract and market portfolio earnings*

The market risk of a non-competitive risk contract, defined in a single-period CAPM framework, by the beta coefficient, β_e, is given by:

$$\beta_e = \frac{\text{covar}(r_e, r_m)}{V_m^{(r)}}$$

$$= \frac{\Sigma p_{em}(r_e - \bar{r}_e)(r_m - \bar{r}_m)}{\Sigma p_m(r_m - \bar{r}_m)^2} \qquad \text{(i)}$$

where,

p_{em} denotes the probability distribution of the returns to contract e and the returns to the market portfolio;

p_m denotes the probability distribution of the returns to the market portfolio

r_e represents a random value of the rate of return on contract e given by

$$r_e = \frac{y_e}{TMV_e} - 1;$$

r_m is similarly defined;

y_e stands for a random value of the cash flow earnings on contract e including any residual value as defined by the single period version of equation (4) on page 47; and,

TMV_e denotes the market value of contract e as also defined by equation (4).

Substituting for r_e and r_m in (i);

$$\beta_e = \frac{\Sigma p_{em}\left\{\left(\frac{y_e}{TMV_e} - 1\right) - \left(\frac{\bar{y}_e}{TMV_e} - 1\right)\right\}\left\{\left(\frac{y_m}{TMV_m} - 1\right) - \left(\frac{\bar{y}_m}{TMV_m} - 1\right)\right\}}{\Sigma p_m\left\{\left(\frac{y_m}{TMV_m} - 1\right) - \left(\frac{\bar{y}_m}{TMV_m} - 1\right)\right\}^2}$$

$$= \frac{\Sigma p_{em}\left(\frac{y_e - \bar{y}_e}{TMV_e}\right)\left(\frac{y_m - \bar{y}_m}{TMV_m}\right)}{\Sigma p_m\left(\frac{y_m - \bar{y}_m}{TMV_m}\right)^2}$$

$$= \frac{\Sigma p_{em}(y_e - \bar{y}_e)(y_m - \bar{y}_m)(TMV_e . TMV_m)^{-1}}{\Sigma p_m (y_m - \bar{y}_m)^2 (TMV_m)^{-2}}$$

$$= \frac{covar(y_e, y_m)}{var(y_m)} . \frac{TMV_m}{TMV_e} \qquad \text{(ii)}$$

That is to say, the beta coefficient of contract e can be expressed as the covariance of its cash flow earnings with those on the market portfolio, *divided by* the variance of the cash flow earnings on the market portfolio, *multiplied* by a scale factor represented by the relative market values of the market portfolio and contract e. In short, an earnings beta is readily derived from a rate of return beta in the single-period case.

(b) *Covariability of market portfolio earnings and contract costs*

In the case of a non-competitive, single-period risk contract, its price, k_e is a deterministic variable which is determined simultaneously with its beta coefficient which, in turn, specifies that contract's rate of return. It is therefore necessary to specify the contract's beta coefficient by reference to the covariability of its costs, O_e, with the earnings on the market portfolio, y_m.

$$\text{Let } y_e = k_e - O_e$$
$$\text{where, } O_e = h_e + (A_e + R_e - Y_e) - H_e. \qquad \text{(iii)}$$

Substituting (iii) into (ii) yields:

$$\beta_e = \frac{covar(-O_e, y_m)}{var(y_m)} . \frac{TMV_m}{TMV_e} \qquad \text{(iv)}$$

TMV_e is explicitly estimated as an integral part of the contract costing procedure, and all other values on the R.H.S. of (iv) can either be estimated from historical time-series data, or observed. Hence, a beta coefficient derived from the single-period CAPM framework can be used as a basis for determining the target rate of return for a non-competitive Government contract. One minor qualification is that the market portfolio needs to be proxied with an index. Using the de Zoete Equity Index, which contains 30 shares, it is possible quickly to arrive at a market value thereof since the equity market values of the 30 constituents are quoted in *The Times* every Monday.

Appendix II

Derivation of the minimum required rate of return for multi-period non-competitive Government contracts where there is serial dependence between periodic cash flows

A general multiperiod solution can be derived from a solution to the two-period case of serial dependence.†

Two-period contract

If there are z possible outcomes in period 1, there will in period 2 be z probability distributions, each with its own expected value, and z joint probability distributions with the market portfolio.

Let the period 2 expected values of contract earnings be $k_2 - \bar{O}_{12}$, $k_2 - \bar{O}_{22}$, ..., $k_2 - \bar{O}_{z2}$.

This definition implies that the second instalment, k_2, of the contract price is independent of the route taken to period 2. This is in fact the essential feature of a non-competitive fixed price contract.

At the end of period 1, the period 2 expected values have market values, MV_{11}, MV_{21}, ..., MV_{z1}, given by:

$$MV_{11} = \frac{k_2 - \bar{O}_{12}}{1 + i + (r_m - i)\frac{covar(-O_{12}, y_2)}{var(y_2)} . \frac{MV_1^{(m)}}{MV_{11}}}$$

$$= \frac{k_2 - \bar{O}_{12} - (\bar{r}_m) - i\frac{covar(-O_{12}, y_2)MV_1^{(m)}}{var(y_2)}}{1 + i} \qquad \text{(v)}$$

etc., etc. for MV_{21}, MV_{31}......MV_{z1}.

where,

O_{12} denotes the random values of the first probability distribution of contract costs in period 2;

y_2 stands for the random values of the earnings on the market portfolio in period 2; and,

$MV_1^{(m)}$ represents the market value of the market portfolio at end-year 1.

To allocate the total contract price, $k_2 + k_1$, over the contract's two-period duration, k_2 and k_1 must be treated as independent and dependent variables respectively.

It should also be noted that the end-period 1 solution values of MV_{11}, MV_{21},......M_{z1}, not only depend upon a chosen value for k_2 but also upon an estimate of the value, $MV_1^{(m)}$, of the market portfolio at the end of period 1. The sensitivity of the values of MV_{11}, MV_{21},......M_{z1}, and therefore of the value of k_1 (first instalment of contract price), to the estimate of $MV_1^{(m)}$ can obviously be tested in the usual way.

The second instalment of the contract price, k_2, (and therefore the solution values of MV_{11}, MV_{21},......MV_{z1}) having been treated as independent variable(s), the solution to the first period problem is the derivation of k_1 given by:

$$MV_o = [p_{11}(k_1 - O_{11} + MV_{11}) + p_{21}(k_1 - O_{21} + MV_{21}) + ... + p_{z1}(k_1 - O_{z1} + MV_{z1})] (1 + \bar{r}_1)^{-1}$$

$$= \frac{k_1 - \bar{O}_1 + \sum_{i=1}^{z} p_{i1}MV_{i1}}{1 + \bar{r}_1}$$

whence,

$$k_1 = MV_0(1 + \bar{r}_1) + \bar{O}_1 - \sum_{i=1}^{z} p_{i1}MV_{i1}$$

where $\bar{r}_1$ is derived as described in Appendix I.

Bibliography

Brealey, Richard & Myers, Stewart, *Principles of Corporate Finance*, McGraw Hill, 1981.

Dimson, E. and Brealey, R., "The Risk Premium on U.K. Equities", *The Investment Analyst*, No. 52, 1978.

Gee, K., "Contract Cost Escalation Clauses", University of Salford, 1981.

Harrington, D., *Modern Portfolio Theory and the Capital Asset Pricing Model – A User's Guide*, Prentice-Hall, 1983.

Lawson, G. H., "Why the current U.D.S. takeover bids became inevitable", *The Accountant*, vol. 188, 1983.

London Business School, Institute of Finance and Accounting, *Risk Measurement Service (1979 – 83)*, LBS Financial Services.

Review Board for Government Contracts, *Report on the third general review of the profit formula for non-competitive Government contracts*, HMSO, 1980.

Stapleton, R. C. & Subrahmanyam, M. G., "A Multiperiod Equilibrium Asset Pricing Model", *Econometrica*, Vol. 46, 1978.

†The conditions under which the multiperiod CAPM hold are in fact quite restrictive. Sufficient conditions for the model to hold are derived in Stapleton and Subrahmanyam (1978).

Specifying a multiperiod, computer-based financial model

by

G. H. Lawson

Contents

Specifying a multiperiod, computer-based financial model

I. REQUIRED OUTPUTS (see pages 18-21 (inclusive))

Sequences of:

(a) projected periodic income statements

(b) projected periodic cash flow statements

(c) projected periodic cash flow statements expressed at end-year 0 prices

(d) projected end-period balance sheets corresponding to (a) and (b).

II. BASIC INPUT DATA (see also pages 17, 18 and 19)

(a) Latest income statement and end-period balance sheet corresponding thereto classified as in the required outputs.

(b) Long- and short-term interest rates.

(c) Book values of inventories and fixed assets in the *beginning-of-year* balance sheet corresponding to the latest income statement.

(d) Book values of assets for tax purposes and tax losses brought forward (if any).

(e) Scenario of estimated relative price changes expressed in money terms, e.g., rates of change of cost of materials, labour, overheads, fixed assets and of selling prices.

(f) Estimated sales volume growth rates.

(g) Capital expenditure intentions.

[The inputted income statement and balance sheet constitute the arithmetic basis to which all the sub-models are linked. This is necessarily the case because the *specification* of a multiperiod financial model is largely, though not entirely, an exercise in multiperiod accounting, i.e., the specification of a company's inter- and intra-period accounting relationships commencing with its financial *status quo* and existing accounting parameters. The latter should of course be adjusted in respect of anticipated future changes thereto.]

III. SUB-MODELS CONSTITUTING THE TOTAL MODEL

III.1.1 Sales model (income statement)

$$d_o \{1+v_1(TM)\}(1+ms_1)(1+sp_1) = d_1$$

or, more generally,

$$d_{j-1} \{1+v_j(TM)\}(1+ms_j)(1+sp_j) = d_j \qquad (1)$$

where, in year j,

d_j = accrued sales;

$v_j(TM)$ = rate of growth in the volume of the total market (measured in physical units);

ms_j = rate of increase in the individual firm's market share. [If the firm merely maintains its market share in year j, ms_j=0. But if it increases its market share from (say) 10% to 15%, $1+ms_j$ = 15/10 = 1 + 0.5].

sp_j = the firm's percentage change in selling price.

III.1.2 Trade receivables (balance sheet)

The end-year trade receivables, TR_j, corresponding to periodic accrued sales, d_j, can be derived from the ratio TR_{j-1}/d_{j-1} which is quantified by the basic input data. Thus,

$$TR_j = d_j \; (TR_{j-1}/d_{j-1}) \qquad (2)$$

Alternatively, and perhaps more reliably, the trade receivables/sales ratio can be estimated from the weighted average of (say) the previous five-year's values of that ratio but allowing for any expected adjustments thereto, e.g., $\sum_{j=-4}^{o} TR_j \; / \sum_{j=-4}^{o} d_j$

III.1.3 Sales receipts (cash flow statement)

The cash, k_j, collected from customers in year j is given by:

$$k_j = TR_{j-1} + d_j - TR_j \qquad (3)$$

III.2.1 Materials component of the cost of sales (income statement)

$$m_o \{1+v_j^{(TM)}\}(1+ms_1)\{1+c_1^{(m)}\} = m_1$$

or, more generally,

$$m_{j-1} \{1+v_j^{(TM)}\}(1+ms_j)\{1+c_j^{(m)}\} = m_j \qquad (4)$$

where, in year j,

m_j = materials component of the cost of sales;

$v_j^{(TM)}$ and ms_j are as defined under III.1.1 (above); and,

$c_j^{(m)}$ = rate of increase in the cost of raw materials.

The materials component of the cost of sales, m_j, is also given by:

$$m_j = a_{j-1}^{(m)} + b_j - a_j^{(m)} \qquad (4a)$$

where, in year j,

b_j denotes purchases of materials

[$a_{j-1}^{(m)}$ and $a_j^{(m)}$ are defined under the next subheading].

III.2.2 Materials inventory model (balance sheet)

$$a_o^{(m)}[\{1+v_1^{(TM)}\}(1+ms_1)]^{½} \{1+c_1^{(m)}\} = a_1^{(m)}$$

or, more generally,

$$a_{j-1}^{(m)} [\{1+v_j^{(TM)}\}(1+ms_j)]^{½} \{1+c_j^{(m)}\} = a_j^{(m)} \qquad (5)$$

where

$a_{j-1}^{(m)}$, $a_j^{(m)}$ represent year j opening and closing materials inventories.

The ½ positive exponent in equation (5) gives effect to the EOQ formula relationship between inventory volume and sales volume, e.g., a 10% increase in sales volume requires a $(1.1)^{½}-1 = 0.04881$ (say 5%) increase in raw materials inventory.

III.2.3 Materials purchased

Rearranging equation (4a); materials purchased, b_1, in period 1 can be expressed as:

$$b_1 = m_1 - a_o^{(m)} + a_1^{(m)}$$

or, more generally,

$$b_j = m_j - a_{j-1}^{(m)} + a_j^{(m)} \qquad (6)$$

N.B. As the materials component, m_j, of the cost of sales is included in the income statement, b_j, $a_{j-1}^{(m)}$ and $a_j^{(m)}$ are not included therein. Materials purchased, b_j, is the basis of the end-year trade payables estimate, TP_j, and the (operating) payment, $h_j^{(m)}$, in respect of materials [See III.2.7 and III.2.8].

III.2.4 Work-in-progress inventories (balance sheet)

$$a_o^{(WIP)}\ [\{1+v_1^{(TM)}\}(1+ms_1)]^{½}\{1+c_1^{(WIP)}\} = a_1$$

or, more generally,

$$a_{j-1}^{(WIP)}\ [\{1+v_j^{(TM)}\}(1+ms_j)]^{½}\{1+c_j^{(WIP)}\} = a_j \qquad (7)$$

where, in year j,

$a_{j-1}^{(WIP)}$, $a_j^{(WIP)}$ = opening and closing work-in-progress; and,

$c_j^{(WIP)}$ = rate of change in the unit book value of work-in-progress.

III.2.5 Periodic changes in work-in-progress (income statement)

$$\Delta\ WIP_j = a_{j-1}^{(WIP)} - a_j^{(WIP)} \qquad (8)$$

N.B. Because the closing book values of work-in-progress and finished goods usually exceed their corresponding opening values, the periodic changes in these values (see also equation (8a)) are normally deductions from the cost side of the income statement.

III.2.6 Finished goods inventories (balance sheet) and periodic changes therein (income statement)

$$a_o^{(FG)}[\{1+v_1^{(TM)}\}(1+ms_1)]^{½}\{1+c_1^{(FG)}\} = a_1^{(FG)}$$

or, more generally,

$$a_{j-1}^{(FG)}[\{1+v_j^{(TM)}\}(1+ms_j)]^{½}\{1+c_j^{(FG)}\} = a_j^{(FG)} \quad (9)$$

where, in year j,

$a_{j-1}^{(FG)}$, $a_j^{(FG)}$ = opening and closing finished goods inventories; and,

$c_j^{(FG)}$ = rate of change in the unit book value of finished goods.

The periodic change in finished goods, ΔFG_j, is given by:

$$\Delta\ FG_j = a_j^{(FG)} - a_{j-1}^{(FG)} \quad (8a)$$

Note: The income statement classification described in this paper distinguishes between opening and closing raw materials inventories which are included in the materials component of the cost of sales (section III.2.1) and the periodic changes in work-in-progress and finished goods inventories which are treated separately as described here and in section III.2.5. Alternatively all three inventories can be included in the materials component of the cost of sales (see equation (4a)) in which case ΔWIP_j and ΔFG_j are not separately included in the income statement.

III.2.7 End-year trade payables (balance sheet)

The end-year trade payables, TP_j, corresponding to periodic accrued purchases, b_j, are conveniently derived from the ratio TP_{j-1}/b_{j-1} (or from an average of the previous years' values of that ratio). Thus,

$$TP_j = b_j\ (TP_{j-1}/b_{j-1}) \quad (10)$$

Note, however, that for the first trade payables (TP_1) to be forecast, purchases b_o first needs to be derived.

However, since, $b_j = m_j - a_{j-1}^{(m)} + a_j^{(m)}$, (6)

we have $b_o = m_o - a_{-1} + a_o$

As indicated by II(a) and II(c) above, m_o, $a_{-1}^{(m)}$ and $a_o^{(m)}$ are basic input data.

III.2.8 Payments to materials suppliers (cash flow statement)

In year j payments to suppliers of materials are given by:

$$h_j^{(m)} = TP_{j-1} + b_j - TP_j \tag{11}$$

III.3.1 Labour costs (income statement)

Labour costs are assumed to be variable with respect to the level of output. (Salaries and any fixed element of labour cost should be classified under fixed expenses). Thus,

$$lab_o\{1+v_1^{(TM)}\}(1+ms_1)\{1+c_1^{(\ell)}\} = lab_1$$

or, more generally,

$$lab_{j-1}\ \{1+v_j^{(TM)}\}(1+ms_j)\{1+c_j^{(\ell)}\} = lab_j \tag{12}$$

where, in year j,

lab_j = labour cost; and,

$c_j^{(\ell)}$ = rate of change in unit labour cost.

III.3.2 Payments in respect of labour cost (cash flow statement)

These can be assumed to be equal to lab_j because any accrued (unpaid) labour cost is included in accrued expenses in the balance sheet. The periodic changes in such balance sheet accruals effectively transform accrued expenditure into cash payments as indicated under section III.4.5.

III.4.1 Fixed expenses (income statement)

Fixed expenses, fex, are defined as expenses which are fixed with respect to the level of output - given the scale of trading and productive capacity. Thus,

$$fex_o \{1+c_1^{(fex)}\} = fex_1$$

or, more generally,

$$fex_{j-1} \{1+c_j^{(fex)}\} = fex_j \tag{13}$$

where in year j,

fex_j = fixed expenses; and,

$c_j^{(fex)}$ = the rate of increase in fixed expenses in money terms.

[If fixed expenses are anticipated to increase step-wise in relation to capacity increments, R_j, and/or large cumulative increases in sales volume, fixed costs expressed as a function of time should be projected accordingly, e.g., fex_1, fex_2, $fex_2\{1+c_3(fex)\}(1+fcs)$, where, fcs denotes a step-wise increase in fixed costs in year 3].

III.4.2 Variable expenses (income statement)

Variable expenses, vex, are defined as expenses which are variable with respect to the level of output. Thus,

$$vex_o \{1+v_1^{(TM)}\}(1+ms_1) \{1+c_1^{(vex)}\} = vex_1$$

or, more generally,

$$vex_{j-1}\{1+v_j^{(TM)}\}(1+ms_j)\{1+c_j^{(vex)}\} = vex_j \tag{14}$$

where,

$c_j^{(vex)}$ = rate of increase in unit variable cost in money terms in year j.

III.4.3 Accrued expenses (balance sheet)

The end-year accrued expenses, AEX_1, corresponding to periodic total expenses, fex_1+vex_1 can reasonably be derived from the ratio $AEX_o/(fex_o+vex_o)$ (or from an average of the previous years' values of that ratio). Thus,

$$AEX_j = [AEX_{j-1}/(fex_{j-1}+vex_{j-1})] (fex_j+vex_j) \tag{15}$$

III.4.4 Payments in advance (balance sheet)

The end-year payments in advance, $PADV_j$, corresponding to periodic total expenses, fex_j+vex_j can also be derived as described in III.4.3. Thus,

$$PADV_j = [PADV_{j-1}/(fex_{j-1}+vex_{j-1})]\ (fex_j+vex_j) \qquad (16)$$

III.4.5 Payments re fixed and variable expenses (cash flow statement)

Payments, $h_j^{(OHD)}$, in period j, in respect of fixed and variable expenses, are given by:

$$h_j^{(OHD)} = (AEX_{j-1}-PADV_{j-1}) + (fex_j+vex_j) - (AEX_j-PADV_j) \qquad (17)$$

III.5 Capital investment, fixed assets, depreciation and disposals

(a) Let the exogenously-determined capital expenditures (excluding the proceeds of assets displaced) that are to appear in the cash flow statement for year j be CE_j (j = 1, 2, 3,...).

(b) Let GBV_{j-1} and CD_{j-1} respectively denote the gross book value of fixed assets and the cumulative depreciation thereon which are reported in the end-year j-1 balance sheet.

(c) Assume that depreciation, L_j, charged in year j's income statement is given by:

$$L_j = (L_{j-1}/GBV_{j-2})\ GBV_{j-1}. \qquad (18)$$

[The *ex post* multiperiod average value of L_j/GBV_{j-1}, or some other depreciation rate, could be used as an alternative to L_{j-1}/GBV_{j-2}.]

(d) Let the gross book value of disposals in year j be $xGBV_{j-1}$ and the cumulative depreciation relating thereto be yCD_{j-1}. The written down book value of disposals, X_j, in year j is therefore given by:

$$X_j = xGBV_{j-1} - yCD_{j-1} \qquad (19)$$

(e) The sales proceeds, Y_j, of assets displaced that are reported in period j's cash flow statement can be expressed as:

$$Y_j = X_j(1+z) = (xGBV_{j-1} - yCD_{j-1})(1+z) \tag{20}$$

(f) The profit or loss $Y_j - X_j$ on assets displaced that is reported in period j's income statement is therefore given by:

$$Y_j - X_j = z(xGBV_{j-1} - yCD_{j-1}) \tag{21}$$

(g) The gross book value, GBV_{j-1}, reported in the end-year j balance sheet is given by

$$GBV_j = GBV_{j-1} - xGBV_{j-1} + CE_j \tag{22}$$

and the cumulative depreciation, CD_j, relating thereto is:

$$CD_j = CD_{j-1} - yCD_{j-1} + L_j \tag{23}$$

The net book value, NBV_j, of fixed assets reported in the end-year j balance sheet can therefore be expressed as:

$$NBV_j = GBV_j - CD_j \tag{24}$$

To model a firm's capital investment, fixed assets, depreciation and disposals in the above manner, it is therefore necessary to know its capital expenditure intentions and have estimates of the x, y and z parameters.

III.6 Corporate taxation

A corporate taxation model can be divided into two parts:

(i) the computation of the charge, t_j, on the taxable earnings of year j which results in a tax payment in that same, or subsequent, year; and,

(ii) the computation of a transfer, t_j^*, to a deferred taxation account.

[Deferred taxation accounting is ignored here on the assumption that it has insignificant economic consequences.]

III.6.1 Corporate income tax charge on taxable earnings (income and cash flow statements)

Corporate taxable earnings TE_j, for any year j can be approximated as follows:

$$TE_j = d_j - (a_{j-1} + b_j - a_j) - F_j + Y_j - ACRS_j \qquad (25)$$

where, in year j,

d_j = accrued sales;

a_j, a_{j-1} = opening and closing inventories;

b_j = purchases;

F_j = corporate interest payments;

Y_j = proceeds of assets displaced; and,

$ACRS_j$ = tax depreciation allowances (including the written down value for tax purposes of assets displaced) computed in accordance with the Accelerated Cost Recovery System introduced by the Tax Reform Act, 1986 (see III.6.2 *infra*).

[N.B. For simplicity it can reasonably be assumed that the written down value of a company's existing assets and all future capital expenditure qualify for ACRS depreciation allowances.

It is also reasonable to assume that tax losses are eligible for relief on a current year basis in the form of tax repayments, i.e., unless the specific purpose of a multiperiod financial model is the analysis of the economic consequences of the corporate tax system, the 3-year carry-back and the 15-year carry-forward provisions can be ignored. This is not a very strong assumption in that the present value of a projected sequence of tax payments and repayments computed on a current-year basis will, as a rule, closely approximate the present value of the sequence that is computed in accordance with the carry-back and carry-forward provisions.]

III.6.2 The computation of ACRS tax depreciation allowances

The ACRS guidelines specify several classes of assets and prescribe a class recovery period (or class life) which is a rough approximation of economic life. The main aspects of the ACRS can be summarized as in Tables 1 and 2.

Table 1 Major Classes and Asset Lives for ACRS under the Tax Reform Act of 1986

Class	Type of Property
3-year	Computers and equipment used in research.
5-year	Automobiles, tractor units, light-duty trucks, computers, and certain special manufacturing tools.
7-year	Most industrial equipment, office furniture, and fixtures.
10-year	Certain longer-lived types of equipment.
27.5 year	Residential rental real property such as apartment buildings.
31.5 year	All nonresidential real property, including commercial and industrial buildings.

Source: Brigham and Gapenski, Financial Management: Theory and Practice, The Dryden Press, 1988, page 36.

III.6.3 ACRS tax deprecation allowances for three-year class investments

The $ACRS^{(3)}$ tax depreciation schedule for three-year class investments can be specified as in Table 3.

As the $ACRS_j$ tax depreciation allowances for the 5-year, 7-year and 10-year class investments are calculated in the same manner as those set out in Table 3, an $ACRS_j$ tax depreciation schedule for all four of these investment classes in any year j is therefore given by:

Table 2 Recovery Allowance Percentages for Personal Property under the Tax Reform Act of 1986

Ownership Year	Class of Investment 3-Year	5-Year	7-Year	10-Year
1	33%	20%	14%	10%
2	45	32	25	18
3	15	19	17	14
4	7	12	13	12
5		11	9	9
6		6	9	7
7			9	7
8			4	7
9				7
10				6
11				3
	100%	100%	100%	100%

Source: Brigham and Gapenski, page 36.

Table 3 Tax Depreciation Schedule for 3-Year Investment Class

capital expenditure	ACRS$^{(3)}$ in year j	j+1	j+2	j+3	j+4	j+5
$CE_j^{(3)}$	$0.33CE_j^{(3)}$	$0.45CE_j^{(3)}$	$0.15CE_j^{(3)}$	$0.07CE_j^{(3)}$		
$CE_{j-1}^{(3)}$	$0.45CE_{j-1}^{(3)}$	$0.15CE_{j-1}^{(3)}$	$0.07CE_{j-1}^{(3)}$			
$CE_{j-2}^{(3)}$	$0.15CE_{j-2}^{(3)}$	$0.07CE_{j-2}^{(3)}$				
$CE_{j-3}^{(3)}$	$0.07CE_{j-3}^{(3)}$					
$CE_{j+1}^{(3)}$		$0.33CE_{j+1}^{(3)}$	$0.45CE_{j+1}^{(3)}$	$0.15CE_{j+1}^{(3)}$	$0.07CE_{j+1}^{(3)}$	
$CE_{j+2}^{(3)}$			$0.33CE_{j+2}^{(3)}$	$0.45CE_{j+2}^{(3)}$	$0.15CE_{j+2}^{(3)}$	$0.07CE_{j+2}^{(3)}$
$CE_{j+3}^{(3)}$				$0.33CE_{j+3}^{(3)}$	$0.45CE_{j+3}^{(3)}$	$0.15CE_{j+3}^{(3)}$
$CE_{j+4}^{(3)}$					$0.33CE_{j+4}^{(3)}$	$0.45CE_{j+4}^{(3)}$
$CE_{j+5}^{(3)}$						$0.33CE_{j+5}^{(3)}$
etc.						

[N.B. each year contains the same four annual depreciation percentages.]

$$ACRS_j = \left[0.33C_j^{(3)} + 0.45C_{j-1}^{(3)} + 0.15C_{j-2}^{(3)} + 0.07C_{j-3}^{(3)}\right]$$

$$+ \left[0.2C_j^{(5)} + 0.32C_{j-1}^{(5)} + 0.19C_{j-2}^{(5)} + 0.12C_{j-3}^{(5)}\right.$$

$$\left. + 0.11C_{j-4}^{(5)} + 0.06C_{j-5}^{(5)}\right]$$

$$+ \left[0.14C_j^{(7)} + 0.25C_{j-1}^{(7)} + 0.17C_{j-2}^{(7)} + 0.13C_{j-3}^{(7)}\right.$$

$$\left. + 0.09C_{j-4}^{(7)} + 0.09C_{j-5}^{(7)} + 0.09C_{j-6}^{(7)} + 0.04_{j-7}^{(7)}\right]$$

$$+ \left[0.1C_j^{(10)} + 0.18C_{j-1}^{(10)} + 0.14C_{j-2}^{(10)} + 0.12C_{j-3}^{(10)}\right.$$

$$+ 0.09C_{j-4}^{(10)} + 0.07C_{j-5}^{(10)} + 0.07C_{j-6}^{(10)}$$

$$\left. + 0.07C_{j-7}^{(10)} + 0.07_{j-8}^{(10)} + 0.06C_{j-9}^{(10)} + 0.03C_{j-10}^{(10)}\right]$$

III.7.1 Cash balance model (balance sheet)

Assuming that companies maintain cash balances for transactions and precautionary purposes, the following (EOQ) cash balance model suggests itself:

$$CB_0[\{1+v_1^{(TM)}\}\ (1+ms_1)]^{\frac{1}{2}}\ (1+g_1) = CB_1$$

or, more generally,

$$CB_{j-1}[\{1+v_j^{(TM)}\}(1+ms_j)]^{\frac{1}{2}}\ (1+g_j) = CB_j \qquad (27)$$

where,

g_j denotes the rate of inflation expected in year j.

[This model assumes that cash is maintained in a non-interest bearing account.]

III.7.2 Periodic liquidity change (cash flow statement)

The liquidity change, H_j, in period j which should be explicitly allowed for in the cash flow statement is given by:

$$H_j = CB_j - CB_{j-1} \qquad (28)$$

III.8 Debt policy (short- and long-term debt financing)

III.8.1 Short-term debt financing

Long-term debt financing is best treated as an exogenous variable whereas, given the level of cash balances, $\sum_{t=-z}^{j} H_t$, the level of short-term debt, $\sum_{t=-z}^{j} M_t$ should be treated as a dependent variable - after allowing for tax payments, dividend payments, and long-and short-term interest payments.

As short-term interest payments, $F_j^{(ST)}$ are also a dependent variable, they need to be computed by reference to the cash flow statement as follows. The cash surplus (or deficit), CS_j, for year j is initially given by:

$$CS_j = (k_j-h_j) - (CE_j-Y_j) - t_j^{\dagger} - H_j - (D_j-B_j) - [F_j^{(L)}-N_j] \qquad (29)$$

where, in year j,

k_j = cash collected from customers;

$h_j = h_j^{(m)} + h_j(\ell) + h_j^{(OHD)}$ = operating payments;

CE_j = capital expenditure;

Y_j = proceeds of assets displaced;

$t_j^{\dagger}$ = previous year's tax payment used as an estimate of the current year's tax payment (or previous year's tax charge payable in arrears (as in the U.K.)).

H_j = liquidity change

D_j-B_j = shareholder cash flow;

$F_j^{(L)}$ = long-term interest payments; and,

N_j = long-term debt raised (or repaid).

Interest, $F_j^{(ST)}$, on average short-term debt for the period is given by:

$$F_j^{(ST)} = \frac{r_d}{2}\left[\sum_{t=-z}^{j-1} M_t + \left[\sum_{t=-z}^{j-1} M_t - CS_j\right]\right]$$

$$= r_d\left[\sum_{t=-z}^{j-1} M_t - \frac{1}{2} CS_j\right] \qquad (30)$$

Closing short-term debt, $\sum_{t=-z}^{j} M_t$, is therefore given by:

$$\sum_{t=-z}^{j} M_t = \sum_{t=-z}^{j-1} M_t\,(1+r_d) - CS_j\left[1+\frac{r_d}{2}\right] \qquad (31)$$

and appears in the balance sheet accordingly. Note that interest $F_j^{(ST)}$ appears in the final cash flow statement for year j as part of total interest, F_j. Thus,

$$F_j = F_j^{(L)} + F_j^{(ST)} \qquad (32)^{\dagger}$$

Moreover, making no distinction between interest paid and interest accrued, <u>F_j also appears in the income statement</u>. It therefore follows that the cash flow statement <u>should be completed before</u> the income statement because the current year's tax <u>charge</u>, t_j, allows for the relief on the current year's interest payments, F_j.

III.8.2 <u>Long-term debt financing</u>

To accommodate an exogenously (or otherwise)-determined long-term debt-financing policy, a row must be reserved in the <u>cash flow statement</u> to record, N_1, N_2,...

The cumulative sum of the latter, $\sum_{t=-x}^{j} N_j$, (including the end-year 0 long-term debt levels) is recorded in the <u>balance sheet</u>.

$$^{\dagger}F_j^{(L)} = r_d^{(L)} \sum_{t=-x}^{j} N_t \qquad (33)$$

III.9 Dividend policy and shareholder cash flows

Several U.K. and U.S. empirical studies covering most of the post-war period suggest that corporate dividend policies are based on post-tax shareholder profits disclosed in the income statement. By contrast, the standard valuation model of financial theory suggests that dividend and debt-financing policies should be simultaneously determined by reference to multiperiod projected entity cash flows. Be this as it may, dividend policy D_1, D_2, D_3,..., needs to be accommodated in both the income statement and cash flow statement (as a constituent of shareholder cash flow) and, to the extent that accrued dividends differ from dividends paid, end-period outstanding dividends should be recorded in the balance sheet.

In that a multiperiod financial model facilitates observations on the relationship between accruals and cash flow variables, it is an ideal vehicle for analyzing the economic consequences of decisions, like the dividend decision, which are are based on accruals accounting numbers. To the extent that equity capital B_1, B_2,..., is raised from, or repaid to, shareholders such amounts need to be accommodated in both the cash flow statement (as components of shareholder cash flow) and balance sheet.

IV. SUMMARY (student work assignment)

Specify separate periodic income and cash flow statements and an end-year balance sheet in symbolic form, as described in the foregoing pages, adopting the classifications illustrated in the financial statements which follow. Also show that a periodic cash flow statement can be derived by differencing successive end-period balance sheets.

SCENARIO & OTHER INPUTS

Year	1	2	3	4	5	6	7	8
Land & Buildings Displacement Percentage	0.0%	0.0%	0.0%	0.0%	0.0%	0.0%	0.0%	0.0%
Plant & Machinery Displacement Percentage	2.0%	2.0%	2.0%	2.0%	2.0%	2.0%	2.0%	2.0%
Other Fixed Assets Displacement Percentage	0.0%	0.0%	0.0%	0.0%	0.0%	0.0%	0.0%	0.0%
Land & Buildings Depreciation Displacement %	0.0%	0.0%	0.0%	0.0%	0.0%	0.0%	0.0%	0.0%
Plant & Machinery Depreciation Displacement %	2.5%	2.5%	2.5%	2.5%	2.5%	2.5%	2.5%	2.5%
Other Fixed Assets Depreciation Displacement %	0.0%	0.0%	0.0%	0.0%	0.0%	0.0%	0.0%	0.0%
Profit % on WDV Of Land & Buildings Displaced	0.0%	0.0%	0.0%	0.0%	0.0%	0.0%	0.0%	0.0%
Profit % on WDV Of Plant & Machinery Displaced	20.0%	20.0%	20.0%	20.0%	20.0%	20.0%	20.0%	20.0%
Profit % on WDV Of Other Fixed Assets	0.0%	0.0%	0.0%	0.0%	0.0%	0.0%	0.0%	0.0%
Total Market Growth Rate	1.5%	1.5%	1.5%	1.5%	1.5%	1.5%	1.5%	1.5%
% Change In Market Share	2.0%	2.0%	2.0%	2.0%	2.0%	2.0%	2.0%	2.0%
% Change In Selling Prices	3.7%	3.2%	2.7%	2.7%	2.7%	2.7%	2.7%	2.7%
% Change In Unit Cost Of Materials	4.1%	3.6%	3.1%	3.1%	3.1%	3.1%	3.1%	3.1%
% Change In Unit Cost Of Work In Progress	3.8%	3.4%	2.9%	2.9%	2.9%	2.9%	2.9%	2.9%
% Change In Unit Cost Of Finished Goods	3.9%	3.5%	3.0%	3.0%	3.0%	3.0%	3.0%	3.0%
% Change In Unit Cost Of Variable Expense	3.9%	3.4%	2.9%	2.9%	2.9%	2.9%	2.9%	2.9%
% Change In Fixed Expenses	4.1%	3.6%	3.1%	3.1%	3.1%	3.1%	3.1%	3.1%
% Change In Unit Labour Cost	3.5%	3.3%	2.8%	2.8%	2.8%	2.8%	2.8%	2.8%
Annual Inflation Rate	4.0%	3.5%	3.0%	3.0%	3.0%	3.0%	3.0%	3.0%
Bank Overdraft Interest Rate p.a.	8.0%	7.5%	7.0%	7.0%	7.0%	7.0%	7.0%	7.0%
Other Short Term Loans Interest Rate p.a.								
Loan & Stock Debenture Interest Rate p.a.	12.0%	12.0%	12.0%	12.0%	12.0%	12.0%	12.0%	12.0%
Corporate Income Tax Rate	35.0%	35.0%	35.0%	35.0%	35.0%	35.0%	35.0%	35.0%
Preference Dividends	0.0%	0.0%	0.0%	0.0%	0.0%	0.0%	0.0%	0.0%
Common Stock Dividend Payout Ratio	48.0%	48.0%	48.0%	48.0%	48.0%	48.0%	48.0%	48.0%
Expenditure On Land & Buildings	0.0%	0.0%	0.0%	0.0%	0.0%	0.0%	0.0%	0.0%
Expenditure On Plant & Machinery	1015.00	1114.00	1225.00	1346.00	1480.00	1626.00	1787.00	1964
Expenditure On Other Assets	0	0	0	0	0	0	0	0
New Preference Share Capital Raised	0	0	0	0	0	0	0	0
New Common Stock Capital Raised	0	0	0	0	0	0	0	0
Treasury Stock Purchases	0	0	0	0	0	0	0	0
Other Short Term Debt Issued	0	0	0	0	0	0	0	0
Other Short Term Debt Repaid	0	0	0	0	0	0	0	0
Minority Interests Profit Percentage	0	0	0	0	0	0	0	0
Long Term Debt Raised	0	0	0	0	0	0	0	0
Long Term Debt Repaid	0	0	0	0	0	0	0	0
Inflation Indexation Factors	0.9615	0.9290	0.9020	0.8757	0.8502	0.8254	0.8014	0.7780

BALANCE SHEET	Input Data									
End-years	-1	0	1	2	3	4	5	6	7	8
Land & Buildings:GBV	2823.0	2823.0	2823.0	2823.0	2823.0	2823.0	2823.0	2823.0	2823.0	2823.0
Cum. Depreciation	338.0	338.0	338.0	338.0	338.0	338.0	338.0	338.0	338.0	338.0
Net Book Value	2485.0	2485.0	2485.0	2485.0	2485.0	2485.0	2485.0	2485.0	2485.0	2485.0
Plant & Machinery:GBV	7937.0	8524.0	9368.5	10295.1	11314.2	12434.0	13665.3	15018.0	16504.6	18138.5
Cum. Depreciation	3425.0	3742.0	4373.0	5060.0	5808.6	6625.1	7516.3	8490.0	9554.3	10718.3
Net Book Value	4512.0	4782.0	4995.5	5235.2	5505.7	5808.9	6148.9	6528.0	6950.4	7420.2
Other Fixed Assets:GBV	2.0	2.0	2.0	2.0	2.0	2.0	2.0	2.0	2.0	2.0
Cum. Depreciation	1.0	1.0	1.0	1.0	1.0	1.0	1.0	1.0	1.0	1.0
Net Book Value	1.0	1.0	1.0	1.0	1.0	1.0	1.0	1.0	1.0	1.0
Fixed Assets	6998.0	7268.0	7481.5	7721.2	7991.7	8294.9	8634.9	9014.0	9436.4	9906.2
Raw Materials Inventory	1434.0	1559.0	1651.3	1740.7	1826.1	1915.6	2009.5	2108.1	2211.5	2319.9
Work In Progress	6338.0	6890.0	7277.0	7656.0	8015.9	8392.7	8787.2	9200.2	9632.6	10085.4
Finished Goods	2330.0	2533.0	2677.8	2820.1	2955.5	3097.4	3246.1	3402.0	3565.4	3736.6
Trade Recievables		3883.0	3850.7	4114.2	4374.4	4651.1	4945.3	5258.1	5590.7	5944.3
Prepayments		390.0	411.3	431.8	451.2	471.7	493.2	515.8	539.5	564.6
Cash		120.0	127.0	133.7	140.1	146.9	153.9	161.3	169.1	177.2
Current Assets		15375.0	15995.1	16896.5	17763.2	18675.3	19635.3	20645.5	21708.9	22828.1
Total Assets		22643.0	23476.6	24617.6	25754.9	26970.2	28270.2	29659.5	31145.2	32734.3
Trade Payables		4600.0	4950.3	5307.9	5663.9	6045.4	6452.5	6887.1	7350.9	7846.0
Accruals		920.0	970.2	1018.6	1064.4	1112.6	1163.3	1216.7	1272.8	1331.8
Corporate Taxes		209.0	328.0	345.0	349.1	368.0	384.9	399.8	411.4	419.2
Dividends		486.0	394.9	422.6	441.0	473.6	506.4	538.3	569.5	599.2
Bank Overdraft		837.0	814.4	1047.0	1282.0	1503.3	1747.2	2018.5	2324.6	2673.0
Other Short Term Loans		0.0	0.0	0.0	0.0	0.0	0.0	0.0	0.0	0.0
Current Liabilities		7052.0	7457.8	8141.1	8800.6	9502.9	10254.3	11060.4	11929.2	12869.2
Net Assets Employed		15591.0	16018.8	16476.6	16954.3	17467.4	18015.9	18599.1	19216.0	19865.1
Minority Interests										
Issued Capital		2308.0	2308.0	2308.0	2308.0	2308.0	2308.0	2308.0	2308.0	2308.0
Reserves		11783.0	12210.8	12668.6	13146.3	13659.4	14207.9	14791.1	15408.0	16057.1
Preference Capital		0.0	0.0	0.0	0.0	0.0	0.0	0.0	0.0	0.0
Loan Stock & Debentures		1500.0	1500.0	1500.0	1500.0	1500.0	1500.0	1500.0	1500.0	1500.0
Treasury Stock Purchases		0.0	0.0	0.0	0.0	0.0	0.0	0.0	0.0	0.0
Funds Employed		15591.0	16018.8	16476.6	16954.3	17467.4	18015.9	18599.1	19216.0	19865.1

INCOME STATEMENT	Input								
For years	0	1	2	3	4	5	6	7	8
Sales	43475.0	46675.0	49869.0	53023.3	56377.2	59943.3	63734.9	67766.3	72052.7
Materials in Cost of Sales	26610.0	28678.9	30760.1	32833.2	35045.9	37407.8	39928.9	42619.9	45492.2
Labour	6362.0	6817.1	7290.7	7759.4	8258.2	8789.1	9354.1	9955.5	10595.5
Variable Expenses	3577.0	3847.7	4119.0	4388.0	4674.7	4980.0	5305.3	5651.9	6021.1
Fixed Expenses	5533.0	5759.9	5967.2	6152.2	6342.9	6539.5	6742.3	6951.3	7166.8
Change In WIP & Other Finished Goods	-755.0	-531.8	-521.3	-495.3	-518.7	-543.2	-568.9	-595.8	-624.0
Operating Expense (Bef. Depr.)	41327.0	44571.7	47615.6	50637.4	53803.0	57173.3	60761.7	64582.7	68651.6
Profit Before Depr. & Interest	2148.0	2103.3	2253.3	2385.9	2574.2	2770.0	2973.1	3183.5	3401.1
Depreciation									
Land & Buildings	0.0	0.0	0.0	0.0	0.0	0.0	0.0	0.0	0.0
Plant & Machinery	661.0	724.5	796.3	875.1	961.7	1056.9	1161.5	1276.5	1402.9
Other Fixed Assets	0.0	0.0	0.0	0.0	0.0	0.0	0.0	0.0	0.0
Profit On Assets Displaced	-1.0	-15.4	-15.6	-15.9	-16.2	-16.6	-17.1	-17.6	-18.2
Interest Expense	281.0	243.5	247.3	258.8	274.2	289.9	307.3	326.9	349.0
Pre-Tax Profit	1207.0	1150.6	1225.3	1267.9	1354.6	1439.8	1521.3	1597.8	1667.4
Corporate Taxation	209.0	328.0	345.0	349.1	368.0	384.9	399.8	411.4	419.2
Profit After Tax	998.0	822.6	880.3	918.8	986.6	1054.9	1121.5	1186.4	1248.3
Dividends:Preferred	0.0	0.0	0.0	0.0	0.0	0.0	0.0	0.0	0.0
:Common	486.0	394.9	422.6	441.0	473.6	506.4	538.3	569.5	599.2
Profit Ascribable To Minorities	0.0	0.0	0.0	0.0	0.0	0.0	0.0	0.0	0.0
Retained Earnings	512.0	427.8	457.8	477.8	513.0	548.5	583.2	616.9	649.1
Purchases Of Materials	26735.0	28771.2	30849.5	32918.5	35135.5	37501.8	40027.4	42723.3	45600.7

Note: Corporate taxation, i.e. tax payment one year later is given by:
corporate taxation = 0.35(pre-tax profit + depreciation + profit on assets displaced - net capital expenditure)
e.g. in year 1, = 0.35(1150.6 + 724.5 - 15.4 - 922.7) = 328

CASH FLOW STATEMENT									
For years	0	1	2	3	4	5	6	7	8
Sales Reciepts		46707.3	49605.5	52763.1	56100.5	59649.1	63422.1	67433.7	71699.1
Materials Paid For		28420.8	30491.9	32562.5	34754.0	37094.6	39592.9	42259.4	45105.6
Wages Paid		6817.1	7290.7	7759.4	8258.2	8789.1	9354.1	9955.5	10595.5
Expenses Paid		9578.6	10058.3	10513.8	10989.8	11490.4	12016.9	12570.9	13153.9
Operating Payments		44816.5	47840.9	50835.7	54002.0	57374.1	60963.9	64785.8	68855.0
Operating Cash Flow		1890.8	1764.6	1927.4	2098.5	2275.0	2458.1	2647.9	2844.1
Capital Expenditure									
Land & Buildings		0.0	0.0	0.0	0.0	0.0	0.0	0.0	0.0
Plant & Machinery		1015.0	1114.0	1225.0	1346.0	1480.0	1626.0	1787.0	1964.0
Other		0.0	0.0	0.0	0.0	0.0	0.0	0.0	0.0
Proceeds Of Assets Displaced		92.3	93.7	95.3	97.3	99.7	102.5	105.7	109.5
Net Capital Expenditure		922.7	1020.3	1129.7	1248.7	1380.3	1523.5	1681.3	1854.5
Corporate Tax Payments		209.0	328.0	345.0	349.1	368.0	384.9	399.8	411.4
Change In Liquidity		7.0	6.7	6.4	6.7	7.1	7.4	7.7	8.1
Entity Cash Flow		752.1	409.5	446.3	494.0	519.6	542.3	559.1	570.1
Minority Interest Cash Flow									
Dividends Paid:Pref.		0.0	0.0	0.0	0.0	0.0	0.0	0.0	0.0
:Common		486.0	394.9	422.6	441.0	473.6	506.4	538.3	569.5
New Equity Raised:Pref		0.0	0.0	0.0	0.0	0.0	0.0	0.0	0.0
:Common		0.0	0.0	0.0	0.0	0.0	0.0	0.0	0.0
Treasury Stock Purchases		0.0	0.0	0.0	0.0	0.0	0.0	0.0	0.0
Shareholder Cash Flow		486.0	394.9	422.6	441.0	473.6	506.4	538.3	569.5
Lender Cash Flow		266.1	14.7	23.7	52.9	46.1	36.0	20.8	0.6
Interest Paid		243.5	247.3	258.8	274.2	289.9	307.3	326.9	349.0
Changes In Bank Overdraft		22.6	-232.6	-235.0	-221.3	-243.9	-271.4	-306.1	-348.4
Increases In Other Short Term Debt		0.0	0.0	0.0	0.0	0.0	0.0	0.0	0.0
Decreases In Other Short Term Debt		0.0	0.0	0.0	0.0	0.0	0.0	0.0	0.0
Long Term Debt Raised		0.0	0.0	0.0	0.0	0.0	0.0	0.0	0.0
Long Term Debt Repaid		0.0	0.0	0.0	0.0	0.0	0.0	0.0	0.0
Lender Cash Flow		266.1	14.7	23.7	52.9	46.1	36.0	20.8	0.6

CASH FLOW STATEMENT AT END YEAR 0 PRICES

For years	0	1	2	3	4	5	6	7	8
Sales Reciepts		44909.1	46083.5	47592.3	49127.2	50713.6	52348.6	54041.4	55781.9
Materials Paid For		27326.6	28327.0	29371.4	30434.1	31537.8	32680.0	33866.7	35092.1
Wages Paid		6554.7	6773.0	6998.9	7231.7	7472.5	7720.9	7978.3	8243.3
Expenses Paid		9209.8	9344.2	9483.4	9623.8	9769.1	9918.7	10074.3	10233.7
Operating Payments		43091.1	44444.2	45853.8	47289.6	48779.5	50319.6	51919.3	53569.2
Operating Cash Flow		1818.0	1639.3	1738.5	1837.7	1934.2	2029.0	2122.0	2212.7
Capital Expenditure									
Land & Buildings		0.0	0.0	0.0	0.0	0.0	0.0	0.0	0.0
Plant & Machinery		975.9	1034.9	1105.0	1178.7	1258.3	1342.1	1432.1	1528.0
Other		0.0	0.0	0.0	0.0	0.0	0.0	0.0	0.0
Proceeds Of Assets Displaced		88.8	87.0	85.9	85.2	84.7	84.6	84.7	85.2
Net Capital Expenditure		887.2	947.9	1019.0	1093.5	1173.6	1257.5	1347.4	1442.8
Corporate Tax Payments		201.0	304.7	311.2	305.7	312.8	317.7	320.4	320.1
Change In Liquidity		6.7	6.3	5.8	5.9	6.0	6.1	6.2	6.3
Entity Cash Flow		723.2	380.5	402.5	432.6	441.8	447.6	448.1	443.5
Minority Interest Cash Flow									
Dividends Paid:Pref.		0.0	0.0	0.0	0.0	0.0	0.0	0.0	0.0
:Common		467.3	366.8	381.2	386.2	402.6	417.9	431.4	443.0
New Equity Raised:Pref		0.0	0.0	0.0	0.0	0.0	0.0	0.0	0.0
:Common		0.0	0.0	0.0	0.0	0.0	0.0	0.0	0.0
Treasury Stock Purchases		0.0	0.0	0.0	0.0	0.0	0.0	0.0	0.0
Shareholder Cash Flow		467.3	366.8	381.2	386.2	402.6	417.9	431.4	443.0
Lender Cash Flow		255.9	13.6	21.4	46.3	39.2	29.7	16.6	0.5
Interest Paid		234.5	229.8	233.5	240.3	246.7	253.9	262.1	271.5
Changes In Bank Overdraft		21.3	-216.1	-212.1	-194.0	-207.5	-224.2	-245.4	-271.0
Increases In Other Short Term Debt		0.0	0.0	0.0	0.0	0.0	0.0	0.0	0.0
Decreases In Other Short Term Debt		0.0	0.0	0.0	0.0	0.0	0.0	0.0	0.0
Long Term Debt Raised		0.0	0.0	0.0	0.0	0.0	0.0	0.0	0.0
Long Term Debt Repaid		0.0	0.0	0.0	0.0	0.0	0.0	0.0	0.0
Lender Cash Flow		255.9	13.6	21.4	46.3	39.2	29.7	16.6	0.5

SOME MANAGERIAL IMPLICATIONS OF WORKING CAPITAL ANALYSIS

by

GERALD H. LAWSON

Contents

1. Introduction

This paper outlines a multiperiod analysis of working capital investment. It also attempts to clarify the objects of working capital management by reference to wealth maximisation orthodoxy.

Total working capital, $\sum p_j$, invested in a firm at end-year j, may be defined as the sum of its trade debtors (including (revenue) payments in advance), $\sum(d_j-k_j)$, minus trade creditors (including accrued (revenue) expenditure), $\sum(b_j-h_j)$, plus the book value, a_j, of its inventories of raw materials, work-in-progress and finished goods at end-year j. With this definition, the amount of working capital invested in a firm may be derived from its balance sheet.

Defining debtors and creditors in a little more detail,

$\sum(d_j-k_j)$ denotes the cumulative difference between periodic accrued sales, d_j, and periodic cash collections, k_j, from customers between the formation of the firm and end-year j, and

$\sum(b_j-h_j)$ stands for the cumulative difference between periodic purchases, b_j, and periodic payments to suppliers, h_j, between the formation of the firm and end-year j.

Periodic working capital investment, p_j, is simply the difference between total working capital invested at the beginning and end of the period in question, that is,

$$p_j = (d_j-k_j) - (b_j-h_j) + (a_j-a_{j-1}).$$

The latter expression is readily interpreted as the algebraic sum of the periodic changes in debtors, creditors and inventories.

A wider definition of working capital investment could include a firm's liquidity level and the multiperiod analysis could also focus on the periodic liquidity adjustments which are usually assumed to be a function of transactions, precautionary and speculative motives. In initially concentrating on periodic working capital investment as the link between pre-depreciation profit and operating cash flow, periodic liquidity adjustments are first ignored.

They are explicitly allowed for when we turn to the more specific managerial implications of working capital analysis.

In attempting to elicit the array of variables, namely, relative price changes, output changes, profit rate differences, periods of trade credit etc., of which periodic working capital is a function, it is initially helpful to recall the basic determinants of trade credit.

The absolute amount of credit given to customers, and outstanding at any given moment in time, clearly depends upon the level of sales transacted on a credit basis and the period of credit given. If, in the normal course of trade, a company allows its customers a period of credit on virtually the entire volume of its invoiced sales, it may require a very significant period of credit from its suppliers (and in respect of other revenue cost items) if it is to emerge as a net credit-taker. This is because, firstly, a company that is profitable in the conventional accounting sense will by definition have a turnover level which exceeds total expenses. Secondly, the period of credit obtainable in respect of certain cost items, e.g., labour, is characteristically very short. In other words, it is very easy to visualise the mechanics of how the many net credit-giving companies get into this condition for perfectly admissible commercial and technical reasons.

The public debate, which was sparked off by the 1974 financial crisis in British industry, strongly suggested that the manner in which inventory investment and net credit given interact, and the effects of this interaction, are much less obvious. Thus, whereas the giving of a net amount of credit causes capital to be deployed in exactly the same way as inventory investment, the point was not widely taken. Initial U.K. interest (and confusion) centered almost entirely on rising inventory book values and the attendant implications for liquidity and the measurement of profitability. Following the publication of the Report of the Inflation Accounting Committee (September

1975), the realisation that there are demonstrable affinities between a firm's inventory investment and its net trade credit position began to emerge. However, it is still not widely appreciated that the relative amount of periodic net credit given or taken varies considerably from company to company and across industries. The same is true of the book value of inventories.

Further aspects of working capital investment that have not been widely appreciated include the economic consequences of its treatment for tax purposes. The recent abolition of U.K. stock relief exacerbates the failure of the previous system (which allowed only the price element of the change in inventory book values as a tax-deductible expense) to comply with the principles of tax neutrality. The consequence is generally an excess of the effective incidence of taxation over the apparent tax burden. Examples of this phenomenon are to be seen in some of the tables which follow.

The progression of illustrations contained in the following section leads first to a base case (Table 4) in which, after year 2, everything including total working capital deployed is constant. Thereafter, the idea is successively to substitute the base-case assumptions with greater realism and to observe the effects on both the periodic and total working capital investments that are respectively recorded in the last two lines of the tables.

2. The mechanics of working capital investment: inventories and trade credit

Even when a firm's financial transactions are entirely conducted on a cash basis, and even if its costs are constant in money terms over time, it will, in maintaining a given level of inventory, tie up capital on a continuing basis. As illustrated arithmetically by Table 1, the amount of capital so invested will remain constant in money terms so long as the other assumptions hold. Note, however, that such investment has an obvious opportunity cost (which is examined briefly in section 7).[1]

Removing the assumption that the company in Table 1 takes no credit, Table 2 postulates that a continuously outstanding amount of credit equal to 1/6 of periodic costs is taken from suppliers. (Such complications as the frequency of deliveries and invoicing are ignored on the grounds that, whilst affecting the time-profile of payments and outstanding credit taken, they do not affect the principle at issue.) The degree to which the negative working capital investment in the form of credit taken offsets working capital deployed in inventories can be clearly seen.

The combined working capital effects of the assumed levels of inventory and credit taken (Table 2) are shown in lines p_j (periodic) and $\sum p_j$ (cumulative). It may also be noted that in this particular case, periodic working capital investment is equal to the amount actually paid out in cash minus (conventionally-measured) cost of sales, that is, line h_j minus line c_j.

The next step in this progression is the addition of an assumption about periodic turnover levels and of the period of credit given. Assume that the product is sold at cost (of sales) plus 6 percent. If the company sells only for immediate settlement in cash, the working capital position shown in Table 2 would in no way be affected and periodic pre-depreciation profit, e_j, would be computed as in Table 3. The difference, line p_j, between periodic profit, e_j, and net operating cash flow, n_j, can be readily interpreted as periodic working capital investment and the cumulative sum of these differences, $\sum p_j$, as total working capital deployed.

The effect of credit given on working capital investment may now be taken into account. It is assumed that debtors equal 20% of periodic sales. Superimposed upon all the other assumptions underlying Tables 1, 2 and 3, the assumption that credit given causes an increase in total working capital deployed produces the situation shown in Table 4. The last two lines are, once again, readily interpreted. Line p_j, periodic working capital investment, is given by periodic inventory investment, $a_j - a_{j-1}$, minus periodic credit taken, $b_j - h_j$, plus periodic credit given, $d_j - k_j$. Similarly, line $\sum p_j$ represents total working capital deployed and is given by total inventory investment to date, a_j, minus total credit received (creditors), $\sum(b_j - h_j)$, plus total credit given (debtors), $\sum(b_j - k_j)$. Stated more concisely (as in the introduction),

$$p_j = (a_j - a_{j-1}) - (b_j - h_j) + (d_j - k_j) \qquad \text{i}$$

and

$$\sum p_j = a_j + \sum\{(d_j - k_j) - (b_j - h_j)\} \qquad \text{ii}$$

All other accounting (profit/cash flow/balance sheet) relationships that are illustrated by Table 4 can of course be stated in symbolic terms.

TABLE 1. PERIODIC AND TOTAL INVENTORY INVESTMENT

Period	1		2		3		4	
	units	£	units	£	units	£	units	£
a_{j-1} opening inventory	—	—	270	203	270	203	270	203
b_j variable costs	1,270	953	1,000	750	1,000	750	1,000	750
b_j fixed costs		250		250		250		250
	1,270	1,203	1,270	1,203	1,270	1,203	1,270	1,203
a_j closing inventory	270	203	270	203	270	203	270	203
$c_j = a_{j-1} + b_j - a_j$ cost of sales	1,000	£1,000	1,000	£1,000	1,000	£1,000	1,000	£1,000
h_j cash paid out		£1,203		£1,000		£1,000		£1,000
$a_j - a_{j-1} = b_j - c_j$ = *periodic inventory investment*		203		—		—		—
a_j *total inventory investment*		203		203		203		203

Assumptions

i. The company in question commences business at the beginning of period 1.
ii. Excluding period 1 when it builds up a permanent inventory of 270 units, the company's periodic production remains at a constant level of 1,000 units.
iii. Costs are constant in money terms.
iv. Inventories are valued at variable cost on a FIFO basis.
v. The company neither gives nor takes credit.

TABLE 2. INVENTORY INVESTMENT AND CREDIT TAKEN

Period	1		2		3		4	
	units	£	units	£	units	£	units	£
a_{j-1} opening inventory	—	—	270	203	270	203	270	203
b_j {variable costs	1,270	953	1,000	750	1,000	750	1,000	750
b_j {fixed costs		250	·	250		250		250
	1,270	1,203	1,270	1,203	1,270	1,203	1,270	1,203
a_j closing inventory	270	203	270	203	270	203	270	203
$c_j = a_{j-1} + b_j - a_j$ cost of sales	1,000	£1,000	1,000	£1,000	1,000	£1,000	1,000	£1,000
h_j cash paid out		£1,002		£1,034		£1,000		£1,000
$a_j - a_{j-1} = b_j - c_j$ periodic inventory investment		203		—		—		—
a_j total inventory investment		203		203		203		203
$b_j - h_j$ periodic credit taken		201		−34		-		-
$\Sigma (b_j - h_j)$ total credit taken		201		167		167		167
$p_j = (d_j - k_j) + (a_j - a_{j-1}) - (b_j - h_j)$ *periodic working capital investment*		2		34		—		—
$\Sigma p_j = a_j - \Sigma(b_j - h_j)$ *total working capital investment*		2		36		36		36

Additional assumption
Total credit taken constitutes $\frac{1}{4}$ of periodic costs, that is, $\Sigma(b_j - h_j) = \frac{1}{4}\, b_j$.

TABLE 3. INVENTORY INVESTMENT, CREDIT TAKEN AND CASH SALES

Period	1		2		3		4	
	units	£	units	£	units	£	units	£
c_j cost of sales	1,000	1,000	1,000	1,000	1,000	1,000	1,000	1,000
$e_j = d_j - c_j$ profit†		60		60		60		60
d_j recorded sales	1,000	£1,060	1,000	£1,060	1,000	£1,060	1,000	£1,060
k_j cash collected	1,000	1,060	1,000	1,060	1,000	1,060	1,000	1,060
h_j cash paid out		1,002		1,034		1,000		1,000
$n_j = k_j - h_j$ net operating cash flow		58		26		60		60
$p_j = e_j - n_j$ *periodic working capital investment*		2		34		—		—
Σp_j *total working capital investment*		2		36		36		36

Additional assumptions
i. Product selling price is £1.06 unit.
ii. All sales are for cash.
† Before depreciation.

TABLE 4. INVENTORY INVESTMENT, CREDIT GIVEN AND TAKEN (CONSTANT COSTS, PRICES, INVENTORIES AND SALES VOLUME)

Period	1		2		3		4	
	units	£	units	£	units	£	units	£
a_{j-1} opening inventory	—	—	270	203	270	203	270	203
b_j {variable costs	1,270	953	1,000	750	1,000	750	1,000	750
b_j {fixed costs		250		250		250		250
	1,270	1,203	1,270	1,203	1,270	1,203	1,270	1,203
a_j closing inventory	270	203	270	203	270	203	270	203
$c_j = a_{j-1} + b_j - a_j$ cost of sales	1,000	£1,000	1,000	£1,000	1,000	£1,000	1,000	£1,000
d_j sales invoiced		1,060		1,060		1,060		1,060
$e_j = d_j - c_j$ profit†	1,000	£60	1,000	£60	1,000	£60	1,000	£60
$a_j - a_{j-1} = b_j - c_j$ periodic inventory investment	270	£203		—		—		—
a_j = total inventory investment	270	£203	270	£203	270	£203	270	£203
h_j cash paid out		£1,002		£1,034		£1,000		£1,000
$b_j - h_j$ periodic credit taken		201		−34		—		—
$\Sigma(b_j - h_j)$ total credit taken		201		167		167		167
k_j = cash collected		848		1,060		1,060		1,060
$d_j - k_j$ periodic credit given		212		—		—		—
$\Sigma(d_j - k_j)$ total credit given		212		212		212		212
$n_j = k_j - h_j$ operating cash flow		−154		26		60		60
$p_j = (a_j - a_{j-1}) - (b_j - h_j) + (d_j - k_j) = e_j - n_j$ *periodic working capital investment*		214		34		—		—
$\Sigma p_j = a_j + \Sigma\{(d_j - k_j) - (b_j - h_j)\}$ *total working capital investment*		214		248		248		248

Additional assumptioin
Total credit given constitutes 20% of periodic sales invoiced, that is, $\Sigma(d_j - k_j) = 0.2d_j$.
†Before depreciation.

3. The effect of relative price changes and output/sales volume growth on working capital investment

In Tables 1 to 4, the assumptions (after period 1) of constant prices, inventory, output and sales volume result in a build-up of total working capital deployed which itself remains constant after period 1. The removal of these assumptions results in situations which can readily be inferred from Table 4. In the interests of precision, the separate effects of relative price changes and growth are next considered individually prior to an examination of the combined effects of the two.

In continuing conditions of rising factor input costs and rising selling prices, the nominal values of all three components of working capital investment are, even assuming zero output growth, likely to be affected and a Table 5-type situation will characteristically emerge. In a multitude of cases in practice there is thus not only a working capital build-up on the commencement of business, but also a continuing need for extra money investment merely to maintain a constant level of production and trading. This does not, of course, preclude the possibility that credit taken may, for a long succession of periods or, as in some branches of the retail trade, permanently exceed credit given.[2]

Table 6 is designed to elicit the effects of output, sales volume and inventory growth on working capital investment in isolation of the effects of changes in the prices of inputs and outputs - given the conditions of credit taken and given, and inventory policy.[3] In that output growth necessitates a continuous deployment of money, it has essentially the same kind of arithmetic effect as cost and price increases on periodic and total working capital invested. (Compare the last two lines of Tables 6 and 5.)

As might be expected, the arithmetic effects of increases in the costs of factor inputs and in the prices of product outputs respectively (on the periodic and total working capital requirements) are compounded by the effects of physical growth. This can be seen by comparing the last two lines of Tables 4, 5, 6 and 7.

4. Differences in the rate of profit and choice between alternatives

Whereas the sales volume growth postulated in Table 7 is combined with the same unit selling prices that are charged in Table 5 (constant sales volume), the unit selling prices for periods 2, 3 and 4 that are assumed in Table 8 represent average total cost plus 6 percent. The respective four-year

TABLE 5. INVENTORY INVESTMENT, CREDIT GIVEN AND TAKEN, COST AND SELLING PRICE INCREASES (CONSTANT SALES AND INVENTORY VOLUMES)

Period	1		2		3		4	
	units	£	units	£	units	£	units	£
a_{j-1} opening inventory	—	—	270	203	270	233	270	268
b_j {variable costs	1,270	953	1,000	863	1,000	992	1,000	1,141
{fixed costs		250		287		331		380
	1,270	£1,203	1,270	£1,353	1,270	£1,556	1,270	£1,789
a_j closing inventory	270	203	270	233	270	268	270	308
$c_j = a_{j-1} + b_j - a_j$ cost of sales	1,000	£1,000	1,000	£1,120	1,000	£1,288	1,000	£1,481
d_j sales invoiced	1,000	1,060	1,000	1,187	1,000	1,365	1,000	1,570
$e_j = d_j - c_j$ profit†	1,000	£60	1,000	£67	1,000	£77	1,000	£89
$a_j - a_{j-1} = b_j - c_j$ periodic inventory investment	270	£203	—	£30	—	£35	—	£40
a_j = total inventory investment	270	£203	270	£233	270	£268	270	£308
h_j cash paid out		£1,002		£1,159		£1,294		£1,488
$b_j - h_j$ periodic credit taken		201		−9		29		33
$\Sigma(b_j - h_j)$ total credit taken		201		192		221		254
k_j = cash collected		848		1,162		1,329		1,529
$d_j - k_j$ periodic credit given		212		25		36		41
$\Sigma(d_j - k_j)$ total credit given		212		237		273		314
$n_j = k_j - h_j$ operating cash flow		−154		3		35		41
$p_j = (a_j - a_{j-1}) - (b_j - h_j) + (d_j - k_j) = e_j - n_j$ *periodic working capital investment*		214		64		42		48
$\Sigma p_j = a_j + \Sigma\{(d_j - k_j) - (b_j - h_j)\}$ *total working capital investment*		214		278		320		368

Additional assumptions

i. Costs increase at 15% annually.

ii. Profit, e_j, constitutes 6% of the cost of sales. The resultant sequence of unit selling prices is readily apparent.

† Before depreciation.

sequences of selling prices in these tables are thus:

Period	1	2	3	4
Tables 5 and 7	1.06	1.187	1.365	1.570
Table 8	1.06	1.163	1.309	1.477

Other things being equal, a reduction in the rate of profit will lower periodic sales, d_j, cash collected, k_j, operating cash flow, k_j-h_j, periodic credit given, d_j-k_j, periodic working capital investment, p_j, and total working capital investment, $\sum p_j$. A comparison of Tables 7 and 8 shows that this is in fact the case. It hardly needs emphasising that the net result is the

TABLE 6. CREDIT GIVEN AND TAKEN, INVENTORY AND SALES VOLUMES GROWTH (CONSTANT COSTS AND PRICES)

Period	1		2		3		4	
	units	£	units	£	units	£	units	£
a_{j-1} opening inventory	—	—	270	203	284	213	298	224
b_j {variable costs	1,270	953	1,114	836	1,224	918	1,346	1,010
{fixed costs		250		250		250		250
	1,270	£1,203	1,384	£1,289	1,508	£1,381	1,644	£1,484
a_j closing inventory	270	203	284	213	298	224	313	235
$c_j = a_{j-1} + b_j - a_j$ cost of sales	1,000	£1,000	1,100	£1,076	1,210	£1,157	1,331	£1,249
d_j sales invoiced	1,000	1,060	1,100	1,166	1,210	1,283	1,331	1,411
$e_j = d_j - c_j$ profit†	1,000	£60	1,100	£90	1,210	£126	1,331	£162
$a_j - a_{j-1} = b_j - c_j$ periodic inventory investment	270	£203	14	£10	14	£11	15	£11
a_j = total inventory investment	270	£203	284	£213	298	£224	313	£235
h_j cash paid out		1,002		1,106		1,154		1,245
$b_j - h_j$ periodic credit taken		201		−20		14		15
$\Sigma(b_j - h_j)$ total credit taken		201		181		195		210
k_j = cash collected		848		1,145		1,259		1,386
$d_j - k_j$ periodic credit given		212		21		24		25
$\Sigma(d_j - k_j)$ total credit given		212		233		257		282
$n_j = k_j - h_j$ operating cash flow		−154		39		105		141
$p_j = (a_j - a_{j-1}) - (b_j - h_j) + (d_j - k_j) = e_j - n_j$ *periodic working capital investment*		214		51		21		21
$\Sigma p_j = a_j + \Sigma\{(d_j - k_j) - (b_j - h_j)\}$ *total working capital investment*		214		265		286		307

Assumptions
i. Constant costs and constant selling prices (unit selling price = £1.06).
ii. Inventory and output volumes increase annually at 5 and 10 per cent respectively.
iii. Total credit taken is ⅙ of periodic cost, b_j.
iv. Total credit given is 20% of periodic sales, d_j.
† Before depreciation.

deterioration in operating cash flow which is recorded in Table 8. An increase in the rate of profit would clearly have the opposite effect. For convenience the relevant profit and operating cash flow figures in Tables 7 and 8 are reproduced here.

Period	1	2	3	4
e_j (Table 7)	60	99	158	238
e_j (Table 8)	60	72	90	111
reduction in e_j	-	27	68	127
n_j (Table 7)	-154	15	88	147
n_j (Table 8)	-154	-7	28	35
reduction in n_j	-	22	60	112

An analysis of the effect of sales volume growth on periodic and total working capital investment should be qualified by reference to the demand curve, i.e., by reference to the effect of higher volumes on the conventional profit mark-up and in turn upon the rate of operating cash flow. Tables 5 and 8 constitute a relevant comparison. Thus, a firm faced with two such alternatives would achieve a superior operating cash flow position were it to choose the Table 5 strategy. That is, hold output constant and charge the (after period 1) higher selling prices assumed in Table 5.

It is interesting that the choice of strategy signalled by a comparison of the respective sequences of historic cost profit, e_j, in Tables 5 and 8 conflicts with the decision indicated by the comparison of operating cash flows. In that profit, e_j, ignores the cost of invested working capital, it is arguable that the cash flow sequence is decisive. Making this point more comprehensively; it might stated that a wealth-maximising firm should choose the alternative plan which offers the sequence of expected cash flows having the highest attainable present value.

It cannot be too strongly emphasised that the superiority of the Table 5 strategy over that depicted in Table 8 is not signalled by the lower levels of working capital (p_j and $\sum p_j$) that are required in the former case. Thus, as a comparison of Tables 7 and 8 makes clear, a situation in which the superior "cash flow" alternative also requires a greater deployment of working capital is eminently possible. A crucial inference, which may now be drawn, is that the level of working capital deployed by a firm is a dependent variable and not a financial objective. That is to say, assuming that, consistent with the maintenance of mutually "agreeable" business relationships with customers and suppliers, a firm minimises the period of credit given, maximises the period of credit taken, and pursues an optimal inventory policy, the absolute levels of its debtors, creditors and inventories depend upon its choice of multiperiod price/output policy. As already indicated, a wealth-maximising firm should base the latter choice on the present value of expected cash flows.

Implicit in the foregoing proposition are the possibilities that alternative price/output policies may sooner or later require the creation of additional productive capacity and that replacement investments are continuously undertaken in keeping capacity intact. Therefore, the absolute level of working capital should, apparently, be determined by reference to the interrelated price/output/investment policies which maximise the present value of expected operating cash flows minus capital investments.

The latter prescription is itself subject to a proviso concerning the liquidity component of working capital deployed. If, as widely assumed (and broadly consistent with observations), corporate liquidity levels are a function of transactions, precautionary and speculative motives, output growth (and therefore, as a rule investment growth) should, <u>ceteris paribus</u>, cause rising liquidity levels, i.e., real periodic liquidity investment (which may be defined as H_j) and vice versa. Moreover, anticipating the focal point of the section which follows, periodic corporate tax payments, t_j, should also be included in the analysis. A firm's objective function should therefore read: maximise the present value of [expected operating cash flows minus capital investment minus liquidity adjustments minus tax payments] or, stated symbolically:

$$\text{Max!} \sum_{j=0}^{\infty} \{(\bar{k}_j-\bar{h}_j) - (\bar{A}_j+\bar{R}_j-\bar{Y}_j) - \bar{t}_j - H_j\}(1+\bar{r})^{-j}$$

where (using bars to denote expected values)

$\bar{A}_j + \bar{R}_j - \bar{Y}_j$ stands for replacement investment, A_j, growth investment, R_j, and the proceeds of assets displaced, Y_j, (all in period j); and

$\bar{r}$ represents the firm's weighted average cost of capital which, for simplicity, is assumed to be constant.

In theory, a firm's planning horizon should be coterminous with the entire life of a business which, as the previous financial objective assumes, may be perpetual. In practice, a corporate financial plan typically covers a five-year sequence, is normally rolled over and generally revised annually. Such practical imperatives do not negate the foregoing wealth maximisation objective itself, nor the cash flow basis of planning which is logically implicit in that objective, nor the inference that the level of working capital should be treated as a dependent variable.

The proposition, that working capital should be treated as a dependent variable from a decision-making standpoint, is not however, the contention that the level of working capital deployed can be left to look after itself. Just as cash flow projections can, and should, be used as a basis for exercising financial control in the implementation of a wealth-maximising plan, the projected working capital levels that are associated therewith should constitute important yardsticks for the exercise of control over actual working capital deployed.

To conclude this discussion on the effect of changes in the profit rate on both working capital deployed and the ranking of alternatives, two further possibilities, which also provide a link with the next section, are considered.

Leaving aside liquidity changes, the composition and determinants of periodic working capital investment are such that it can generally be regarded as a 'feature of the system'. This is another way of stating that the (characteristic) periodic excess of pre-depreciation profit over periodic operating cash flow contributes to a cumulative permanent excess and does not constitute a self-reversing timing difference. Consequently, a situation in which conventionally-calculated pre-depreciation profit is positive and operating cash flow is negative on a continuing basis cannot be ruled out.[4]

In the latter circumstances (and even aside from the characteristic excess of periodic capital expenditure over depreciation which exacerbates the problem) an apparently profitable company simply would not be financially viable.

A closely-related possibility, with rather more subtle and pernicious, macroeconomic implications, is a situation in which a reduction in conventional profit mark-ups not only lowers the absolute level of conventionally-calculated profit but also causes operating cash flow to go negative. It was to exactly this danger that British firms were exposed during the 1973-79 U.K. regime of statutory price and profit margin controls. There is every reason to believe that this policy contributed not only to the rise in U.K. debt ratios during that period, but also to an increase in the effective incidence of corporate taxation.

Finally, it should also be emphasized that the break-even price-output levels that are signalled by the conventional accounting model are generally lower than their cash flow break-even counterparts. Thus, even in the absence of capital expenditure, "conventional" break-even conditions do not constitute a sufficient condition for "break-even" self-financing.[5]

5. Working capital and the incidence of taxation

A significant difference between Tables 7 and 8 stemming directly from differences in their respective profit rates, is reflected in the relationship (in both cases) between the previous period's pre-depreciation profit,, e_{j-1}, and the current period's operating cash flow, n_j.[6] For example, in Table 7, the pre-depreciation profits of periods 2 and 3 constitute 112.5 and 107.5 percent of the operating cash flows of periods 3 and 4 respectively. That is to say,

$$e_2/n_3 = 99/88 = 1.125$$

and

$$e_3/n_4 = 158/147 = 1.0748$$

TABLE 7. CREDIT GIVEN AND TAKEN: COST AND SELLING PRICE INCREASES COMBINED WITH OUTPUT, INVENTORY, AND SALES VOLUME GROWTH

Period	1		2		3		4	
	units	£	units	£	units	£	units	£
a_{j-1} opening inventory	—	—	270	203	284	245	298	296
b_j {variable costs	1,270	953	1,114	961	1,224	1,214	1,346	1,535
b_j {fixed costs		250		288		331		381
	1,270	£1,203	1,384	£1,452	1,508	£1,790	1,644	£2,212
a_j closing inventory	270	203	284	245	298	296	313	357
$c_j = a_{j-1} + b_j - a_j$ cost of sales	1,000	£1,000	1,100	£1,207	1,210	£1,494	1,331	£1,855
d_j sales invoiced	1,000	£1,060	1,100	£1,306	1,210	£1,652	1,331	2,090
$e_j = d_j - c_j$ profit†	1,000	£60	1,100	£99	1,210	£158	1,331	£235
$a_j - a_{j-1} = b_j - c_j$ periodic inventory investment	270	£203	14	£42	14	£51	15	£61
a_j = total inventory investment	270	£203	284	£245	298	£296	313	£357
h_j cash paid out		1,002		1,242		1,495		£1,855
$b_j - h_j$ periodic credit taken		201		7		50		61
$\Sigma(b_j - h_j)$ total credit taken		201		208		258		319
k_j = cash collected		848		1,257		1,583		2,002
$d_j - k_j$ periodic credit given		212		49		69		88
$\Sigma(d_j - k_j)$ total credit given		212		261		330		418
$n_j = k_j - h_j$ operating cash flow		-154		15		88		147
$p_j = (a_j - a_{j-1}) - (b_j - h_j) + (d_j - k_j) = e_j - n_j$ *periodic working capital investment*		214		84		70		88
$\Sigma p_j = a_j + \Sigma\{(d_j - k_j) - (b_j - h_j)\}$ *total working capital investment*		214		298		368		456

Assumptions
i. Costs increase at 15% p.a.
ii. Unit selling prices for periods 1, 2, 3 and 4 are £1.06, £1.187, £1,365 and £1.57 respectively as in Table 5.
iii. See Table 6, assumptions ii, iii and iv.
† Before depreciation.

The corresponding relationships in Table 8 are:

$$e_2/n_3 = 72/28 = 2.571$$

and

$$e_3/n_4 = 90/35 = 2.571$$

In other words, other things being equal, the lower the rate of profit, $e_j/(a_{j-1}+b_j-a_j)$, on the cost of sales, the higher is the multiple by which the previous period's pre-depreciation profit, e_{j-1}, exceeds the current period's operating cash flow, n_j.

TABLE 7A. CREDIT GIVEN AND TAKEN: COST AND SELLING PRICE INCREASES COMBINED WITH OUTPUT, INVENTORY, AND SALES VOLUME GROWTH (POSITIVE PROFITS AND NEGATIVE CASH FLOWS) 16

Period	1		2		3		4	
	units	£	units	£	units	£	units	£
a_{j-1} opening inventory	--	--	270	203	284	245	298	296
b_j [variable costs	1270	953	1114	961	1224	1214	1346	1535
fixed costs]		250		288		331		381
	1270	£1203	1384	£1452	1508	£1709	1644	£2212
a_j closing inventory	270	203	284	245	298	296	313	357
$c_j = a_{j-1} + b_j - a_j$ cost of sales	1000	£1000	1100	£1207	1210	£1494	1331	£1855
d_j sales invoiced	1000	£1030	1100	£1243	1210	£1539	1331	1911
$e_j = d_j - c_j$ profit†	1000	£ 30	1100	£ 36	1210	£ 45	1331	£ 56
$a_j - a_{j-1} = b_j - c_j$ periodic inventory investment	270	£ 203	14	£ 42	14	£ 51	15	£ 61
a_j = total inventory investment	270	£ 203	284	£ 245	298	£ 296	3313	£ 357
h_j cash paid out		1002		1242		1495		1855
$b_j - h_j$ periodic credit taken		201		7		50		61
$\sum(b_j-h_j)$ total credit taken		201		208		258		319
k_j = cash collected		824		1200		1480		1837
$d_j - k_j$ periodic credit given		206		43		59		74
$\sum(d_j-k_j)$ total credit given		206		249		308		382
$n_j = k_j-h_j$ operating cash flow		-178		-42		-15		-18
$p_j = (a_j-a_{j-1}) - (b_j-h_j) + (d_j-k_j) = e_j-n_j$ periodic working capital investment		208		78		60		74
$\sum p_j = a_j + \sum\{(d_j-k_j) -(b_j-h_j)\}$ total working capital investment		208		286		346		420

Assumptions

i. Costs increase at 15% p.a.

ii. Unit selling prices for periods 1, 2, 3 and 4 are £1.03, £1.13, £1.272 and £1.44 respectively.

iii. See Table 6, assumptions ii, iii and iv.

† Before depreciation.

TABLE 8. CREDIT GIVEN AND TAKEN: COST AND SELLING PRICE INCREASES COMBINED WITH OUTPUT, INVENTORY, AND SALES VOLUME GROWTH

Period	1		2		3		4	
	units	£	units	£	units	£	units	£
a_{j-1} opening inventory	—	—	270	203	284	245	298	296
b_j {variable costs	1,270	953	1,114	961	1,224	1,214	1,346	1,535
b_j {fixed costs		250		288		331		381
	1,270	£1,203	1,384	£1,452	1,508	£1,790	1,644	£2,212
a_j closing inventory	270	203	284	245	298	296	313	357
$c_j = a_{j-1} + b_j - a_j$ cost of sales	1,000	£1,000	1,100	£1,207	1,210	£1,494	1,331	£1,855
d_j sales invoiced	1,000	1,060	1,100	1,279	1,210	1,584	1,331	1,966
$e_j = d_j - c_j$ profit†	1,000	£60	1,100	£72	1,210	£90	1,331	£111
$a_j - a_{j-1} = b_j - c_j$ periodic inventory investment	270	£203	14	£42	14	£51	15	£61
a_j = total inventory investment	270	£203	284	£245	298	£296	313	£357
h_j cash paid out		1,002		1,242		1,495		1,855
$b_j - h_j$ periodic credit taken		201		7		50		61
$\Sigma(b_j - h_j)$ total credit taken		201		208		258		319
k_j = cash collected		848		1,235		1,523		1,890
$d_j - k_j$ periodic credit given		212		44		61		76
$\Sigma(d_j - k_j)$ total credit given		212		256		317		393
$n_j = k_j - h_j$ operating cash flow		−154		−7		28		35
$p_j = (a_j - a_{j-1}) - (b_j - h_j) + (d_j - k_j) = e_j - n_j$ *periodic working capital investment*		214		79		62		76
$\Sigma p_j = a_j + \Sigma\{(d_j - k_j) - (b_j - h_j)\}$ *total working capital investment*		214		293		355		431

Assumptions
i. Profit constitutes 6 per cent of the cost of sales.
ii. Other assumptions as in Table 7.
† Before depreciation.

If corporation tax is assessed on a preceding year basis on pre-depreciation profit, e_j, (less tax depreciation allowances)[7] an excess of e_{j-1} over n_j will clearly exert an upward leverage on the effective rate of tax on cash flow earnings, ETR_j. This point is readily illustrated by imposing a tax at the rate of 35 percent on e_2 and e_3 in Tables 7 and 8 respectively. The results are shown in Tables 9 and 10. (Assumed capital expenditure and the tax depreciation allowances thereon are as indicated in the tables).

The tax rate leverage effect in Tables 9 and 10 expressed in terms of effective tax rates, ETR_j, is given by:

TABLE 9. THE IMPACT OF TAXATION AND CAPITAL ALLOWANCES ON TABLE 7

Period	2		3		4	
	£		£		£	
e_j profit (before depreciation)	99		158		235	
$A_j + R_j$ capital expenditure	20		22		24	
$e_j - (A_j + R_j)$ pre-depreciation profit minus capital expenditure	79		136		211	
t_{j+1} tax charged† @ 35% on $e_j - 0.67(A_j + R_j)$	30	(38%)	50	(37%)	77	(36%)
$e_j - (A_j + R_j) - t_{j+1}$ profit after tax and capital expenditure	49		86		134	
n_j operating cash flow			88		147	
$A_j + R_j$ capital expenditure			22		24	
$n_j - (A_j + R_j)$ pre-tax cash flow earnings			66		123	
t_j tax paid			30		50	
$n_j - (A_j + R_j) - t_j$ post-tax cash flow earnings			36		73	
$t_j/n_j - A_j - R_j)$ effective tax rate, ETR_j			45%		41%	

TABLE 10. THE IMPACT OF TAXATION AND CAPITAL ALLOWANCES ON TABLE 8

Period	2		3		4	
	£		£		£	
e_j profit (before depreciation)	72		90		111	
$A_j + R_j$ capital expenditure	20		22		24	
$e_j - (A_j + R_j)$ pre-depreciation profit minus capital expenditure	52		68		87	
t_{j+1} tax charged† @ 35% on $e_j - 0.67(A_j + R_j)$	21	(40%)	26	(38%)	33	(38%)
$e_j - (A_j + R_j) - t_{j+1}$ profit after tax and capital expenditure	31		42		54	
n_j operating cash flow			28		35	
$A_j + R_j$ capital expenditure			22		24	
$n_j - (A_j + R_j)$ pre-tax cash flow earnings			6		11	
t_j tax paid			21		26	
$n_j - (A_j + R_j) - t_j$ post-tax cash flow earnings			−15		−15	
$t_j/n_j - A_j - R_j)$ effective tax rate, ETR_j			350%		236%	

$$ETR_j = \left[\frac{e_{j-1} - 0.67(A_{j-1} + R_{j-1})}{n_j - (A_j + R_j)}\right] 0.35$$

Thus, in the case of Table 9,

$$ETR_3 = \left[\frac{99 - (0.67)(20)}{88 - 22}\right] 0.35 = 0.45 \text{ (i.e., 45 percent)}$$

and

$$ETR_4 = \left[\frac{158 - (0.67)(22)}{147 - 24}\right] 0.35 = 0.41 \text{ (i.e., 41 percent)}$$

The effective tax rates, ETR_3 and ETR_4, in Table 10 of 350 percent and 236 percent respectively, are calculated in the same way.

The above analysis suggests that when the level of periodic working capital investment is such that the deviation between $e_{j-1} - 0.67(A_{j-1} + R_{j-1})$ and $n_j - (A_j + R_j)$, is relatively low, the time lag between the charging and payment of tax may prevent significant upward leverage on the effective tax rate, $t_j/(n_j - A_j - R_j)$. When periodic working capital expenditure is relatively high (in the sense just mentioned), the delay in the payment of taxes may not prevent the effective tax rate being levered to confiscatory levels as illustrated in Table 10.

The foregoing discussion thus provides some indication of the safeguards that need to be built into any corporate tax system to preclude positive (and negative) leverage on the effective tax rate on cash flow earnings in order, thereby, to obviate the direct threat to corporate financial viability posed by the basis of taxation alone. These include the requirements that all periodic working capital expenditure, p_j, and all capital expenditure, $A_j + R_j$, not merely some proportion thereof, should be allowed as tax deductible expenses.[9] In these circumstances, a preceding year basis of taxation could only constitute a necessary condition for upward tax rate leverage in a situation in which last year's cash flow earnings, $n_{j-1} - (A_{j-1} + R_{j-1})$, exceed the current year's cash flow earnings, $n_j - (A_j + R_j)$. Such an excess may be caused by $n_{j-1} > n_j$ and/or $A_{j-1} + R_{j-1} < A_j + R_j$. Since the latter conditions may persist over a long sequence of periods, a complete safeguard against upward tax leverage is clearly a current year basis of taxation and the measurement of taxable capacity on a cash flow basis. This also implies that, in periods in which firms generate negative cash flow earnings, they should receive tax rebates. Otherwise, the tendency for relatively high cash flow earnings to be associated with relatively low tax payments and vice versa cannot be precluded. Such negative correlation increases the volatility of post-tax cash flow earnings, i.e., increases their characteristic degrees of risk.[10] It should also be stated that a neutral corporate tax system does not allow debt interest to be treated as a tax-deductible expense.

Unfortunately, neither the previous, nor present, U.K. corporate tax regimes satisfy the above neutrality conditions. Both systems therefore, discriminate across companies, and over time, and do not preclude corporate fiscal drag which may rise to confiscatory levels.

The practical significance of the foregoing propositions is very dramatically emphasised by the post-war financial history of U.K. quoted companies. As the record clearly shows, the effective incidence of taxation has, throughout most of this period, been very much higher than that suggested by the tax charges disclosed in their published accounts. The dispersion of effective tax rates about the average has, for reasons illustrated in this paper, also been very significant. In other words, the legislator's failure to allow fully for the cost of working capital as a tax-deductible expense has contributed to corporate fiscal drag in a most inconsistent manner across public-quoted companies. The evidence also implies that unquoted companies will have suffered in precisely the same way.[11]

It is therefore, difficult to avoid the inference that the corporate tax changes that were introduced by the Finance Act 1984 are underpinned neither with a rigorous economic analysis nor assessment of the evidence.

6. Differences in the terms of trade credit

Having considered the separate and combined effects of relative price changes, varying profit margins and sales volume growth on working capital investment given the terms of trade credit, the significance of the latter should also be examined.

Any sample of published company accounts is likely to reveal quite significant variations in the relative amounts credit given and taken both across

TABLE 11. CREDIT GIVEN AND TAKEN: COST AND SELLING PRICE INCREASES COMBINED WITH OUTPUT, INVENTORY, AND SALES VOLUME GROWTH

Period	1		2		3		4	
	units	£	units	£	units	£	units	£
a_{j-1} opening inventory	—	—	270	203	284	245	298	296
b_j {variable costs	1,270	953	1,114	961	1,224	1,214	1,346	1,535
b_j {fixed costs		250		288		331		381
	1,270	£1,203	1,384	£1,452	1,508	1,790	1,644	2,212
a_j closing inventory	270	203	284	245	298	296	313	357
$c_j = a_{j-1} + b_j - a_j$ cost of sales	1,000	£1,000	1,100	£1,207	1,210	£1,494	1,331	£1,855
d_j sales invoiced	1,000	1,060	1,100	1,279	1,210	1,584	1,331	1,966
$e_j = d_j - c_j$ profit†	1,000	£60	1,100	£72	1,210	£90	1,331	£111
$a_j - a_{j-1} = b_j - c_j$ periodic inventory investment	270	£203	14	£42	14	£51	15	£61
a_j = total inventory investment	270	£203	284	£245	298	£296	313	£357
h_j cash paid out		1,103		1,245		1,520		1,885
$b_j - h_j$ periodic credit taken		100		4		25		31
$\Sigma(b_j - h_j)$ total credit taken		100		104		129		160
k_j = cash collected		954		1,257		1,554		1,927
$d_j - k_j$ periodic credit given		106		22		30		39
$\Sigma(d_j - k_j)$ total credit given		106		128		158		197
$n_j = k_j - h_j$ operating cash flow		−149		12		34		42
$p_j = (a_j - a_{j-1}) - (b_j - h_j) + (d_j - k_j) = e_j - n_j$ *periodic working capital investment*		209		60		56		69
$\Sigma p_j = a_j + \Sigma\{(d_j - k_j) - (b_j - h_j)\}$ *total working capital investment*		209		269		325		394

Assumptions

i. Total credit taken constitutes $\frac{1}{12}$ of periodic costs, that is, $\Sigma(b_j - h_j) = \frac{1}{12}\, b_j$.
ii. Total credit given constitutes 10 per cent of periodic sales, that is, $\Sigma(d_j - k_j) = 0.1\, d_j$.
iii. Other assumptions as in Table 8.
† Before depreciation.

and within different industries. Some companies are, in varying degrees, persistent net credit takers (as in certain branches of the retail trade), others are net credit givers whilst, taking one year with another, many companies succeed in balancing credit given against credit taken. In short, there is quite considerable dispersion about the (weighted) average relative magnitudes that are revealed in aggregate statistics. Moreover, in the case of U.K. listed companies, the pattern of trade credit has changed quite dramatically over the last two or more decades.

Aside from credit taken (1/12 of periodic cost, b_j, compared with 1/6 in Table 8) and credit given (10 percent of d_j, as opposed to 20 percent in Table 8), Table 11 reflects all the other assumptions which underlie Table 8. A comparison of these two tables suggests that two companies which, aside from the terms of trade credit they give and take, are in every other respect identical, will always show the same historic cost (pre-depreciation) profit, e_j. However, the operating cash flow, n_j, of the one company, and therefore, the size of its proprietor cash flow stream will, if Table 8 and 11-type assumptions persist, always be lower than the operating cash flow and proprietor cash flow stream of the other. Hence, the value of the first company must be lower than the value of the second. This situation is the familiar indictment of the historic cost accounting model which, in the comparison just postulated, fails to satisfy a simple test of common sense.

7. The cost of working capital

The failure on the part of the historic cost accounting method to satisfy a common sense criterion stems from the fact that this, and indeed other, accounting models, do not take cognisance of the cost of all invested working capital. To correct the historic cost profit & loss account in respect of this omission, the cost of working capital can be calculated in either of two ways which, economically speaking, are formally equivalent. Either, interest should be calculated on total working capital invested throughout an entire accounting period at the cost of capital to the enterprise in question,[12] or periodic working capital investment, p_j, should be treated as a periodic cost.[13] In either event, an adjustment is made to the profit and loss account.

The effect of the first alternative can be illustrated by assuming that the cost of working capital to two companies, represented by Tables 8 and 11

TABLE 12. ADJUSTMENT OF TABLE 8 FOR THE COST OF WORKING CAPITAL

Period	1	2	3	4
	£	£	£	£
$e_j = d_j - c_j$ profit (before depreciation)	60	72	90	111
less cost of working capital (see note i)	0	43	59	79
adjusted pre-depreciation profit (see note ii)	60	29	31	40

Notes to Tables 12 and 13

i. Cost of working capital $= r\sum p_{j-1}$ where $r = 0.2$.

ii. Adjusted profit $= e_j - r\sum p_{j-1}$

TABLE 13. ADJUSTMENT OF TABLE 11 FOR THE COST OF WORKING CAPITAL

Period	1	2	3	4
	£	£	£	£
$e_j = d_j - c_j$ profit (before depreciation)	60	72	90	111
less cost of working capital (see note i)	0	42	54	65
adjusted pre-depreciation profit (see note ii)	60	30	36	46

is (say) 20 percent per annum in money terms. The respective e_j lines would be adjusted as in Tables 12 and 13.

After Tables 8 and 11 have been corrected in respect of the omitted cost of working capital (as shown in Tables 12 and 13) the respective sequences of profits provide an interfirm comparison which is consistent with what is known to exist, namely, a difference between the respective values of the two enterprises.

Note that the adjusted profits, $e_j - r\sum p_{j-1}$, in Tables 12 and 13 do not coincide with the respective operating cash flows shown in Tables 8 and 11 as would be the case were periodic working capital investment, p_j, to be taken as the cost of working capital. However, the present values of the adjusted profits illustrated by Tables 12 and 13 will coincide with the present value fo the corresponding operating cash flows over the entire life of a business. In other words,

$$\sum_{j=1}^{w} e_j - r\sum_{j=0}^{w} p_{j-1}\,(1+r)^{-j} = \sum_{j=1}^{w} n_j(1+r)^{-j},$$

where, r is the cost of capital which, for convenience, is here assumed to be constant, and w is the (finite) life of the business in question.

It is important to emphasise that the cost of working capital should be allowed for regardless of the manner in which a company is financed. A company's capital structure determines the division of entity income between lenders and shareholders - information that should be reported in the appropriation section of the profit and loss account rather than in the operating account itself.

8. Conclusion

An analysis of the mechanics and determinants of periodic working capital investment, p_j, is essentially concerned with the relationship between pre-depreciation historic cost profit, e_j, and operating cash flow, n_j. Stated in greater detail, this relationship is:

$$p_j \equiv [d_j - (a_{j-1} + b_j - a_j)] - (k_j - h_j)$$

As the illustrations in this paper have shown, periodic working capital investment, p_j, is a function of a number of different variables:

changes in inventory, output and sales volume,

selling price changes,

cost changes,

the period of credit given to customers,

the period of credit taken from suppliers, and

the rate of profit expressed as a percentage of the cost of sales.

As a function of an array of such different variables as these, it is clearly naive to assume that the relative magnitude of p_j, that is

$p_j/[d_j - (a_{j-1} + b_j - a_j)]$, is the same, or similar for firms in general or for the same firm over time. Hence, profit measured in accordance with the historic cost accounting model (which ignores the cost of working capital) is neither an admissible index for intercompany comparisons nor, even in the absence of inflation, for inter-period comparisons. The historic cost accounting model ought not, therefore, to be used as a multiperiod valuation framework since, aside from the inaccuracy that pervades all estimates, that model is characterised by an inherent measurement error which behaves perversely.

Given the affinities between multiperiod valuation analysis and wealth maximisation, it also follows that the historic cost accounting model is not a valid planning framework for a wealth maximising firm.

The seriously debilitating and potentially perverse economic consequences of taxable earnings which ignore the cost of working capital should disqualify all such measures for tax purposes.

It may also be suggested, though this is possibly a subject for a separate paper, that any accounting model that fails fully to give effect to the cost of working capital, or perhaps more precisely, only partially allows for the cost of working capital, is more or less deficient in the respects elaborated above.

Finally, it should perhaps be repeated that the notion of efficient working capital management is essentially relative to a firm's corporate financial objective. A wealth-maximising firm should plan on a cash flow basis and, having chosen a plan which seems to maximise the present value of expected entity cash flows, its level of working capital investment is, given the periods of credit given and taken, to and from customers and suppliers, a dependent variable. As already emphasised, this does not mean that the level of invested working capital can be left to take care of itself. One of the essential features of any plan is its role as a basis for positive managerial action in the form of financial control. Working capital investment is no exception to this notion.

Notes

[1]It is not difficult to show that the inclusion of the cost of working capital in the (historic cost) profit & loss account is one of the two correctives that are necessary to convert that statement into a cash flow earnings statement or a statement which is mathematically equivalent to a cash flow statement. See Lawson and Stark (1975).

[2]See The Economist (January 22, 1977).

[3]In Table 6, sales volume increases at an annual rate of 10 percent whilst the physical inventory level is assumed to increase at an annual rate of 5 percent. The latter rate is also used in Tables 7, 7A 8 and 11, and is derived from the economic order quantity, EOQ, given by:

$$EOQ = \sqrt{\frac{2AD}{rC}}$$

Where A is the cost of placing an order, D, annual sales volume, r, cost of capital and C, unit variable cost.

[4]This possibility is illustrated by Table 7A.

[5]See Schweitzer, Trossmann and Lawson (1991), pp. 256-277.

[6]In all of the Tables in this paper the situation 'stabilises' in terms of profit, e_j, from the outset. The first two periods are characterised by start-up influences which are reflected in the cash flows of those periods. For this reason, this comparison utilises the cash flows of periods 3 and 4 only.

[7]This is basically the corporate tax regime reintroduced by the Finance Act 1984. The following section is intended to show briefly the major shortcomings of such a regime and to identify the respects in which it violates the classic principle of tax neutrality.

[8]Note to Tables 9 and 10. The assumed tax depreciation allowance, 0.67 $(A_j + R_j)$, represents the present value, PVA, of a reducing balance sequence of annual allowances (delayed one year) expressed as a percentage of the present value, PV, of a 100 percent write-off delayed one year. Thus, PVA is given by:

$$PVA = \frac{\alpha A}{1+r} + \frac{\alpha A(1-\alpha)}{(1+r)^2} + \frac{\alpha A(1-\alpha)^2}{(1+r)^3} + \ldots \text{ ad inf.}$$

$$= \frac{\alpha A}{r+\alpha}$$

whereas,

$$PV = \frac{A}{1+r}$$

where,

A is eligible capital expenditure,
α stands for the rate of annual allowance,
r represents a discount rate expressed in money terms and given by $r = i + (r_m - i)\beta$,
i denotes the risk free interest rate expressed in money terms,
$(r_m - i)$ is the excess return on the market portfolio, and
β denotes the market risk of the firm in question.

Putting $\alpha = 0.25$ and $r = 0.2$ (i.e., $i = 0.11$, $r_m - i = 0.09$ and $\beta = 1$ (average market risk))

$$\frac{\alpha A}{r + \alpha} / \frac{A}{1 + r} = \frac{0.25}{0.45} / \frac{1}{1.2} = 0.67$$

[9]Otherwise the corporate tax system will discriminate against working capital intensive companies, e.g., companies in manufacturing industries.

[10]This line of argument is pursued further in Lawson (1979).

[11]See Lawson (1980), (1981) and Lawson and Stark (1981). For a comparison with American and German companies see Lawson, Möller and Sherer (1982).

[12]Using this method, the cost of working capital may be approximated (as in Table 12) by calculating interest on the total working capital deployed at the beginning of the individual period in question.

[13]If this second alternative is adopted, e_j is converted to n_j. This measure of financial performance immediately reflects the difference between the respective values of the two enterprises. The economic rationale for the proposition that periodic working capital investment, p_j, constitutes the periodic cost of invested working capital is discussed in Lawson and Stark (1975).

References

The Economist, 22nd January 1977.

Inflation Accounting Committee, Report Cmnd 6225, H.M.S.O., September 1975.

Lawson, G. H. Company profitability and the U.K. stock market - an exercise in cash flow accounting, Manchester Business School Research Report, March 1979.

__________, "The measurement of corporate profitability on a cash flow basis," International Journal of Accounting Education and Research, Fall, 1980.

__________, "The cash flow performance of U.K. companies: Case studies in cash flow accounting, in Essays in British Accounting Research (eds. Bromwich and Hopwood), Pitman, 1981.

Lawson, G. H., Möller, P. and Sherer, M., "On the use of conventional accounting statements in the measurement of corporate debt capacity, taxable earnings and the formulation of dividend policies," published in German in Lück and Trommsdorff (eds.) Internationalisierung der Unternehmung, Erich Schmidt Verlag, Berlin 1982.

Lawson, G. H. and Stark, A. W., "The concept of profit for fund-raising," Accounting and Business Research, Winter 1975.

__________, "Equity values and inflation: dividends and debt financing," Lloyds Bank Review, No. 138, January, 1981.

Schweitzer, M., Trossmann, E. and Lawson, G. H., Break-even analyses: Basic Model, Variants, Extensions, John Wiley & Sons, 1991, pp. 256-277.

Zones Ltd

GERALD H. LAWSON, Manchester Business School and Southern Methodist University, Texas

The traditional approach to breakeven analysis can be described as: the determination of the level of output for some forthcoming period, typically one year, at which, using its existing scale of productive capacity, a firm breaks even in the historic-cost (accruals) accounting sense of the expression. As is now widely appreciated, accruals measures of costs and revenues generally deviate from their cash flow counterparts and usually, though not always, profit measured on an accruals basis exceeds earnings measured on a cash flow basis.

Given such a characteristic deviation, it may be tempting to assume that the level of output at which a company breaks even in a cash flow sense will usually be higher than that determined by reference to accruals measures of costs and revenue. If so, a firm is not self-financing at the 'accruals' breakeven level of output and, unless it has continuous access to an external source of finance, such a firm cannot assume that continuous attainment of the conventional accruals breakeven level of output will ensure its continuing existence as a going concern.

In the following case, the characteristics of the cash flows of Zones Ltd are such that the breakeven point determined by the initially proposed cash flow model is highly sensitive to Zones Ltd's working capital position. An alternative breakeven cash model is proposed. It is tentatively concluded that, at least in the case of Zones Ltd, the single-period approach to breakeven analysis is not reliable and that breakeven considerations need to be examined in the context of a multiperiod financial model that is capable of generating sequences of projected income, cash flow and balance sheet statements. Such a model can analyse the financial implications of alternative revenue and cost structure sequences. Examples of such sequences are included in the questions which follow the concluding section of the case.

Initial Financial Position

The balance sheet of Zones Ltd on 31 December 1984 was as shown in Exhibit 1. Other financial data include the following:

Exhibit 1 *Balance Sheet (as at 31.12.84)*

	£
Fixed Assets	
Tangible assets	123,113
Participation	43,200
	166,313
Current Assets	
Petty cash	166
Intergroup debtors	35,623
Trade debtors	630,698
Bank	20,011
	686,498
	852,811
Capital and Reserves	
Share capital	10,000
Retained earnings:	
Last year	15,504
This year	18,953
	44,457
Provisions for Taxes	16,622
Current Liabilities	
Banks	292,802
Intergroup creditors	234,302
Trade creditos	62,879
Payroll creditors	201,749
	791,732
	852,811

(i) the level of fixed costs expected in the year to 31 December 1985 is £325,000;

(ii) bank overdraft interest is to be calculated at the rate of 13 per cent p.a.;

(iii) customers receive three months' credit, i.e. outstanding debtors constitute 25 per cent of the previous year's sales;

(iv) Zones Ltd obtains an average credit period of 36.4 days in respect of both fixed and variable costs, i.e. outstanding trade creditors constitute 10 per cent of the previous year's fixed costs and outstanding payroll creditors constitute 10 per cent of the previous year's variable costs.

Traditional Breakeven versus Cash Flow Breakeven

Traditional Breakeven Approach

The traditional approach to breakeven analysis is based upon the conventional historic cost accounting measure of profit, HCP_j, which, in the case of Zones Ltd is given by:

$$\begin{aligned} HCP_j &= d_j - 0.85d_j - FC_j - Int_j \\ &= 0.15d_j - FC_j - Int_j \end{aligned} \tag{1}$$

where d_j denotes turnover in year j;
$0.85d_j$ stands for variable cost in year j;
$0.15d_j$ represents the total contribution on sales d_j in year j;
FC_j denotes fixed costs in year j;
Int_j represents interest payable in year j and reflects the year's average borrowing level.

Adopting the conventional breakeven approach, the breakeven level of turnover is the value of $d_j^{(BE)}$ which satisfies the equation:

$$0 = d_j^{(BE)}(1-0.85) - FC_j - Int_j$$

whence

$$d_j^{(BE)} = \frac{FC_j + Int_j}{0.15} \tag{2}$$

Putting FC_j = £0.325 m and Int_j = (0.13) £0.3 m:

$$\begin{aligned} d_j^{(BE)} &= \frac{0.325+0.039}{0.15} \\ &= £2.427 \text{ m} \end{aligned}$$

Cash Flow Breakeven Approach

The breakeven level of sales signalled by equation (2) does not allow for the period of credit given to customers nor for the period of credit taken from suppliers. It does not therefore indicate the annual level of turnover at which the company is self-financing, i.e. just generating enough cash to meet its payments in any individual year. Thus, the net amount of cash, CFE_j, generated in year j is given by:

$$CFE_j = \{\phi d_{j-1} + (1-\phi)d_j\}$$

$$- \gamma(0.85d_{j-1}+FC_{j-1})-(1-\gamma)(0.85d_j+FC_j) - Int_j \qquad (3)$$

where ϕ stands for the period of credit given to customers, expressed as a percentage of the previous year's sales, e.g. 3 months' credit = 0.25;

γ denotes the period of credit taken in respect of variable and fixed costs e.g. γ=0.1 denotes an average period of credit taken of 36.4 days.

To illustrate equation (3) in a little more detail, put ϕ=0.25, therefore $1-\phi$=0.75. In other words, the cash collected in any individual year j is represented by 25 per cent of the previous year's sales, d_{j-1}, and 75 per cent of the current year's sales d_j. Similarly, if γ=0.1, the amount of cash paid in respect of costs in any year j is equal to 10 per cent of the previous year's costs, $0.85d_{j-1}+FC_{j-1}$, and 90 per cent of the current year's costs, $0.85d_j+FC_j$.

Note, however, that if the previous financial year-end balance sheet (balance sheet for end-year $j-1$) is already available, the debtors shown therein should be substituted for ϕd_{j-1}; and, end-year $j-1$ creditors should be substituted for $\gamma 0.85d_{j-1}$ (payroll) and γFC_{j-1} (trade).

Using equation (3) to determine the cash flow breakeven level of turnover, it is necessary to determine the value of $dj^{(CBE)}$ which satisfies the equation:

$$0 = \phi d_{j-1} + (1-\phi)d_j^{(CBE)} - \gamma(0.85d_{j-1}+FC_{j-1}) - (1-\gamma)\,[0.85d_j^{(CBE)}+FC_j] - Int_j$$

whence

$$dj^{(CBE)} = \frac{\gamma FC_{j-1}+(1-\gamma)FC_j+Int_j-d_{j-1}(\phi-\gamma 0.85)}{(1-\phi) - (1-\gamma)\,0.85} \qquad (4)$$

Putting γ = 0.1, ϕ = 0.25, ϕFC_{j-1} = £62,879 (trade creditors), FC_j = £325,000, Int_j = £39,000†, ϕd_{j-1} = £630,698 (trade debtors), and $\gamma 0.85d_{j-1}$ = £201,749 (payroll creditors),

$$d_j^{(CBE)} = \frac{62{,}879+(0.9)(325{,}000)+39{,}000-630{,}698+201{,}749}{0.75 - 0.765}$$

$$= \frac{-34{,}570}{-0.015} = £2{,}304{,}667$$

† Interest can be based on the opening bank overdraft, i.e. 0.13 × £300,000, because at the breakeven level of cash flow the overdraft would be constant.

It should be noted that if the periods of credit given (ϕ) and taken (γ) are constant, the value of the cash flow breakeven level of sales, $d_j^{(CBE)}$, defined by equation (4) is highly sensitive to the value of the numerator on the right-hand side of that expression. Farthermore, the relationship between the periods of credit given ($\phi=0.25$) and taken ($\gamma=0.1$) and the variable cost of sales ($=0.85d_j$) is such that equation (4) produces results which at first sight appear to be counterintuitive.

For example, if instead of taking trade debtors on 31 December 1984 as £630,698 they are approximated as

$$\phi d_{j-1} = (0.25)\ £2,824,904 = £706,226$$

namely 25 per cent of 1984 turnover, the cash flow breakeven sales level, $d_j^{(CBE)}$, would have been given by:

$$d_j^{(CBE)} = \frac{-34,570-(706,226 - 630,698)}{-0.015}$$

$$= £7,339,867$$

The apparent paradox that the breakeven level of sales is higher, the higher the level of opening debtors is readily explained. Thus, substituting the *alternative* levels of opening debtors just considered (£630,698 and £706,226) and the corresponding cash flow breakeven levels of sales (£2,304,667 and £7,339,867) into equation (3) (treating cash paid to creditors, overhead payments and interest as a constant), we obtain:

cash from debtors	+	cash from current year's sales	−	cash paid to creditors

(*i*) $CFE_j = 630,698 + (0.75)(2,304,667) - 201,749 - 62,879$

— payroll payments — overhead payments — interest

$- (0.9)(0.85)(2,304,667) - (0.9)(325,000) - 39,000$

$= 630,698 + 2,304,667\ (0.75 - 0.765) - \lambda$

$= 596,128 - \lambda$

(*ii*) $CFE_j = 706,226 + 7,339,861\ (0.75-0.765) - \lambda$

$= 596,128 - \lambda$

Comparing (*i*) and (*ii*) we see that in any *individual* year every £1 of sales actually contributes a negative amount of cash, namely 0.75−0.765 =

0.015.[†] Hence, at the higher level of opening debtors, higher sales are necessary to generate a higher absolute *negative* cash contribution from sales.

The main feature of equation (4) that needs to be emphasised is that it lacks robustness, i.e. it contains three parameter values, namely ϕ, γ and 0.85, which make the value of $d_j^{(CBE)}$ highly sensitive to the values of FC_{j-1} and d_{j-1}, which in turn determine the opening creditors and opening debtors. The latter values must therefore be chosen with great care in using equation (4) to determine breakeven and target sales levels.

An Alternative Cash Flow Approach

Because equation (3) is highly sensitive to the absolute values of opening debtors and creditors, i.e. opening working capital, it is arguable that the cash flow breakeven level of turnover should be computed on a modified basis. Thus, the opening working capital position mainly reflects the level of turnover that was achieved in the previous period, whereas the essence of a periodic cash flow breakeven approach is that it is, or should be, concerned with the level of turnover that needs to be achieved in the forthcoming period to cover the cash outlays associated therewith.

However, to the extent that the forthcoming level of turnover exceeds the previous year's turnover, *additional* working capital investment in debtors, which has an opportunity cost, will become necessary. This cost will be offset to a greater or lesser extent by the negative opportunity cost of the associated increases in trade and payroll creditors. Additionally, the fixed capital and working capital deployed at the beginning of any financial year has an opportunity cost which should be taken into account separately from the opportunity cost of *changes* in the level of working and other capital.

Adopting this alternative approach, a second cash flow equation, CFE_j^*, can be formulated as follows. In any year j, accrued sales d_j have an average

† This can be demonstrated mathematically by simplifying equation (3) and putting $\phi=0.25$ and $\gamma=0.1$. Thus:

$$CFE_j=\phi d_{j-1}+d_j-\phi d_j-\gamma 0.85d_{j-1}-\gamma FC_{j-1}-0.85d_j+\gamma 0.85d_j$$
$$-\ FC_j+\gamma FC_j-Int_j$$
$$=d_{j-1}(\phi-\gamma 0.85)+d_j(1-\phi-0.85+\gamma 0.85)-\gamma FC_{j-1}(1-\gamma)-\gamma FC_{j-1}-Int_j$$

Putting $\phi = 0.25$ and $\gamma = 0.1$ then

$$CFE_j = 0.165d_{j-1}-0.015d_j-0.1FC_{j-1}-0.9FC_j-Int_j$$

The term $0.165d_{j-1}$ represents trade debtors *minus* payroll creditors at end-year $j-1$; and $0.1FC_{j-1}$ represents trade creditors on the same date.

Exhibit 2

	31.12.84 (£)
Total assets	852,811
Less Provision for taxes	16,622
Intergroup creditors	234,302
Trade creditors	62,879
Payroll creditors	201,749
	337,259
Financed by:	
Capital and reserves	44,457
Bank loans	292,802
	337,259

due date which, if a company is giving its customers three months' credit, is nine months after the beginning of year j. The cash value of those sales k^*_{j-1} at end-year $j-1$ is therefore given by:

$$k^*_{j-1} = \frac{d_j}{(1+r)^{9/12}} \tag{5}$$

Similarly, the cash value of the company's costs, h^*_{j-1}, is (assuming average credit taken of 36.4 days, and therefore an average due date of 36.4 + 364/2 = 218.4 days from the beginning of the year (=0.6 of a year)) given by:

$$h^*_{j-1} = \frac{0.85d_j + FC_j}{(1+r)^{0.6}} \tag{6}$$

The capital employed at the beginning of the 1985 financial year in the case of Zones Ltd is represented by the figures given in Exhibit 2.

The opportunity cost of using this capital in the forthcoming year can be expressed as the notional interest thereon payable one year hence, namely $r337{,}259$.[†] This notional interest payment has a present value, PVI_{j-1}, at end-year $j-1$ given by:

$$PVI_j = \frac{r337{,}259}{1+r} \tag{7}$$

† This includes the interest on the bank overdraft.

The alternative cash flow equation can now be written as:

$$CFE_j^* = k_{j-1}^* - h_{j-1}^* - PVI_j$$

$$= \frac{d_j}{(1+r)^{0.75}} - \frac{0.85d_j + FC_j}{(1+r)^{0.6}} - \frac{r337,259}{1+r} \quad (8)$$

Using this formulation, the cash flow breakeven level of forthcoming turnover $d_j^{(CBE^*)}$ is therefore given by:

$$d_j\,(\mathrm{CBE}^*) = \frac{\dfrac{FC_j}{(1+r)^{0.6}} + \dfrac{r337,259}{1+r}}{\dfrac{1}{(1+r)^{0.75}} - \dfrac{0.85}{(1+r)^{0.6}}} \quad (9)$$

Putting $FC_j = 325,000$ and $r = 0.2$ (i.e. a cost of capital of 20 per cent p.a. in money terms),

$$d_j(\mathrm{CBE}^*) = \frac{\dfrac{325,000}{(1.2)^{0.6}} + \dfrac{67,451.8}{1.2}}{\dfrac{1}{(1.2)^{0.75}} - \dfrac{0.85}{(1.2)^{0.6}}}$$

$$= \frac{291,323 + 56,210}{0.872196 - 0.7619}$$

$$= £3,150,912$$

The latter value compares with the £2,427 million generated by the conventional approach, i.e. equation (2).

It should be noted that the value of equation (9) is not highly sensitive to the opportunity cost of capital (the firm's cost of capital, r). Thus, if r is increased from 0.2 (i.e. 20 per cent) to 0.25, $d_j^{(CBE^*)}$ rises by about 4.8 per cent to £3,302,734. Similarly, if r is reduced to 0.15 (i.e. 15 per cent), $d_j^{(CBE^*)}$ falls by about 4.5 per cent to £3,007,912.

Plausibility of the Alternative Approach: Breakeven Turnover

The plausibility of the above (cash flow) breakeven turnover levels, $d_j^{(CBE^*)}$, can be tested by substituting them back into equations (1) and (3). In other words, we use $d_j^{(CBE^*)}$ to determine the profit and loss account, the cash flow statement and end-year balance sheet for 1985, using the notion of (cash flow) breakeven outlined in this alternative approach.

First substituting into equation (3) with $d_j^{(CBE*)}$ = £3,150,912:

$$\begin{aligned} CFE_j &= \{630{,}698+(0.75)(3{,}150{,}912)\} \\ &\quad - 201{,}749 - 62{,}879 - (0.765)(3{,}150{,}912) \\ &\quad - (0.9)(325{,}000) - Int_j \\ &= £26{,}306 - Int_j \\ &= -£12{,}694 \text{ (since } Int_j \text{ on the bank loan } = £39{,}000) \end{aligned}$$

Next substituting $d_j^{(CBE*)}$ = £3,150,912 into equation (1):

$$\begin{aligned} HCP_j &= (0.15)3{,}150{,}912 - 325{,}000 - 39{,}000 \\ &= £108{,}637 \end{aligned}$$

Turning to the end-year 1985 balance sheet, with $\phi=0.25$ and $\gamma=0.1$, end-year 1985 trade debtors, trade creditors and payroll creditors would be respectively: (0.25)(3,150,912)=787,728; (0.1)(325,000)=32,500; and (0.1)(0.85)(3,150,912)=267,828. The end-year 1985 balance sheet would, assuming no change in provisions for taxes, intergroup debtors and creditors, fixed assets, cash at bank and petty cash, therefore be as shown in Exhibit 3.

Plausibility of Turnover Levels Exceeding the Cash Flow Breakeven Turnover Level

Choosing some turnover level in excess of the breakeven turnover level $d_j^{(CBE*)}$ (=£3,150,912), say d_j=£5,000,000, and substituting in turn into equation (8) (with $r=0.2$), equation (3) and equation (1), we obtain:

$$CFE_j^* = 0.110276d_j - 0.8964FC_j - 0.167CE_{j-1}$$

(where CE_{j-1} denotes capital employed at the beginning of year j)

$$\begin{aligned} &= (0.110276)(5{,}000{,}000) - (0.8964)(325{,}000) - (0.167)(337{,}295) \\ &= £203{,}722 \end{aligned}$$

(The latter value measures the financial viability of a £5 million turnover in the current year.)

Next, putting d_j=£5 million in equation (3):

$$\begin{aligned} CFE_j &= \{630{,}698+(0.75)(5{,}000{,}000)\} \\ &\quad - 201{,}749-62{,}897 - (0.765)(5{,}000{,}000) \end{aligned}$$

Exhibit 3 *Breakeven Cash Flow: Projected Balance Sheet (as at 31.12.85)*

		£
Fixed Assets		166,313
Current Assets		
Petty cash		166
Intergroup debtors		35,623
Trade debtors		787,728
Bank		20,011
		£1,009,841
Capital and Reserves		
Opening balance	44,457	
Annual profit	108,637	153,094
Provisions for Taxes		16,622
Current Liabilities		
Banks: Opening	292,802	
Deficit	12,694	305,496
Intergroup creditors		234,302
Trade creditors		32,500
Payroll creditors		267,828
		£1,009,842

$$-(0.9)(325{,}000) - Int_j$$
$$= - £1{,}430 - Int_j$$
$$= - £40{,}340 \text{ (since } Int_j = £39{,}000)$$

Finally, putting d_j=£5 million in equation (1):

$$HCP_j = (0.15)(5{,}000{,}000) - 325{,}000 - 39{,}000$$
$$= £386{,}000$$

Turning to the end-year 1985 balance sheet, with $\phi=0.25$ and $\gamma=0.1$ end-year 1985 trade debtors, trade creditors and payroll creditors would be respectively: (0.25)(5,000,000)=1,250,000; (0.1)(325,000)=32,500; and (0.1)(0.85)(5,000,000)=425,000. The end-year 1985 balance sheet would, again assuming no change in provisions for taxes, intergroup debtors and creditors, fixed assets, cash at bank and petty cash, therefore be as shown in Exhibit 4.

Exhibit 4 *Sales of £5 million: Projected Balance Sheet (as at 31.12.85)*

		£
Fixed Assets		166,313
Current Assets		
Petty cash		166
Intergroup debtors		35,623
Trade debtors		1,250,000
Bank		20,011
		£1,472,113
Capital and Reserves		
Opening balance	44,457	
Annual profit	386,000	430,457
Provisions for Taxes		16,622
Current Liabilities		
Banks: Opening	292,802	
Deficit	40,430	333,232
Intergroup creditors		234,302
Trade creditors		32,500
Payroll creditors		425,000
		£1,472,113

Reconciliation of Apparent Conflict between Alternative Cash Flow Approaches

We can now reconcile the apparent conflict between the values given by CFE_j (equation (3)) and CFE_j^* (equation (8)). The former, i.e. CFE_j, is entirely concerned with the cash arising in an individual year, including the net amount received from opening debtors *minus* opening creditors. The latter, i.e. CFE_j^*, is concerned with the cash flow generated by periodic turnover, allowing for the fact that some of that cash arises in the following period. As described earlier, CFE_j^* also allows for the cost of capital employed. Hence, in order to observe the pure cash flow effects of a turnover level which seems healthy when judged against the CFE_j^* criterion, it is necessary to extend the analysis for at least a further year. But such an extension requires a further assumption, namely the turnover level in that second year. Perhaps the most neutral assumption is that the second year's turnover is the same as that of the previous year. However, many alternative turnover levels can be analysed, as can different assumptions about the rate of increase in costs. Moreover, to gain greater insights into the cash flow properties of the cost and revenue functions, the analysis should be extended over a number of periods.

To complete the comparison of CFE_j and CFE_j^* we therefore extend the previous example one further year, i.e. generate projections for 1986, assuming that turnover remains at £5 million and that costs remain constant in money terms. With $r=0.2$, $\phi=0.25$ and $\gamma=0.1$, CFE_j^* for 1986 would be:

$$CFE_j^*(1986) = (0.110276)(5{,}000{,}000) - (0.8964)(325{,}000) - (0.167)(763{,}689)^{\dagger}$$
$$= £132{,}514$$

The value of CFE_j for 1986 would exceed that of 1985. Thus:

$$CFE_j(1986) = \{1{,}250{,}000 + (0.75(5{,}000{,}000)\} - 425{,}000 - 32{,}500 - (0.765)(5{,}000{,}000) - (0.9)(325{,}000) - Int_j$$
$$= £425{,}000 - £15{,}698^{\dagger\dagger}$$
$$= £409{,}302$$

Conventional profit for 1986 would also be £409,302, namely:

$$HCP_j(1986) = (0.15)(5{,}000{,}000) - 325{,}000 - £15{,}698$$
$$= £409{,}302$$

Finally, the balance sheet at the end of 1986 would, on the foregoing assumptions, be as shown in Exhibit 5.

Conclusions

Three main inferences can be drawn from the foregoing analysis:

(1) The breakeven level of turnover for Zones Ltd is currently about £3.2 million. (If this is maintained for both 1985 and 1986, the bank overdraft would in fact be reduced to about £200,000 at the end of 1986. However, taxes would need to be provided for, which would probably restore the end-year 1986 overdraft to its end-year 1984 level of £292,802.)

† £763,689 is the value of capital employed on 31.12.85.

†† £15,698 represents interest at 13 per cent on an average bank overdraft of ½ (−£333,232+0) for 9.41 months and an average bank balance of ½ (0+£91,768) for 2.59 months.

Exhibit 5 *1986 Sales of £5 million: Projected Balance Sheet (as at 31.12.86)*

		£
Fixed Assets		166,313
Current Assets		
Petty cash		166
Intergroup debtors		35,623
Trade debtors		1,250,000
Bank		20,011
		£1,472,113
Capital and Reserves		
Opening balance	430,457	
Annual profit	409,302	839,759
Provisions for Taxes		16,622
Current Liabilities		
Banks: Opening	333,232	
Less Surplus	409,302	(76,070)
Intergroup creditors		234,302
Trade creditors		32,500
Payroll creditors		425,000
		£1,472,113

(2) The relationship between the periods of credit given and taken and gross margin has rather curious cash flow properties which need exploring in further detail. (This analysis requires a multiperiod framework and alternative assumptions about turnover levels, turnover growth rates, and rates of cost change.)

(3) If Zones Ltd can attain a turnover of about £5 million in both 1985 and 1986, it should enjoy a very healthy improvement in its cash flow generating capacity. At this level of activity, the bank overdraft would probably be eliminated, though some provision for corporation tax that would become payable on 1 October 1986 should be made.

Questions

1. Using the equations contained in the case you are required to build a mathematical model which will generate sequences of balance sheets, profit and loss accounts and two kinds of cash flow statement.

2. Examine the multiperiod turnover levels at which the company breaks even on accruals and cash flow bases respectively.
3. In addition to the various turnover levels that are considered in the case (in relation to one or more annual accounting periods), you are asked to explore the following:

   (a) sales of £5 million in 1985 coupled with sales of £4 million and £4.25 million in 1986 and 1987 respectively;
   (b) variable costs constituting 87.5 per cent of sales in 1985 and 90 per cent of sales in 1986 and 1987 respectively;
   (c) overhead costs (excluding depreciation and foreign exchange differences) of £382,000, £289,000 and £312,000 in 1985, 1986 and 1987 respectively;
   (d) a reduction in the period of credit given to customers from three months to two months in conjunction with the sales and variable costs mentioned in (a) and (b).

This case focuses upon and emphasizes, six aspects of break-even analysis, namely:

i. the conventional single-period approach to break-even analysis which uses cost and revenue variables that are measured on an accruals basis;

ii. a single-period approach to break-even analysis, in which the variables are measured on a cash-flow basis, that attempts to determine the level of turnover at which, for any given debt ratio that must be serviced, a firm is exactly self-financing;

iii. the deviation, and its determinants, between accruals-based and cash-flow based break-even points;

iv. the possibility that the properties of a firm's cash flow earnings, i.e., the relationship between the period of credit given to customers, the period of credit taken from suppliers (including employees) and the conventional profit mark-up, may not be robust enough to facilitate the calculation, on a direct cash flow basis, of reliable single period break-even turnover levels;

v. a modified, more robust, single period cash flow approach to break-even analysis;
and,

vi. the conclusion that, in the absence of a robust (unmodified) single-period break-even cash flow model, it is advisable to undertake a detailed exploration of a firm's financial future using a multiperiod model.

The full financial implications of break-even levels of activity can only be captured by projected sequences of profit and loss, cash flow and balance sheet statements which are part of the case requirement. (Note, however, that the modified cash flow break-even calculation is outside the double-entry accounting of the multiperiod outputs.)

The arrangement of the case is that each of the six aspects enumerated above can first be taught and discussed in turn. They can be integrated in a later part of the case discussion.

Once students have begun to entertain sufficient doubts about the single-period approach to break-even analysis, and come to realize that aspects of break-even analysis constitute one particular managerial use of multiperiod financial model, the question of managerial uses of such models can be raised at a more general level. Such uses are generally based on alternative financial and economic scenarios concerning (multiperiod):

a) expected inflation and expected relative price changes

b) expected interest rates and the "Fisher effect"

c) expected sales volume growth

d) existing capacity constraints and the creation of additional capacity as a function of c).

The case is intended to be completely self-contained, i.e., should not require reference to additional material, and contains a number of cues to stimulate class discussion. Most of these should become apparent on a first reading.

Whilst they are shorn mathematical complexity, experience suggests that the teacher will find it fruitful to explain each equation in turn and to illustrate each with numbers that are included in the text.

The firm in question is the (small) U.K. subsidiary of a foreign parent and is engaged in North Sea oil ancillary activities. All figures given in the case were taken directly from the subsidiary's internal accounting records.

Sonderdruck aus:

Eduard Gaugler/Hans Günther Meissner
Norbert Thom (Hrsg.)

Zukunftsaspekte der anwendungsorientierten Betriebswirtschaftslehre

Erwin Grochla
zum 65. Geburtstag gewidmet

C. E. Poeschel Verlag Stuttgart

239

*Gerald H. Lawson**

The Valuation of a Business as a Going Concern

CORRIGENDUM

Page 167, 2nd para., line 2: "rat" should be "rate"
Page 167, 3rd para., line 3: "depriciation" should be "depreciation"
Page 171, 2nd para., line 1: "qualification" should be "quantification"

* Prof. *Gerald H. Lawson*, Manchester Business School, Un:versity of Manchester.

A. Introduction

Most market economies are replete with going concern valuation problems. This includes economies which enjoy a stock market that is efficient in the sense of the semi-strong version of the efficient market model. No more than an extremely small sub-set of joint stock companies is quoted on the world's stock markets, many of which are anyway not believed to be efficient at impounding new information into security prices.

This paper is primarily concerned with some of the theoretical aspects of the valuation problem which appear to be gaining interest among Anglo-Saxon practitioners. It considers alternative bases of valuation on the one hand and aspects of valuation accounting methodology on the other.

B. Valuation theory and practice

A familiar normative going concern valuation model can be specified in detailed operational terms, as in equation (1).

$$\sum_{j=1}^{\infty} \frac{(\bar{k}_j - \bar{h}_j) - (\bar{A}_j + \bar{R}_j - \bar{Y}_j) - \bar{t}_j - \bar{H}_j}{\prod_{t=1}^{j} (1 + \bar{r}_t)} = \sum_{j=1}^{\infty} \frac{\bar{F}_j - \bar{N}_j - \bar{M}_j}{\prod_{t=1}^{j} \{1 + \bar{r}_t^{(d)}\}} + \sum_{j=1}^{\infty} \frac{\bar{\bar{D}}_j - \bar{B}_j}{\prod_{t=1}^{j} \{1 + \bar{r}_t^{(e)}\}} \qquad (1)$$

or, V_o	= $V_o^{(d)}$		$V_o^{(e)}$
that is, market value of entity	= market value of debt	+	market value of equity
or, present value of entity cash flows	= present value of lender cash flows	+	present value of shareholder cash flows

where (using bars to denote expected values), and expressing everything in money terms

- $k_j - h_j$ denotes operating cash flow in year j represented by cash collected from customers, k_j, and operating cash outflows h_j;
- $A_j + R_j - Y_j$ stands for replacement investment, A_j, growth investment, R_j, and the proceeds from assets displaced, Y_j, in year j;
- t_j stands for all taxes assessed on the corporation that are actually paid in year j;
- H_j denotes liquidity change in year j;
- F_j represents period j interest payments;
- N_j is medium and/or long term debt raised or retired in year j;
- M_j is short term debt raised or repaid in year j;
- D_j represents dividends paid to shareholder in year j;
- B_j is equity capital raised or repaid in year j; and,
- $\bar{r}_t \bar{r}_t^{(d)}, \bar{r}_t^{(e)}$ denote the single period costs of entity, lender and shareholder capital respectively.

Whereas $\bar{r}_t^{(d)}$ and $\bar{r}_t^{(e)}$, and therefore $V_o^{(d)}$ and $V_o^{(e)}$, are a function of the debt ratio $V_o^{(d)}/V_o$, $\bar{r}_t$ may, in a neutral tax regime, be assumed to be independent of $V_o^{(d)}/V_o$. For analytical convenience (1) can be rewritten as:

$$\sum_{j=1}^{\infty} \frac{\overline{ENCF}_j}{(1+\bar{r})^j} = \sum_{j=1}^{\infty} \frac{\overline{LCF}_j}{(1+\bar{r}_d)^j} + \sum_{j=1}^{\infty} \frac{\overline{SHCF}_j}{(1+\bar{r}_e)^j} \quad (2)$$

i.e. we are now assuming that the firm's (entity) cost of capital, the cost of debt and the cost of equity are constant over time. (This does not necessarily imply that the debt ratio $V_o^{(d)}/V_o$ is serially constant.) As above, we still have,

$$V_o = V_o^{(d)} + V_o^{(e)}.$$

Replacing $V_o^{(e)}$ with the more familiar P_o;

$$P_o = V_o - V_o^{(d)} \quad (3)$$

That is to say, the main focus of business valuation, namely, the market value of a firm's equity, is given by:

$$\text{market value of equity} = \text{market value of entity} \ \underline{\text{minus}} \ \text{market value of debt}$$

Assuming that entity cash flows change at an annual rate that can be approximated with a constant rate $\bar{g}$, (expressed in money terms);

$$\sum_{j=1}^{\infty} \frac{\overline{ENCF}_j}{(1+\bar{r})^j} = \frac{\overline{ENCF}_j}{1+\bar{r}} + \frac{\overline{ENCF}_1(1+\bar{g})}{(1+\bar{r})^2} + \ldots\ldots\ldots \text{ad inf.}$$

$$= \frac{\overline{ENCF}_1}{\bar{r}-\bar{g}} \ (\text{provided } \bar{r} > \bar{g}) \quad (4)$$

A normative valuation framework is usually advanced as a theory of the homogeneous expectations that are formed by stock market participants; and of the capitalisation process whereby those expectations are converted into observable market values. In that the capitalisation rate is assumed to be exactly commensurate with the degree of risk which characterises a firm's expected cash flow stream, firms are assumed to be valued at a price that will yield no more or less than a risk-commensurate rate of return i.e. zero net present value represented by the present value of expected entity cash flows *minus* the currently observable market value of debt and equity capital.

If this is the case, it is not easy to explain why stock market transactions are undertaken on a continuing basis. Once the homogeneous expectations assumption is dropped, deviations between individual discounted cash flow expectations and quoted market values can be accommodated. In a large market many investors will conclude that an individual company is overvalued and many will draw the opposite conclusion. A significant volume of business may therefore be transacted at a market price which shows little or no movement. Thus, individuals who transact in both efficient and inefficient stock markets are actively pursuing net present values. Whether, even assuming they are rational in the formation of their expectations, they consistently outperform the market, is of course another matter.

The same kind of analysis is applicable to unquoted firms even though they are not valued at a frequency that facilitates continuous ownership changes via transactions in financial instruments in secondary capital markets. Unquoted firms are, as a rule, valued for sale or acquisition as real economic entities by entrepreneurs who seek positive net present values from economic activity. Such positive net present values are usually inaccessible to the investing public. Stated in alternative normative terms; a potential purchaser will buy an unquoted firm for which he may have his own commercial intentions if his (subjectively-determined) discounted entity cash flow expectations exceed the price at which it can be acquired. The latter price can, in turn, be defined as the best »open market« price that can be negotiated by a potential seller given the number of potential buyers.

A potential acquirer's discounted cash flow expectations can also be regarded as the upper limit he will impose on a negotiated acquisition price. Similarly, if the subjectively-determined discounted cash flow expectations of one or more potential buyers exceed those of a potential seller, the business will be sold. However, net disposal values, i. e. the net amount that would be realised on an orderly sale of a firm's assets on an open market basis and discharge of its liabilities, may influence the decisions of both buyers and sellers; especially if, as can occasionally be inferred from the takeovers of quoted companies, a firm's net disposal value exceeds its going concern value. Moreover, the expected realisable values of individual assets may be characterised by relatively low degrees of risk. Hence, disposal values can provide some indication of the amount of capital that is truly at risk when a business is acquired at a (higher) going concern value.

The replacement value of a business, i. e. the cost of replicating it elsewhere, and the degree to which a replica may compete away business from an existing undertaking [1], which might be acquired too, may also enter the decisions of buyers and sellers. The upshot of the foregoing paragraphs is that potential buyers and sellers of unquoted firms should always hold four notions of value clearly in view, namely, discounted cash flow expectations, possible »open market« acquisition price, net disposal value and replacement value.

Whilst raising formidable forecasting problems, the so-called »fundamentalist« approach to going concern valuation, that is, the estimation of each of the previously-defined components of expected entity cash flows, has undoubtedly gained increasing use in recent years. But it must also be emphasised that in practice some confusion over the distinction between cash flow and historic cost (accruals) accounting variables, or the apparent belief that the latter are accurate approximations of the former, may have compounded the forecasting error. In that the accruals basis of measurement directly influences the price/earnings approach to valuation, the accruals-cash flow distinction deserves explicit attention.

C. Accruals-based historic cost accounting model

The cash flow basis of measurement which is the essence of the familiar normative valuation model can readily be contrasted with the accruals-based historic cost accounting model. Historic cost profit, E_j, for any period j is given by:

$$E_j = d_j - (a_{j-1} + b_j - a_j) - L_j - F_j + (Y_j - X_j) - t_{j+1} \tag{5}$$

where,

d_j denotes accrued sales in year j;
a_{j-1}, a_j denote inventory book values at the beginning and end of year j;
b_j ist total accrued revenue expenditure in year j;
L_j stands for depreciation based on historic cost in year j;
t_{j+1} denotes corporation tax charged in period j that is payable in period j+1; and,
$Y_j - X_j$ denotes the accounting profit on assets displaced (X_j represents their written down book value).

For any year j entity cash flows, $ENCF_j$, are as indicated by the LHS of (1), given by:

$$ENCF_j = (k_j - h_j) - (A_j + R_j - Y_j) - t_j - H_j \tag{6}$$

Ignoring taxes and assuming the case of a wholly equity-financed company; the difference between periodic entity cash flows and historic cost profit, E_j–$ENCF_j$, is given by:

$$E_j - ENCF_j = (d_j - k_j) + (a_j - a_{j-1}) - (b_j - h_j) + (A_j + R_j - L_j - X_j) + H_j \tag{7}$$

that is,
$E_j - ENCF_j$ = periodic change in (debtors, inventories and creditors)
+ periodic depreciation shortfall + periodic liquidity change.

The constituents of this difference are such that there are strong *a priori* reasons for assuming that E_j will characteristically overstate $ENCF_j$. This contention can also be demonstrated empirically [2] and by generating hypothetical data using the kind of multiperiod computer-based simulation models that are now commonly used in going concern valuation problems. Thus, contrary to common supposition, a characteristic excess of historic cost profit over cash flow earnings tends to be a permanent difference rather than a self-reversing timing difference.

The upshot of the foregoing analysis is (again assuming a wholly equity-financed company) that a capitalised earnings method based on $\bar{E}_l$, instead of $EN\bar{C}F_l$, will in the absence of a commensurate discount rate adjustment, cause an upward valuation bias, VB_o, given by:

$$VB_o = \frac{\bar{E}_l - EN\bar{C}F_l}{\bar{r} - \bar{g}} \tag{8}$$

An adjusted discount rate that would compensate for the capitalisation of $\bar{E}_l$, rather than $EN\bar{C}F_l$, is apparently the value of $\bar{r}^*$ which satisfies (9).

$$\frac{ENCF_l}{\bar{r} - \bar{g}} = \frac{\bar{E}_l}{\bar{r}^* - \bar{g}} \tag{9}$$

$$\text{whence, } \bar{r}^* = \frac{\bar{E}_l(\bar{r} - \bar{g})}{EN\bar{C}F_l} + \bar{g}$$

However, under conditions of either real or nominal growth, the upward bias defined by (8) is only accurately measured if $\bar{E}$, and $EN\bar{C}F_l$ change at the same annual rate $\bar{g}$. This is not a safe assumption; $ENCF_j/E_j$ is generally not serially constant.

D. The price/earnings approach

Notwithstanding the enormous dispersion about published average price-earnings ratios, the $P_o/\bar{E}_l$ approach to valuation is commonly encountered. It is reported to be especially influential in the fixing of the first quoted prices of companies that obtain a listing on either the Unlisted Securities Market (U.S.M.) or on the London Stock Exchange. [3] The dispersion about the average of the second day premia, by which newly quoted shares generally rise, further attests to the shortcomings of this method.

The foregoing analysis provides a means of explaining why companies, which are apparently similar, can have significant P_o/E_l differences. Using equations (3), (4) and (5), the price-earnings ratio can be written

$$\frac{P_0}{\bar{E}_1} = \frac{\dfrac{EN\bar{C}F_1}{\bar{r}-\bar{g}} - V_0^{(d)}}{\bar{d}_1-(\bar{a}_0+\bar{b}_1-\bar{a}_1)-\bar{L}_1-\bar{F}_1-\bar{t}_2+(\bar{Y}_1-\bar{X}_1)} \tag{10}$$

Inspection of (10) reveals that $P_0/\bar{E}_1$ differences between companies can be explained by:

- intercompany differences in the ratio of current earnings before interest, i. e. $\bar{E}_1+\bar{F}_1$, to entity cash flows $EN\bar{C}F_1$
- intercompany debt ratio differences
- intercompany differences in expected entity cash flow growth rates
- intercompany differences in the cost of capital which reflect differences in characteristic degrees of market risk.

It is perhaps interesting to note that a change in a firm's debt ratio may either increase or decrease its $P_0/\bar{E}_1$ ratio depending upon the level of the nominal debt interest rat. Thus, changes in interest rates will change $P_0/\bar{E}_1$ ratios and, depending upon intercompany debt levels, may also change $P_0/\bar{E}_1$ ratio rankings.

Additionally noteworthy is the possibility that intercompany differences in the ratio of current earnings, $\bar{E}_1+\bar{F}_1$, to entity cash flows, $EN\bar{C}F_1$, may be ascribable either to intercompany accounting policy differences e. g. differences in depriciation and inventory valuation policies; or, to real events e. g. differences in periods of trade credit given and/or taken and/or in inventory levels.

E. The horizon value problem

In using the discounted cash flow method to estimate the value of a going concern the practitioner is apparently faced with a choice between equations (1) and (4). The use of equation (1) is, as mentioned earlier, a fundamentalist approach. It requires separate estimates pertaining to future conditions in:

- end-product markets, e. g. total market growth, market share, development of selling prices
- the markets for labour, materials, energy, capital goods etc.
- the fiscal environment.

Moreover, future liquidity requirements are a function of each of these variables and need to be estimated accordingly.

As regards the use of equation (4) it is not immediately obvious how a practitioner can (directly) estimate rates of change in future entity cash flow without first adopting a fundamentalist approach to estimate each of its determinants. In the absence of such individual estimates, the practitioner must inevitably resort to the guessing of a range of reasonable values for $\bar{g}$; or, alternatively, to extrapolating from *ex post* rates of change in entity cash flow.

The major shortcoming of the fundamentalist approach (equation [1]) is that it apparently requires the forecasting of a perpetual stream of entity cash flows. Needless to say, this is a wholly unrealistic notion and, in practice, entity cash flows can only ever be projected for a finite sequence of periods. But if the valuation problem is truncated in this way a horizon valuation problem arises. That is to say, the left-hand side of equation (2) needs to be rewritten as:

$$V_o = \sum_{j=1}^{n} \frac{\overline{ENCF}_j}{(1+\bar{r})^j} + \frac{\bar{V}_n}{(1+\bar{r})^n} \tag{11}$$

where $\bar{V}_n$ denotes the expected entity value of the company as a going concern at end-year n. Assuming that n represents the number of entity cash flows that can be estimated with a tolerable degree of accuracy, an important practical question is whether the present value of a firm's end-year n value as a going concern is likely to constitute a significant proportion of V_o. This clearly depends upon the rate of change in the first n entity cash flows in conjunction with: the values of n, the discount rate, $\bar{r}$, and the expected horizon value $\bar{V}_n$. Even more important is the question of how $\bar{V}_n$ is to be estimated.

If $\bar{V}_n$ is really intended as a going concern valuation, it should reflect the post-horizon expected entity cash flows, $\overline{ENCF}_{n+1}$, $\overline{ENCF}_{n+2}$... ad. inf. But if the post-horizon cash flows are defined as those that cannot realistically be projected using a fundamentalist approach, $\bar{V}_n$ can only be estimated from $\overline{ENCF}_n$ in conjunction with direct estimates of the post-horizon expected rate of change in entity cash flows, $\bar{g}$. That is to say, $\bar{V}_n$ is given by:

$$\bar{V}_n = \frac{\overline{ENCF}_{n+1}}{\bar{r}' - \bar{g}'} \text{(provided } \bar{r}' > \bar{g}'\text{)} \tag{12}$$

If $\bar{g}'$ is specified in real terms so too must the post-horizon discount rate $\bar{r}'$.

Assuming a constant annual rate of change, $\bar{g}$, in the first n expected entity cash flows, followed by a constant annual rate of growth $\bar{g}'$ in the post-horizon cash flows, the valuation formula can be written:

$$V_o = \frac{\overline{ENCF}_1}{\bar{r} - \bar{g}} \left[1 - \frac{(1+\bar{g})^n}{(1+\bar{r})^n}\right] + \frac{\overline{ENCF}_1 (1+\bar{g})^n}{(1+\bar{r})^n (\bar{r}' - \bar{g}')} \tag{13}$$

With $\bar{r} = \bar{r}'$, $\bar{g} = \bar{g}'$ and $\bar{r}' > \bar{g}'$,

then, with $n = 1$, $V_o = \dfrac{\overline{ENCF}_1}{1+\bar{r}} + \dfrac{\overline{ENCF}_1 (1+\bar{g})}{(1+\bar{r})(\bar{r}-\bar{g})}$

and, with $n = 2$, $V_o = \dfrac{\overline{ENCF}_1}{(\bar{r}-\bar{g})}\left[1 - \dfrac{(1+g)^2}{(1+r)^2}\right] + \dfrac{\overline{ENCF}_1 (1+\bar{g})^2}{(1+\bar{r})^2 (\bar{r}-\bar{g})}$ etc.

That is to say, expressed as a percentage of V_o, the discounted expected horizon value, V_n decreases at the annual rate of $1 - (1+\bar{g})/(1+\bar{r})$. Thus, after n years, the present value of V_n will, on the foregoing assumptions, constitute the proportion $(1+\bar{g})^n/(1+\bar{r})^n$ of the total value V_o. For example, putting $\bar{g} = 0.05$, $\bar{r} = 0.09$ and $n = 7$, $(1+\bar{g})^n/(1+\bar{r})^n = (1.05/1.09)^7 = 0.77$. However, with $\bar{g} = 0.01$ and $\bar{r} = 0.09$, the present value of V_7 would constitute 59 per cent of V_o. Present values of $\bar{V}_n$ (expressed as a decimal fraction of V_o) for alternative values of n and $\bar{g}$ are given in Table 1.

Table 1 leaves no doubt that the discounted horizon value of a company will invariably constitute a significant proportion of its value as a going concern. Although this is essentially the logic of valuation arithmetic, it is nevertheless one of the main reasons why many practitioners dislike the discounted cash flow valuation method.

Alternative horizon values that are not infrequently advocated include historical and current cost net book, net replacement, and net disposable values. Estimated horizon price/earnings ratios, $\bar{P}_n/\bar{E}_{n+1}$, are also used as a means of arriving at horizon values. Moreover, in addition to

$\bar{V}_n/(1+\bar{r})^n V_0 = (1+\bar{g})^n/(1+\bar{r})^n$								
	$100\bar{g}$	−5	−3	−1	0	1	3	5
	$\bar{r} = 0.06$							
n								
5		0.58	0.64	0.71	0.75	0.79	0.87	0.95
7		0.46	0.54	0.62	0.67	0.71	0,82	0.94
9		0.37	0.45	0.54	0.59	0.65	0.77	0.92
11		0.30	0.38	0.47	0.53	0.59	0.73	0.90
13		0.24	0.32	0.41	0.47	0.53	0.69	0.88
15		0.09	0.26	0.36	0.42	0.48	0.65	0.87
	$\bar{r} = 0.09$							
n								
5		0.50	0.56	0.62	0.65	0.68	0.75	0.83
7		0.38	0.44	0.51	0.55	0.59	0.67	0.77
9		0.29	0.34	0.42	0.46	0.50	0.60	0.71
11		0.22	0.28	0.35	0.39	0.43	0.54	0.66
13		0.17	0.22	0.29	0.33	0.37	0.48	0.62
15		0.13	0.17	0.24	0.27	0.32	0.43	0.57
	$\bar{r} = 0.12$							
n								
5		0.44	0.49	0.53	0.57	0.60	0.66	0.72
7		0.32	0.37	0.42	0.45	0.48	0.56	0.64
9		0.23	0.27	0.33	0.36	0.39	0.47	0.45
11		0.16	0.21	0.26	0.29	0.32	0.40	0.49
13		0.12	0.15	0.20	0.23	0.26	0.34	0.43
15		0.08	0.12	0.16	0.18	0.21	0.28	0.38

Table 1: Discounted expected horizon value expressed as a proportion of total value

their use as a means of estimating horizon values, these alternatives are often used in parallel with the discounted cash flow method to generate a range of end-year 0 values for the guidance of potential buyers and sellers.

Accounting book values can only be of relevance to business valuations to the extent that they are reasonable approximations – essentially an empirical question – of replacement, disposal and going concern values. All of the latter reflect values that can be realised in markets and the evidence for quoted companies [4] suggest that they are not even consistently related to accounting book values. Moreover, the last three (market) value concepts are only of direct relevance to valuation problems to the extent that they reflect courses of action which buyers and sellers actually intend to pursue.

F. Estimating the cost of capital

The discounted cash flow expectations of a firm are prone to two separate forecasting errors. Errors in the estimation of a firm's expected cash flow stream will either be compounded or reduced by errors in estimates of the cost of capital. The degree of compound error may be exacerbated if, as may be the usual case in practice, periodic cash flows are serially dependent. As already mentioned, it is usually assumed that a firm's cost of capital is commensurate with its characteristic degree of risk. [5] The conventional textbook approach is that the latter risk premium, namely, a premium for market risk is specified by the capital-asset pricing model (CAPM). Thus, in the CAPM formulation the rate of return, $\bar{r}_e$, expected from a risky asset, e, is equal to the risk-free interest rate, i, plus a risk premium that reflects the covariability of the values of, or rates of return on, that asset and the market portfolio, that is,

$$\bar{r}_e = i + (\bar{r}_m - i)\,\beta_e \tag{14}$$

where,

$$\beta_e = \frac{\text{covar.}\,(r_e, r_m)}{\text{var.}\,(r_m)}$$

The CAPM risk premium is therefore a measure of an individual asset's risk relative to average risk i.e. the risk inherent in a portfolio that is diversified across the market as a whole. It follows directly from equation (14), that a firm of average risk has a beta coefficient of unity; and that firms of above-average or below-average risk have beta coefficients of $\beta > 1$ and $\beta < 1$ respectively.

As usually formulated, the CAPM is a single-period model. In fact the conditions on which the single-period model can be extended to a multiperiod framework are quite restrictive. [6] The single-period model nevertheless appears to be gaining increasing practical usage in the quantification of the cost of capital for multiperiod analysis. [7] To quantify the cost of capital for an individual firm, it is, as indicated by (14), necessary to estimate the riskfree interest rate, i, the excess return on the market portfolio, $\bar{r}_m - i$, and the one value that is peculiar to the individual firm, namely, its beta coefficient.

Whereas spot riskfree interest rates, expressed in money terms, for periods of up to thirty years or more, can be estimated from the redemption yields on Government bonds, estimates of the excess return, $\bar{r}_m - i$, and of beta coefficients can only be based on historic time-series data. An indication of the reliability of past data as a basis for forecasting is provided by the temporal stability of the distributions from which they are drawn. The historic excess return on the U. K. market portfolio is usually measured by the average difference between the one-year return on the de-Zoete-Equity-Index [8] and the one-year rate of interest obtained from consecutive investments in ninety-one day Treasury Bills. Whilst the historic excess return on the U. K. market portfolio has not been completely stable over the last 66 years, it is probably the best available guide to the future excess return (see Table 2). The predictive power of beta coefficients that have been derived from joint historic returns (on investment in quoted companies and in the market portfolio) is at least dubious. In the case of unquoted firms the beta estimation problem is even more acute.

Since 1919 the excess of the one-year rate of return on U. K. equities over the riskfree interest rate has averaged 8.8 percentage points (before personal taxes) in real terms, i. e. 6.16 percentage points in real terms net of tax in the case of a basic rate taxpayer. [9] The comparative average for the U. S. A. takes on a similar value. [10] The U. K. averages for inter-war and post-war periods are given in Table 2.

	nominal rate of return on equities %	nominal Treasury Bill rate %	average real excess return %
1919–28	17.3	4.1	13.2
1929–38	6.1	1.7	4.4
1939–45 (7 yrs)	9.8	1.1	8.7
1946–55	10.7	1.3	9.4
1956–65	13.2	4.8	8.4
1966–75	17.8	7.8	10.0
1976–84 (9 yrs)	19.0	11.7	7.3
1919–84	13.5	4.7	8.8

Table 2: The excess return on U. K. equities 1919–1984

Returning to the estimation of beta coefficients; beta values derived from past (joint) returns on individual quoted companies and the market portfolio are nowadays regularly published in the U. K. and elsewhere. [11] A measure of the predictive accuracy of historic beta coefficients is the sequence of periodic abnormal returns each of which is represented by the difference between the expected periodic return predicted with equation (14) (using a historic beta value) and the actual periodic return. If betas are good predictors, a sequence of (say) twenty quarterly abnormal returns should sum to zero. An analysis of a broad data set shows that this is invariably *not the case*. Nevertheless in the present state of knowledge betas derived from historic time-series data are probably the best beta estimates that are available.

The qualification of the beta coefficients of unquoted firms is perhaps even more problematical. One approach is to use the beta coefficient of a similar quoted firm as a surrogate. As the value of a firm's beta coefficient reflects a combination of economic, political and psychological influences on market value behaviour, the affinities between a possible quoted surrogate and its unquoted counterpart should be analysed accordingly. Assuming that the market values of two comparable firms are affected to a similar degree by psychological and political factors, their respective covariabilities with the market portfolio depend upon their respective products, product mixes, cost structures including operating leverage and financial leverage. [12] If these are similar, there are grounds for using the beta of a comparable quoted company as a proxy for that of the unquoted counterpart.

In the absence of a surrogate quoted company, the beta quantification problem can possibly be circumvented by allowing that of an unquoted company to take on low, average and high values respectively. Allowing for personal taxes at the rate of 30 per cent, and expressing all values in real terms, such calculations can be illustrated as follows:

Let i (riskfree interest rate) = 0.5;

$\bar{r}_m - i$ (excess return on the market portfolio) = 9; and

$\beta_e = 0.5$.

Therefore $\bar{r}_e = [0.5 + 9(0.5)](1 - 0.3) = 3.5$ per cent.

Alternatively, with $\beta_e = 1$,

$\bar{r}_e = [0.5 + 9(1)](1 - 0.3) = 6.65$ per cent;

and with $\beta = 1.5$,

$\bar{r}_e = [0.5 + 9(1.5)](1 - 0.3) = 9.8$ per cent.

It is hardly necessary to add that variations in the cost of capital on this scale generate significant differences in the values of discounted cash flows. For example, assuming as in a case in which the writer was recently involved, a company is expected to generate a perpetual annual cash flow (expressed in real terms net of corporation tax at the rate of 35 per cent) of £ 11.3 million [13], its respective capitalised (market) values at the above three costs of capital would be:

11.3/0.035 = £ 323 million
11.3/0.0665 = £ 170 million
11.3/0.098 = £ 115 million.

Allowances for errors in the estimation of the company's expected cash flow stream will obviously widen the above range. On the other hand, if the life estimate is arbitrarily shortened to 15 years, the last three values fall to £ 130 mill., £ 105 mill., and £ 87 mill. respectively.

G. Conclusion

Whereas this paper has focused almost entirely on valuation analysis for acquisition or merger, it would be remiss not to refer to the going concern valuations that are continuously needed in taxation, arbitration and inheritance cases etc. [14] An important difference between these two categories is the greater scope for negotiation that may characterise the determination of the transfer price for an acquisition or merger.

Valuations for legal purposes are usually more constrained by case law precedents, and statutory provisions, than are the freely-negotiated transfers of business undertakings in the normal course of commercial activity. Legal valuations may in a sense, be more objectively determinate whilst to a significant extent departing from the normative valuation model of the textbook which is anyway not capable of generating a uniquely »correct« value.

The textbook analysis nevertheless provides a powerful framework that not only elucidates the character of valuation problems but offers a practical means of analysing prospective cash flows which, in turn, may facilitate such contentions as, »... this firm is worth at least £ 50 million because it is likely to repay that amount over the next three years and to continue as a cash flow generator for many years thereafter.«

Notes

1 This is a subject in itself which cannot be pursued further here.
2 See *Lawson/Möller/Sherer*(Bemessung).
3 See *Rutherford*(Stock Exchange).
4 See *The Stock Exchange*(Quarterly).
5 Doubts have recently been voiced about this assumption. See *Keane*(Mystery).
6 See *Stapleton/Subrahmanyam*(Multiperiod).

7 See, for example, *Lawson/Stapleton* (Pricing).
8 See *de Zoete/Bevan* (Equity-Gilt).
9 See *Merrett/Sykes* (Finance) and *de Zoete/Bevan* op cit.
10 See *Ibbotson/Sinquefield* (Stocks).
11 See, for example, *London Business School* (Risk).
12 See *Rubinstein* (Synthesis). An alternative, though somewhat similar form of analysis is proposed by *Franks/Broyles* (Finance).
13 Note that under the U.K. imputation system of corporation tax cash flows that are expressed net of corporation tax are, because part of that corporation tax is imputed to shareholders, also net of income tax at the basic rate. Hence, in allowing for personal taxes at the basic rate, the discount rate alone needs to be reduced by 30 per cent.
14 *Eastaway* (Unquoted Shares).

References

De Zoete/Bevan (Equity-Gilt): The de Zoete Equity-Gilt Study: A study of the relative performance of Equity and Fixed Interest Investment from 1919 to 1984, 30th Annual Edition, London, January 1985.

Eastaway, N. (Unquoted Shares): The art of valuing unquoted shares. In: The Accountant, 18th April, 1985.

Franks, J. R./*Broyles*, J. E. (Finance): Modern Managerial Finance. New York u. a. 1979.

Ibbotson, R. C./*Sinquefield*, R. (Stocks): Stocks, Bonds, Bills and Inflation. Financial Analysts research Foundation, Charlottesville, Va., 1979.

Keane, S. M. (Mystery): The mystery of January and small firms. In: The Accountant's Magazine. July 1985.

Lawson, G. H./*Möller*, P./*Sherer*, M. (Bemessung): Zur Verwendung anschaffungswertorientierter Aufwand-Ertrag-Rechnungen als Grundlage für die Bemessung von Zinsen, Steuern und Dividenden. In: *Lück*, W./*Trommsdorff*, V. (Hrsg.): Internationalisierung der Unternehmung, Berlin 1982.

Lawson, G. H./*Stapleton*, R. C. (Pricing): The Pricing of Non-competitive Government Contracts. In: Managerial Finance. Vol. 10, No. 3/4, 1984.

London Business School (Risk): Risk Measurement Service. LBS Financial Services, 1979–85, London.

Merrett, A. J./*Sykes*, A. (Finance): The Finance and Analysis of Capital Projects. 2nd ed. London 1973.

Rubinstein, M. (Synthesis): Mean Variance Synthesis of Corporate Financial Theory. In: Journal of Finance, Vol. 28, 1969.

Rutherford, J. (Stock Exchange): Introduction to Stock Exchange Investment. London 1983.

Stapleton, R. C./*Subrahmanyam*, M. G. (Multiperiod): A Multiperiod Equilibrium Asset Pricing Model. In: Econometrica, Vol. 46, 1978.

Sieben, G./*Schildbach*, T.: Zum Stand der Entwicklung der Lehre von der Bewertung ganzer Unternehmungen. In: DStR, Heft 16/17, 1979.

Stock Exchange (Quarterly): The Stock Exchange Quarterly. London, December 1984.

Was Woolworth ailing?

F W Woolworth has been courting financial disaster with a 'somewhat perverse' dividend policy, argues GERALD H LAWSON, FCCA professor of business finance at Manchester Business School.

THE recently proposed change in the ownership of F W Woolworth is widely assumed to be ascribable to economic 'badwill' — a situation in which the disposible (or exchange) value of a firm's assets minus current liabilities (excluding overdrafts) exceeds its value as a going concern (market value of debt plus market value of equity).

If its CCA balance sheet is anything to go by, Woolworth's exchange value was about £939 million on January 31 last, at which time its going concern value was somewhere in the region of £350 million.

In these situations it is always interesting to question whether a sharp deterioration in financial viability finally brought about the ownership change.

Any notion of financial viability must clearly have something to do with a firm's internal cash flow generating ability. Hence, to assess whether Woolworth's cash flow generating ability has declined in recent years it is necessary to analyse its financial performance on a pure cash flow basis for the years in question. However, if various elements of a firm's cash flow performance are to be tracked and evaluated over time, its cash flow statements need to be restated at a base-year price level as illustrated by Table 2.

The conceptual foundation of cash flow accounting, which regrettably is not generally well understood in accounting circles, is pre-eminently a theory of valuation deriving from both classical and modern capital market theory. Modern evaluation theory makes the explicit distinction between a firm's total corporate value (alias entity value) on the one hand which is equal to the sum of the market values of its debt and equity on the other.

The market value of an entity is assumed to be given by the present value of its expected (entity) cash flows whilst the market values of its debt and equity represent the present values of its lender and shareholder cash flows respectively. Commencing with a company's total cash flow statement for some past year *j*, these relationships can be represented as: entity cash flows ≡ lender cash flows + shareholder cash flows. (See panel)

This identity can be slightly adjusted to read:

expected entity cash flows ≡ expected lender cash flows + expected shareholder cash flows

and the valuation identity is, as already stated:

present value of expected entity cash flows ≡ present value of expected lender cash flows + present value of expected shareholder cash flows

ie entity market value ≡ market value of debt + market value of equity.

From the above outline it can be readily inferred that an entity as such is financially viable, and has a market value as a going concern, if, taking one year with another, it can generate positive entity cash flows (net of all periodic capital expenditure — after disposals) and hold out the continuing prospect of so doing.

But the effect of continuously revised market expectations, influenced no doubt by actual cash flow performance, may be such that, like Woolworth's, an entity's going concern value falls below its net asset value. That is to say, the entity remains financially viable as a going concern whilst becoming financially weaker and has ceased to represent the best deployment of its fixed assets.

Although the total (entity) market value of Woolworth declined by about 26 per cent in real terms between January 1977 and January 1982, (from roughly £454 million to approximately £337 million) it is highly probable that its disposable value exceeded the former value throughout the entire period.

Multiperiod cash flows analysis

A multiperiod *ex post* cash flow statement re-expressed at a base-year price level can not only highlight the individual factors that have contributed

Total cash statement for year j.

$$(k_j - h_j) - (A_j + R_j - Y_j) - H_j - t_j \equiv (F_j - N_j - M_j) + (D_j - B_j)$$

that is,

entity cash flows ≡ lender cash flows + shareholder cash flows

where,

$k_j - h_j$	denotes operating cash flow in year j represented by cash collected from customers, k_j, and operating cash outflows, h_j
$A_j + R_j - Y_j$	stands for replacement, investment A_j, growth investment, R_j, and the proceeds from assets displaced, Y_j, in year j
H_j	denotes liquidity change in year j†
t_j	stands for all taxes assessed on the corporation that are actually paid in year j
F_j	represents period j interest payments
N_j	is medium and/or long-term debt raised or retired in year j
M_j	is short-term debt raised or repaid in year j;
D_j	represents dividends paid to shareholders in year j
B_j	is equity capital raised or repaid in year j.

† *It is assumed that firms maintain liquidity for transactions, precautionary and speculative motives. Hence liquidity changes are a legitimate component of periodic entity cash flows and reflect changing expectations about risk, future transactions levels and speculative opportunities.*

to any deterioration in an entity's cash flow generating capability, it can also reveal whether such a deterioration has in any sense been exacerbated by its dividend and debt-financing policies.

As the above identities make abundantly clear, dividend and debt-financing policies represent the division of entity cash flows, (which when investment is substantial may take on negative values) between lenders and shareholders.

Now if, even leaving aside any commitments in the form of contractual interest and loan/overdraft repayments, dividends (net of equity capital raised) are set at levels which consistenly exceed post-tax entity cash flows, an entity clearly self-imposes two unnecessary burdens on its cash-flow generating capacity.

In the first place the excess of shareholder cash flows over entity cash flows is an immediate strain that must be debt-financed and, in turn, adds both to future contractual interest payments and loan/overdraft repayments. The second strain stems from the further debt that is required to finance current contractual interest payments and current loan/overdraft repayments.

Woolworth is an interesting example of a company which, in the face of a declining cash flow generating capacity, adopted a dividend/debt financing policy which was a stick for its own back. These contentions are illustrated by reference to Table 2.

The trend of an entity's operating cash flow must be regarded as the paramount index of its financial performance. Firms engage in business for the exclusive purpose of organising profitable productive and trading activity. The ability of any firm to survive and grow in a profitable economic sense must therefore by definition depend upon the level of cash collected from customers minus the associated operating payments in respect of materials, labour, energy, overheads etc.

Taking one year with another, operating cash flow is the fund from which all capital expenditures, all tax payments and all liquidity adjustments must be financed, not to mention risk-commensurate returns to lenders and shareholders.

The sequence of operating cash flows in Table 2 suggests that the viability of Woolworth's real trading activity has been under continuous pressure and that something of a collapse occurred in the year to January 1982.

The serial relationship between (real) operating cash flow and (real) investment is also an important focus for performance evaluation. In general it can be said that higher investment is undertaken now in the expectation of commensurately higher operating cash flows in the future.

But a constant or declining real operating cash flow that is paralleled by a consistently upward real investment level, implying an inherent decline in entity cash flow generating ability, may well exercise a strong influence on market expectations of future entity cash flows and existing market values will impound such expectations accordingly.

After allowing for tax payments and liquidity changes, Woolworth's post-tax entity cash flow performance for the five years to January 1982 (see Table 2) does not look particularly scintillating. An average (real) entity cash flow of £18.345 million was characterised by a pronounced downward trend.

The real decline in Woolworth's

Table 1 F W Woolworth and Co plc: total cash flow statements (£000s)

Years to January 31	1978	1979	1980	1981	1982
funds from trading	+54,143	+61,355	+67,404	+49,229	+33,596
change in working capital	−13,380	−33,194	−25,354	− 2,025	−14,784
	+40,763	+28,161	+42,050	+47,204	+18,812
interest paid	+ 5,450	+ 5,219	+10,213	+15,024	+16,333
1 *operating cash flow*	+46,213	+33,380	+52,263	+62,228	+35,145
investment	−10,637	−16,684	−26,116	−50,151	−48,151
disposals	+ 2,607	+ 3,865	+ 4,750	+29,701	+24,657
2 *capital investment*	− 8,030	−12,819	−21,366	−20,450	−23,494
3 = 1 − 2	+38,183	+20,561	+30,897	+41,778	+11,651
tax paid	−12,189	−11,527	−15,180	−12,377	−13,693
liquidity change	− 151	− 5,946	+ 7,255	−11,733	− 6,008
post-tax entity cash flows	+25,843	+ 3,088	+22,972	+17,668	− 8,050
dividends (less new capital)	−14,934	−15,785	−17,363	−17,594	−17,906
lender cash flow	+10,909	−12,697	+ 5,609	+ 74	−25,956
represented by:					
interest	− 5,450	− 5,219	−10,213	−15,024	−16,333
overdraft/loans	− 5,459	+17,916	+4,604	+14,950	+42,289
	−10,909	+12,697	− 5,609	− 74	+25,956

Table 2 F W Woolworth and Co plc: total cash flow statements restated at January 1982 prices (£000s)

Years to January 31	1978	1979	1980	1981	1982	5-year averages	revised 5-year averages
1 *operating cash flow*	+78,095	+52,337	+70,853	+72,147	+36,741	+62,035	assuming 56pc cut in average dividend payment
investment	−17,975	−26,159	−35,405	−58,145	−50,337	−37,604	
disposals	+ 4,405	+ 6,060	+ 6,440	+34,435	+25,776	+15,423	
2 *capital investment*	−13,570	−20,099	−28,966	−23,710	−24,561	−22,181	
3 = 1 − 2	+64,525	+32,238	+41,887	+48,437	+12,180	+39,854	+39,854
tax paid	−20,598	−18,073	−20,580	−14,350	−14,315	−17,583	−19,988
liquidity change	− 255	− 9,323	+ 9,836	−13,603	− 6,281	− 3,925	− 3,925
post-tax entity cash flow	+43,672	+ 4,842	+31,143	+20,484	− 8,415	+18,345	+15,941
dividend (less new capital)	−25,237	−24,749	−23,539	−20,398	−18,719	−22,528	−10,000
lender cash flow	+18,435	−19,908	+ 7,604	+ 86	−27,134	− 4,183	+ 5,941
represented by:							
interest	− 9,210	− 8,183	−13,846	−17,419	−17,075	−13,147	− 8,526
overdraft/loans	− 9,225	+28,090	+ 6,242	+17,333	+44,209	+17,329	+ 2,586
	−18,435	+19,908	− 7,604	− 86	+27,134	+ 4,183	− 5,941
*indexation factors**	1.6899	1.5679	1.3557	1.1594	1.0454		

**Retail price index at January 1982 divided by the July index level for the individual accounting year in question*

entity cash flows was paralleled by the behaviour of its real market value (see Table 4). Thus, the 26 per cent real decline in Woolworth's entity market value between 1977 and 1982 was represented by something like a 44 per cent real *increase* in the market value of its debt (absolute increase of about £36 million at January 1982 prices) and a 41 per cent real *decline* in the market value of its equity (absolute decline of roughly £153 million at January 1982 prices).

The latter decline compares with an 8 per cent real decline in the de Zoete Equity index over the same period.

Dividend and debt-financing policies
The Table 2 relationship between Woolworth's post-tax entity cash flows and its shareholder cash flows (dividends less new equity) is much more striking albeit somewhat perverse. In paying shareholders about 23 per cent more than the entity actually generated (before charging interest let it be emphasised), Woolworth was in excellent company (see Lawson and Stark, *Lloyds Bank Review*, January 1981.)

Viewing the position from the lenders' standpoint', far from receiving some part of post-tax entity cash flows, lenders were net contributors over the five-year period. This is another way of saying that lenders not only financed the excess of shareholder cash flows over entity cash flows, but also financed their own interest payments. (This is of course exactly the practice of some Western banks in respect of their lending to the Communist world).

Sagacious financial management generally requires that the size of the policy variables on the right hand side of the (multiperiod) cash flow identity be simultaneously determined by reference to each other subject to the expected level of entity cash flows on the left hand side.

To ignore this prescription, and to determine dividend levels by reference to some other yardstick, when entity cash flows are under increasing strain from intensifying competition, or whatever, is to court financial trouble.

Nevertheless, many firms seem to be convinced that the maintaining of a 'well-established dividend policy — even when under severe commercial pressures on entity cash flow generating capacity — is a ***sine qua non*** for 'financial respectability' and the preclusion of 'undesirable' fluctuations in their equity market values. Nothing could be further from both commensense and observable reality.

Table 3A Woolworth's average accounting and cash flow performance 1977-82

	HCP	CF	
pre-depreciation profit	1,000	669	operating cash flow
depreciation	148	239	capital expenditure
profit before interest	852	430	
less interest	142	142	
pre-tax profit	710	288	
tax charged (32 per cent)	227	190	tax paid
post tax profit	483	98	
dividends (52 per cent)	251	243	dividends (net of new equity)
		42	liquidity change
retained earnings	232	(187)	debt-financed deficit

Table 3B Historic cost (HCP) and adjusted cash flow (CF) performance

	HCP	CF	
pre-depreciation profit	1,000	669	operating cash flow
depreciation	148	239	capital expenditure
		42	liquidity change
profit before interest	852	388	
tax charged (27 per cent)	227	190	tax paid (49 per cent)
less interest	142	28	*less* real interest
post tax profit	483	170	
dividends (52 per cent)	251	243	dividends (net of new equity)
retained earnings	232	(73)	real debt-financed deficit

Note: The values in the published profit and loss accounts were first restated at January 1982 prices and then averaged. This transformation does not however give economic meaning to an original profit sequence which itself lacks economic validity. However, the average of a multiperiod sequence of restated historic cost profits can legitimately be compared with average restated cash flows in order to depict the average relative magnitude of the permanent difference between historic cost profit and cash flows.

Table 4 Woolworth's market values restated at January 1982 prices (£000s)

calendar year	1977	1978	1979	1980	1981
equity* : high	440,921	432,979	448,484	315,754	276,983
low	303,662	349,787	282,098	214,788	162,375
(a) average	372,287	391,383	365,291	265,271	219,679
(b) debt: average balance sheet values**	81,310	85,346	89,059	88,590	117,061
(c) average entity value	453,597	476,729	454,350	353,861	336,740
(d) debt ratio = (b) ÷ (c)	18%	18%	20%	25%	35%

*Source: Extel British Company Service
**Mainly short term overdrafts the balance sheet value of which represents their market value

Effect of lower dividends
What level of dividends would have been appropriate in the five years to January 1982? Assuming an annual net distribution of £10 million to shareholders, the average five-year cash flow performance of Woolworth would have been as in the last column of Table 2. The following comments on these revised five-year averages are apposite.

The (revised) averaged post-tax entity cash flow would have been £2.404 million lower, which reduction represents tax relief at 52 per cent on the difference between the actual and revised interest payments.

However, this decline in average post-tax entity cash flow would have been partially offset by the personal tax that would have been saved on the difference between the actual and revised interest payments. Calculated at the basic rate, this saving would have been 0.3 (13.147 − 8.526) = £1.386 million a year. On these assumptions the net reduction in annual tax savings would therefore have been 2.404 − 1.386 = £1.018 million.

A distinct advantage that could have been set against the additional

Continued on page 32

Continued from page 14

net annual tax payment averaging £1.018 million would have been the reduction in the financial stress stemming from a decline in the preferential contractual interest charge on post-tax entity cash flows[1] of (13.147 – 8.526) = £4.621 million complemented by a reduction (averaging £12.528 million) in the dividend commitment.

It can reasonably be questioned whether a non-neutral corporate tax regime, which effectively gives a 22 percentage points advantage to interest payments over dividends, should be allowed to dominate the simultaneous determination of dividend and debt-financing policies if, at the end of the day, the securing of that tax advantage imposes very considerable strains on continuing financial viability.

Better, it might be argued, for the Government to abolish the differential corporate tax relief on interest payments (whilst simultaneously lowering the corporate tax rate) in an attempt to stop companies playing games with the tax system which might ultimately result in direct threats to corporate financial viability.

As a final comment on the last two columns of Table 2, it might be said that they highlight two radically contrasting situations. In the five years to January 1982 an excess of shareholder cash flows over entity cash flows was debt-financed, as were the whole of interest payments.

The alternative (hypothetical) dividend policy would have been wholly internally-financed and lenders would also have been net recipients, *ie* interest payments would have exceeded debt raised. The latter policies would have been more defensible in that they are consistent with the maintaining of a stable long term debt ratio.

By contrast, if shareholder cash flows persistently exceed entity cash flows a company's directorate may inadvertently be selling equity interests to lenders and continuously escalating its debt ratio. Measured on a market value basis, Woolworth's debt ratio (market value of debt ÷ entity market value) rose from about 18 per cent in 1977 to 35 per cent in 1982.

Economic consequences of accounting

To conclude we consider how, in reality, shareholder cash flows can turn out to be uncovered to the degree illustrated by the penultimate column of Table 2. In practice dividend levels are invariably determined by reference to post-tax published profit (with contractual interest payments recorded as a cost 'above the line').

But if, like Woolworth, companies are habitually net working capital investors (see the second line of Table 1) and charge annual depreciation in their profit and loss accounts which, as in Woolworth's case, typically constitutes 62 per cent of capital expenditure, the potential for uncovered dividends is quite enormous.

> ‘In paying shareholders about 23 per cent more than the entity actually generated (before charging interest) Woolworth was in excellent company’

This is readily demonstrated by juxtaposing, as in Table 3A, Woolworth's average accounting performance for the five years to January 1982 with its average cash flow performance for the same period.

The left hand side of Table 3A gives the unmistakable impression that Woolworth's housekeeping was, taking one year with another, on a sound footing for the five years to January 1982. Thus, the company's interest payments were seemingly well covered, taxes were apparently charged at the relatively modest rate of 32 per cent and the dividend pay-out ratio was little over 50 per cent.

A somewhat different incidence of interest taxes and dividends on corporate cash flow generating capacity is suggested by the right hand side of Table 3A.

One must however hasten to add that as an indication of the economic consequences of accounting, the right hand side of Table 3A is not strictly accurate; and, if it is to give faithful indications of effective interest cover, the true incidence of corporate taxation and effective dividend cover needs to be adjusted in one important respect.

As is well known, market interest rates respond to inflation. When inflation is high, interest rates are high, roughly speaking. The inflationary element of the interest rate merely serves to maintain lenders' capital intact and can therefore be regarded as the repayment of lenders' principal.

For example, if corporate interest rates average (say) 15 per cent when inflation is 12 per cent, it is arguable that 80 per cent of contractual interest payments represents the repayment of lenders' principal and that the remaining 20 per cent constitutes real interest.

Using these assumptions to partition the contractual interest payments shown in Table 3A, the position can be restated as in Table 3B.

The right hand side of Table 3B can now be interpreted as follows:

- Woolworth's effective real (*ie* economic) interest cover averaged (388-190) ÷ 28 = 7 over the five year period in question and not 852 ÷ 142 = 6 as suggested by the left hand side of Table 3A.
- Woolworth's effective tax rate (*ie* computed in accordance with the principles of tax neutrality) was 190 ÷ 288 = 49 per cent and not 32 per cent as indicated by the left hand side of Table 3A.

Woolworths dividends were only 70 per cent internally financed and not twice covered as suggested by the left hand side of Table 3.

Conclusion

The principal inference that can be drawn from the forgoing analysis of Woolworth's financial performance, for the five years to January 1982, is that accruals accounting numbers have some seriously misleading properties.

In particular it cannot be assumed that a good accounting performance will guarantee a good cash flow performance and that accounting numbers will generally lead to the same set of decisions as would be signalled by a cash flows analysis.

In short, a mastery of the multi-period relationship between accounting numbers and cash flow numbers is a pre-requisite for efficient financial management not to mention reliable interpretations of financial performance and financial policies.□

[1]Tax payments are determined by reference to taxable earnings (net of allowable interest) and not by reference to pre-tax entity cash flows. Moreover, tax payments take precedence over interest payments. Hence, contractual interest represents a charge on *post-tax* entity cash flows.

Why the current UDS takeover bids became inevitable

The rather dramatic collapse of operating cash-flow in the year to January 1982 brought the United Drapery Stores group under close stock market scrutiny, and stimulated takeover plans. Opening his two-part look at cash-flow analysis, GERALD H. LAWSON, FCAA, professor of business finance at Manchester Business School, examines the group's performance and potential.

Table 1 UDS Consolidated source and application of funds statement

Year to January 31	1978	1979	1980	1981	1982
Source of funds					
Profit before taxation	19,158	27,818	24,115	16,244	13,744
Extraordinary items	(899)	(3,663)	(4,564)	(2,485)	(7,320)
	18,259	24,155	19,551	13,759	6,424
Adjustments for items not involving the movement of funds					
Depreciation and amortisation	4,709	4,583	5,626	6,592	6,819
Profit on sale of fixed assets and investments				(7,502)	(3,443)
Profits retained in associated companies	(1,145)	(1,347)	(1,460)	(678)	(1,861)
	3,564	3,236	4,166	(1,588)	1,515
Total generated from trading	21,823	27,391	23,717	12,171	7,939
Disposl of fixed assets and investments	8,051	25,435	32,769	14,373	8,485
Disposal of trade debtors				24,278	
Proceeds of rights issue			34,397		
Long and medium term loans	3,000	17,544			5,000
Excess of net tangible assets over cost of subsidiary companies acquired			3,068		
	32,874	70,370	93,951	50,822	21,424
Application of funds					
Purchase of fixed assets	(9,146)	(11,077)	(45,632)	(16,008)	(14,521)
Dividends paid	(7,442)	(7,781)	(8,612)	(11,843)	(11,843)
Taxation paid	(7,323)	(5,728)	(6,750)	(7,432)	(6,240)
Purchase of own debentures, investments and repayment of medium term loans	(141)	(27,502)	(9,115)	(1,631)	(7,714)
	(24,052)	(52,192)	(70,109)	(36,914)	(40,318)
Decrease/(increase) in working capital					
Stock	(8,284)	(4,558)	(9,460)	6,942	(3,548)
Debtors	(8,025)	(14,343)	(17,234)	4,951	(1,003)
Creditors	3,143	7,483	14,417	(5,202)	(492)
	(13,166)	(11,418)	(12,277)	6,691	(5,043)
Net inflow/(outflow) of funds	(4,344)	6,760	11,565 •	20,599	(23,937)
Represented by:					
Net liquid resources/(short term borrowings)					
At beginning of year	16,796	21,140	14,380	(2,815)	16,119
At end of year	21,140	14,380	(2,815)	16,119	(7,818)
Re-classification of long term borrowing				1,665	
	(4,344)	6,760	11,565	20,599	(23,937)

ACTUAL case studies provide the most convincing ways of illuminating the arguments about the analysis and interpretation of corporate financial behaviour and performance.

This week, while takeover bids are being revealed, the UDS example shows how cash-flow problems can bring about the scrutiny of investors in different ways. Compare, for example, the dividend and debt financing policies of the group which directly contrast with those of Woolworth (see *The Accountant*, November 4, 1982) while having as their similar root cause the dramatic collapse of operating cash-flow.

Analysis of UDS

The published consolidated funds flow statements of the UDS Group plc and subsidiaries for the five years ended January 30, 1982, are shown in Table 1. The cash-flow statements derived therefrom are presented in actual money terms and restated at January 1982 prices in Tables 2A and 2B.

Apart from this conversion process, two additional adjustments to the UDS consolidated funds flow statements are apposite, namely, the separate disclosure of

(a) rental revenue from properties not in the group's occupation (see note 2 in notes to the accounts); and,

(b) investments included in the funds flow item:

'Purchase of own debentures, investments and repayment of

> 'If the group's balance sheets are anything to go by, the disposable net asset value of UDS' equity is about 67 to 100 per cent higher than its current market value'

Table 2A total cash-flow statements (£000s)

Year to January 31	1978	1979	1980	1981	1982
funds generated from trading	+21,829	+27,391	+23,717	+12,171	+7,939
change in working capital	-13,172	-11,418	-12,277	+6,691	-5,043
disposal of trade debtors				+24,278	
interest paid	+6,967	+7,729	+8,610	+9,619	+8,263
1. operating cash-flow	+15,624	+23,702	+20,050	+52,795	+11,159
represented by:					
rental revenue	+1,779	+1,920	+2,557	+3,296	+4,002
cash from other trading	+13,845	+21,782	+17,493	+49,463	+7,157
purchase of fixed assets*	-9,146	-11,077	-42,564	-16,008	-14,521
purchse of investments	-1,486	-5,912			-3,732
disposal of fixed assets	+8,051	+25,435	+32,769	+14,373	+8,485
disposal of investments			+859	+3,579	
2. capital investment	-2,581	+8,446	-8,936	+1,944	-9,768
3. = 1-2	+13,043	+32,148	+11,114	+54,703	+1,391
tax paid	-7,442	-5,728	-6,750	-7,432	-6,240
liquidity change	-2,362	-2,299	-21,911	-10,832	+17,191
post-tax entity cash-flows	+3,239	+24,121	-17,547	+36,439	+12,342
dividends (less new equity raised)	-7,323	-7,781	+25,785	-11,843	-11,843
lender cash-flow	-4,084	+16,340	+8,238	+24,596	+499
represented by:					
interest paid	-6,967	-7,729	-8,610	-9,619	-8,263
medium/long term loans raised (less repaid)	+4,345	-4,150	-9,974	-5,210	+1,018
change in overdrafts	+6,706	-4,461	+10,346	-9,767	+6,746
short-term loans	+4,084	-16,340	-8,238	-24,596	-499

**including those acquired via company acquisitions*

medium-term loans'. (The difference, representing purchase of own debentures and repayment of medium-term loans, is also separately recorded in the cash-flow statements).

For 1982, the latter adjustment is:

Long and medium term loans as shown in consolidated balance sheet:

On January 30, 1982	34,988
On January 30, 1981	33,970
increase	1,018
Long and medium term loans raised (as shown in consolidated funds flow statement	5,000
Therefore long and medium term loans repaid	3,982
Purchase of own debentures, investments and repayment of medium term loans (as shown in funds flow statement)	7,714
Therefore investments purchased	3,732

> 'It seems hardly necessary to conclude that the current takeover plans for UDS are not surprising'

In interpreting the 1977-81 real cash-flow performance of UDS (Table 3) the two components of its operating cash-flow are an obvious starting point.

Whilst the annual revenue from properties not in the group's occupation was constant over the five-year period, other trading operations seemed to be on the decline.

In the absence of a significant sale of debtors in the year to January 1981 (£28.1 million at January 1982 prices), trading operations would only have generated a £23.6 million average in real terms and would have shown a distinct downward trend.

As in the recent Woolworth's case, a rather dramatic collapse of operating cash-flow in the year to January 1982, probably brought the UDS group under close stock market scrutiny, and stimulated takeover plans.

The somewhat extreme fluctuations in the UDS group's sequence of capital expenditure during 1977-81 largely refects its dealings in freehold properties. It can readily be inferred, from the group's published fixed asset schedules, that the realised market values of freehold land and buildings consistenly outweighed the proceeds of other assets displaced.

In that the group has for some years disclosed its property and in-

> 'Only through a comparison of real and monetary rates of return can the true impact of inflation and the illusory character of monetary values really be brought out into the open'

vestment transactions as a major activity and shows the profits thereon in its divisional turnover and profit report, one can hardly level the accusation that 'exceptional' or 'extraordinary' items are propping up the group and are in some sense reprehensible.

In each of the five years in question, the group's operating cash-flow exceeded its capital expenditure and, in two of those years, (because of property dealings) the latter expenditure actually constituted a net inflow.

After allowing for tax payments and annual liquidity adjustments, UDS generated an average real (entity) cash-flow of £14.937 million from which a rather modest dividend (less new equity) averaging £3.159 million was paid.

The difference (£11.778 million) constituted a net payment (mainly contractual interest payments) to lenders.

The dividend and debt financing policies of the UDS group thus contrast starkly with those of Woolworth. Over the same five-year period Woolworth made net payments to shareholders which were financed to the tune of 23 per cent by lenders who were therefore net contributors.

Summing up the interpretation of UDS group's real cash-flow performance during the five-year period to January 31, 1982 we see that the group demonstrated a positive (entity) cash-flow generating capability throughout the five years though, as in the Woolworth's case, its operating

Table 2B Total cash-flow statements restated at January 1982 prices (£000s)

Years to January 31	1978	1979	1980	1981	1982	5-year averages
1 operating cash-flow	+26,402	+37,162	+27,182	+61,169	+11,666	+32,717
represented by:						
rental revenue	+ 3,006	+ 3,010	+ 3,467	+ 3,821	+ 4,184	+ 3,498
cash from other trading	+23,396	+34,152	+23,715	+57,348	+ 7,482	+29,219
purchase of fixed assets	−15,456	−17,368	−57,704	−18,560	−15,180	−24,854
purchase of investments	− 2,511	− 9,269			− 3,901	− 3,136
disposal of fixed assets	+13,605	+39,880	+44,425	+16,664	+ 8,870	+24,690
disposal of investments			+ 1,165	+ 4,149		+ 1,063
2. capital investment	− 4,362	+ 13,242	−12,115	+ 2,254	−10,211	− 2,237
3. = 1-2	+22,040	+50,405	+15,067	+63,423	+ 1,454	+30,480
tax paid	−12,576	− 8,981	− 9,151	− 8,617	− 6,523	− 9,170
liquidity change	− 3,992	− 3,605	−29,705	−12,559	+17,971	− 6,378
post tax entity cash-flows	+ 5,472	+37,819	−23,788	+42,247	+12,902	+14,932
dividends (less new equity raised)	−12,375	−12,200	+34,957	−13,731	−12,380	− 3,146
lender cash flow	− 6,903	+25,619	+11,169	+28,516	+ 522	+11,786
represented by						
interest paid	−11,774	−12,118	−11,673	−11,152	− 8,638	−11,072
medium/long-term loans raised (less repaid)	+ 7,343	− 6,507	−13,522	− 6,040	+ 1,064	− 3,533
change in overdrafts/ short-term loans	+11,332	− 6,994	+14,026	−11,324	+ 7,052	+ 2,819
	+ 6,902	−25,619	−11,169	−28,516	− 522	−11,786
indexation factors	1.6899	1.5679	1.3557	1.1594	1.0454	

Table 3A UDS actual market values (£ million)

as at end-January	1977	1978	1979	1980	1981	1982
(a) equity	94.4	141.8	138.8	144.4	127.7	135.3
(b) debt*	61.0	76.0	63.0	64.0	50.0	56.0
(c) entity	155.5	217.8	201.8	208.4	177.7	191.3
(d) debt ratio = (b) ÷ (c)	39%	35%	31%	31%	28%	29%

Table 3B. UDS market values (£ million) expressed at January 1982 prices

as at end January	1977	1978	1979	1980	1981	1982
(a) equity	170.3	232.4	208.1	182.8	143.0	135.3
(b) debt*	109.9	124.6	94.4	81.0	56.0	56.0
(c) entity	280.2	357.0	302.5	263.8	199.0	191.3

**balance sheet value of short-term borrowings plus estimated market value of medium and long term loans*

cash-flow declined rather spectacularly in the final period.

Unlike Woolworth, the UDS group constrained its dividend policy (net of new equity) to the group's internal cash-flow generating capacity and did not therefore allow dividend payments to cause an escalating debt ratio (see Table 3A).

Whilst it may be tempting to conclude that the above description adds up to a picture of good husbandry, the recent activities of the Bassishaw predators suggest another conclusion.

As in the Woolworth takeover, UDS is yet another company whose going concern value (market values of debt and equity) apparently lies signifiacantly below the realisable value of its net assets.

If the group's historic and current cost balance sheets are anything to go by, the disposable net asset value (excluding intangibles of UDS's equity is about 67 to 100 per cent higher than its current market value.

The implication is that, notwithstanding its financial viability during 1978-82, the group's cash-flow performance was not sufficient to satisfy the stock market. This is another way of saying that the group's cash-flow performance contributed to the formation of pessimistic expectations about the level of future cash-flows which, in turn, were reflected in poor market value performance.

The half matrices of (real) entity, lender and shareholder rates of return shown in Tables 5A, 5B and 5C seem to bear this out.

Thus, the real entity rates of return (DCF returns on total capital) were negative in 11 of the 15 holding periods, as were shareholder rates of return. Lenders did rather better. In 10 of the 15 holding periods they enjoyed real positive rates of return. Negative real rates of return can be interpreted as the annual real rate of erosion of proprietorship wealth.

Incidentally, it is only through a comparison of real and monetary rates of return (and real and actual market values) that the true impact of inflation and the illusory character of monetary values can really be brought out into the open.

Interpreted in conjunction with the group's cash-flow performance and its dividend and debt-financing policies, the achieved rates of return lead to an interesting conclusion.

This is namely that, whereas UDS managed the right hand side of its cash-flow identity (dividend and debt policies) with some skill, the performance recorded on the left hand side facilitated adequate returns for lenders but left shareholders in the lurch.

‘UDS managed its dividend and debt policies with some skill facilitating adequate returns for lenders, but it left shareholders in the lurch’

‘As in the Woolworth takeover, UDS is yet another company whose going concern value lies significantly below the realisable value of its net assets’

Table 4A UDS entity rates of return (per cent per annum)
sold on January 31

		1978	1979	1980	1981	1982
	1977	42.15	21.58	12.62*	10.09	10.85
bought	1978		3.73	−0.69	0.47	3.43
on	1979			−5.43	−1.24	3.32
31st	1980				2.75	7.98
January	1981					14.60

* *See footnote to Table 4c.*

Table 4B. UDS lender rates of return (per cent per annum)
sold on January 31

		1978	1979	1980	1981	1982
	1977	17.90	10.75	11.87	12.82	12.84
bought	1978		4.40	8.33	10.97	11.29
on	1979			14.66	15.55	14.93
31st	1980				16.56	15.12
January	1981					13.00

Table 4C. UDS shareholder rates of return (per cent per annum)
sold on January 31

		1978	1979	1980	1981	1982
	1977	57.8	28.48	13.12	8.31	9.68
bought	1978		3.37	−5.76	−4.88	−0.14
on	1979			−14.54	−8.59	−1.24
31st	1980				−3.36	5.13
January	1981					15.23

The rate of return for any holding period is derived from the entry and exit market values (see Table 3) and cash-flows (see Table 2) corresponding thereto. For example, the three-year entity rate of return of 12.62% pa for 31.1.77. to 31.1.80. is the value of r which satisfies the equation:

$$155.5 = \frac{3.239}{1+r} + \frac{24.121}{(1+r)^2} + \frac{(208.4-17.547)}{(1+r)^3}$$

Table 5A UDS entity rates of return (per cent per annum) expressed at January 1982 prices

		sold on January 31				
		1978	1979	1980	1981	1982
	1977	29.36	11.19	0.39	−1.90	−1.15
bought	1978		−4.67	−12.54	−11.20	−6.33
on	1979			−20.66	−14.54	−9.67
31st	1980				−8.55	−3.65
January	1981					2.61

Table 5B. UDS lender rates of return (per cent per annum) expressed at January 1982 prices

		sold on January 31				
		1978	1979	1980	1981	1982
	1977	7.10	1.41	0.31	1.11	1.09
bought	1978		−3.68	−3.10	−1.07	−0.76
on	1979			−2.36	0.72	0.77
31st	1980				4.34	2.97
January	1981					0.93

Table 5C. UDS shareholder rates of return (per cent per annum) expressed at January 1982 prices

		sold on January 31				
		1978	1979	1980	1981	1982
	1977	43.73	17.43	0.45	−3.88	−2.46
bought	1978		−5.21	−17.57	−16.35	−11.75
on	1979			−28.96	−21.21	−13.75
31st	1980				−14.26	−6.28
January	1981					3.27

> ‘Some rationalisation, ie asset stripping, may become inevitable’

In other words, shareholders suffered from reverse leverage — a situation in which the returns on total capital were generally lower than the preferential returns to lenders.

It seems hardly necessary to conclude that the current takeover plans for UDS are not surprising. Whether a new or rejuvenated management can raise its cash-flow generating capacity to a level that is commensurate with its realisable asset value remains to be seen. Some rationalisation ie asset stripping, may become inevitable.

CONVICTION

Even though predators may have convinced themselves that, after gaining control, they intend to continue to operate a target company as a going concern, at its existing or other level of activity, a handsomely valued fall back position must always constitute an enormous takeover stimulus.

Moreover, if on realistic assumptions the market value of a company's assets is likely to continue to exceed its value as a going concern, there is a powerful economic argument for asset stripping since the implication is that those assets can be more efficiently deployed elsewhere.

Alternatively, a degree of asset stripping may be justified depending upon the piecemeal *ex ante* financial viability of a company's individual trading establishments.

But in all cases the best interests of the shareholders of a target company ought to be the paramount consideration of its directorate.

That is to say, if the exchange value of a company's assets exceeds their value as a going concern, it is incumbent upon its directorate to ensure that the lion's share of the excess of former value over the latter is not given away to predators.

The Measurement of Corporate Performance on a Cash Flow Basis: A Reply to Mr. Egginton

G. H. Lawson

Introduction

In recently enlarging upon his perceptions of the deficiencies of cash flow accounting/analysis (hereafter CFA), Mr. Egginton (1984) mainly concentrates on the earlier work of its two longstanding UK protagonists—Lawson and Lee. As a more careful reading of their later contributions would have revealed, both have developed their ideas well beyond those contained in the papers which are the main focus of Egginton's criticisms.

Furthermore, there are genuine differences between the respective CFA models that are currently advocated by Lawson and Lee. Nor is this likely to be the end of the story. CFA protagonists will doubtless break new ground in the near future. Thus, given its affinities with, not to say origins in, classical capital theory, one might reasonably speculate that, noting the development of modern capital market theory, CFA will become the first accounting system that measures performance on two dimensions—risk and profitability (in some sense of the latter).[1]

So much for the future. The purpose of this paper is to examine Egginton's recent robust criticisms of CFA by reference to the currently-advocated Lawson model.

Egginton's main allegations are:

(i) CFA is incapable of measuring *ex post* performance.
(ii) CFA cannot cope with the impact of inflation on financial performance.
(iii) CFA is exclusively concerned with flows and largely ignores the need of a financial position statement disclosing asset and liability values.
(iv) CFA cannot avoid the ownership emphasis: 'The usual presentations of CFA retain an ownership viewpoint.'
(v) CFA does not wholly circumvent the allocation problem.
(vi) *Ex ante* CFA has severe limitations.

The first five of these criticisms can be examined in an *ex post* framework leaving the last to be looked at separately. A more detailed version of Egginton's Royal Dutch/Shell example is used to emphasise the particular weaknesses of his attempted interpretation of that company's financial performance during 1974–81. It is also used to illustrate aspects of financial behaviour that normally escape 'conventional' interpretations of corporate performance. These also point to some of the respects in which corporate disclosure is (arguably) deficient.

The Lawson CFA model

In the present Lawson scheme of things, CFA is essentially a system for measuring multiperiod (*ex post*) performance. It also reveals entity, lender and shareholder returns, for all possible holding periods within any multiperiod sequence, and thereby attempts to link short, medium and long term measures of performance. Like all financial performance measurement systems which utilise periodic opening and closing values, CFA is not expectations free. Hence, *ex post* CFA cannot be completely detached from performance viewed *ex ante*.

A multiperiod *ex post* CFA model can be derived directly from the normative *ex ante* corporate (cash flow) valuation model which has been at the centre of financial theory for half a century or more. As is well known, two of the more recent applications of the normative valuation model have been its uses as a vehicle for illustrating the Modigliani-Miller hypothesis and the Miller-Modigliani dividend irrelevance proposition. Whereas the MM theories facilitate incisive *interpretations* of financial behaviour, the specification of their basic valuation model has practical limitations. Thus, whilst distinguishing explicitly be-

[1] One might also speculate that the addition of the risk dimension to value added statements can hardly fail to add rigour to an analysis that is essentially concerned with the partitioning of a risky earnings stream in a pre-determined order of priorities.

tween entity and proprietor (lender and shareholder) cash flows, their model does not specify this identity in detail. Expressed in detail, a firm's total cash flow statement for any year j can be represented as:

$$(k_j - h_j) - (A_j + R_j - Y_j) - H_j - t_j \equiv (D_j - B_j) + (F_j - N_j - M_j) \quad (1)$$

that is

entity cash flows ≡ shareholder cash flows + lender cash flows

where

$k_j - h_j$ denotes operating cash flow in year j represented by cash collected from customers, k_j, and operating cash outflows, h_j;

$A_j + R_j - Y_j$ stands for replacement investment, A_j, growth investment, R_j, and the proceeds from assets displaced, Y_j, in year j;

t_j stands for all taxes assessed on the corporation that are actually paid in year j;

H_j denotes liquidity change in year j;

F_j represents period j interest payments;

N_j is medium and/or long term debt raised or retired in year j;

M_j is short term debt raised or repaid in year j;

D_j represents dividends paid to shareholders in year j; and

B_j is equity capital raised or repaid in year j.

Whereas the variables contained in a firm's periodic cash flow statement can be specified in a wholly objective manner, its classification is, or should be, intended to facilitate interpretation. A multiperiod version of the LHS of (1) discloses economic information on three separate decision areas, namely, trading and production, capital investment and liquidity. It can also reveal the effective *incidence* of taxation on corporate cash flows. The RHS provides information on dividend and debt/equity financing policies. In other words, the LHS of a multiperiod version of (1) is concerned with *economic performance*[2] whereas the RHS has to do with matters of *financial policy* (over which management can perhaps exercise considerable discretion), namely, the levels of dividends and debt financing respectively.

Making use of the *ex ante* multiperiod version of (1), the 1958 MM hypothesis may, under a neutral corporate tax regime, be expressed as:

$$\sum_{j=1}^{\infty} \frac{(\bar{k}_j - \bar{h}_j) - (\bar{A}_j + \bar{R}_j - \bar{Y}_j) - \bar{t}_j - \bar{H}_j}{\prod_{t=1}^{j}(1+\bar{r}_t)} \equiv \sum_{j=1}^{\infty} \frac{\bar{D}_j - \bar{B}_j}{\prod_{t=1}^{j}\{1+\bar{r}_t^{(e)}\}} + \sum_{j=1}^{\infty} \frac{\bar{F}_j - \bar{N}_j - \bar{M}_j}{\prod_{t=1}^{j}\{1+\bar{r}_t^{(d)}\}} \quad (2)$$

or, $V_o \equiv V_o^{(e)} + V_o^{(d)}$

that is, market value of entity ≡ market value of equity + market value of debt

or, present value of entity cash flows ≡ present value of shareholder cash flows + present value of lender cash flows

where (using bars to denote expected values),
$\bar{r}_t$, $\bar{r}_t^{(e)}$ and $\bar{r}_t^{(d)}$ denote the single period costs of entity, shareholder and lender capital respectively; and, $\bar{r}_t$ and V_o are independent of the ratio $V_o^{(d)}/V_o$.

It is hardly necessary to recall MM's (1958, 1961) basic intentions. In using a normative valuation model to demonstrate (1958) that, in a neutral tax régime, a firm's total market value and its weighted average cost of capital are independent of its debt ratio, they also show that an independent choice of debt ratio automatically determines the relative market values of debt and equity. On the other hand, their 1961 paper effectively shows that the relative market values (debt ratio) of debt and equity depend upon the way in which dividend payments are financed. The 1958 and 1961 MM papers are therefore *a powerful aid in the interpretation of* a firm's cash flow performance, its past dividend/debt financing policies and the interaction of such policies with the *ex post* market values of its debt and equity capital.[3]

In using the *ex post* version of a normative valuation model as a basis for measuring multiperiod cash flow performance, two (rather than

[2]To *measure* economic performance the multiperiod LHS of (1) needs to be supplemented with market values as described hereafter.

[3]Positive empirical corroboration is not a necessary condition for using a normative theory as an aid to interpretation. Put more simply, the point is that a normative financial theory may suggest the right kind of questions for the analysis of financial behaviour and performance.

one) market values must be included in the computation, namely, the entity market values V_o and V_n, at the beginning and end of the n-year sequence respectively. The basic multiperiod *ex post* cash flow computation can therefore be incorporated into the familiar *ex post* internal rate of return (IRR) equation. Thus,

$$V_o = \sum_{j=1}^{n} \frac{(k_j - h_j) - (A_j + R_j - Y_j) - t_j - H_j}{(1+r)^j} + \frac{V_n}{(1+r)^n} \quad (3)$$

or

$$V_o^{(d)} + V_o^{(e)} = \sum_{j=1}^{n} \frac{(F_j - N_j - M_j) + (D_j - B_j)}{(1+r)^j} + \frac{V_n^{(d)} + V_n^{(e)}}{(1+r)^n} \quad (3a)$$

The internal rate of return, r, in (3) and (3a) can be interpreted as the *ex post* rate of return (expressed in money terms if actual values are used) on entity (i.e. total corporate) capital for the n-year sequence in question. From an entity standpoint it is a convenient device for tying together the two elements of its economic performance (for any sequence of periods), namely, distributed entity cash flow (LHS of (1)) and the change in its market value (i.e. change in the value of the business). This implies that the IRR automatically allows for the unexhausted benefits of capital expenditure. We return to this point below.

Viewing past performance from the respective standpoints of lenders and shareholders, their *ex post* rates of return, r_d and r_e, are given by:

$$V_o^{(d)} = \sum_{j=1}^{n} \frac{F_j - N_j - M_j}{(1+r_d)^j} + \frac{V_n^{(d)}}{(1+r_d)^n} \quad (4)$$

and

$$V_o^{(e)} = \sum_{j=1}^{n} \frac{D_j - B_j}{(1+r_e)^j} + \frac{V_o^{(e)}}{(1+r_e)^n} \quad (5)$$

Lender and shareholder rates of return, r_d and r_e, can be interpreted in much the same way as the entity rate of return, r. The former tie together the cash flow and market value change components of the respective returns to lenders and shareholders.

Multiple sign-change complications aside, internal rates of return can be computed for any holding period. For any n-year sequence there are therefore:

$n + (n - 1) + \ldots + 1$ internal rates of return.

The *ex post* computations represented by (1) (the total cash flow statement) and equations (3), (4) and (5) are incontrovertible statements of observable reality. There is no other way of expressing *either* the true *ex post* financial relationship between a firm and its proprietors or the true *ex post* relationship between income and capital. One or two practical inferences seem to follow, namely, that companies should *inter alia*:

(i) Disclose multiperiod cash flow statements, classified in accordance with identity (1), covering a minimum period of (say) 5 years. The basic purpose of such a statement is, as already implied, to show the recent development of the components of entity cash flows as well as revealing how they were distributed between lenders and shareholders.

(ii) Include statements, or charts, of the market values of their debt and equity capital (based on (say) weekly or monthly observations) in their interim and final accounts.

(iia) Disclose net realisable asset values on a continuing basis so that, by comparing the latter with the value of their company as a going concern, shareholders can judge whether continuation or dismantling would be in their better interests.

(iii) Disclose half matrices of internal rates of return in order systematically to tie together both components of lender, shareholder and entity returns.

(iv) Disclose the statements mentioned in i, ii, iia, and iii in real terms (more precisely, at a base-year price level) to eliminate the illusory effects of inflation and thereby facilitate multiperiod comparisons.

Except for a multiperiod statement of net realisable assets and half matrices of internal rates of return expressed in money terms, each of the above statements is illustrated in the Royal Dutch/Shell example.[4]

One might also argue, though this is perhaps too contentious for some, that cash flow performance should be juxtaposed with accruals performance to highlight the relative values of cash flow and accruals magnitudes and to draw attention to possible economic consequences of accounting.[5]

Technicalities and the interpretation of cash flow performance

Measuring Performance in Real Terms

In considering whether, and how, performance should be measured in real terms, the distinction between inflation and relative price changes should be made.

If any two, or more, time-series of factor prices are stated in money terms, those series automatically capture relative price changes. Thus, unlike the historic cost accounting model, a multiperiod cash flow statement expressed in money terms records actual prices in the individual periods in which those prices obtain and therefore

[4]See Tables 1 to 7.

[5]See Lawson (1982).

embodies relative price changes in exactly the same way. Hence in restating an actual (multiperiod) cash flow statement in real terms, it is merely necessary to allow for changes in the purchasing power of money using an index of general inflation.[6] The use of industry indices for the latter indexation exercise is clearly incorrect.

For a number of obvious reasons, measures of financial performance expressed at a base year price level are more informative than performance measures expressed in money terms. For example, interperiod comparisons of individual cash flow variables, market values and rates of return are only meaningful when expressed in constant purchasing power. Thus, a real decline in operating cash flow, which may be symptomatic of a need for radical changes in production, product mix, strategies for new product development etc., can easily be masked by an actual operating cash flow which steadily increases in money terms. Similarly, assuming that the paramount objective of a business undertaking is the creation of real wealth, a leading question is the rate at which real wealth has recently been created or eroded. This is signalled by positive or negative rates of return respectively.

The Unexpired Benefits and Financing of Capital Expenditure

It is reasonable to contend that, even when expressed at a base year price level, a multiperiod cash flow statement ignores the opening and closing unexpired benefits of capital expenditure.

A separate, though related, stricture is the contention that to deduct periodic capital expenditure from operating cash flow is to ignore the fact that a significant part of that expenditure may be financed with debt.

The second objection can conveniently be discussed first. It may be entirely valid when attention is focused on a single period, or perhaps even on a sequence of two or three periods, in isolation. But on a multiperiod dimension the contention that the inclusion of total capital expenditure in a cash flow statement ignores the extent to which that expenditure is financed with debt reflects a confusion over the distinction, illustrated by identity (1) and equation (2), between the performance of an entity *per se* and the manner in which that entity is financed by lenders and shareholders. More specifically it is a confusion that apparently overlooks the fact that an entity with a mixed capital structure not only finances a portion of its multiperiod capital expenditure with debt but also some part of its multiperiod post-tax operating cash flows and multiperiod liquidity adjustments.

[6]Because it is an admixture of many different purchasing powers, historic cost profit is not amenable to such an index number transformation.

The value of the unexpired benefits of a firm's past capital expenditure is represented *either* by the values that would be realised if its assets were to be sold in secondhand markets (value in exchange); *or*, by the cash flows that combination of assets is expected to generate in the future. Expectations do, however, have a market value which, if a company's debt and equity are traded, is observable.[7] In that value in exchange and value in use are concepts which relate to mutually exclusive courses of action, the former value can only validly be used as a terminal value if a company actually has terminated its activities by selling its assets in secondhand markets.[8] To the extent that firms have been undertaking capital expenditure, that expenditure is objectively reported in multiperiod cash flow statements. But the magnitude, timing and value of the unexhausted benefits of such expenditure is a question that is best left to the market place. Put more simply: if past capital expenditure is still of value it will be reflected in the market value of the business in question. Past capital expenditure, no matter how heavy, will only enhance the value of a business if the market is convinced of its 'quality'. Any judgment that the accountant or anybody else chooses to make about the unexhausted benefits of capital expenditure is entirely beside the point.

The foregoing line of argument seems to suggest that opening and closing *total* market values should be included in a multiperiod cash flow statement in order to make the connection between capital investment and changes in the value of a business. This is merely an alternative route to an inference that has already been drawn from equations (1) to (5) (inclusive). In that investors are continuously interested in such market value changes, there may be a stronger argument for the disclosure of (say) weekly or monthly market values in a chart or separate annex (like Table 3). Thus, a preface to the half matrices of IRRs could emphasise that the latter values tie together that part of proprietorship returns (entity cash flows) that is delivered directly by a company to its proprietors with the changes in the market value of a business that can only be accessed through market transactions.

Interpretation of Royal Dutch/Shell (RDS) performance 1975–81

Table 1 can be regarded as the basic work sheet for *ex post* cash flow analysis. It illustrates how a total

[7]The market value of variable interest rate debt is always equal to its nominal value.

[8]As already mentioned, equations (3), (3a), (4) and (5) include opening and closing market values, and therefore explicitly allow for the unexpired benefits of capital expenditure at the beginning and end of the n-year sequence, as does each of the IRRs in Tables 4 to 7 (inclusive).

Table 1
Royal Dutch/Shell: cash flow statement 1975-81

Years to 31st December	*1975* £m	*1976* £m	*1977* £m	*1978* £m	*1979* £m	*1980* £m	*1981* £m
Funds from operations	+ 1612	+ 2366	+ 2218	+ 2314	+ 4685	+ 4183	+ 4168
Currency translation effects	+ 213	+ 432	− 185	− 13	− 309	− 338	+ 886
Change in working capital*	− 485	− 269	+ 25	+ 458	− 1384	− 1409	− 301
Tax paid	+ 2361	+ 1973	+ 2150	+ 1689	+ 1383	+ 2468	+ 2961
Interest paid	+ 197	+ 253	+ 295	+ 350	+ 358	+ 399	+ 627
1 *Operating cash flow*, $k_j - h_j$	+ 3898	+ 4755	+ 4503	+ 4798	+ 4733	+ 5303	+ 8341
Purchase of property, plant & equipment	− 1333	− 1829	− 2222	− 2368	− 4075	− 2969	− 3965
Investment in associated companies	− 124	− 116	− 7	− 66	− 38	− 361	− 384
Other funds applied (less provided)	− 9	− 19	− 72		+ 60	− 62	− 157
Disposal of fixed assets	+ 340	+ 118	+ 82	+ 128	+ 107	+ 399	+ 405
2 *Net capital outlay*, $A_j + R_j - Y_j$	− 1126	− 1846	− 2219	− 2306	− 3946	− 2993	− 4101
3 = 1 + 2 $(k_j - h_j) + (A_j + R_j - Y_j)$	+ 2772	+ 2909	+ 2284	+ 2492	+ 787	+ 2310	+ 4240
Tax paid, t_j	− 2361	− 1973	− 2150	− 1689	− 1383	− 2468	− 2961
Liquidity change, H_j	− 191	− 540	+ 233	− 178	− 161	+ 542	− 949
Post-Tax Entity Cash Flows $(k_j - h_j) - (A_j + R_j - Y_j) - t_j - H_j$	+ 220	+ 396	+ 367	+ 625	− 757	+ 384	+ 330
Minority Interests, MI_j	− 147	− 14	− 30	+ 81	− 53	− 77	− 102
Dividends less New Equity Raised, $D_j - B_j$	− 303	− 428	− 507	− 537	− 608	− 604	− 587
Lender Cash Flow $F_j - N_j - M_j$	− 230	− 46	− 170	+ 169	− 1418	− 297	− 359
Represented by:							
Capitalised lease obligations, N_j	—	+ 30	+ 12	− 42	− 26	+ 2	+ 20
Interest paid, F_j	− 197	− 253	− 295	− 350	− 358	− 399	− 627
Medium/long term loans raised, N_j	+ 538	+ 491	+ 655	+ 594	+ 1682	+ 664	+ 1010
Medium/long term loans repaid, N_j	− 203	− 347	− 244	− 328	− 291	− 370	− 502
Change in overdrafts/short term loans, M_j	+ 92	+ 126	+ 43	− 43	+ 411	+ 400	+ 458
$F_j - N_j - M_j$	+ 230	+ 47	+ 170	− 169	+ 1418	+ 297	+ 359

*Including increase in receivables and deferred charges.

cash flow statement expressed in actual money terms is derived, and classified in accordance with identity (1), by re-ordering a published funds flow statement. If, as in the RDS example, the latter statement does not disclose tax payments, they can usually be derived from the corresponding balance sheets and profit and loss accounts. Thereafter the tax payments are added to both sides of the funds flow identity. Interest payments should also be added to both sides of the funds flow identity in preparing the total cash flow statement.

Whilst automatically capturing relative price changes, Table 1 does *not* facilitate multiperiod comparisons.[9] This is the purpose of Table 2 which, as indicated, is a simple index number transformation of Table 1.

The main inferences and questions that are suggested by Table 2 are concerned with the trends and relative magnitudes of the four constituents of post-tax entity cash flows.

[9]Mr. Egginton seems a little ambivalent about this. Notwithstanding a 125 per cent rise in the general level of prices between June 1975 and December 1981, he refers to the 'vast' net operating receipts generated by Royal Dutch/Shell and ignores the 30 per cent real decline in this series over the six years to December 1980.

Table 2
Royal Dutch/Shell: cash flow statement 1975–81 expressed at December 1981 prices

	1975 £m	*1976* £m	*1977* £m	*1978* £m	*1979* £m	*1980* £m	*1981* £m	*ave.* £m
Operating cash flow	+ 8780	+ 9413	+ 7574	+ 7513	+ 6656	+ 6163	+ 8707	+ 7829
Net capital outlay	− 2536	− 3654	− 3732	− 3611	− 5549	− 3478	− 4281	− 3834
Tax paid	− 5318	− 3906	− 3616	− 2645	− 1945	− 2868	− 3091	− 3341
Liquidity change	− 430	− 1069	+ 392	− 279	− 226	+ 630	− 991	− 282
Post-Tax Entity Cash Flows	+ 496	+ 784	+ 618	+ 978	− 1064	+ 447	+ 344	+ 372
Minority Interests	− 331	− 28	− 50	+ 127	− 75	− 89	− 106	− 79
Dividends less New Equity Raised	− 682	− 847	− 853	− 841	− 855	− 702	− 613	− 770
Lender Cash Flow	− 517	− 91	− 285	+ 264	− 1994	− 344	− 375	− 477
Interest payments	− 444	− 501	− 496	− 548	− 503	− 464	− 654	− 516
Debt raised (+) repaid (−)	+ 961	+ 592	+ 781	+ 284	+ 2947	+ 808	+ 1029	+ 993
Indexation factors	2.2524	1.9795	1.6819	1.5659	1.4062	1.1622	1.0439	

Table 3
Royal Dutch/Shell: estimated market values of debt and equity capital 1974–81

As at 31st December	*1974* £m	*1975* £m	*1976* £m	*1977* £m	*1978* £m	*1979* £m	*1980* £m	*1981* £m
Market value of loans and overdrafts								
Short term	638	773	907	990	946	1375	1799	2368
Long term	1430	1936	2534	2732	3243	4281	4215	5518
Total debt capital	2068	2709	3441	3722	4189	5656	6014	7886
Market value of Royal Dutch equity	2201	3965	5428	4659	5846	4757	5771	4934
Market value of Shell equity	1468	2644	3618	3106	3898	3172	3848	3289
Total equity capital	3669	6609	9046	7765	9744	7929	9619	8223
Minority interests	660	593	736	898	1159	1329	1513	1579
Total Market Value	6397	9911	13,223	12,385	15,092	14,914	17,146	17,688

Market values restated at December 1981 prices

	1974 £m	*1975* £m	*1976* £m	*1977* £m	*1978* £m	*1979* £m	*1980* £m	*1981* £m
Minority interests	1744	1255	1352	1472	1752	1714	1695	1579
Total debt capital	5463	5730	6325	6101	6335	7296	6739	7886
Total equity capital	9692	13,978	16,627	12,727	14,735	10,228	10,778	8223
Total Market Value	16,889	20,963	24,304	20,300	22,822	19,238	19,212	17,688
Indexation factors	2.6416	2.1151	1.8381	1.6391	1.5122	1.2899	1.1205	1.0000

Notes

(i) The market value of short term debt is (accurately) approximated by using its balance sheet values.

(ii) The long term debt is not listed on stock exchanges. Its market value is assumed to be equal to its balance sheet value. Its currency spread and nominal interest rate composition is such that this approximation is reasonable.

(iii) The market value of Royal Dutch equity is taken from *The Times* Monday capitalisation table. The equity market value of Shell is taken as two-thirds of the value of Royal Dutch equity.

(iv) In the absence of the necessary stock exchange quotations, the market values of minority interests are assumed to be equal to their balance sheet values.

Operating cash flow declined by 30 per cent in real terms during 1974-80 before recovering to its 1975 real level. Capital expenditure increased by 119 per cent in real terms between 1975 and 1979 before falling by 23 per cent over the two years to 1981. A leading question is therefore: how have the operating cash flow performance, the capital expenditure programme, and therefore the expected (future) operating cash flow performance as at December 1981, contributed to the value of the business during 1974-1981? Table 3 provides the answer. Over the seven-year period to December 1981, the real total market value of RDS increased by about 5 per cent.[10] This change in real market value together with the stream of real entity cash flows (distributed debt and equity cash flows) constitute the two elements which fully describe RDS's *going concern* performance on the financial (as opposed to risk) dimension during 1974–81.

Turning to the periodic liquidity changes shown in Table 2, RDS's liquidity steadily increased in real terms during 1974-81. In that its operating cash flow remained roughly constant in real terms,[11] the liquidity increase could, given the expectations that were apparently impounded in its total market value as at December 1981, hardly be ascribed to transactions motives. An alternative explanation might have been that, in the second half of the risk-laden seventies, RDS increased its liquidity as a precaution.

Computed from Table 2 in accordance with the principles of tax neutrality, the effective incidence of taxation on RDS during 1974–81 was 90 per cent, i.e. 3341/(372 + 3341).[12] Given an effective tax burden of this magnitude as a feature of the system, and only a modest increase in total market value (which probably embodied tax expectations that were similar), there must be serious doubts as to whether RDS could have provided adequate (i.e. risk-commensurate) returns during 1974-81. Such doubts are reinforced by the fact that, given the separate (accruals) basis of taxable earnings, assessed taxes constitute a preferential claim on entity cash flows, i.e. tax payments are characterised by a lower degree of risk than lender and shareholder returns and introduce an element of financial leverage risk.

Given the serial behaviour of a firm's total market value, evidence of the adequacy of entity cash flows may be provided by the (multiperiod) financing of its dividend policy (more precisely, the financing of shareholder cash flows).[13] As indicated by Table 2, shareholder cash flows exceeded post-tax entity cash flows by a factor of 2.07 during 1974–81. The equity cash flow shortfall was (by definition) financed by lenders who also financed their own interest payments.

The accumulation of debt caused by uncovered dividends and the fact that RDS's total market value remained roughly constant over the seven-year period have clear implications for its debt ratio. Unless there had been a significant countervailing rise in interest rates causing a commensurate decline in the market value of its debt, RDS's debt ratio would have risen. Table 3 shows that this was indeed the case. Measured on a market value basis, the increase was 13 percentage points, i.e. 32 per cent to 45 per cent.

An unambiguous answer to the question of the adequacy of real entity, shareholder and lender returns is provided by Tables 4, 5, 6, and 7.[14] Fourteen of the 28 real rates of return in Table 4 are negative and a further two are close to zero. RDS was therefore not consistently profitable over all investor holding periods during 1974–81.

Focusing on the seven possible holding periods to December 1981 (1981 columns), the *seven-year* entity (Table 4) and equity (Table 6) real rates of return were both positive but those for all shorter holding periods were negative. This is largely explained by the historically low equity market values that were caused by the 1974 stock market collapse which accompanied the corporate financial crisis in that year.

For shareholders (Table 6) buying after 1974, i.e. after the 1974 aberration, there were 7 out of 21 possible holding periods with positive real returns. The same can be said of the real entity rates of return (Table 4) but, as already mentioned, two of these positive rates were close to zero.

A further comparison of the 1981 columns of Tables 4, 5 and 6 suggests the presence of a reverse leverage effect (lenders being subsidised by shareholders) for the 5, 4, 3, 2 and one-year holding periods to 1981. A reverse leverage effect is always a serious possibility if there is debt-equity substitution caused by uncovered dividends when a firm's total market value is not increasing in real terms.

Mr. Egginton's criticisms of CFA

Turning finally to Mr. Egginton's criticisms of CFA, it is hardly necessary to deal with each in

[10]The reader needs no reminding that values expressed in money terms are usually the main focus of financial commentators. Royal Dutch/Shell's 177 per cent actual total market value increase is almost entirely illusory.

[11]The linear regression line fitted to the operating cash flows in Table 2 falls slightly and is given by y = 8920 – 273x.

[12]The validity of this computation is demonstrated elsewhere (Lawson (1981), Lawson, Möller and Sherer (1982)) and need not be repeated here.

[13]This is an interpretation of Table 2 which, in effect, requires a comparison of the LHS of the total cash flow identity with the equity and lender components on the RHS.

[14]Here we ignore the minorities' half matrix because their returns may be strongly influenced by the balance sheet values that have been used as illustrative proxies for their market values.

Table 4
Royal Dutch/Shell: entity rates of return (real terms)

Sold / *Bought*	*1975*	*1976*	*1977*	*1978*	*1979*	*1980*	*1981*
1974	26.98	23.32	9.81	11.54	4.82	4.39	2.88
1975		19.68	1.78	6.54	−0.52	0.01	−1.01
1976			−13.93	0.24	−6.89	−4.67	−4.97
1977				17.24	−2.94	−1.23	−2.48
1978					−20.37	−9.49	−8.39
1979						2.19	−2.02
1980							−6.14

Table 5
Royal Dutch/Shell: lender rates of return (real terms)

Sold / *Bought*	*1975*	*1976*	*1977*	*1978*	*1979*	*1980*	*1981*
1974	−4.58	2.20	−1.48	1.00	−2.78	−4.99	−2.09
1975		8.80	−0.04	2.72	−2.38	−5.05	−1.76
1976			−8.05	−0.09	−5.74	−7.86	−3.44
1977				8.16	−4.59	−7.81	−2.46
1978					−16.31	−14.04	−5.22
1979						−12.35	−0.87
1980							11.46

Table 6
Royal Dutch/Shell: shareholder rates of return (real terms)

Sold / *Bought*	*1975*	*1976*	*1977*	*1978*	*1979*	*1980*	*1981*
1974	51.27	37.84	16.95	18.16	9.27	9.67	6.19
1975		25.01	1.64	7.73	−0.71	1.42	−1.53
1976			−18.32	−0.61	−8.94	−4.55	−7.04
1977				22.38	−3.32	1.24	−3.43
1978					−24.79	−8.78	−11.77
1979						12.25	−3.56
1980							−18.02

Table 7
Royal Dutch/Shell: minorities rates of return (real terms)

Sold / *Bought*	1975	1976	1977	1978	1979	1980	1981
1974	−9.06	−1.05	2.94	4.60	4.10	4.10	3.47
1975		9.98	11.27	10.99	8.62	7.70	6.33
1976			12.61	11.52	8.16	7.13	5.60
1977				10.40	6.01	5.37	3.90
1978					2.09	3.06	1.88
1979						4.08	1.77
1980							−0.61

detail. The contention that the CFA model currently advocated by the writer is incapable of measuring *ex post* performance, and that it cannot cope with the impact of inflation on financial performance, are views that do not stand up to serious analysis.

There is also no substance to the objection that CFA is exclusively concerned with flows and largely ignores the need of a financial position statement disclosing asset and liability values. As illustrated above, the financial position statement of a going concern is a statement showing the debt and equity components of its total market value. Market values represent the best unbiased estimates of the value of the unexpired benefits of its existing asset stock. The relative market values of debt and equity also provide an incisive indication of additional debt-raising capacity, i.e. the ability to substitute further debt for equity. This is not to deny the importance of a statement of the realisable values of a firm's assets and liabilities—its value in exchange. Should the latter consistently exceed its going concern value (value in use) the implication may be that the firm should be dismembered or at least put under new management. The appropriate foundations for representing these mutually exclusive courses of action are well established in economics. It is therefore rather naive to argue, that '. . . for cash flow the corresponding stock at the end of the accounting period must be the entity's cash holding'.

Apropos of the criticism that CFA cannot avoid the ownership emphasis, two points can be made. In the first place, the case for avoiding the ownership emphasis in corporate reporting is by no means clear cut. If personal or institutional ownership is an observable fact of life, the interests of accountability (in every sense of the word) are not served by pretending that the situation is somehow different. This is not to gainsay the fact that employees may, albeit with limited tenure, have prior claims on expected cash inflows. But, in the second place, the Lawson CFA model makes the clear distinction between economic, i.e. entity, performance on the one hand, and the financing of the firm on the other. A further analysis of operating cash flows is the remaining short step to a unidimensional (cash flow) value added statement.

The contention that CFA does not circumvent the allocation problem is, in the writer's view, a complete red herring. The CFA model advocated by Lawson is entirely allocation free. There is no matching problem. Payments and receipts are recorded at the points in time at which they are made and received respectively. No form of allocation whatsoever is involved in this process. To describe the classification problem as an allocation problem is to confuse things that may occasionally be subject to classification error with costs and/or revenues that can only be allocated, as in the classical example of joint costs in the chemical industry, on a basis which is wholly arbitrary. To criticise CFA because it reports operating cash flows, capital expenditure, liquidity changes and tax payments as separate components of entity cash flows, on the grounds that such a classification requires allocations, is to ignore unambiguously definable classification criteria and to play semantic games. Classification is the crucial aspect of financial statement presentation that is intended to facilitate performance interpretation. Hence, any suggestion that classification should be abandoned as a means of circumventing a dubiously defined allocation problem throws out the baby with the bath water.

All forms of arbitrary allocation can and should be avoided. Thus, the assignment of data to specific sub-divisions of an entity can always be based on clearly defined principles and never needs to be tainted with arbitrary bases of allocation. There is absolutely no need for the arbitrary allocations advocated by the FASB in its recommendation on segment reports which themselves can be suitably classified.

The contention that *ex ante* CFA has severe limitations can be levelled against any form of *ex ante* accounting. There is clearly nothing in CFA which gives it special predictive power and, as far as is known, nobody has ever claimed that it has. What can however be argued is that companies should plan on a multiperiod cash flow basis. It is not difficult to demonstrate that, under fairly general conditions, there can be significant differences between the ranking of alternative plans on accruals and cash flow bases respectively. This is another way of saying that, used as corporate financial objectives, wealth maximisation and (multiperiod) ROI maximisation will not signal the same set of decisions. Any attempt to demonstrate the superiority of an ROI objective function would need to controvert established economic orthodoxy.

Mr Egginton's suggestion that cash flows are not uniquely amenable to discounting, because a 'suitably-adjusted' all-embracing income measure also has this property, in no way rebuts the foregoing proposition. The 'suitable adjustment' in question is a transformation which ensures that, given the firm's cost of capital, the present value of income is equal to the present value of the corresponding sequence of cash flows.

In conclusion it is appropriate to emphasise the importance of Mr. Egginton's recent challenge to CFA. As recently suggested elsewhere, CFA is here to stay. It has not only gained an increasing number of adherents in recent years, but has also been developed in different directions by a number of its proponents. It is important that its present rapid evolution should be held clearly in view. Replying to Mr. Egginton helps to achieve this.

References

Egginton, D. A., 'In Defence of Profit Measurement: Some Limitations of Cash Flow and Value Added as Performance Measures for External Reporting', *Accounting and Business Research*, Spring 1984.

Lawson, G. H., 'Was Woolworth Ailing?' *Accountant*, November 4, 1982.

Lawson, G. H., 'Why the Current UDS Takeover Bids Became Inevitable', *Accountant*, February 10, 1983.

Lawson, G. H., 'Call for SSAP 10 Reform', *Accountant*, February 17, 1983.

Lawson, G. H., Möller, H. P., and Sherer, M., 'Zur Verwendung anschaffungswertorientierter Aufwand-Ertrag-Rechnungen als Grundlage für die Bemessung von Zinsen, Steuern und Dividenden', in Lück and Trommsdorff (eds.), *Internationalisierung der Unternehmung*, Erich Schmidt Verlag, Berlin, July 1982.

Lawson, G. H. and Stark, A. W., 'Equity Values and Inflation Dividends and Debt Financing', *Lloyds Bank Review*, January 1981.

Lee, T. A., *Cash Flow Accounting*, Van Nostrand Reinhold (UK), 1984.

Miller, M. H. and Modigliani, F., 'Dividend Policy, Growth and the Valuation of Shares', *Journal of Business*, October 1961.

Modigliani, F. and Miller, M. H., 'The Cost of Capital, Corporation Finance and the Theory of Investment', *American Economic Review*, June 1958.

Call for SSAP 10 reform

A company's economic and financial performance, and the nature and effects of its dividend and debt financing policies can be elucidated by the use of multiperiod cash-flow analysis. The analysis of Woolworth and UDS *The Accountant* (November 4, 1982 and February 10, 1983) showed how revealing this technique can be.

The multiperiod cash-flow analysis is based on the following identity: Entity cash-flows = lender cash-flows + shareholder cash-flows.

Sound financial management and the maintenance of a stable debt ratio dictates that dividend and debt financing policies (right hand side of the identity) should be simultaneously determined by reference to each other — subject to the level of expected entity cash-flows on the left hand side.

When these conditions have not been met, eg if firms consistently fail to generate positive entity cash-flows and/or finance uncovered dividends with debt, the individual factors that have caused the situation, or indeed any other, can be highlighted by a suitably classified multiperiod cash-flow statement supplemented by a statement of the market values of the company's debt and equity for the same sequence of periods.

The qualification 'suitably classified' is important since classification is intended to facilitate an interpretation reflecting an underlying notion of financial performance which, in turn, derives from a corporate financial objective.

Cash-flow accounting is the accounting method implicit in the objective of wealth (or market value) maximisation or, in more familiar operational terms, the maximisation of the present value of expected proprietorship (lenders and shareholders)

'The funds flow statement needs to be adjusted or supplemented in at least seven respects'

In his second article on cash-flow analysis professor GERALD LAWSON argues that if an SSAP 10 type funds flow statement is to stimulate interpretations of financial performance and behaviour, it needs to be radically reformed.

cash-flows. The left hand side of a company's cash-flow identity can thus be regarded as a set of variables, the magnitudes of which management should attempt to optimise by judicious selection from alternative feasible plans (multiperiod price, output and investment strategies) that are characterised by different cash-flow time profiles.

By contrast, the shareholder and lender cash-flows on the right hand side of the cash-flow identity are, as already emphasised, policy variables over which, subject to the magnitude of the left hand side, financial managers can exercise not inconsiderable discretion.

ASPECTS

A suitable classification of the left hand side of the cash-flow identity should therefore reflect four aspects of business behaviour that are common to all going concerns, namely:

(i) The use of existing capacity (including a work-force and an array of managerial and other capabilities) in undertaking trading (sales and buying) and productive activity to generate a net inflow of cash from operations (operating cash-flow *equals* sales receipts *minus* operating cash outflows);

(ii) that, in using existing productive and trading capacity, firms are continuously confronted with the need to replace constituents of their existing assets and may also uncover expansionary and new product opportunities requiring 'growth' capital expenditure;

(iii) the generation of taxable earnings which result in payments to the tax collectors;

(iv) the maintaining, and periodic adjustment of, liquidity levels (cash and related assets) in response to transactions, precautionary and speculative motives.

Entity cash-flows having been defined and classified in accordance with the above decision-making areas, the right hand side of a firm's cash-flow identity by definition discloses the total cash-flows that are divisible between shareholders and lenders respectively.

Thus, reiterating in a slightly different form of words; if a firm's investment decisions are generally well based then, taking one year with another, the level of operating cash-flows should at least be such that the left hand side of the cash-flow identity constitutes a net inflow facilitating net returns ie net payments, to both lenders and shareholders.* The classification of a multiperiod cash-flow statement should directly facilitate this kind of interpretation.

Hence, the cash-flow format that was proposed in the previous article, namely,

operating cash flow *less* **investment** *less* **tax paid**

less **liquidity change** = **lender cash flows** *plus* **shareholder cash flows**

Converting funds flow statements to cash-flow statements

Whereas neither British nor American companies are required to disclose cash-flow statements, the latter can be derived from the obligatory

**This is a necessary condition. The sufficient condition (illustrated later) is that the level of entity cash-flows should provide lenders and shareholders streams of net payments that are commensurate with the respective risks which then they bear.*

funds flow statements. This derivation is principally the reordering and reclassification of the numbers in funds flow statements, supplemented with adjustments in respect of interest paid and liquidity changes.

(The US statement of changes in financial position starts with post-tax profit and does not disclose tax paid. The latter therefore needs to be separately computed from a taxation account reconstructed from opening and closing tax balances in the balance sheet and the tax charge in the profit and loss account corresponding to the period in question.)

The above arithmetic is readily illustrated by commencing with an SSAP 10-type funds flow statement expressed in identity form, ie:

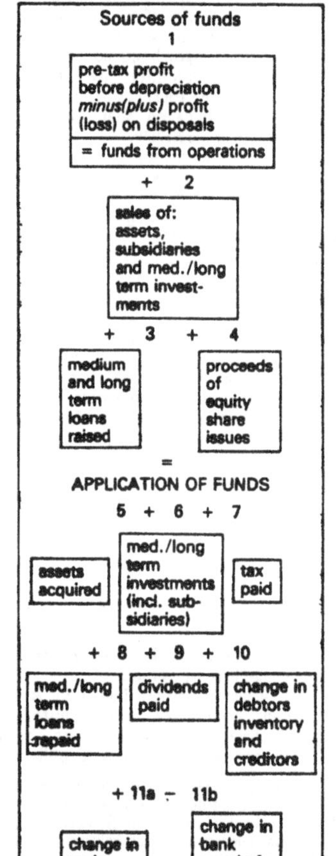

Taking the derivation of the cash-flow statement from the funds flow statement in two stages; the items in the above identity should first be reordered as follows:

$$(1-10)-(5+6-2)-7-11a=$$
$$(8+11b-3)+(9-4)$$

Thereafter, both sides of the identity should be adjusted in respect of interest paid (which is a constituent of lender cash-flows) since pre-tax profit includes that interest as a cost 'above the line'.

Thus, interest paid, F, should be added both to $(1-10)$ and to $(8-11b-3)$. This implies that interest received should be treated as an operating cash (in) flow which is indeed the case since it results from a conscious managerial decision to deploy capital externally in interest-bearing securities as opposed to internal real capital projects.

The groupings of outlays and receipts associated with internal and external investment and disinvestment $(5+6-2)$, and the adjustments to the right hand side of the funds flow statement (which effect the classification of lender and shareholder cash-flows as initially described) require no further amplification.

PRINCIPLE

By contrast, adjustments in respect of periodic working capital investment, $(1-10)$, and periodic changes in cash, $-11a$, raise important matters of principle.

Apropos of the working capital adjustment, the reader is first reminded that it converts (the accruals-based) funds from operations into cash from operations. Rather more important is the reason for the adjustment.

An inherent weakness of the funds flow statement is that it gives the erroneous impression that funds generated from operations constitute part of a pool which, at management's discretion, can then be deployed in alternative uses including periodic working capital investment.

Far from being independent of funds generated from operations, periodic working capital investment is a direct function thereof, and should be linked with funds from operations accordingly.

Consider first a situation in which, whilst a firm's level of physical trading activity, represented by (say) purchases and sales of merchandise, remains constant, its costs and prices increase in money terms. (The number of units of inventory investment is also assumed to be constant — as are the periods of credit given to and received from customers and suppliers respectively).

In these circumstances the periodic change in working capital (changes in debtors, creditors and inventory values) is a *function* of the level of pre-depreciation historic cost profit which itself is a function of the rates of change of the firm's costs and selling prices.

The recognition that a continuous deployment of working capital (measured in money terms) is necessary to sustain a constant volume of activity when costs and prices are increasing has, of course, led to the emergence and acceptance, of the cost of sales and monetary working capital adjustments that are now an integral part of SSAP 16.

It is only a further short step to the realisation that, if a company's level of physical activity changes over time, the effects on working capital will be the same as those that are caused by changing costs and changing selling prices.

That is to say, changes in physical activity levels affect the magnitudes in the profit and loss account which, in turn, affect the level of total working capital deployed.

For example, assume that whilst a company's costs and prices remain constant over a succession of accounting periods, its volume of trading activity increases.

Under these conditions there will be periodic increases in its accrued sales (historic) cost of sales, inventory volumes, debtors and creditors. Given the respective periods of credit given and taken, periodic increases in the individual elements of working capital (debtors, creditors and inventories) will be observed.

Again, it must be emphasised that, far from being *independent* of the profit and loss account, the change in

'SSAP 10 by no means makes it clear what questions the funds flow statement is designed to answer'

working capital is a *function* of the level of reported profit. Note, however, that this particular change in working capital is a function of both historic cost and current cost profit.

The arguments for showing liquidity changes (11a) as a separate item in a funds flow statement have already been adduced and require little further emphasis. What can be underscored is that the deducting of changes in bank overdrafts from changes in cash balances to disclose a so-called 'net movement of liquid funds' is objectionable in that it confuses two separate things.

The transactions, precautionary and speculative motives for maintaining and adjusting any level of liquidity, are common to all firms, regardless of the way in which they are financed.

By contrast, the level of a bank overdraft is a policy question concerned with the exercise of managerial discretion with respect to a company's overall debt level including the short, medium and long term composition thereof.

The substance of the foregoing paragraphs is that if an SSAP 10-type funds flow statement is to stimulate interpretations of multiperiod financial performance and financial behaviour which are:

(a) Consistent with the objective, and determinants, of market value maximisation; and,
(b) elucidate dividend and debt-financing policies, then that statement needs to be adjusted or supplemented in at least seven respects,* namely:
(i) Interest received should be treated as a constituent of operating income whereas interest paid should be shown as a separate item in the funds statement.
(ii) Both the price and volume elements of periodic changes in working capital should be directly linked to pre-depreciation profit in the funds statement.
(iii) 'Assets and subsidiaries acquired' and 'assets and subsidiaries sold' should be summarised in a single section of the funds statement.
(iv) Periodic changes in cash balances (including short term investment) should be shown separately from periodic changes in bank overdrafts.
(v) Companies should be required to disclose multiperiod (covering say five years) cash flow/funds statements expressed in both money and real terms.
(vi) The financing of interest, taxes and dividends should be made explicit by reference to a multiperiod cash flow/funds flow statement.
(vii) SSAP 10 should be supplemented with diagrams showing the market values of debt, equity and entity capital in both real and money terms over a ten-year period.

It is occasionally objected by 'efficient market' theorists that, because published accounts do not contain 'new' information, no amount of revamping or arithmetical reordering can alter that fact. Valid though such a contention may be, it does not negate the proposition that accounting statements should directly facilitate interpretations of corporate performance and financial behaviour by the public in general.

Table 1. UDS shareholder rates of return (per cent per annum) expressed at January 1982 prices (See last week's issue (page 16) for all the half matrices).

		sold on January 31				
		1978	1979	1980	1981	1982
	1977	43.73	17.43	0.45	−3.88	−2.46
bought	1978		−5.21	−17.57	−16.35	−11.75
on	1979			−28.96	−21.21	−13.75
31st	1980				−14.26	−6.28
January	1981					3.27

Half matrices of rates of return

A logical extension of (v) and (vii), and directly derivable from the data required thereunder, are half matrices of both real and nominal achieved DCF rates of return for lenders, shareholders and the company as a whole. Table 1 indicates how such half matrices might be disclosed.

The case for the disclosure of achieved proprietorship rates of return lies in the fact that they tie together the two constituents of the returns to shareholders and lenders, namely:

(a) A stream of cash-flows delivered directly by a company to its proprietors; and,
(b) the capital appreciation (or depreciation) resulting from the capital market transactions whereby individuals or institutions acquire (or divest themselves of) proprietory rights in companies.

(As Table 1 shows, a five-year half matrix shows every rate of return for all possible holding periods within and including, the five-year sequence.)

It is perhaps important to emphasise that the computational basis of a proprietorship DCF rate of return differs fundamentally from that of the rate of return of capital employed that is often published in company accounts.

Finally, it should be questioned whether the disclosure of funds flow statements in accordance with the (two-year) basis recommended by SSAP 10 is intended to promote some alternative form of interpretation. SSAP 10 by no means makes it clear what questions the funds flow statement is designed to answer. One is thus left wondering whether a statement that;

(a) treats interest paid as an operating cost rather than as an allocation of achieved earnings to lenders;
(b) mixes up operating, financing and capital investment transactions on both sides of the identity;
(c) gives the unmistakable impression that periodic working capital investment is independent of funds generated from operations; and,
(d) defines the periodic change in liquid resources as the net difference between periodic cash-flows that reflect an economic decision (liquidity adjustment) on the one hand and a policy decision (change in short-term debt) on the other

can be a defensible basis for disclosing the changes in a company's financial position. This is an aspect of funds flow statements that has not escaped the attention of others including Professor Busse von Colbe and Von Wysochi, who have for many years strongly advocated a funds flow classification which clearly separates operating, investment and financing transactions.□

Equity Values and Inflation: Dividends and Debt Financing

by G H Lawson and A W Stark

In his article in last July's issue of this *Review*[1], Professor Basil Moore purports to show that, contrary to widespread belief, there has been no significant secular decline in UK real corporate profitability. The real decline in UK equity values since 1969 is apparently ascribable to the real reduction in the absolute level of dividend payments, stemming from a combination of government and corporate action. Moreover, management has seemingly reinvested a real 'dividend shortfall' in capital projects 'bringing too low a rate of return'.

The purpose of this article is to show:

a) that the 'dividend shortfall' hypothesis is at odds with the facts;
b) that, even allowing for the element of lender's capital which was repaid via contractually-determined interest payments, a significant proportion of UK dividends was debt-financed during 1961-77; and
c) that such (real) debt-equity substitution probably accounts for about 38 per cent of the real decline in equity values between 1961 and 1978.

A fourth important factor which emerges from our analysis is that the effective tax burden, ie the incidence of taxation, on UK companies was significantly higher than that suggested by the tax charges disclosed in their published accounts. For reasons briefly outlined in the penultimate section, such fiscal drag probably contributed in no small way to the decline in real equity values.

The authors are respectively Professor of Business Finance at the Manchester Business School, University of Manchester, and Lecturer in Accounting and Business Finance, Faculty of Economics and Social Studies, University of Manchester. Professor Lawson was on leave of absence at the Ruhr University, Bochum, between September and December, 1980, and is currently at the University of Texas at Dallas.

[1] Professor Moore's reply to this article and to a letter from Professor Peter Wiles is on pages 55-57 of this issue.

The implication is that the increase in real dividends which is advocated by Professor Moore could, in the absence of a commensurate reduction in the corporate tax burden (which in our view is still too high), be financed only from further real absolute increases in debt capital. Such additional increases in debt would merely reinforce the real decline in equity values that has taken place since 1969.

As Professor Moore's analysis to some extent reflects a new conventional wisdom on corporate profitability which appears to be gaining credence in both official and other quarters, it is important that it should be examined in its own right. However, if two analyses of the same problem yield diametrically opposed conclusions, the implications are none too comfortable from a corporate and public policy standpoint. Thus, in the pages which follow, we first consider some of the technicalities raised, and conclusions drawn, by Professor Moore. Thereafter, in presenting our own results, we attempt to highlight the main differences between his approach and ours.

Equity Values and Reinvestments

According to Professor Moore, the real return on (total) fixed investment, including the returns on new projects 'bringing too low a rate of return', has remained roughly constant whilst real equity values have simultaneously declined. If this were so, the returns on new projects could have been inadequate only in the sense that they failed to provide risk-commensurate rates of return, ie new projects earned much the same return as 'old' assets but were more risky. Shareholders respond to increasing risks by adjusting their discount rates and will allow for perceived quality changes in the returns to ongoing operations in the same way. Professor Moore rejects the increasing risks argument and, notwithstanding the fact that dividend yields have long been discredited as a proxy for the cost of equity capital, concludes from their relative stability that shareholders have only slightly increased the rates at which they discount expected dividend income.

It is legitimate to question how new projects which neither reduced the return on total capital, nor raised over-all risk, nevertheless yielded an inadequate return and, simultaneously, reduced share values via some undefined process in which shareholder discount rates apparently did not rise.

A closely related analytical issue requiring clarification concerns the effect on equity values *over time* of '... a reduction in dividend payouts' which is '... in practice associated with a rise in both retentions and corporate investment expenditure rather than a reduction in new issues' (page 14). It is not generally correct to argue, as does Professor Moore, that if two companies, which we may term a 'reinvestor' and an 'earnings distributor', begin with the same capital stock, the 'reinvestor' will, should it fail to earn risk-commensurate rates of return on its reinvestment projects, tend to have a lower value over time than the 'income distributor'.

In a sense, this kind of comparison is invalid precisely because of the capital stock changes which take place in the one case compared with the other. Thus, the 'inefficient' reinvestment of disposable shareholder income within a company might be assumed to affect its observable value in the following way. Assume that a company reinvests 100 of disposable earnings in a project offering a negative net present value of 30. The market value of the company can be expected to fall by the latter amount since it has exchanged 100 of cash for an asset worth only 70. The value of the company's real asset stock has nevertheless increased by 70. By comparison, the distribution of the 100 as a dividend would have resulted in capital stock and market values both of which were 70 lower than under the reinvestment alternative.

To be sure, shareholders are better off in the second case since they are personally able to reinvest their 100 dividend at risk-commensurate rates of return in investments worth 100 and can thereby enjoy wealth that is 30 greater than under the first alternative. But it is nevertheless the case that the observable value of the 'reinvestor' will exceed the observable value of the 'earnings distributor' and, on the foregoing assumptions, a continuation of their respective reinvestment and distribution policies will cause a continuous divergence of their market values over time.

It therefore seems difficult to argue, as does Professor Moore, that a reduction in dividend payments causing expansionary investment results in lower market values than those that would have emerged in the absence of such expansion. If dividend policy is to be made one of the culprits for the decline in real equity values, some other explanation appears to be necessary. However, before pursuing the role of dividend policy further, certain aspects of the major accounting technicality raised by Professor Moore, namely, the correction of reported earnings in an inflationary environment, need to be considered.

Inflation and Profitability

Whilst most inflation accounting protagonists would probably agree that historic cost profit needs to be adjusted in respect of a depreciation shortfall and stock appreciation, Professor Moore obscures two separate methodological questions in suggesting (page 5) that '. . . few accountants or businessmen today would be prepared to defend such "partially adjusted" figures as an unbiased estimate of true profits in an inflationary environment'.

One of the most significant conceptual improvements that has emerged from the last decade's debate on inflation accounting, and now formally reflected in SSAP 16, is the distinction between (current cost pre-interest) operating profit and shareholder profit. This dichotomy corresponds to the distinction between the entity and equity bases of profit measurement and, in principle, facilitates inter-company comparisons regardless of differences in debt/equity ratios. Thus, the entity (ie SSAP 16 operating profit) basis of profit measurement is concerned with the profitability of the totality of economic activity organized by a business entity. By contrast, in viewing profitability from a shareholder standpoint, the equity basis deals with the division of entity income between lenders and shareholders.

To represent an equity concept of profitability as a notion of profitability in a fundamental economic sense is to confuse the level of achieved economic (entity) income with the ratio in which that income is distributed between lenders and shareholders. It is, of course, perfectly true that shareholders occasionally benefit at the expense of lenders and *vice versa* but that has little or nothing to do with company economic performance *per se.*

The upshot of the foregoing paragraphs is that each of the array of gearing adjustments described by Professor Moore is irrelevant to the measurement of economic performance. Moreover, if, as Professor Moore repeatedly tells us, equity market values depend upon prospective dividend streams, notions of equity profit are also irrelevant and gearing adjustments can again be left severely alone.

In using the type of dividend valuation model described by Professor Moore, the leading question concerns the division of an entity's sustainable cash flows between payments to lenders, to the tax collectors and to shareholders. For this purpose, an entity's cash flow should be defined as annual operating cash flow (sales receipts less payments in respect of operating costs) *minus* annual total capital expenditure[1].

[1] It may be mentioned *en passant* that a company is profitable in an *ex ante* economic sense if the present value of its expected operating cash flow stream exceeds the present value of its expected capital expenditures.

Dividends, Debt Financing and Equity Values

To draw inferences about the role of dividend policy in the equity valuation process it is, among other things, necessary to:

a) analyse past (multi-period) entity cash flow performance,
b) ascertain the past division of achieved entity cash flows between lenders, the tax collectors and shareholders; and
c) to determine whether there are particular 'features of the system' which will result in a similar, or changing, division of entity cash flows in the future.

Tests of efficient market theory suggest that there is good reason to suppose that, at the level of aggregation considered by Professor Moore, these three steps constitute an integral part of the process whereby investors collectively form expectations about future dividends, thereby exerting a corresponding influence on the equity market valuation process. Consider, for example, the likely effect on equity market values of a situation in which dividend payments (less new equity capital raised) consistently exceed post-tax entity cash flows and, in the modern jargon, necessitate a continuous borrowing requirement. Such debt-equity substitution is of a similar character to that which takes place when an American corporation raises a loan in the capital market to finance the purchase of its own shares in the stock market. The result is an increase in the market value of the corporation's debt and a decline by a similar amount of the market value of its equity[1].

An analysis of the cash flow performance of the official sample of quoted companies adopted by Professor Moore is shown in Table 2 (page 48). It leaves little doubt that, since 1961, their dividend payments have been financed with debt to a significant degree[2]. However, before looking at the cash flow data, it ought perhaps to be emphasized that the repayment of shareholder capital via dividend policy should not usually cause any loss of shareholder wealth. Indeed, it may actually give shareholders corporate tax benefits. When dividend payments are debt-financed, companies effectively repurchase their own shares at (unbiased) market values.

At least two objections to debt-financed dividends, in addition to the one mentioned by Professor Moore (wealth transfers from bondholders to shareholders when new

[1] Cumulative debt-equity substitution may be associated with a constant, increasing or declining entity value and may be expected to exert the most pronounced effect on real equity values in the latter case.

[2] A similar analysis of their seven years' previous performance leads to the same conclusion for that period.

tranches of debt are raised on conditions which lower the quality of existing corporate debt), do however suggest themselves. Debt-financed dividends are objectionable if, as has apparently been the case in the UK, the related debt-financing is unintentional. The evidence suggests that UK companies have hitherto based their dividend policies on historic cost profits[1] and, in distributing roughly 40 per cent thereof during 1961-77, failed to realize that dividends on this scale exceeded post-tax entity cash flows.

A somewhat less serious objection to debt-financed dividends is that they represent unsolicited adjustments to investor portfolios.

Cash Flow Performance

The 17-year cash flow performance shown in Table 2 is derived from the annual aggregated accounts of listed companies engaged in manufacturing and distribution etc. which hitherto were published in *Financial Statistics*[2]. The derivation is a simple two-stage process. In the first stage, the funds table is converted into a cash flow table as illustrated by the lay-out of Table 1. Thereafter, the entire sequence of 17 annual cash flow statements is restated at a base-year price level using the retail price index to measure the decline in the purchasing power of money. The latter operation is illustrated by the second column of Table 1 overleaf. The 1977 indexation factor of 0.6484 is equal to the level of retail price index at December 1974 divided by the corresponding level at April 1977[3], ie 116.9/180.3.

The basic intention in expressing a multi-period cash flow performance statement in real terms is the derivation of time sequences of absolute numbers which facilitate both intra- and inter-period comparisons (and therefore time-series averages). It is also important to note that each of the items in any individual periodic cash flow statement that emerges in the first stage is expressed in terms of that period's purchasing power. Hence, a sequence of cash flow statements expressed in money terms automatically captures relative price changes taking place over time, ie changes in the relative prices of labour, material, capital etc. The second stage preserves the changing relative price structure that is captured in the first stage, since it

[1] See M Theobald, 'Intertemporal Dividend Models — An Empirical Analysis Using Recent UK Data', *Journal of Business Finance & Accounting*, 1978.

[2] Due to impending changes in the sample's composition, the latest available data, namely those for 1977, were published in July 1979.

[3] April 1977 is the approximate average due date of the aggregate cash flows arising during the tax year 1977. The latter year covers the twelve-month period to April 1978, and the aggregation process includes the accounts of companies whose financial years end within it.

Table 1 *Income and Finance of Listed Companies: Cash Flows of Companies engaged in Manufacturing and Distribution etc*

Accounts for year 1977 for 975 companies		£m actual	*£m at Dec 1974 prices*
gross income		+11 522.0	*(indexation*
add back short-term interest		+ 1 129.0	*factor = 0.6484*
deduct periodic working capital investment			*see note v)*
increase in debtors	−1 879.9		
increase in inventory	−2 710.0		
increase in creditors	+2 170.0	− 2 419.9	
Operating Cash Flow		+10 231.1	*+6 633.8*
deduct total investment (see note i)		− 5 924.7	*−3 841.6*
Pre-tax Entity Cash Flow		+ 4 306.4	*+2 792.2*
deduct increase in liquidity		− 755.4	*− 489.8*
total interest paid		− 1 817.5	*−1 178.5*
tax paid (see note ii)		− 2 020.6	*−1 310.2*
dividends paid (see note iii)		− 942.1	*− 610.9*
Deficit		1 229.2	*797.0*
Financed by:			
increase in amounts owing to banks		638.8	*414.2*
increase in short-term loans		24.9	*16.1*
increase in long-term debt (see note iv)		565.6	*366.7*
		1 229.2	*797.0*

Notes

i) Derived as explained on page 48.

ii) Tax paid comprises: corporation tax payments of £2 208.1m minus other capital receipts (chiefly cash grants) of £275.7m and an increase in tax reserve certificates of £88.2m.

iii) Dividends paid are net of new equity capital amounting to £597.7m but include 70 per cent of 'acquisition of subsidiaries by cash' ie 70 per cent of £295.3m (= £206.7m).

iv) The increase in long-term debt is net of 30 per cent of 'acquisition of subsidiaries by cash' (= £88.6m).

v) The December 1974 values are equal to the products of the respective adjacent actual values and the 0.6484 indexation factor which is also explained in the text (see page 45).

Table 2 *UK Listed Companies: Entity and Proprietorship Cash Flows Expressed at December 1974 Prices*

£m	Entity Cash Flows							Debt Proprietorship			Equity Proprietorship
accounts for year	1 operating cash flow	2 total invest-ment	3=1−2 pre-tax entity cash flow	4 personal tax on interest	5 tax paid	6 change in liquidity inc(−)dec(+)	7=3−4−5+6 =10+11 post-tax entity cash flow	8 interest paid net of personal tax	9 new debt finance	10=8+9 post-tax lender cash flow	11=7−10 dividends less new capital plus capital repaid
1961	5 104	2 826	2 278	71	1 895	+ 88	400	237	− 390	− 153	553
1962	5 343	2 814	2 529	75	1 854	− 91	509	251	− 627	− 376	885
1963	5 496	2 554	2 942	77	1 717	− 229	919	259	− 416	− 157	1 076
1964	5 450	2 653	2 797	92	1 698	+ 118	1 125	307	− 499	− 192	1 317
1965	5 719	3 141	2 578	114	1 866	+ 94	692	382	−1 203	− 821	1 513
1966	5 588	2 985	2 603	141	1 845	− 71	546	471	−1 295	− 824	1 370
1967	5 699	2 888	2 811	155	1 654	− 261	741	520	− 910	− 390	1 131
1968	6 170	3 151	3 019	171	1 768	− 173	907	573	− 711	− 138	1 045
1969	6 007	3 310	2 697	195	1 851	− 133	518	652	−1 052	− 400	918
1970	6 134	3 404	2 730	207	1 937	+ 65	651	692	−1 077	− 385	1 036
1971	7 124	3 217	3 907	197	1 752	− 528	1 430	661	− 278	+ 383	1 047
1972	7 403	3 529	3 874	226	1 453	−1 188	1 007	758	− 612	+ 146	861
1973	7 165	4 280	2 885	304	1 506	− 715	360	1 017	−2 170	−1 153	1 513
1974	6 464	4 196	2 268	381	1 673	+ 458	672	1 274	−1 907	− 633	1 305
1975	7 197	3 655	3 542	338	1 181	− 828	1 195	1 133	− 339	+ 794	401
1976	6 233	3 858	2 374	303	862	− 990	219	1 015	−1 212	− 197	416
1977	6 634	3 842	2 792	271	1 310	− 490	721	908	− 797	+ 111	611
average 1961/77	6 172	3 312	2 860	195	1 636	− 287	742	654	− 911	− 257	999

Notes

i) The personal tax shown in column 4 on interest paid is calculated at the rate of 23 per cent.
ii) Corporate tax paid (column 5) is net of cash grants received. To facilitate comparability with the other eleven years, the years 1967-72 (inclusive) include tax at the standard rate on (gross) dividends paid.
iii) As short-term interest was first published in 1972, the first eleven payments included in column 8 include estimated short-term interest.
iv) The dividends included in column 11 are net of tax at the standard (now basic) rates payable at the time.

merely constitutes the multiplication of each of the cash flows within an individual period by the same factor.

Three aspects of Table 1 can usefully be clarified. First, the total (actual) investment of £5 924.7m is the sum of five items disclosed in the official sources and uses table, namely:

	£m
tangible fixed assets	5 270.2
adjustments due to consolidation	3.0
intangible assets	46.2
other expenditure	277.0
investments (ie portfolio investments)	328.3
total investment	£5 924.7

'Expenditure on the acquisition of subsidiaries by issue of shares and loans' is not included in the above total investment on the assumption that it relates to intra-sample take-overs. If so, such expenditure merely involves the exchange of new paper for old, does not change the sample's economic composition, and is cancelled out by an equal amount on the sources side of the sources and uses table.

To the extent that the intra-sample mergers assumption causes an understatement of total investment incurred during the 17-year period it will also cause an overstatement of entity cash flow performance. That is to say, if some of the takeovers were in fact extra-sample mergers, part of the 'expenditure on acquisition of subsidiaries by issue of shares and loans' ought to be included in the total investment that is matched with the extra-sample income that would automatically be aggregated with the other (major) component of sample income. For reasons that need not be pursued here, the removal of the intra-sample take-over assumption would strengthen our conclusions.

'Expenditure on the acquisition of subsidiaries by cash' is treated as the repayment of debt and equity capital since it clearly represents a cash outflow from the standpoint of the sample as a whole. Whilst most of this cash would have been paid to shareholders in the acquisition of majority interests, some of it would have been used to repay debenture and loan stockholders. Though the matter is of little consequence, it is not possible to determine from the official sources and uses table how this cash outflow was in fact divided between lenders and shareholders. We have assumed that it was repaid in the ratio 3:7 though it would be surprising if lenders received much more than 10 per cent of the repayment. The substitution of a 1:9 ratio for the 3:7 ratio used here would also add strength to our conclusions.

Cash Flows, Taxes, Debt and Dividend Policy

Apart from being expressed at a base-year price level and showing items in a somewhat different order, Table 2 differs from Table 1 only in that it discloses gross interest paid in two components. Column 4 of Table 2 shows personal tax calculated at the rate of 23 per cent on gross interest paid whereas column 8 contains the net of (personal) tax interest component.

There are two reasons for this adjustment. First, if lenders are to be compared with shareholders, both should be placed on a net-of-tax footing. Secondly, to the extent that investors succeed in shifting their personal taxes forward into interest rates and required equity returns, such personal taxes are ultimately a charge on entity income and should be treated as such. Judging from the evidence[1], the 23 per cent rate used in Table 2 is probably a conservative estimate of the extent to which lenders shifted taxes forward during 1961-77. By contrast, it may be inferred from the well-known 'clientele effect', eg the preference of high rate taxpayers for capital gains suffering taxes at relatively low rates, that shareholders suffered taxes at higher rates — hence the assumption that shareholders were standard rate taxpayers (see Table 2, note iv). This assumption is also supported by the evidence.

Apart from the adjustment just described, Table 2 is largely self-explanatory[2]. Basically, it shows how the post-tax entity cash flows disclosed in column 7 were divided between lenders (column 10) and shareholders (column 11) during 1961-77. In all but four of those seventeen years, namely 1971/2/5 and 1977, shareholder cash flows exceeded entity cash flows. On average, 26 per cent, ie 257/999, of equity cash flows were financed with debt. Alternatively, it might be said that on average net payments to shareholders exceeded post-tax equity cash flows by 257/742 = 35 per cent.

In that some part of the net interest shown in column 8 probably represents a premium for risks borne by lenders, that premium should be deducted from column 7 in determining the degree to which the net payments to shareholders were uncovered by internally generated cash flows. But, it may be objected, internally generated cash flows should not be stated net of total investment for this purpose since a

[1] Sources of evidence are cited in R C Stapleton and C M Burke, 'Tax systems and corporate financing policy', *Monograph series in finance and economics*, New York University, 1978.

[2] Post-tax entity cash flows are shown net of periodic liquidity changes which can be regarded as periodic investments (or disinvestments) for transactionary, precautionary and speculative purposes.

Table 2-type cash flow statement seemingly ignores the unexpired benefits of capital expenditure at the terminal date[1].

In examining this objection it should be questioned whether the unexpired benefits of capital expenditure, namely, some part of *future* operating cash flows, are likely to alter the kind of consistent multi-period relationship between operating cash flows and capital expenditure depicted by columns 1 and 2 of Table 2. In other words, do the relative magnitudes of columns 1 and 2 constitute a consistent feature of the continuing (perpetual) system with which we are here concerned[2]? If so, it cannot be assumed that, in the absence of dividend policy changes, the unexhausted benefits of capital expenditure will ever obviate the degree of dividend-induced debt financing that is present in Table 2.

Turning to the past effects of dividend-induced debt-equity substitution; if an excess of dividends (less new equity plus capital repayments) over post-tax entity cash flows has (*ex definitio*) been consistently debt-financed, company debt ratios might be expected to reveal the situation accordingly. Whereas, in practice, corporate debt ratios tend to be computed by reference to balance sheet values, it is arguable that they are more correctly measured on a market value basis. In any event, the market values of both equity and medium/long-term debt automatically incorporate the effect of post-issue changes in the interest rate structure, thereby impounding the financial advantages (or disadvantages) of debt-financing from both a lender and shareholder standpoint.

Both the actual and base-year market values that are shown in Table 3 are indicative of a significant degree of debt-equity substitution during 1961-77. The following comparison of the (re-expressed) 1961 and 1977 market values isolates the real effect of the debt-equity substitution over the 17-year period.

	Debt £m	Equity £m	Entity £m
1961	4 006	37 110	41 116
1977	9 277	23 140	32 419
change	5 271	(13 970)	(8 699)

[1] But what about the unexpired benefits of capital expenditure at the commencing date? These should arguably be treated as an additional charge against cash flow income.

[2] It can be usefully emphasized that an assessment of the likelihood that entity cash flows will continue to be divided between lenders, tax collectors and shareholders as in the past is not the same thing as the measurement of multi-period (entity) cash flow performance. Nevertheless, it may be noted that in any finite multi-period case for which there are entry and exit capital stock values, an economic depreciation rate can, with the help of a little algebra, be shown to be closely approximated by aggregate multi-period capital expenditure divided by the sum of the other corresponding sequences of post-tax entity cash flows. This is virtually another way of stating that, from a multi-period performance appraisal standpoint it is legitimate to match the sequence of capital expenditures with the other sequences of cash flows.

Table 3 *Market Values of Debt and Equity 1961-77*

	Actual			*At December 1974 prices*		
year	debt	equity	entity	*debt*	*equity*	*entity*
	1	2	3	*4*	*5*	*6*
1961	1 727	16 000	17 727	*4 006*	*37 110*	*41 116*
2	1 963	14 306	16 269	*4 322*	*31 495*	*35 817*
3	2 301	17 432	19 733	*4 963*	*37 597*	*42 560*
4	2 695	19 417	22 112	*5 697*	*41 046*	*46 743*
5	2 918	17 599	20 517	*5 841*	*35 228*	*41 069*
6	3 489	16 402	19 891	*6 741*	*31 692*	*38 433*
7	4 204	15 795	19 999	*7 888*	*29 638*	*37 526*
8	4 383	24 829	29 212	*7 871*	*44 585*	*52 456*
9	4 531	23 897	28 428	*7 710*	*40 663*	*48 373*
1970	5 287	20 686	25 973	*8 525*	*33 354*	*41 879*
1971	6 046	26 187	32 233	*8 902*	*38 555*	*47 457*
2	6 553	33 716	40 269	*9 077*	*46 700*	*55 777*
3	7 552	30 707	38 259	*9 586*	*38 976*	*48 562*
4	9 050	16 275	25 325	*9 971*	*17 932*	*27 903*
5	9 634	23 343	32 977	*8 724*	*21 137*	*29 861*
6	12 122	30 049	42 171	*9 232*	*22 885*	*32 117*
7	14 307	35 688	49 995	*9 277*	*23 140*	*32 417*

Notes

i) An indication of the effect of rising interest rates on the market value of debt is provided by a comparison of the values in column 1 with the nominal values of short-, medium- and long-term debt disclosed in company balance sheets. The 1977 balance sheet value of long-term loans, bank overdrafts and short-term loans was £18 731 millions.

ii) The values in column 1 are the sum of long-term interest capitalized at the redemption yield for the year in question and the same year's balance sheet value of bank overdrafts and short-term loans.

iii) The equity values in column 2 are taken directly from Professor Moore's Table 2.

iv) The values in columns 4, 5 and 6 are derived from those in columns 1, 2 and 3 respectively using the indexation procedure described on page 45.

That is to say, 38 per cent of the decline in the value of equity can be ascribed to the £5 271m real increase in the market value of debt[1]. Taken together, Tables 2 and 3 leave little doubt that, given the level of investment that was undertaken during 1961-77, higher dividends could have been financed only with debt. Such action would

[1] If, in order to avoid results that are sensitive to 'capricious' entry and exit values, the former are derived from averages of the 1961 and 1962 (real) values and exit values are derived in like manner, the apparent degree of debt-equity substitution rises to 45 per cent of the real decline in equity values.

simply have heightened the degree of debt-equity substitution that actually took place and caused a commensurate fall in real equity values.

In fairness to Professor Moore, it should be recalled that he explicitly rejects the 'given level of investment assumption' arguing that it had been too high and inadequately profitable at the margin. He also dismisses the possibility of any decline in the quality of shareholder returns. But if, as we have illustrated, debt-financed dividends probably lowered equity values whilst, at the aggregate level, new projects 'bringing too low a (by implication positive) rate of return' probably had the opposite effect, could any other factors have contributed to the 1961-77 decline in equity and entity values?

The Incidence of Taxation

The Table 2 relationship, between column 3 on the one hand and columns 4 and 5 on the other, is indicative of a significant degree of fiscal drag, ie effective rates of tax that were in excess of the nominal rates at which taxes were actually assessed during 1961-77.

The effective rate of tax which measures the true incidence of taxation on an entity's multi-period cash flows is a discounted cash flow rate. Supplementing a modicum of algebra with a little sensitivity analysis, it can be shown that the multi-period rate of tax, T, on entity cash flows is closely approximated by:

$$\frac{\text{average tax payment (Table 2: col 4 + col 5)}}{\text{average pre-tax entity cash flows (Table 2: col 7 + col 4 + col 5)}}$$

The effective rate of tax on entity cash flows for the seventeen years covered by Table 2 is thus:

$$T \simeq \frac{195 + 1\,636}{742 + 195 + 1\,636} \simeq 71 \text{ per cent per annum.}$$

During 1970-77 the value of T averaged 70 per cent per annum, whereas, since the amelioration of the UK corporate tax burden following the initial introduction of stock appreciation relief in November 1974, the effective rate of tax on entity cash flows for the last three years recorded in Table 2 was 67 per cent per annum.

In that these effective tax rates are expressed as percentages of entity cash flows, ie with net interest 'below the line', whereas nominal tax rates are based on some notion of shareholder profit with gross interest 'above the line', it can be stated with some conviction that the corporate tax burden is still of debilitating proportions. Moreover, it cannot be too strongly emphasized that the effective entity tax rates cited here are not only multi-period rates but also represent the cross-sectional averages for a large sample of listed companies. Multi-period cash flow analyses of individual companies leave little doubt that the dispersion about these averages is quite spectacular[1].

Since 1974 the UK incidence of corporation tax has not only been radically non-neutral; it has actually caused effective tax rates exceeding 100 per cent in specific cases[2]. A non-neutral corporate tax regime which is prone to causing confiscatory taxation, ie capable of causing effective tax rates in excess of 100 per cent, is *prima facie* a sufficient condition for the kind of situation contemplated by Professor Moore. This is a situation in which, by accepting new capital projects, a company can cause its market value to fall below that which it would have obtained had it distributed a dividend as an alternative to the capital expenditure incurred[3]. But in these circumstances the cash flows generated by an entity's existing operations are also taxed away, and the need for further debt to finance tax payments becomes virtually inescapable. A further financial pressure comes from existing contractually-determined interest payments and, as the level of debt increases, this pressure will be reinforced. Under these conditions, dividend payments can therefore be expected to make a further contribution to debt-equity substitution.

Conclusion

By way of conclusion, we reaffirm our rejection of Professor Moore's contention that the remedy for the declining real value of UK equities is higher pay-out ratios and lower levels of investment. In our view, the facts suggest that the combination of a relatively high absolute tax burden on entity cash flows and increasing interest payments, coupled with dividend policies based on historic cost profits has, especially in the last decade, led to a significant repayment of real equity capital. Equity market values have reflected the situation accordingly. In that there has been a general decline in real entity values since the early 'sixties, the doubling of the real market value of corporate debt has had a particularly strong real debt-equity substitution effect.

[1] See G H Lawson, 'The Measurement of Corporate Profitability on a Cash-flow Basis', *The International Journal of Accounting Education and Research*, Fall, 1980.

[2] As discussed elsewhere, the UK corporate tax system also amplifies the volatility of post-tax entity cash flows. See G H Lawson, *Company profitability and the UK Stock Market — an exercise in cash flow accounting*, Manchester Business School, Research Report, March, 1979.

[3] There can be little doubt that during 1973-77 price controls seriously arrested the rate of growth of real operating cash flows (see Table 2, column 1) and exacerbated fiscal drag.

In forming expectations about the future behaviour of real equity values, investors are, as always, confronted with the question of the real values which might emerge in each of the first seven columns of Table 2. The multi-period behaviour of future equity values will be influenced by the proportions in which company directorates allocate post-tax entity cash flows (column 7) between lenders (column 10) and shareholders (column 11).

Corporate taxation is likely to remain a dominating influence on the returns to investors and changes therein will affect market values accordingly. The UK corporate tax system fails to comply with tax neutrality criteria to a degree that has long assumed epidemic proportions; it discriminates against the manufacturing sector in a particularly pernicious manner. In the absence of corporate tax reforms which alter both the cross-sectional incidence and the sheer weight of taxation on the manufacturing sector, it is likely that total (entity) market values will continue on their downward path. In these circumstances, a continuation of past dividend policies will, whilst returning capital to shareholders, cause the rate of decline in real equity values to exceed the rate at which real entity values will fall.

We have also attempted to show that the relationship between dividend policy and equity values is essentially a financial problem that should be analysed on a multi-period basis in financial, ie cash flow, terms. Put another way: the determinants of shareholder cash flows are themselves cash flows and it is rather pointless to pretend that accounting variables somehow or other constitute the entrails of a dividend valuation model.

Journal of Management Studies 25:5 September 1988
0022-2380 $3.50

BANKRUPTCY PREDICTION - AN INVESTIGATION OF CASH FLOW BASED MODELS[1]

Abdul Aziz
Humboldt State University, California

David C. Emanuel
The University of Texas at Dallas and Chicago Mercantile Exchange

Gerald H. Lawson
Manchester Business School

INTRODUCTION

Ratios included in bankruptcy prediction models are based on a type of *ad hoc* pragmatism rather than a sound theoretical work. Altman, Haldeman and Narayanan (1977) used financial ratios and measures found helpful in providing statistical evidence of impending failures in other studies plus new measures thought to be potentially helpful. Dambolina and Khoury (1980) have used similar criteria for ratio selection but added that data availability for the calculation of ratios across firms and across years was an additional consideration. This also applies to such other studies as Beaver (1967), Deakin (1972), Edminster (1972) and Altman (1968). Pinches *et al.* (1975), and Chen and Shimerda (1981) list and analyse the multitude of ratios used by various researchers. Blum (1974) points out that in the absence of a theory of symptoms one cannot use statistical analysis of financial ratios and expect a sustained correlation between independent variables and the event to be predicted. Ball and Foster (1982) also criticize this brute empiricism approach using stepwise discriminant/regression analysis as a result of which the selected variables tend to be sample-data specific and the empirical findings do not permit generalization. Wilcox (1973), Vinso (1979) and Emanuel, Harrison, and Taylor (1975) have tried to arrive at a single measure - the probability of bankruptcy based on theoretical approaches to avoid 'brute empiricism'. Casey and Bartzack (1984, 1985) have investigated the use of operating cash flows as a possible predictor of bankruptcy. More recently Gentry, Newbold and Whitford (1985) have used a cash-based fund flow model developed in 1972 by Helfert (1982) to obtain a set of financial ratios and measures for generating a multivariate bankruptcy model. Our study is similar to that of Gentry *et al.* (1985). However, instead of using Helfert's fund flow model we have used a cash flow identity developed by Lawson (1971).

The basic difference between Helfert's fund flow statement and Lawson's cash flow identity is the objective of the two relations - the former is designed to provide analysis by 'area of management attention' while the latter is for 'firm

Address for reprints: Dr. Abdul Aziz, Department of Business Administration, College of Business and Technology, Humboldt State University, Arcata, CA 95521, USA.

valuation'. Since corporate bankruptcy is closely related to firm valuation Lawson's identity is likely to provide better predictors.

LAWSON'S IDENTITY

Lawson's identity is based on simple logic and is described as follows:

entity cash flows = lender cash flows + shareholder cash flows

The left hand side may be broken further as follows:

operating cash flow − net investment in fixed assets − liquidity changes − taxes actually paid

Symbolically the identity may be stated as:

$$(k_j - h_j) - (A_j + R_j - Y_j) - H_j - t_j = (F_j - N_j - M_j) + (D_j - B_j)$$

where,

$k_j - h_j$ denotes operating cash flow in year j represented by cash collected from customers, k_j, and operating cash outflow, h_j;

$A_j + R_j - Y_j$ stands for net capital investment, represented by replacement investment, A_j, growth investment, R_j, and the proceeds from assets displaced, Y_j in year j;

t_j stands for all taxes assessed on the corporation that are actually paid in year j;

H_j denotes liquidity change in year j;

F_j *represents period* j interest payments;

N_j is medium and/or long term debt raised or retired in year j;

M_j is short-term debt raised or repaid in year j;

D_j represents dividends paid to shareholders in year j;

B_j is equity capital raised or repaid in year j.

This identity is basic to the theory of corporate valuation which may be stated as

$$\text{total market value, } TMV_0 = \text{market value of debt } MV^{(d)} + \text{market value of equity } MV^{(e)} \qquad (1)$$

or

the present value of expected entity cash flows (after tax) = present value of expected lender cash flows + present value of expected shareholder cash flows

or symbolically

$$\sum_{j=1}^{\infty} \frac{(K_j - h_j) - (A_j + R_j - Y_j) - H_j - t_j}{(1+\bar{r})^j} = \sum_{j=1}^{\infty} \frac{F_j - N_j - M_j}{(1+\bar{r}_d)^j} + \sum_{j=1}^{\infty} \frac{D_j - B_j}{(1+\bar{r}_e)^j} \qquad (2)$$

where,

the bars denote expected values; and $\bar{r}$, $\bar{r}_d$ and $\bar{r}_e$ represent the firm's weighted average cost of capital, its cost of debt, and the cost of its equity respectively.

From identities (1) and (2), it may be inferred that a firm is financially viable, and has a market value as a going concern, if on a continuing basis it generates positive entity cash flows (after net capital expenditure) and holds out the prospect of continuing to do so.

Additionally, if the dividend and equity financing policies of a firm are persistently such that $(D_j - B_j) > (k_j - h_j) - (A_j + R_j - Y_j) - t_j - H_j$, *i.e.* the company pays uncovered dividends then the difference must, by definition, be persistently financed with debt.

If $(k_j - h_j) - (A_j + R_j - Y_j) - H_j - t_j$, and MV_j, the market value of firm in year j are constant in real terms then, *ceteris paribus*, continuous debt-equity substitution will result in a serial decrease in MV_j[e]. With the passage of time, these changes become more rapid and observable leading to creditor control of the firm – an indication of bankruptcy. Thus, theoretically speaking, entity cash flows provide vital information on a firm's financial performance as well as its bankruptcy potential.[2]

The quality of signals as given by the cash flow based (CFB) variables and historic-cost accounting measures of performance may be assessed from the following example.[3]

AM International, McLouth Steel, Nucorp Energy, Sambo's Restaurants, Saxon Industries, Seatrain Lines and Wickes, in 1981, had price–earnings multiples significantly higher than market but their cash flows were not encouraging. They all filed bankruptcy petitions under chapter 11 in 1982.

Thus, a theoretical and empirical rationale exists for formulating a hypothesis about corporate bankruptcy in terms of cash flow variables.

COMPUTATION OF THE CFB VARIABLES

Using definitions of the data items provided by the COMPUSTAT, the CFB variables were computed as follows:

$$k_j - h_j = \text{FOP}_j + [\Delta\text{CL}]^j_{j-1} + H_j + t_j + F_j - [\Delta\text{CA}]^j_{j-1} - [\Delta\text{STD}]^j_{j-1}$$
$$A_j + R_j - Y_j = (k_j - h_j) - H_j - t_j - (D_j - B_j) - (F_j - N_j - M_j)$$
$$t_j^3 = [\Delta\text{TL}]^j_{j-1} + \text{tax expense}_j$$
$$H_j = [\Delta\text{CMS}]^j_{j-1}$$
$$D_j - B_j = \text{cash dividend}_j + [\Delta\text{CPS}]^j_{j-1}$$
$$F_j - N_j - M_j = F_j - [\Delta\text{LTD}]^j_{j-1} - [\Delta\text{STD}]^j_{j-1}$$

where subscript j stands for the jth year and $[\Delta]^j_{j-1}$ for the change in a variable from year $j-1$ to j.

FOP is funds from operations, CMS stands for cash and marketable securities, CA is current assets, CL is current liabilities, STD stands for short-term debt, CPS is common and preferred stock, LTD is long/medium-term debt, and TL[4] is tax liability.

Thus a positive value of $(k_j - h_j)$ represents cash inflow but positive values of all other CFB variables represent cash outflow.

When using the above variables in the model, scaling the data is necessary to avoid the problem of heteroscedasticity. In a great deal of previous work, balance sheet values have been used as a basis for scaling data. This is a crude basis. After all, cash flows affect market value much more than book value. Hence the firm's total market value (MV debt plus MV equity) should be used to scale data on predictors from the cash statement. However, there is a serious difficulty in valuing unquoted debt and preferred stock. Therefore, we have also used book value of the firm for scaling purposes. Hopefully the robustness of models will mitigate the influence of this approximation.

SAMPLE SELECTION

We used Standard and Poor's 1983 Industrial Annual COMPUSTAT Research File[5] to determine the companies that failed during the period 1971–82. The population of bankrupt companies carried on file forms a subset of companies assigned Code 02. Companies with this code are the ones which have been deleted from the active COMPUSTAT files due to bankruptcy, mergers, exchanged or liquidated and those which stopped trading for having sold assets to other firms. A company belonging to this set and having filed bankruptcy under chapter 10 or 11 or otherwise declared bankruptcy was a candidate for inclusion in the sample. However, a company was included in the sample if it satisfied· the following conditions:[6]

(1) the equity of the company must have been traded on some stock exchange or over the counter;
(2) at least two years data must be available from COMPUSTAT (Research or Active) files in the period five years prior to bankruptcy declaration date for the bankrupt or its matching firm, if the firm is non-bankrupt; and
(3) the firm does not belong to financial institutions or utilities group.

A paired sample design based on the criteria of industry classification and asset size was used to select matching non-bankrupt firms. Zmijewski (1984) has investigated the influence of such non-random sampling on the conclusions drawn in bankruptcy studies. He found that higher (than available in population) distressed firm sample frequency rates cause lower distressed firm estimated error rates but, in general, do not affect the statistical inferences or the overall classification rates for the distress model and the samples tested. Still, for cost effectiveness reasons such sampling is quite common in bankruptcy studies. Moreover, the cost of predicting a bankrupt firm as non-bankrupt is much higher, implying that the bias due to non-random sampling is rather 'beneficial'. Thus we have used a one-to-one matching process in the sample selection.

This study does not restrict sample with reference to asset size of firm. It has also included firms from service and transportation industries. Firms included in the sample are listed in table IX.

ANALYSIS

In order to determine the suitability of Lawson's identity components for discrimination between bankrupt and non-bankrupt firms Multiple Discriminant Analysis (MDA) and Logistic Regression (LR) techniques were used. Components were calculated for one, two, three, four, and five years prior to bankruptcy occurrence date.

Overview of Data

Characteristics of the variables useful in a discriminant function ought to be different for the different classes/groups. The larger the difference the more efficiently would the variables work as discriminators.

Table I presents data to enable a comparison between the profiles for the bankrupt (B) and non-bankrupt (NB) groups. Unweighted group means for each separate independent variable and the tests for significant differences between the group means are given. Inspection of this table shows that $k_j - h_j$, the cash flow from operations, and t_j, taxes assessed and actually paid in cash are consistently significant at a very high level from fifth year to first year prior to bankruptcy. Other variables significant at high levels are $F_j - N_j - M_j$, the lender cash flows and $A_j + R_j - Y_j$, the net investment in long-term investment, in years one and two prior to bankruptcy. H_j, cash used for liquidity changes, is significant beyond 5 per cent in the fifth year prior to bankruptcy and $D_j - B_j$, the stockholder cashflows, is not significant in any year. These observations are substantiated by drawing time-series graphs of these variables (see figure 1).

Inspection of table I and figure 1 brings out the following:

(1) All cash flows, except shareholders and liquidity change are consistently higher for non-bankrupt firms than for bankrupt firms for each of the five years prior to bankruptcy.
(2) Liquidity change cash flows are higher for non-bankrupt firms than for bankrupt firms in each of the five years except for year one prior to bankruptcy.
(3) Shareholder cash flows for bankrupt and non-bankrupt firms do not follow any pattern.

Thus, except for H_j and $(D_j - B_j)$ we observe a clear divergence in the group means of variables as bankruptcy approaches. It is, therefore, logical to assume that apart from theoretical considerations, empirical evidence also supports the development of a classificatory model using components of Lawson's identity.

Discriminant Models

Two types of discriminant functions are commonly available. The first may be represented as

$$Z_i = b_0 + b_1X_1 + b_2X_2 + \ldots + b_nX_n$$

where the discriminant score Z_i is a linear function of the independent variables. It allows a clear interpretation of the effect of each of the independent variables. The second type is called a non-linear discriminant function and it may be stated as

$$Z'_i = a + \mathrm{b}X_i + cX_i^2 + dY_i + ezy_i^2 + fX_iY_i$$

assuming that X_i and Y_i are the two independent variables. This is a more complex function and isolating the effect of each variable is not easy. For example, the effect on Z'_i of increasing X_i *by one unit depends upon the values of* X, b, c,f, and even Y_i.

Table I. Profile analysis of predictors and significance tests

Variable	*Group*	Years prior to bankruptcy and univariate F ratios									
		1	*f*	*2*	*f*	*3*	*f*	*4*	*f*	*5*	*f*
$K_j - h_j$	B	0.04508	26.11[a]	0.06023	23.55[a]	0.08737	21.89[a]	0.1117	10.18[b]	0.08856	14.07[a]
	NB	0.19201		0.18729		0.18623		0.17426		0.17927	
$A_j + R_j - Y_j$	B	−0.03635	8.227[b]	0.07144	2.368	0.06649	2.106	0.05191	1.478	0.05235	0.07208
	NB	0.09865		0.10025		0.08782		0.07482		0.05975	
t_j	B	0.00325	37.26[a]	0.01348	19.32[a]	0.0189	26.12[a]	0.02014	34.52[a]	0.01096	17.35[a]
	NB	0.05607		0.05793		0.06338		0.05852		0.05728	
H_j	B	0.01626	0.02959	0.00178	0.0718	−0.0068	1.451	−0.00145	1.611	0.00701	3.675[c]
	NB	0.01294		0.00494		0.01373		0.01699		0.03607	
$D_j - B_j$	B	0.06422	1.996	−0.02449	1.967	0.00321	0.1779	0.03740	1.835	0.01429	0.0509
	NB	0.0079		0.00977		−0.00417		0.00925		0.01890	
$F_j - N_j - M_j$	B	−0.00231	28.07[a]	−0.00198	4.166[c]	−0.00055	3.563[d]	0.00370	5.380[c]	0.00394	0.09684
	NB	0.02357		0.01441		0.02547		0.01468		0.00724	

[a] Significant beyond the 0.0005 level
[b] Significant beyond the 0.005 level
[c] Significant beyond the 0.05 level
[d] Significant beyond the 0.1 level

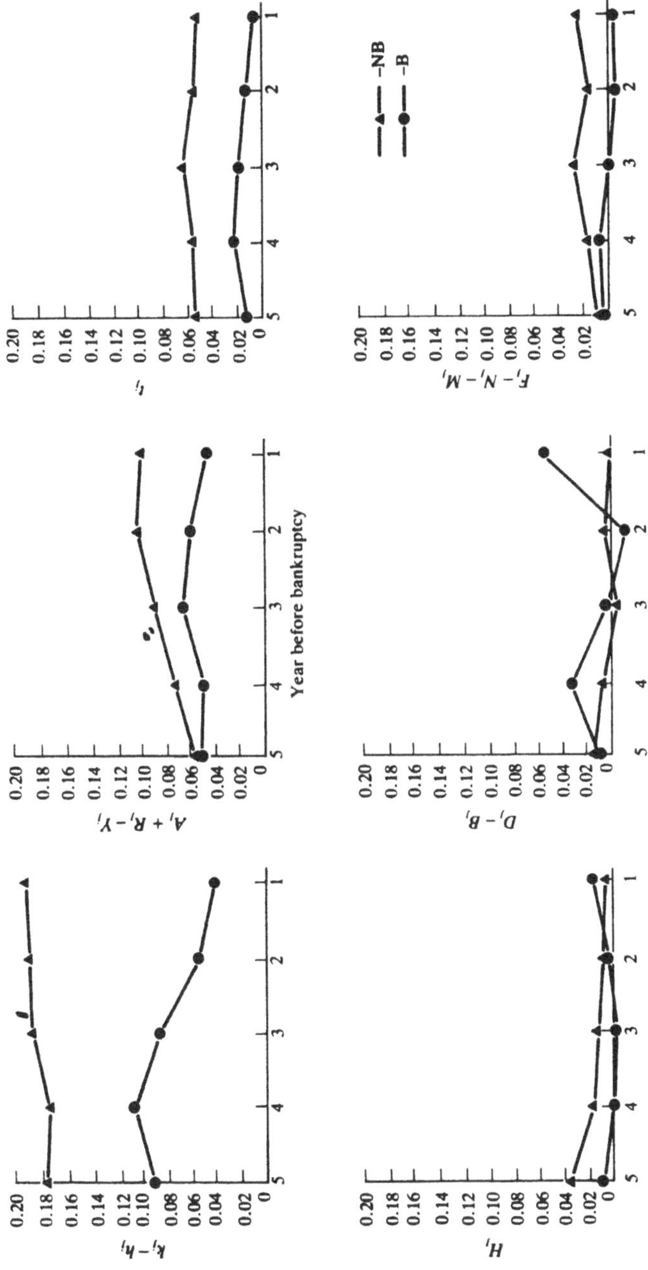

Figure 1. Graphic analysis of variables

Thus, for interpretation, a linear discriminant function is very desirable. For this reason we have limited our investigation to a linear discriminant function.[7]

Results of Discriminant Analysis

To construct discriminant functions, assess their significance and test their validity the following procedure was followed:

(1) Develop models for each of the five years prior to bankruptcy using the Discriminant method. However, $D_j - B_j$, the stockholders' cash flow was excluded to avoid statistical over-identification. This variable was selected for exclusion because it was found always insignificant. The option METHOD = DIRECT of the procedure discriminant analysis of SPSSX was used to develop models.
(2) Partial models were constructed using the option METHOD = RAO of discriminant analysis procedure of SPSSX.
(3) Partial models were obtained using the BMDP7M-Stepwise discriminant analysis procedure.

The objectives of the first and second steps of this procedure were to obtain canonical loading, classification matrices, and generalized chi-square values to test the significance of discriminant functions. Tables II and III present a summary of the results of these two steps. The third step provides the classification matrix as well as a jack-knifed classification (based on Mickey–Lauchenbruch validation technique) in addition to U- and F-statistics. Whereas the U- and F-statistics provide an alternate method to X^2 statistic to test the significance of the discriminant function, the jack-knifed classification presents an almost unbiased validation technique.

Table II shows that the variable t_j, taxes assessed and actually paid in cash, is the most important contributor to discriminant function in four out of five years, the next important variable is $k_j - h_j$ (operating cash flow). However, ranks are unstable for other variables. This implicitly confirms the findings of Mensah (1984) that previous bankruptcy prediction studies using MDA of financial ratios exhibit a lack of consistency in the values of the coefficients.

Table II. Canonical loading and ranking of variables by importance

Years prior to bankruptcy	*Variables*					
	$k_j - h_j$	$A_j + R_j - Y_j$	t_j	H_j	$D_j - B_j$	$F_j - M_j - N_j$
1	0.347	0.356	0.646	–	–	0.512
	(4)	(3)	(1)			(2)
2	0.657	–	0.524	–	–	0.256
	(1)		(2)			(3)
3	0.581	–	0.564	–	−0.232	–
	(1)		(2)		(3)	
4	–	0.548	0.881	0.462	–	0.357
		(2)	(1)	(3)		(4)
5	0.386	–	0.839	0.530	–	–
	(3)		(1)	(2)		

Figures in parentheses represent rank by importance

Table III. Various goodness of fit tests for discriminant models

Full models (SPSSX): Year	% Correct	X^2	*(Panel 1)* d.f.	Significance level
1	88.8	61.576	5	0.0000
2	80.6	30.338	5	0.0000
3	72.5	27.603	5	0.0000
4	77.1	40.975	5	0.0001
5	80.9	29.633	5	0.0001
Partial models (SPSSX):			*(Panel 2)*	
1	89.8	61.867	4*	0.0000
2	82.7	30.197	3	0.0000
3	74.5	27.525	3	0.0000
4	78.1	40.951	4	0.0000
5	78.7	29.250	3	0.0000

Full models (BMDP): *(Panel 3)*

	Accuracy (%)				
Year	*Analysis sample*	*Jack-knifed classification*	*U. Stat.*	*F. Stat.*	*d.f.*
1	88.8	88.8	0.5176	17.149	5,92
2	81.6	78.6	0.7229	7.053	5,92
3	77.6	74.5	0.7444	6.319	5,92
4	79.2	75.0	0.6390	10.168	5,90
5	78.7	73.0	0.7042	6.973	5,83

* Degrees of freedom are equal to the number of variables included in the final discriminant function

Significance of the Discriminant Functions

Since the sample includes an equal number of bankrupt and non-bankrupt firms, the maximum chance criterion provides 50 per cent as the accuracy of classification by a random model. Examination of table III shows that discriminant models, both full as well as partial, correctly classify firms with a high degree of accuracy up to five years before bankruptcy is declared. X^2 values are significant for all the years. This goodness of fit conclusion is also confirmed by *F*- and *U*-statistics and the jack-knifed classification given in panel 3 of table III. Thus we feel justified in continuing to the interpretation stage. We do not compare the classifying power of the model developed here to that of the other models (such as Altman, Gentry *et al.*, *etc.*) because, as we show further, in our study the discriminant models are not the best possible. Here we only state that variables extracted from Lawson's identity provide a viable alternative set, based on theoretical grounds, for input to a discriminant device.

Results of Logistical Regression Analysis

According to Press and Wilson (1979) logistic regression (Logit) analysis is theoretically more appealing than the discriminant analysis when criterion variables are binary.[8] Its applications to bankruptcy prediction is recommended by Ohlson (1980). Also the requirement of equality of dispersion matrices is not applicable in the case of the logit technique. In addition, we have used logit analysis for the following reasons:

(a) To see if the conclusions of discriminant analysis are confirmed by another technique.[9]
(b) To obtain an optimal model by comparing the accuracy of logit and discriminant models.

For each year full logit models were developed. Again to avoid over-identification, $D_j - B_j$, stockholders cash flows, was excluded from the analysis. BMDPLR (stepwise logistic regression) procedure of Biomedical Program package was used. The procedure was constrained to include all the variables in the final model. Table IV gives the coefficients of the variables, along with relevant asymptotic 't' ratios. Overall predictive accuracy of logit models developed from data from each year ranges from 91.8 per cent to 78.6 per cent and is given in table V.[10] The classification is dependent upon the critical probability which the program generates to minimize the misclassification rate. If the probability of any firm going bankrupt is greater than the critical probability, the firm is classified as bankrupt, otherwise non-bankrupt.

Comparison of results of logit analysis as given in table V and those of discriminant analysis given in table III shows that the former are marginally superior. Thus the results of this study confirm the findings of Gentry *et al.* (1985) that logit models are somewhat superior to discriminant models.

Interpretation of the Coefficients of the CFB Models

If $f(x)$ is a linear multivariate logit function the probability of bankruptcy of a firm is given by $e^{f(x)}/(1 + e^{f(x)})$. A lower value of $f(x)$ indicates a lower bankruptcy potential of the firm. In the computation of the cash flow variables we have taken operating cash (in)flows as positive and all other cash (in)flows as negative. Therefore, in the logit model, the signs of coefficients of all the cash flow variables, except $D_j - B_j$, are expected to be negative. However, the data to compute the CFB variables are obtained from an identity, and hence not controlled for multicollinearity. In such a situation full logit models can provide regression coefficients that are far out of line with what was expected and may even have the opposite sign from what they should be.[11] To overcome this problem and interpret the coefficients we developed partial-logit models for each of the five years prior to bankruptcy.[12] The coefficients obtained are given in table VII (panel 2) and in each year are as expected.

From similar reasoning it can be inferred that the signs of the variables in a partial discriminant model are expected to be positive. Actual signs obtained are shown in table VII, panel 1. These signs not only conform to the empirical evidence but also make economic sense, *i.e.* a potentially non-bankrupt firm generates higher operating cash flows, invests more in capital assets, pays out more in taxes, and is capable of carrying more debt than a matching bankrupt firm.

Validation of the CFB Model

A model becomes acceptable for practical use if it passes the validation test. To validate logit models and obtain an optimal one we tested models developed from

Table IV. CFB models: logit coefficients and asymptotic T ratios

Year	$K_j - h_j$	$A_j + R_j - Y_j$	t_j	H_j	$F_j - M_j - N_j$	Constant
1	−6.601 (−1.065)	−5.183[c] (−1.689)	−32.200[b] (−2.166)	5.823 (0.6866)	−121.44[a] (−3.300)	3.007[a] (3.650)
2	−7.5775[b] (−2.344)	−0.35799 (−0.1183)	−23.588[a] (−2.924)	−2.994 (−0.5807)	−10.033 (−1.282)	1.8161[a] (3.674)
3	−3.1925 (−0.9271)	−2.5741 (−0.7377)	−29.743[a] (−3.223)	−5.5319 (−1.103)	−15.793[c] (−1.776)	1.8457[a] (3.540)
4	−1.1195 (−0.3924)	−8.9282[b] (−2.195)	−39.837[a] (−4.033)	−8.3838[c] (1.805)	−23.413 (−1.688)	2.4722[a] (4.094)
5	−7.7429[c] (−1.987)	0.57494 (0.1840)	−32.343[a] (−3.620)	−17.863[b] (−2.193)	2.0766 (0.2627)	2.2448[a] (3.594)

[a] Significant at 1% level
[b] Significant at 5% level
[c] Significant at 10% level

Table V. Accuracy matrix of different CFB only logit models (%)

Model year	Test year 1			2			3			4			5		
	O	*B*	*N*	*O*	*B*	*N*	*O*	*B*	*N*	*O*	*B*	*N*	*O*	*B*	*N*
1	91.8	85.7	97.9	78.6	79.6	77.6	77.6	75.5	79.6	77.1	72.9	81.25	71.91	78.26	65.12
2	78.1	85.4	70.8	84.7	85.7	83.7	76.5	81.6	71.4	80.2	85.4	75.0	76.4	82.6	69.8
3	82.7	85.7	79.6	79.6	81.6	77.6	78.6	79.6	77.6	79.2	81.3	77.1	75.3	80.4	69.8
4	84.6	89.8	79.6	76.5	75.5	77.6	74.5	73.5	75.5	80.2	81.3	79.2	75.3	78.3	72.1
5	73.5	81.6	65.3	73.5	83.7	62.5	75.5	81.6	69.4	77.1	81.3	72.9	80.9	84.8	76.7

O – correct overall classification
B – correct bankrupt firm classification
N – correct non-bankrupt firm classification

Table VI. Classification matrix and critical probabilities–logit models

Years before bankruptcy	*Overall*	*Accuracy (%) bankrupt*	*Non-bankrupt*	*Critical probability**
1	91.8	85.7	98.0	0.508
2	84.7	85.7	83.7	0.458
3	78.6	79.6	77.6	0.525
4	80.2	81.3	79.2	0.508
5	80.9	84.8	76.7	0.508

* In three out of the five years more than one value of critical probability values gave the same overall accuracy. We have chosen the one closest to 0.5 as the critical probability in each case

year one data on data from years two, three, four and five. Models developed from other years data were similarly tested. Results of this validation procedure are given in table VI. Analysis of this table shows that if the objective is to optimize the average accuracy of prediction of the model then year one model is *appropriate*. Its range of prediction accuracy is 74.5 per cent, in the fifth year before bankruptcy, to 91.8 per cent of the first year. If the objective is to optimize the predictive accuracy of the model with reference to identification of bankrupt firms – this is a valid objective as the cost of misclassifying a bankrupt firm is generally higher than misclassifying a non-bankrupt firm, then the model developed from data on the second year before bankruptcy is superior. Critical probabilities of these models are given in table V.

Comparison with the Gentry et al., *Z, and ZETA Models*

Comparing predictive accuracy of bankruptcy models is not easy. Samples and periods studied differ among various studies. Gentry *et al.* (1985) give predictive accuracy of the model for the period one year before bankruptcy only. The average accuracy is 83.33 per cent and the hit ratio for bankrupt firms is 78.79 per cent. As against this our model has 91.8 per cent and 98 per cent figures respectively.

Comparison with ZETA[13] model (Altman *et al.*, 1977) is available for periods one to five years prior to bankruptcy. Table VIII part (a) presents the overall accuracy comparison.

ZETA model has significant superiority over our model in year two prior to bankruptcy; for other years the overall prediction accuracy of the two models is statistically comparable. On the other hand the Z model, with recomputed coefficients provides somewhat inferior results than the CFB model in four out of five years.

Another important comparison of the models can be made in the context of bankrupt firm identification. The importance of this comparison is due to the fact that a much larger loss may be incurred if a decision is based on misclassifying a potentially bankrupt firm than a non-bankrupt one. Table VIII, part (b) shows the accuracy of the CFB Model as compared with the Z and ZETA models. The CFB model outperforms the Z model significantly in three out of five years and even in the other two years has higher accuracy though not statistically significantly. However, the performance of the ZETA and CFB models is statistically equal though the latter turns in slightly better results than the former in three out of five years.

Table VII. Partial models

(Panel 1)

*Partial discriminant models**
Unstandardized canonical discriminant function coefficients

Years before bankruptcy	Variables						
	$k_j - h_j$	$A_j + R_j - Y_j$	t_j	H_j	$D_j - B_j$	$F_j - N_j - M_j$	Constant
1	2.441	1.526	15.089	–	–	21.192	- 1.010
2	5.069	–	10.461	–	–	6.435	- 1.041
3	5.555	–	13.089	–	- 2.678	–	- 1.210
4	–	5.938	27.539	6.491	–	15.403	- 1.651
5	3.387	–	15.993	7.420	–	–	- 1.138

(Panel 2)

*Partial logit models** coefficients*

Years before bankruptcy	Variables						
	$k_j - h_j$	$A_j + R_j - Y_j$	t_j	H_j	$D_j - B_j$	$F_j - N_j - M_j$	Constant
1	–	- 6.6805	- 39.707	–	–	- 125.93	2.5683
2	–	- 7.7143	–	–	- 5.2996	- 17.375	0.71614
3	- 5.2842	–	- 27.739	–	–	–	1.6552
4	–	- 9.6254	- 40.595	- 9.1608	–	- 24.380	2.4263
5	–	–	- 34.141	- 19.230	–	–	1.3946

The variables are defined on pages 420–1
* Using SPSSX discriminant procedure METHOD = RAO
** Using BMDP logit procedure

Table VIII. Comparative classification accuracy between CFB model and ZETA and Z models (%)

Years prior to bankruptcy	*Overall accuracy* ZETA model**	Z***	CFB model	*(Panel 1)* ZETA [t] CFB	Z [t] CFB
1	92.8	88.8	91.8	0.276	-0.710
2	89.0	82.7	78.6	1.98*	0.727
3	83.5	74.5	77.6	1.06	-0.508
4	79.8	70.8	77.1	0.884	-0.994
5	76.8	67.4	71.9	0.375	-0.653

* Significant at about 5% level
** Original sample accuracy as reported in Altman *et al.* (1977)
*** Logit form with coefficients computed using our investigation sample

Years prior to bankruptcy	*Bankrupt firm identification accuracy* Z***	ZETA***	CFB	*(Panel 2)* ZETA [t] CFB	Z [t] CFB
1	79.6	96.2	85.6	1.866	-0.797
2	75.5	84.9	79.6	0.702	-0.486
3	55.1	74.5	75.5	-0.117	-2.121*
4	52.1	68.1	72.9	-0.528	-2.105*
5	52.2	69.8	78.3	-0.959	-2.629*

* Significant at 1%
** Original sample accuracy as reported in Altman *et al.* (1977)
*** Logit form with coefficients recomputed using out investigation sample

Table IX. Sample of bankrupt firms and matching non-bankrupt firms

Bankrupt firm	*Year of bankruptcy*	*Matching non-bankrupt firm*
Allied Artists	1979	Technicolor
Allied Supermarkets	1978	Giant Foods Inc.
Am. Mfg. Co.	1980	Adams Millis
A. M. International	1982	Eagle Picher
APCO Oil	1977	Amerada Hess
Arctic Enterprises	1981	Am. Shipbuilding
Armac Enterprises	1976	AMF Corp.
Austral Oil	1978	Sabine Corp.
Bobbie Brooks	1982	Russ Togs
Braniff Int'l	1982	Delta Air
Combustion Equip. Assoc.	1980	Zurn Ind.
Cooper Jarrett	1981	Carolina Freight
De Jur Amsco	1978	Bearings Inc.
Eagle Cloth	1977	Blue Bell
Eastern Freight	1976	Overnite Transp.
EDG Oil	1977	OKC Corp.
Fabien Corp.	1979	Cone Mills
Fishman (M. H.)	1974	Wal-Mart
Frier	1976	Caressa
Frigitemp Corp.	1977	Fischback
Gladding	1977	Canadian Marconi
Gruen	1976	Talley Ind.
KDT Ind.	1982	Heck's Inc.
Kirby Ind.	1976	Tidewater Inc.
Mansfield Tire & Rub.	1979	Pope & Talbot
Mays (J. W.)	1982	Dillard
Mego Int'l	1982	Tandycrafts
Merchants Inc.	1979	Telecom
Nelly Don	1978	Garan Inc.
Novo	1978	Altamil Corp.
Overseas National Air	1978	World Overseas Air
PASCO	1976	Cities Services
Piedmont Ind.	1979	Schrader (Abe)
Reeves Telecom	1980	Storer Broadcasting
Richton Int'l	1980	Lenox
Royal Castle System	1975	Saga Corp.
Saxon Ind.	1982	Hammermill
Shenandoah Oil	1978	Summit Energy
Shulman Transport	1978	Transway Int'l.
Sitkin Smelting	1978	Harsco
Stelbar Ind.	1976	Milton Bradley
Supronics	1976	Chesborough Ponds
Tennessee Forging	1978	Hoffman
Universal Container	1978	Crown Cork & Seal
UNR Ind.	1982	Northwestern Steel
Western Orbis	1976	Conner Homes
White Motors	1980	CCI Corp.
Wicke's	1982	Evans Products
Wyly	1977	Automated Data Processing

SUMMARY AND CONCLUSIONS

The CFB model compares favourably with the ZETA and Z models. First, overall accuracy is approximately equal. Second, compared with the Z model the CFB model is substantially more likely to predict a bankruptcy up to five years prior to the event. When compared with the ZETA model, the CFB model is more likely to provide early warning three or more years before the event. However, the ZETA model is superior in the two years immediately preceding bankruptcy. The value of these conclusions is enhanced when considered that the coefficients of the ZETA model are not publicly available. Moreover the cost of misclassifying a potentially bankrupt firm is much higher than misclassifying a potentially non-bankrupt firm. Given that the CFB model incorporates only a theory-based fixed set of variables there is merit in investigating further Lawson's identity for building more efficient bankruptcy prediction models.

NOTES

[1] We wish to acknowledge the encouragement by the General Editors of the *Journal* and the helpful comments and suggestions from two anonymous referees.

[2] For more detailed arguments see Lawson, Moller and Sherer (1981).

[3] See Greene and Bornstein (1982). For arguments in greater detail in this direction, see Lawson (1971).

[4] TL for year *j* is 'income taxes payable' (COMPUSTAT data item 71) plus 'deferred taxes and investment tax credit' (COMPUSTAT data item 35). Tax expense is 'total income taxes' (COMPUSTAT data item 16).

[5] We also examined 1985 Industrial Annual COMPUSTAT Research File to identify companies which declared bankruptcy after 1982. We found a very small number of additional firms on which data were available. Most of the others were under file code 13 and data on those are not available to university subscribers.

[6] This study used data derived from Fund Flow statement items which are available only after 1970 for most of the firms. This is when SEC made it mandatory for such data to be included in financial statements.

[7] Altman *et al.* (1977), after developing both the linear and nonlinear discriminant functions, found the former superior. This is in spite of the fact that statistical reasons require the latter over the former.

[8] However, Effron (1975) on the other hand concludes that MDA is more efficient than LOGIT under certain circumstances.

[9] Sheth (1979) recommends that in order to avoid the danger of making inferences about realities which may be an artefact solely due to peculiarities of just one multivariate method, the same data should be subjected to at least two multivariate techniques.

[10] See the next section for a discussion on and interpretation of the coefficients of the CFB model.

[11] Younger, Mary Sue, *A Handbook of Linear Regression*, Duxbury Press, Massachusetts, 1979, p. 499.

[12] For a detailed discussion regarding the suitability of this procedure see Goldberg, *Topics in Regression Analysis*, Macmillan, London, 1968, pp. 33–8.

[13] It is noted here that the accuracy of the Zeta model is stated with reference to the original sample as reported in Altman *et al.* (1977). Model's effectiveness cannot be tested on our sample because the coefficients of Zeta model being proprietory are not available.

REFERENCES

Altman, E. (1968). 'Financial ratios, discriminant analysis and the prediction of corporate bankruptcy'. *Journal of Finance*, September, 589-609.

Altman, E., Haldeman, R. and Narayan, P. (1977). 'ZETA analysis: a new model to identify bankruptcy risk of corporations'. *Journal of Banking and Finance*, June, 29-53.

Ball, R. and Foster, G. (1982). 'Corporate financial reporting: a methodological review of empirical research'. *Journal of Accounting Research*, **20** (supplement), 161-234.

Beaver, W. (1967). 'Financial ratios as predictors of failure'. *Empirical Research in Accounting: Selected Studies, 1966*. Supplement to *Journal of Accounting Research*, **4**, 71-111.

Blum, M. (1974). 'Failing company discriminant analysis'. *Journal of Accounting Research*, Spring, 1-25.

Casey, C. and Bartszak, N. (1984). 'Cash flow – it's not the bottom line'. *Harvard Business Review*, **62**, July/August, 60-6.

Casey, C. and Bartczak, N. (1985). 'Using operating cash flow data to predict financial distress: some extensions'. *Journal of Accounting Research*, **23**, 1, 384-401.

Chen, K. U. and Shimerda, T. A. (1981). 'An empirical analysis of useful ratios'. *Financial Management*, **10**, Spring, 51-60.

Dambolena, I. G. and Khoury, S. J. (1980). 'Ratio stability and corporate failure'. *Journal of Finance*, September, 1017-26.

Deakin, E. B. (1972). 'A discriminant analysis of predictors of business failure'. *Journal of Accounting Research*, Spring, 167-79.

Drucker, P. F. (1980). *Managing in Turbulent Times*. New York: Harper & Row.

Edminster, R. O. (1972). 'An empirical test of financial ratio analysis for small business failure prediction'. *Journal of Financial and Quantitative Analysis*, March, 1477-98.

Effron, B. (1975). 'The efficiency of logistic regression compared to normal discriminant analysis'. *Journal of American Statistical Association*, **70**, 892-8.

Emanuel, D. C., Harrison, J. M. and Taylor, A. J. (1975). 'A diffusion approximation for the ruin functions of a risk process with compounding assets'. *Scandinavian Actuarial Journal*, 240-7.

Gentry, J. A., Newbold, P. and Whitford, D. T. (1985). 'Classifying bankrupt firms with fund flow components'. *Journal of Accounting Research*, Spring.

Greene, R. and Bornstein, P. (1982). 'A better yardstick'. *Forbes Magazine*, September.

Helfert, E. A. (1982). *Techniques of Financial Analysis*, (5th Ed.). Homewood, IL: Irwin, Ch. 1.

Lawson, G. H. (1971) 'Accounting for financial management: some tentative proposals for a new blueprint'. In Shone, R. (Ed.), *Problems of Investment*. Oxford: Blackwell.

Lawson, G. H. (1982). 'Was Woolworth ailing?'. *The Accountant*, November, 12-14.

Lawson, G. H., Moller, P. and Sherer, M. (1981). 'On the use of conventional accounting statements in the measurement of corporate debt capacity, taxable earnings and the formulation of dividend policies'. Paper presented to the 4th Annual Conference of European Accounting Association in Barcelona, April.

Mensah, Y. M. (1984). 'An examination of the stationarity of multivariate bankruptcy prediction models: a methodological study'. *Journal of Accounting Research*, Spring, 380-95.

Ohlson, J. A. (1980). 'Financial ratios and the probabilistic prediction of bankruptcy'. *Journal of Accounting Research*, Spring, 109-31.

Pinches, G. E., Eubank, A. A., Mingo, K. A. and Caruthers, J. K. (1975). 'The hierarchical classification of financial ratios'. *Journal of Business Research*, October, 295-310.

Press, S. J. and Wilson, S. (1979). 'Choosing between logistic regression and discriminant analysis'. *Journal of American Statistical Association*, **73**, December, 699-705.

SHETH, J. N. (1979). 'How to get the most out of multivariate methods'. In Hair, Anderson, Tatham, and Grablowsky (Eds.), *Multivariate Data Analysis*. Tulsa: Petroleum Publishing Company, Ch. 1.

VINSO, J. D. (1979). 'A determination of the risk of ruin'. *Journal of Financial and Quantitative Analysis*, March, 77–100.

WILCOX, J. (1973). 'A prediction of business failure using accounting data'. *Empirical Research in Accounting: Selected Studies, 1973* Supplement to *Journal of Accounting Research*, **11**.

ZMIJEWSKI, M. D., (1984). 'Methodological issues related to the estimation of financial distress prediction models'. *Journal of Accounting Research*, **22** (supplement), 59–86.

GLOSSARY OF SYMBOLS

The symbols defined below include those that are used principally in the INTRODUCTION to this book and in Papers 1, 2, 6, 9, 11 and 14. Most of these symbols, and a few others, are also adopted, to a greater or lesser extent, in the other papers but with occasional slight differences in usage that are clearly apparent from the specific definitions given in individual contexts.

a_{j-1}, a_j	beginning and ending inventory values in year j
A_j	replacement investment in year j
b_j	accrued purchases in year j
$b_j^{(f)}, b_j^{(v)}$	fixed and variable components of accrued purchases in year j
B_j	equity capital raised, or repaid, in year j
$B_j^{(MI)}$	equity capital raised from, or repaid to, minority shareholders in year j
c_j	cost of sales (before depreciation) in year j
$c_j^{(v)}$	variable cost of sales (before depreciation) in year j
d_j	accrued sales in year j
D_j	dividend payments in year j
$D_j^{(MI)}$	dividend payments to minority interests in year j
e_j	(used only in Paper 6 = $d_j - c_j$ = HCP_j^*)
$ENCF_j$	post-tax entity cash flow in year j
$ENCF_j^*$	post-tax entity cash flow in a neutral corporate tax regime in year j
$ENPROF_j$	economic profit in year j
ETR_j	tax rate leverage effect in year j
fc_j	rate of change in fixed costs in year j
F_j	interest payments in year j (usually assumed to be equal to interest expense)
h_j	operating payments in year j
$h_j^{(f)}, h_j^{(v)}$	operating payments in year j in respect of the fixed and variable components of purchases (excluding inventory adjustments)

$h_j^{(i)}$	operating payments in respect of inventory adjustments in year j
H_j	liquidity change in year j
HCP_j	historic cost profit (after interest, depreciation and corporate tax expenses and including the profit or loss on assets displaced) in year j
$HCP_j^{\dagger}$	entity net profit in year j, viz., HCP_j plus year j interest expense
HCP_j^*	funds from operations, i.e., historic cost profit before interest, depreciation and corporate tax expenses and profit or loss on assets displaced ($=e_j$)
I_j	general definition of entity income in year j (regardless of beginning and end-year valuation bases)
k_j	sales receipts in year j
L_j	historic cost-based depreciation expense in year j
LCF_j	lender cash flow in year j
M_j	short-term debt raised or repaid in year j
MI_j	group profit ascribable to minority interests in year j
$MICF_j$	minority interests' cash flow in year j
$MV_o^{(e)}$	market value of corporate equity at end-year 0
$MV_o^{(d)}$	market value of corporate debt at end-year 0
$MV_o^{(MI)}$	market value of group minority interests at end-year 0
N_j	medium or long-term debt raised or repaid in year j
n_j	(used only in Paper 6 $= k_j - h_j = OCF_j$)
NW_j, $NW_j^{(en)}$	book value of net worth (book values of equity and interest-bearing debt) at end-year j
OCF_j	operating cash flow in year j (see n_j)
p_j	incremental working capital investment in year j
PVA	present value of tax depreciation allowances calculated on a reducing balance basis (Paper 6)
$\bar{r}, \bar{r}_d, \bar{r}_e, \bar{r}^{(MI)}$	entity, (group) lender, shareholder and minority interest costs of capital respectively

RE_j	retained earnings in period j
sp_j	rate of change of selling price in year j
$SHCF_j$	shareholder cash flow in year j
t_j	corporate income tax payments in year j
t_j^*	corporate income tax expense in year j
T_j	corporate income tax rate in year j
T^*	(serially constant) corporate income tax rate in a neutral corporate tax regime
TE_j	corporate taxable earnings in year j
TMV_o	total market value at end-year 0
v_j	rate of change in sales volume in year j
vc_j	rate of change in unit variable costs in year j
x_j	inventory volume at end-year j
X_j	written down book value of assets displaced in year j
y_j	unit inventory (book) value at end-year j
Y_j	cash proceeds of assets displaced in year j
z_j	sales volume in year j
α	annual rate of adjustment of dividends to current earnings (Papers 1 and 2) <u>and</u> annual tax depreciation rate applicable to reducing written down value (Paper 6)
β	market risk coefficient
γ	period of credit allowed by suppliers expressed as a fraction of the previous year's purchases (INTRODUCTION) and target pay-out ratio (Papers 1 and 2)
ϕ	period of credit given to customers expressed as a fraction of the previous year's sales

For Product Safety Concerns and Information please contact our EU representative GPSR@taylorandfrancis.com Taylor & Francis Verlag GmbH, Kaufingerstraße 24, 80331 München, Germany